Valuing Undivided Interests in Real Property

Partnerships and Cotenancies

Readers of this text may also be interested in the following publications from the Appraisal Institute:

- *The Appraisal of Real Estate*, 12th edition
- *A Business Enterprise Value Anthology*, edited by David C. Lennhoff, MAI, SRA
- *Appraising Partial Interests*, by David Michael Keating, MAI
- *The Dictionary of Real Estate Appraisal*, 4th edition

Valuing Undivided Interests in Real Property

Partnerships and Cotenancies

by Dennis A. Webb, MAI, ASA

Appraisal
Institute®

Professionals Providing
Real Estate Solutions

Reviewers: Jeffrey A. Johnson, MAI
Michael S. MaRous, MAI, SRA
John A. Schwartz, MAI
Vanita Spaulding, CFA, ASA
Vice President, Educational Programs and Publications: Larisa Phillips
Director, Publications: Stephanie Shea-Joyce
Editor: Mark Boone
Manager, Book Design/Production: Michael Landis
Production Specialist: Lynne Payne

For Educational Purposes Only

The material presented in this publication has been reviewed by members of the Appraisal Institute; however, the opinions and views expressed herein are the author's views and opinions and are not necessarily endorsed or approved by the Appraisal Institute as Appraisal Institute policy. While substantial care has been taken to provide accurate and current data and information, the Appraisal Institute does not warrant the accuracy or timeliness of the data and information contained herein. Further, the general principles and conclusions presented in this publication are subject to court decisions and to local, state and federal laws and regulations and any revisions of such laws and regulations. This publication is sold for educational purposes with the understanding that the Appraisal Institute is not engaged in rendering legal, accounting or other professional services. If expert advice is required, the services of a competent professional should be sought.

Nondiscrimination Policy

The Appraisal Institute advocates equal opportunity and nondiscrimination in the appraisal profession and conducts its activities in accordance with applicable federal, state, and local laws.

Printed in the United States of America

Library of Congress Cataloging-in-Publication Data
Webb, Dennis A. 1946–
  Valuing undivided interests in real property : partnerships and cotenancies / by Dennis A. Webb.
    p. cm.
  Includes bibliographical references and index.
  ISBN 0-922154-81-3
  1. Real property–Valuation. 2. Business enterprises–Valuation. 3. Limited partnership. 4. Joint tenancy. 5. Real property–Valuation–United States. 6. Business enterprises–Valuation–United States. 7. Limited partnership–United States. 8. Joint tenancy–United States. I. Title.

HD1387.W36 2004
333.33'2–dc22

2004057366

Contents

About the Author

Dennis A. Webb, MAI, ASA, is the owner of Primus Valuations, a Los Angeles regional valuation firm. Primus is a member of the American Business Appraisers® national network, a consortium of independently owned and managed business appraisal practices, which includes many nationally known valuation experts. Mr. Webb has been active in real estate appraisal since 1988 and in business valuation since 1994.

Before specializing in valuation, Mr. Webb was co-owner of an NASD broker/dealer firm, which provided real estate investment syndication, analysis, and consulting services. He held licenses as a registered representative and general securities principal and was responsible for due diligence investigations. Mr. Webb received a bachelor of science degree in engineering from the University of California at Los Angeles with a minor in economics and worked for 15 years as a systems and design engineer.

Dennis Webb has written numerous articles on discount-related topics published in *The Appraisal Journal, Valuation Strategies,* and *Estate Planning,* and wrote the Appraisal Institute's two-day seminar on fractional interest case studies. He teaches extensively on partnership and common tenancy interest valuation. He is a California State Certified General Real Estate Appraiser and a member of the Appraisal Institute, the American Society of Appraisers, the Institute of Business Appraisers, and the Institute of Electrical and Electronics Engineers. A native of Los Angeles, Dennis and his wife, Christel, reside in San Juan Capistrano, California.

Foreword

Interdisciplinary valuation is growing and is an essential part of appraisal practice. It is driven by the profession's mission to serve the public's need for an accurate and meaningful understanding of value in an increasingly complex business environment. *Valuing Undivided Interests in Real Property: Partnerships and Cotenancies* addresses two of the most basic interdisciplinary applications: the family limited partnership and common tenancy ownership of real property. This book demonstrates the need for teamwork between business appraisers and real estate appraisers and for the involvement of accounting and legal professionals.

Appraising real property and valuing business interests rely on similar principles, but otherwise, they are two very different disciplines. Business valuations that involve real estate holding companies require contributions from each discipline, but the real estate appraiser needs to be aware of the business valuation's requirements, and business valuers should be aware of how the real property influences the valuation, to ensure that their work is compatible, and its conclusions are reliable.

Valuing Undivided Interests in Real Property: Partnerships and Cotenancies was written to bridge the gap that exists between the appraisal of real property and the valuation of fractional interests in such property. With a case study as its focus and numerous direct applications of the concepts presented, this practical text spotlights two commonly held forms of real property ownership, family limited partnership and common tenancy, and illustrates the steps involved in reaching a value conclusion for each.

Valuing Undivided Interests in Real Property: Partnerships and Cotenancies provides a clear and straightforward analysis of a potentially complex subject. It is intended for real property and business appraisers, accountants who perform business valuations, attorneys and other professionals who use valuations. This publication will encourage consistency and reliability in client outcomes in this specialized interdisciplinary valuation field, which makes it a welcome contribution to the art and practice of fractional interest valuation.

Gary P. Taylor, MAI, SRA
2004 President
Appraisal Institute

Acknowledgments

I have always enjoyed and been challenged by working in multiple disciplines, and partnership and common tenancy valuation is certainly no exception. Just as it is not possible to engage in this book's valuation process without enlisting the support of other practitioners, it would not have been possible to complete this book without the support of many contributors.

I would like to extend many thanks to those who have reviewed this work and to those who have provided other technical help and inspiration. I have leaned on practitioners in law and accounting—Gerald E. Lunn, Jr., Esq.; Alan J. Stern, CPA; and William Johnson, EA—and on real estate, business, and other interdisciplinary appraisers—including Vanita Spaulding, CFA, ASA; Lari B. Masten, CPA, MSA, CVA; Henry J. Wise, MAI, CBA; Rand M. Curtiss, FIBA, MCBA, ASA; Alan Karbousky, ASA; Thomas J. Cuccia, CFA, ASA; and Jeffrey A. Johnson, MAI. Earlier versions received major contributions from Lawrence A. Salzman, MAI, JD, and Charles W. Rex III, MAI.

I dedicate this book to my wife, Christel, my life partner and personal editor, who now knows more about valuation topics than she ever thought she would. She provides the unwavering support that is essential for my enthusiasm and professional curiosity.

Preface

Real estate appraisal and business valuation are two disciplines that share a common heritage, but have otherwise developed almost entirely independent of each other. This is of concern from time to time with respect to industry-wide standards, definitions, interactions between professional associations, and other topics that are indirectly related to valuation. Moreover, the different curricula upon which these disciplines are built frequently lead real estate and business appraisers to apply appraisal principles in ways that are sometimes misunderstood by one another.

The need for discipline integration applies for many applications, including valuation for financial reporting and valuation of asset-heavy enterprises generally. This book demonstrates this through two of the most basic cases: family limited partnerships and common tenancy. Both cases show that 1) the business appraiser/valuer must have a reasonable understanding of the facts and circumstances associated with the property itself, well beyond simply adding its appraised value to the balance sheet, and 2) the real estate appraiser should have a good idea of the sort of information the business valuer needs, as well as the assignment's underlying premise. Integrating the disciplines becomes important to the credibility of the analysis and the resulting value opinions.

This book also is intended for attorneys and accountants who wish to better understand issues that underlie value. It effectively recommends a team approach that can often have a major financial impact for the client.

The book demonstrates the entire valuation process under two different scenarios: first an FLP that holds an office building, and then ownership of the same office building in common tenancy. The similarities and differences between the two types of valuations are highlighted. Additional topics are addressed in this book, which can be a starting point for valuing more complex situations such as partnerships that hold multiple assets. This is *not* a complete work with respect to applicable valuation art and science, and reference is made throughout to essential business valuation and real estate appraisal works that are required for practitioners.

Valuing Undivided Interests in Real Property: Partnerships and Cotenancies contains an introduction followed by two parts. The introduction provides an overview of the ownership structures, defines the term *levels of value*, and discusses appropriate valuation standards, comparing and contrasting those that apply to real property appraisal with those that apply to business appraisal. Part I (Chapters 1-5), Valuing Limited Partnership Interests, is devoted to the family limited partnership scenario, and Part II (Chapters 6-8), Valuing Common Tenancy Interests, addresses the common tenancy scenario. Examples are included throughout the chapters, with source documents and other references included in the appendixes.

Each case study application is progressive, and content for subsequent chapters is dependent on information presented earlier. Although the chapters can be read independently, it is recommended that they be read in sequence, unless the reader is an appraiser experienced in valuing family limited partnerships and common tenancy interests. Although the concepts presented here may be elementary for one group, they may not be familiar to other readers. Some issues are given fairly brief treatment, and the reader is encouraged to refer to the footnoted references for a more complete tutorial on topics with which he or she may be unfamiliar.

Chapter 1, Beginning the Limited Partnership Valuation, examines the appraisal report, the facts and circumstances of the case, partnership and other agreements, and potential legal concerns that may arise. *Chapter 2, Appraising the Real Property,* summarizes the real estate appraisal methodology used in this case, guides business valuers through the appraisal process and important sections of the report, and shows real estate appraisers how to prepare reports that support valuations.

Chapter 3, Developing the Partnership's Net Asset Value, begins the valuation of the business, examining the partnership's income statements, the balance sheet, and application of the asset approach. *Chapter 4, Developing the Discount for Lack of Control,* introduces the valuation of minority interests, with a complete analysis of the discount for lack of control–the second valuation component of the asset approach. *Chapter 5, Developing the Discount for Lack of Marketability,* is intended for application to asset holding companies, but it has general application for more complex business valuations.

Chapter 6, Beginning the Common Tenancy Valuation, and *Chapter 7, Developing the Common Tenancy Asset-Level Value,* show parallels between the valuation process that was followed for the family limited partnership ownership structure and the common tenancy structure. Both illustrate the heavy dependence of the valuation process on the facts and circumstances of the real estate. *Chapter 8, Developing the Discount for Cotenancy Interests,* like Chapter 5, identifies and brings into the same valuation process the unusual character of property rights held by the cotenant. It also presents additional valuation methods. The appendix provides documents and data that support the valuation process explained and illustrated in this book.

This book is not a complete treatise on either real estate appraisal or business valuation; it is concerned with only their integration and very narrow application; considerable further study and training is required. Real estate appraisers wishing to develop partnership and common tenancy valuation as a practice area are encouraged to build a library of the footnoted references, and complete basic educational offerings in business valuation at a minimum, as a prerequisite for developing competency in the field.

Valuing Undivided Interests in Real Property: Partnerships and Cotenancies addresses a narrow field of practice, but one that affects a large number of clients. Asset valuation has been the subject of considerable controversy when the purpose of the business appraisal involves gift and estate taxation, income tax issues (charitable contributions, establishing tax basis), marital dissolution, partner buyouts, and other situations where discounts are a big, and sometimes costly, issue. Some of the basic principles set forth here also have broader applications, such as public company financial reporting, where asset valuations are becoming more important, and where the interaction between the specific characteristics of the real property and business interests is not well understood. It is my hope that practitioners serving clients who own undivided interests in real estate will begin to realize a more consistent valuation process and body of knowledge, and that the differences between them will narrow, leading to less uncertainty, and more reliable outcomes for the client.

Real Property Ownership Structures and Valuation Standards

Ownership of real property constitutes a bundle of rights, the complete set of which is title in fee. This ownership is a fee simple interest, subject only to governmental powers of taxation, eminent domain, police power, and escheat. The rights to real property may be divided in many ways. Real estate assets may be held in fee simple or divided into a set of property rights.[1] For example, when rights are divided between a lessor and a lessee, the lessor's right of occupancy has been assigned to the lessee, and the lessor holds a leased fee interest. *Valuing Undivided Interests in Real Property: Partnerships and Cotenancies* focuses on undivided property rights, such as those held by partners and common tenants. The notion of a bundle of property rights is useful for analysis because one can think of the whole bundle (fee simple) being diminished as specific rights are transferred to others, and further diminished as they are divided between owners, between a general partner and limited partners, or between majority and minority stockholders.

When more than one owner holds interests in real estate, problems can occur. Multiple ownership complicates property rights and greatly expands the appraisal process. The basic business ownership structures for real property are shown in Figure I.1, Basic Business Ownership Structures for Real Property. The ownership entities shown in the figure are legal mechanisms for apportioning rights to multiple undivided owners, just as leases are mechanisms for apportioning rights associated with occupancy. The ownership structures shown include partnership/limited liability company (LLC), corporation, and common tenancy.

---

1. For an overview of both divided and undivided property rights, see *The Appraisal of Real Estate*, 12th ed. (Chicago: Appraisal Institute, 2001), 67–90.

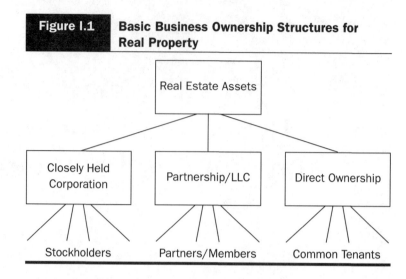

Figure I.1 Basic Business Ownership Structures for Real Property

The case study presented in this book is structured as a limited partnership in Part I and as a common tenancy in Part II. Many of the same principles that apply to partnerships and common tenancies are applicable to corporate structures, but their analysis is not within the scope of this book. These basic ownership forms exhibit strong similarities but also striking differences, which continue to create misunderstanding and confusion.

Partnership/Limited Liability Company

A partnership is characterized by an agreement that generally specifies management responsibilities and sets forth the partners' rights, including the voting structure for the sale of assets and the termination and admission of partners, capital requirements, and cash distributions. A partnership may be either general or limited. General partners are jointly and severally liable and typically participate in management; limited partners have limited liability, contribute capital, receive distributions, and may vote on certain issues but do not participate in day-to-day management decisions.

Members of a limited liability company avoid some of the restrictions imposed on partnerships, but are not authorized to operate in all states. The LLC is similar to the limited partnership in that partnerships and LLCs both usually exist for a specified term and are pass-through entities with earnings taxed at the interest-holder level.

There are important structural differences from an analytical standpoint, and for the purposes of this book only, limited partnerships and LLCs are treated as similar. Therefore, references to the word *partnership* may be taken generally to include LLCs. This does not mean, however, that the ideas expressed here should be applied to LLCs without consulting appropriate state laws.[2]

Corporation

A corporation is governed by a board of directors, has centralized management, and can exist in perpetuity. Stocks representing proprietary ownership may be transferred freely or may be restricted. A corporation may be taxed at the corporate and stockholder levels, or it may be a tax pass-through structure organized under subchapter S of the Internal Revenue Code (an S corporation).

Because the focus of this book is on real property interests, references to corporations are limited to closely held asset holding companies. Corporations that hold other types of assets or are characterized by more active operations often have intangible assets and require valuation methods that are beyond the scope of this book.

Common Tenancy

When ownership in real property is held through a holding company, the interest is held indirectly. Direct, or deeded, ownership by more than one person can take several forms: joint tenancy, tenancy by the entirety, and tenancy-in-common (common tenancy, or cotenancy). The first two generally allow for rights of survivorship, so valuations of separate interests are not often needed. In common tenancy, the undivided interests are independent of one another and may be transferred without permission or knowledge of the other cotenant(s). It is this transferable form of tenancy that often requires valuation and is one focus of this book. Common tenancy is further characterized by the following attributes:

- Typically, no agreement exists between the parties.
- Voting rights are unspecified, and one owner may block nearly any decision.
- No restrictions exist on interest transfers.
- Each common tenant has the right to bring legal action to either partition the property or force its sale.

Common tenancy is still a form of association, however, and, in many important respects, may be treated as if it were an "ownership entity." This treatment is convenient for business valuation because the method of analysis used for partnerships can be applied to common tenancy, with adjustments made for the differences described above. A surprisingly broad range of valuation techniques can be applied to common tenancy, further allowing comparisons with important market data.

2. It is essential for the appraiser to work closely with counsel when an assignment involves LLCs.

Other Business Entities

Other descriptive names may be applied to agreements between property owners, such as *syndication* or *joint venture*, but these are generally considered partnerships for tax purposes.[3] Other similar business entities can pose interesting problems for valuers, since the agreement between the parties may limit control and marketability in ways that indicate that the entity should be valued as a partnership or a common tenancy. Partnership interests would be valued by the methods presented in Chapters 2 through 5, Part I, and common tenancy interests should be valued using the methods presented in Chapters 6 through 8, Part II. Characterizing the entity is a critical step in the valuation process, which can take legal as well as valuation expertise to properly understand.[4]

Levels of Value

The concept of "levels of value" is fundamental to organizing and understanding the valuation process. It shows the relationship between the value of a whole enterprise and the transferable ownership interests, which may be valued at less or more than the whole. For example, a business may be sold for $100 per share to a buyer who acquires all the shares, or at least enough shares to control the enterprise. Shares that confer limited rights, such as small minority interests (typically market-traded shares of public companies), generally trade at a lower value. The levels of value concept has been developed in great detail by many valuation experts including Shannon Pratt[5] and Chris Mercer,[6] but to an extent unnecessary for this book's limited scope. This section presents a basic version of the concept, and later chapters will introduce modifications to suit specific valuation steps.

Figure I.2. shows the flow associated with this concept. The top level is the value of the whole. For a limited partnership or any asset holding company, it is usually the net asset value (*NAV*), or equity, of the enterprise.[7] For common tenancy, it would be generally the real estate itself less any loan balance. The levels of value are often shown in two steps, as on the left side of Figure I.2.

---

3. Section 7701(a)(2) of the Internal Revenue Code (IRC) provides (for estate and gift tax purposes) that partnership includes... a syndicate, group, pool, joint venture, or other unincorporated organization through or by means of which any business, financial operation, or venture is carried on, and which is not, within the meaning of this title, a trust, estate or corporation..."

4. See Appendix E, "Working with Attorneys and Other Client Intermediaries," by Gerald Lunn, Esq.

5. Shannon P. Pratt, DBA, CFA, FASA, et al, *Valuing a Business, The Analysis and Appraisal of Closely Held Companies*, 4th. ed. (Chicago: Irwin Professional Publishing, 2000), 347.

6. Christopher Z. Mercer, ASA, CFA, *Quantifying Marketability Discounts* (Memphis, TN: Peabody Publishing, 1997), 19.

7. Net asset value is generally defined as the value of an enterprise's tangible assets (excluding excess assets and nonoperating assets), less the value of its liabilities. We are assuming little or no identifiable intangible value, and the operation is defined as holding assets. Thus, the definition applies to the value of assets (real property, securities, and cash) less the value of its liabilities (mortgage, security deposits, loans and others). *NAV* is usually equal to the owners' equity.

Figure I.2 Levels of Value

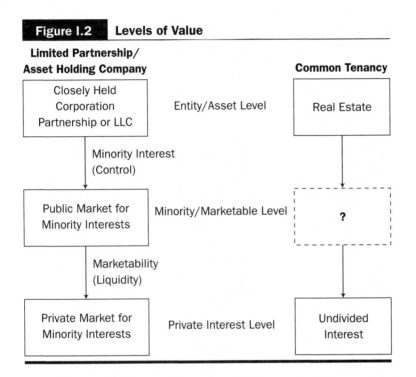

Limited Partnership/
Asset Holding Company

Common Tenancy

| Closely Held Corporation Partnership or LLC | Entity/Asset Level | Real Estate |

Minority Interest (Control)

| Public Market for Minority Interests | Minority/Marketable Level | ? |

Marketability (Liquidity)

| Private Market for Minority Interests | Private Interest Level | Undivided Interest |

Fewer rights are associated with a minority interest in an asset holding company than those associated with direct ownership of its assets and liabilities.[8] The market value of a minority interest is less than its simple pro rata proportion of the partnership's equity because potential buyers discount the pro rata value of the interests to reflect various factors that limit their ability to control the assets or enterprise or to dispose of their interest. The most important limitations are lack of control and lack of marketability. If property rights are limited due to restrictions on control or marketability, a higher yield will be required to compensate the buyer, reducing the market price for the investment and increasing the discount.

Each level of value is conceived largely because of the need for comparability with the various types of market data available. Minority values can be obtained from market trades of shares in public entities such as limited partnerships and public corporations. Applying these data to the subject partnership or corporation results in a hypothetical value for the interest as if it were publicly traded, i.e., the minority-marketable level. The next step is to develop the discount associated with the interest's privately held status. This discount is determined based on data from the market trading of private interests in public entities. Thus, the property rights associated with the whole are reduced first for the interest's lack of

---

8. The term *minority* is usually defined as less than a 50% interest in an enterprise. This book uses an expanded notion of *minority* as meaning *noncontrolling*. *Minority* is used commonly, but is a potential source of confusion.

control (or impaired control), and then for its lack of marketability (or impaired liquidity).

For common tenancy, net asset value (*NAV*), or the owners' equity, is also used as the starting point. Lack of control and lack of marketability characterize these interests, but the two-step process does not apply in the same way. Figure I.2, Levels of Value, shows common tenancy as having a mystery level–that is, the minority-marketable level does not apply for common tenancy. The discount for such interests can be determined based on impaired control, adjusted for lack of marketability, or on impaired marketability, adjusted for lack of control, but using both discounts in sequence has little meaning. In Part II of this book, both points of view are discussed in relation to common tenancy, and several valuation methods are demonstrated to arrive at a single discount.

Valuation Standards

Establishing the value of a limited partnership or a common tenancy interest is an interdisciplinary process in which the valuation of the business entity falls within the domain of business valuation and the appraisal of the assets falls under real property appraisal.[9] Professional appraisal standards are essential in promoting ethical behavior and defining accepted practices and procedures for completing a business valuation assignment. Standards that address valuation issues include:

- Uniform Standards of Professional Appraisal Practice
- Standards of the Business Valuation Committee of the American Society of Appraisers (ASA)
- Standards of the Institute of Business Appraisers (IBA)
- Standards of the National Association of Certified Valuation Analysts
- Standards of the American Institute of Certified Public Accountants.[10]

Uniform Standards of Professional Appraisal Practice (USPAP)

The Uniform Standards of Professional Appraisal Practice (USPAP) are issued by the Appraisal Foundation. Depending on the purpose and intended use of the business valuation, individual appraisers are subject to the standards of the organizations to which they belong and may also be subject to various sections of USPAP, based on the organization's rules

---

9. The term *appraisal* is used throughout the standards, and *valuation* is used sometimes to refer to business appraisals. For clarification, this book uses the term *appraisal* to refer to the real estate analysis and report, and *valuation* for the business analysis and report.

10. These standards may be found in Fishman, Jay E., MBA, ASA, CRA, et al., *Guide to Business Valuation*, 7th ed. (Fort Worth, TX: Practitioners Publishing Company, 1997), Section 100 Appendix, or on the Web sites of the respective associations.

and the licensing requirements of state law. Appraisers who hold multiple affiliations may be required to conform to the requirements of more than one set of standards. Regardless of affiliation, standards offer guidance

> *Appraisers who hold multiple affiliations may be required to conform to the requirements of more than one set of standards.*

that can be helpful in building a convincing case for value and upholding the basic ethical standards that support the profession.

The pertinent rules of ethics and competency and the standards that apply to appraising real estate limited partnerships are described in the sections that follow. Because USPAP is revised annually, these sections are not intended to be a substitute for the Standards themselves; for the most up-to-date standards, readers are encouraged to consult the latest edition of USPAP.[11]

Rules of Ethics and Competency

The Code of Professional Ethics of the Appraisal Institute must be followed by all of its members. Canon 1 of the code sets forth the Appraisal Institute's expectations:

> It is unethical to knowingly: (b) use, or permit an employee or third party to use, a misleading analysis, opinion, conclusion, or report; (c) communicate or permit an employee or third party to communicate, any analysis, opinion, conclusion, or report in a manner that is misleading.

An appraiser who prepares business valuation should indicate the activities that he or she did and did not perform, and while the appraiser may disclaim responsibility for the contents of the underlying report, he or she must still review it to determine that it is not misleading, according to Ethics Rule 1-1(b).

Problems can arise when the data in the real estate appraisal are insufficient to complete the valuation analysis; when the data have been recorded for another, incompatible use, under an incompatible definition of value; or when the data are inadequate with respect to applicable standards.

---

11. In its April 26, 2004 draft on proposed revisions to the 2005 USPAP, the Appraisal Standards Board addressed the issue of certification for multi-discipline reports. These are reports that may contain assignment results developed by real property, personal property, and/ or intangible asset (business) appraisers. The ASB proposes to edit the language in the comments that accompanies each standards rule pertaining to certification so that the focus is on the discipline of the appraiser who develops the assignment result and not on the appraisal discipline of the assignment results themselves. This amendment to the language effectively would relieve an appraiser involved in a multidisciplinary assignment from accepting full responsibility for all the elements of the assignment results or for the entire content of the appraisal report.

Applicable Standards for Valuing Limited Partnerships

Appraisers should be familiar with USPAP standards that apply to the valuation of real estate limited partnerships, which include Standards 1, 2, 3, 9, and 10. Standard 1 pertains to developing a real property appraisal; Standard 2 addresses communicating the results of a real property appraisal; Standard 3 concerns performing an appraisal review; Standard 9 pertains to developing a business or intangible asset appraisal; and Standard 10 covers business appraisal reporting.

Standards 1 and 2. Developing and Reporting an Appraisal.

Standards 1 and 2 are applicable to the case study in Part I because a limited partnership that holds real property is the focus of the assignment, and data and conclusions from a real property appraisal will be incorporated into the business valuation. Specifically, under Standards Rule 1-4 (g), when the value of a non-realty item—in this instance, the rights and restrictions associated with the interest being valued—is significant to the overall value, a separate evaluation is required,[12] developed in compliance with the standard pertinent to the type of property involved.

Standard 3. Performing an Appraisal Review.

Standard 3 addresses appraisal review, defined by USPAP as "the act or process of developing and communicating an opinion about the quality of all or a part of a completed work or service performed by another appraiser." Standard 3 is potentially applicable to valuing a business entity because it addresses reports prepared by others containing data that could be incorporated into the appraisal. According to the standard, real property appraisals prepared by others must still conform to applicable standards, even in instances where the use of extraordinary assumptions come into play in an assignment. This requirement of conformance applies also to the appraiser performing the valuation (who is bound by USPAP), even if he or she did not appraise the real property.

Reliance on Reports Prepared by Others.

A problem might arise concerning this standard if the client feels that a real property appraiser, in performing a partnership valuation, should review the appraisal of the underlying assets, which may have been performed by another real property appraiser. The reviewing appraiser must carefully determine the appropriate scope of work for the review process and describe the precise scope of the review in the report. The requirements of Standard 3 do not extend to

---

12. A separate valuation does not necessarily mean a separate report; however, there are good reasons for preparing a physically separate report. A separate valuation can establish the fact that two distinct disciplines are involved, helping to avoid confusion and possibly misleading results.

- Reviewing or auditing reports from other professions such as accounting, law, and underwriting, and from corporate decision makers

> *...the appraiser should be sufficiently knowledgeable about legal and accounting issues to know when obtaining additional supporting documentation from such professionals is required.*

- An appraiser's review of work prepared by other experts, such as engineers or consultants, or work prepared by an appraiser in a consulting assignment under Standards 4 and 5
- Reviews of an appraiser's work by nonappraisers, such as administrative reviews

Given that valuations often include legal and accounting documents and statements that are typically beyond the appraiser's expertise, he or she may generally accept the information, unless there is reasonable doubt that the documents were prepared by recognized professionals. Nonetheless, any apparent discrepancies between the appraiser's investigation and the information must be disclosed in the appraisal report. When nonprofessionals provide such information, the appraiser should exercise care and consider their qualifications. As an added precaution, the appraiser should be sufficiently knowledgeable about legal and accounting issues to know when obtaining additional supporting documentation from such professionals is required. Guide Note 4 of USPAP provides additional direction to appraisers who must rely on reports prepared by others.

Real Property Appraisal Standards and Business Valuation Standards Compared

The appraisal of real property and the valuation of limited partnerships and common tenancy interests, though similar in many ways, represent distinct disciplines and are guided by two different sets of standards. Though the standards are all contained in the USPAP document and are parallel in some instances, in other instances they are not. The similarities and differences between the two sets of standards are described below so that real estate appraisers who perform holding company valuations can become conversant with the standards that apply to this domain, and business valuers can better understand the value influence of real property assets.

Standard 9. Business Appraisal Development
Standards Rule (SR) 9-1

> In developing a business or intangible asset appraisal, an appraiser must identify the problem to be solved and the

scope of the work necessary to solve the problem and correctly complete the research and analysis steps necessary to produce a credible appraisal.

This binding rule is identical for all appraisal applications covered by USPAP.

Standards Rule 9-2 (a) through (c)

In developing a business or intangible asset appraisal, an appraiser must identify:

(a) the client and any other intended users of the appraisal and the client's intended use of the appraiser's opinions and conclusions

(b) the purpose of the assignment, including the standard of value (definition) to be developed; and

(c) the effective date of the appraisal;

This is also a binding rule. The first items—client, purpose, and date—are similar to Standards Rule 1-2.

Standards Rule 9-2 (d)

In developing a business or intangible asset appraisal, an appraiser must identify the business enterprises, assets, or equity to be valued:

(i) any buy-sell agreements, investment letter stock restrictions, restrictive corporate charter or partnership agreement clauses, and any similar features or factors that may have an influence on value; and

(ii) ascertain the extent to which the interests contain elements of ownership control.

This refers to the partnership and requires that the partnership's assets and equity be identified. The work required to meet this requirement will be demonstrated in detail later in this book.

This rule also requires that the appraiser identify restrictive agreements and elements of control, both of which distinguish a partnership interest valuation from a real property appraisal performed under Standard 1. This also will be illustrated in the case study.

Standards Rule 9-2 (e) through (g)

In developing a business or intangible asset appraisal, an appraiser must identify

(e) the scope of the work that will be necessary to complete the assignment;

(f) any extraordinary assumptions necessary in the assignment; and

(g) any hypothetical conditions necessary in the assignment.

These items–scope of work, extraordinary assumptions, and hypothetical conditions–are identical to Standards Rule 1(f) through (h).

Standards Rule 9-3

In developing a business or intangible asset appraisal relating to an equity interest with the ability to cause liquidation of the enterprise, an appraiser must investigate the possibility that the business enterprise may have a higher value by liquidation of all or part of the enterprise than by continued operation as is. If liquidation of all or part of the enterprise is the indicated basis of valuation, an appraisal of any real estate or personal property to be liquidated may be appropriate.

This rule is based on the valuation of a business entity as an ongoing enterprise, in which case market value usually exceeds liquidation value. For a real estate holding company, the opposite is typically true. A minority or noncontrolling interest increases in value if its holder can force the sale of the underlying assets and distribution of the proceeds–actions that usually terminate the partnership. Minority holders realize the value of their interests earlier than they would otherwise, and value is greater.

Most real estate appraisals assume an orderly sale of the assets, so this rule would not require any special directions for the asset appraisals, which already conform to Standards 1 and 2. There may be cases in which the real property appraiser assumes a longer holding period, however, and it is possible that a real estate appraisal based on liquidation value may be needed.

Standards Rule 9-4 (a)

An appraiser must develop value opinions(s) and conclusions(s) by using one or more approaches that apply to the specific appraisal assignment.

This rule requires that all relevant approaches to value be applied. It does not specify the approaches because, although they fall into the same three general approaches applied in all appraisal disciplines, the breakdown is somewhat more complex for business valuations.

Standards Rule 9-4 (b)

An appraiser must develop value opinion(s) and conclusion(s) by use of one or more approaches that apply to the specific appraisal assignment; and include in the analyses, when relevant, data regarding:
(i) the nature and history of the business
(ii) financial and economic conditions affecting the business enterprise, its industry, and the general economy

(iii) past results, current operations, and future prospects of the business enterprise;

(iv) past sales of capital stock or other ownership interests in the business enterprise being appraised;

(v) sales of similar business or capital stock of publicly held similar businesses;

(vi) prices, terms, and conditions affecting past sales of similar business equity; and

(vii) economic benefit of tangible assets

This list of items to include in the analysis follows Revenue Ruling 59-60. The intangible assets provision does not apply to the case study, and other elements covered in the discussion of Revenue Ruling 59-60 are covered elsewhere in Standard Rule 9.[13] Although the intangible assets item does not generally apply, the appraiser must be able to recognize when it does apply and take steps to comply with the competency rule.

Standards Rule 9-5

> In developing a business or intangible asset appraisal, an appraiser must reconcile the indications of value resulting from the various approaches to arrive at the value conclusion.

This rule requires a reconciliation of value indications, and departure is not permitted.

Standard 10. Business Appraisal, Reporting

Standards Rule 10-1

> In reporting the results of a business or intangible asset appraisal, an appraiser must communicate each analysis, opinion, and conclusion in a manner that is not misleading.

Like Standards Rule 2-1, this binding rule is identical for all appraisal applications covered by USPAP.

Standards Rule 10-2

> Each written business appraisal or intangible asset appraisal report must be prepared in accordance with one of the following options and prominently state which option is used: Appraisal Report or Restricted Use Appraisal Report.

This is a binding rule. Appraisal reports for business valuations are similar in content level to summary reports for real property appraisals; most of the items in Standards Rule 10-2 are identical to those found in Standards Rule 2-2 (b). A self-contained report is not included as an option. The requirements for an appraisal report are the minimum requirements; the report may contain more detail than the minimum required.

---

13. For example, in 59-60 §8.0, Restrictive Agreements and the portion of §4.01(g) having to do with control, which were covered by SR 9-2(d), and §6.0; capitalization rates appear only in Standards Rule 1-4(c) (iii).

Standards Rule 10-3

> Each written business or intangible asset appraisal report must contain a signed certification that is similar to that published on page 81 of the USPAP.

This binding rule is similar to the requirement for Standards Rule 2-3, except that the reference to property inspection has been removed. Members of the Appraisal Institute are also required to add the statements regarding continuing education and review by the Appraisal Institute's duly authorized representatives to the certification under the Certification Standard.

Standards Rule 10-4

> An oral business or intangible asset report must, at a minimum, address the substantive matters set forth in Standards Rule 10-2 (a).

Revenue Ruling 59-60

The partnership appraisal process should conform to the requirements of Revenue Ruling 59-60.[14] Although this ruling specifically addresses the stock of closely held corporations for estate and gift tax purposes, the same principles can be applied to the valuation of other security interests, including interests in private limited partnerships and LLCs.

Revenue Ruling 59-60 has been generally adopted as a business valuation standard and is codified in USPAP Standards Rule 9-4(b). The ruling itself is not a mandatory requirement. It states that all relevant factors affecting the fair market value should be considered (§ 4.01), and also acknowledges the art and science of appraisal in the following language:

> A determination of fair market value, being a question of fact, will depend upon the circumstances in each case. No formula can be devised that will be generally applicable to the multitude of different valuation issues arising in estate and gift tax cases. Often, an appraiser will find wide differences of opinion as to the fair market value of a particular stock. In resolving such differences, he should maintain a reasonable attitude in recognition of the fact that valuation is not an exact science. A sound valuation will be based upon all the relevant facts, but the elements of common sense, informed judgment and reasonableness must enter into the process of weighing those facts and determining their aggregate significance.[15]

14. Revenue Ruling 59-60, 1959-1 CB 237 is included in Appendix F. A revenue ruling is an interpretive regulation issued by the IRS. Rulings represent the position of the IRS on various matters, but do not have the force of law. Regulations, on the other hand, are also formulated by the IRS, but are approved by the Secretary of the Treasury and add to the body of law that governs taxation issues.
15. Revenue Ruling 59-60, §3.01.

Asset holding companies represent a special case of the generalized problem in business valuation addressed by the ruling. Provisions that should be considered when evaluating these entities include:

§4.01(a)[16] *The nature of the business and the history of the enterprise from its inception*

This provision addresses the nature and history of the real estate assets, diversification, and management's record (particularly as to payment of distributions). Items that affect risk levels are of the greatest concern. While much of this would be covered in the real estate appraisal, the nature and history of the partnership itself may have an additional effect on value.

§4.01(b) *The economic outlook in general and the condition and outlook of the specific industry in particular*

This provision pertains to risk level, the specific type of real estate, and to real estate in general. This element is usually covered in the real estate appraisal.

§4.01(c) *The book value of the stock and the financial condition of the business*

Financial condition pertains to the ability of the partnership to fulfill its current and anticipated obligations. This section of the revenue ruling discusses the importance of balance sheet analysis generally, stating: "In computing book value... assets of the investment type should be revalued on the basis of their market price...."

§4.01(d)(e) *The earning and dividend-paying capacity of the company*

This provision includes the income-generating potential of the partnership's assets and its past and expected future distributions.[17] Actual distributions are less important than the earning capacity of an entire operating company, partnership, or individual asset, which is reflected in its appraised value. However, purchasers of noncontrolling interests would generally place the greatest weight on actual distributions that have been paid and that could be reasonably expected in the future. When management operates with impunity, which is not uncommon, the expectation that the partnership's earnings would be paid, as distributions may be unrealistic, since they might be accumulated or reinvested. Earnings and expected distributions affect value at all levels.

---

16. Factors are listed in §4.01, and descriptions follow under the same letters in §4.02.

17. The terms *dividend* and *distribution* are synonymous for the purposes of this book. The term *distribution* is used here to be consistent with the terminology commonly used in referring to partnerships.

§4.01(g) The sales of the stock and the size of the block to be valued
This provision refers to sales of any ownership interests in the entity and to the degree of control represented by the subject interest.

§4.01(h) The market price of stocks of corporations engaged in the same or a similar line of business having their stocks actively traded in a free and open market, either on an exchange or over the counter
This provision suggests that comparative company valuation methods be used and stresses that they be reasonably comparable. Limited partnerships can satisfy this provision by using data from the trading of units of public limited partnerships that hold similar assets as well as from the trading of comparable real estate company stock.

§6.0 Capitalization rates
According to the ruling, determination of the proper capitalization rate presents one of the most difficult problems in valuation. The most important factors influencing capitalization rates are the nature of the business, the risk involved, and stability or irregularity of earnings.

§8.0 Restrictive agreements
This provision requires that consideration be given to any agreement restricting the sale or transfer of stock or other security interest. The case study addresses several issues that come into play with this provision.

All of these provisions can be satisfied through the appraisal process, including the asset appraisal and valuation of the business entity. When data and conclusions presented in asset appraisals are incorporated into a partnership valuation, they become an integral part of the final product and must conform to all standards that apply to the valuation. This means that the scope of work, assumptions, and limitations of asset appraisals become a part of the valuation and must be suitable for the intended use. Revenue Ruling 59-60 provides an accepted framework for evaluating the process, and for determining whether important elements that influence value have been adequately considered.

Part I

Valuing Limited
Partnership Interests

CHAPTER 1

Beginning the Limited Partnership Valuation

The case study in Part I of this book concerns Suburban Office Partners, II, a family limited partnership, and generally follows the format of a business valuation report. This chapter covers the front portion of the report, from the description of the assignment through definitions, scope of work, and a detailed description of the partnership. The purpose and intended use are particularly important because they underlie the scope of work since the subject is a real estate holding company. The facts and circumstances associated with the property are also made prominent at this stage.

Definitions of Value

In valuing a limited partnership, many definitions of value can be applied, depending on the facts and the use of the report. The definitions used should be compatible with both the real estate appraisal and the partnership valuation. USPAP Standards Rule 1-2 (c) and Standards Rule 9-2 (b) require that the valuer identify both the definition of the value used and its source. A valuation report may be based on market value, fair market value, fair value, or other defined values.

Market Value

Market value is defined as "the most probable price, as of a specified date, in cash or in terms equivalent to cash or in other precisely revealed terms, for which the specified property rights should sell after reasonable exposure in a competitive market under all conditions requisite to a fair sale, with the buyer and seller each acting prudently, knowledgeably, and for self-interest, and assuming that neither is under undue duress."[1] A substantially similar definition used by many real estate appraisers for collateral lending is:

> The most probable price which a property should bring in a competitive and open market under all conditions requisite to a fair sale, the buyer and seller each acting prudently, knowledgeably, and assuming the price is not affected by undue stimulus. Implicit in this definition is the consummation of a sale as of a specified date and the passing of title from seller to buyer under conditions whereby buyer and seller are typically motivated; both parties are well informed or well advised, and each acting in what he considers his own best interest; a reasonable time is allowed in the open market; payment is made in terms of cash in U.S. dollars or in terms of financial arrangements comparable thereto; and the price represents normal consideration of the property sold unaffected by special or creative financing or sales concessions granted by anyone associated with the sale.[2]

Fair Market Value

Fair market value is the price at which the property would change hands between a willing buyer and a willing seller, neither being under any compulsion to buy or to sell and both having reasonable knowledge of the relevant facts.[3] Fair market value is typically used for gift and estate purposes and is the legal standard in many other situations.

Fair Value

Fair value is a legally created standard that is typically applied to situations involving dissenting shareholder and minority oppression.[4] Minority and marketability discounts may or may not apply, depending on the facts, court direction, and case law.

Other Definitions of Value

Other definitions of value include intrinsic value and liquidation value. Intrinsic value is the inherent worth of a thing.[5] In valuing divided interests in a business entity, it constitutes the inherent worth to the owner. Intrinsic value is related to investment value, defined as the specific value of an investment to a particular investor or class of investors based on individual investment requirements, as distinguished from market value, which is impersonal and detached.[6]

---

1. *The Dictionary of Real Estate Appraisal*, 4th ed. (Chicago: Appraisal Institute, 2002).
2. Financial Institutions Reform, Recovery, and Enforcement Act of 1989, Title XI, Pub. L. 101-73, 103 Stat. 183, 12 U.S.C. 331 et seq. (1989) § 323-2(f).
3. Internal Revenue Service Regulations §20.2031-1(b). This definition also comports with the ASA business valuation standards definition.
4. Shannon P. Pratt, DBA, CFA, FASA, et al. *Valuing a Business, The Analysis and Appraisal of Closely Held Companies*, 4th ed. (Chicago: Irwin Professional Publishing, 2000).
5. *The Dictionary of Real Estate Appraisal*, 4th ed. (Chicago: Appraisal Institute, 2002).
6. Ibid.

Liquidation value is the price that an owner is compelled to accept when a property must be sold without reasonable market exposure. If the equity interest being valued has sufficient control to cause the termination of the partnership and the sale of its assets, liquidation value might be required. If the real property is readily marketable, then market value may be adequate to establish the liquidation value, but if it has a limited market and a lengthy marketing time, the real estate appraiser may have to consider a forced sale under USPAP Standards Rule 9-3.

> *If the equity interest being valued has sufficient control to cause the termination of the partnership and the sale of its assets, liquidation value might be required.*

Definitions of Interest

USPAP Standard Rule 9-2 (d) (ii) stipulates that the valuer, in developing a business appraisal, must identify the business enterprise's assets, or equity, to be valued and ascertain the extent to which the interests contain elements of ownership control. Some of the most important types of interest characteristic of a limited partnership include minority interests, limited partner interest, and assignee interests.

Minority Interest

Minority interest is generally defined as ownership of less than a 50% voting interest in an enterprise and is a nonmanaging interest.

Limited Partner Interest

A limited partner interest is defined by agreement, which generally provides that the holder be admitted as a limited partner to be entitled to its associated rights and privileges.

Assignee Interest

Assignee interest is the ownership that an interest holder assigns, through written agreement, to another as permitted by state law. An assignee who does not become a substituted limited partner generally has no right to require any information or account of the partnership transactions, to inspect the partnership books, or to vote on any of the matters on which a limited partner would be entitled to vote. The assignee is entitled only to receive the share of the profits or other income compensation, or the return of his contributions, to which his assignor would otherwise be entitled.[7]

---

7. Uniform Limited Partnership Act. All states except Vermont and Louisiana have adopted some form of the Uniform Act, which sets forth basic provisions, but they have also enacted extensive modifications of their own.

The subject may be an assignee interest before the transfer, or the conversion to assignee status may be a potential outcome for the buyer, depending on the provisions of the agreement and the circumstances of the case. If the seller is an assignee, he or she would be limited in the ability to help the buyer with due diligence because the assignee typically has no right to examine the books and records of the partnership. Nor would the assignee have the right to request a §754 election step-up basis for the transaction. Uncertainty about these rights may cause concern for the buyer, so the valuer will usually have to work closely with legal counsel in this area. The business valuer's need to confer with counsel is discussed in Appendix E, Working with Attorneys and Other Client Intermediaries, by Gerald Lunn, Jr., Esq.[8]

Valuation Approaches and Scope of Work

Three traditional valuation approaches are considered to establish levels of value. Each level can present very different problems. These approaches are the asset approach, the comparative company approach, and the income approach. Thus, three approaches times three levels of value equals nine possible combinations of approaches available to value a partnership.

The scope of work describes the methods that the valuer has selected, explains why others were rejected, and indicates how deeply the valuer must delve into each method to arrive at an opinion of value. Scope of work establishes the level of reliability needed and, consequently, the extent of the process that must be followed.

The valuation process involves two or three steps characterized by one or more of the traditional approaches to value. The two-step process requires the valuer to develop value for the partnership at the minority-marketable level directly and then develop the discount for lack of marketability. The three-step process requires that the valuer develop value for the partnership as a whole (for a real estate partnership, using an asset approach), develop the discount for lack of control (to the minority-marketable level of value), and then develop the discount for lack of marketability.

Asset Approach

Two methods for applying the asset approach are the net asset value method and the liquidation method.

Net asset value method. With the net asset value method, the partnership's assets and liabilities are adjusted to current fair market values (or other appropriately defined values) to determine the value of the partnership's equity, or *NAV* (sum of its assets, less the sum of its liabilities). This method is most

---

8. See Appendix E.

appropriate when tangible assets represent the partnership or company's principal value and labor or intangible assets add little value. If the net asset value method is to be the principal method for establishing value, the buyer of a minority interest must expect to realize the pro rata share of the asset's value sometime during an anticipated holding period.

This method would be less appropriate if the assets were being liquidated or if such action could be forced in the near future. In this instance, the liquidation method may be preferable. The net asset value method would also be less appropriate if the partnership owned multiple properties, was in the business of buying and selling properties, or was engaged in an enterprise other than holding fixed assets (in which case the comparative company or income approach would be preferable). Revenue Ruling 59-60 stipulates that when valuing a closely held investment or real estate holding company, the valuer should place greatest weight on adjusted net worth.[9]

Liquidation method. The liquidation method is a variation of the net asset value method and is based on a liquidation value. The gross amount of proceeds from the liquidation of the partnership's assets is first determined and then reduced by direct and indirect selling expenses and net profit or loss during the period. The liquidation value of the partnership's liabilities is deducted, and the amounts are discounted to present value. The real estate valuation may produce a different value under this definition if the property cannot be sold within a short marketing period. This asset liquidation method is most appropriate if the subject interest has the degree of control necessary to force such a sale.

Comparative Company Approach

The comparative company approach, generally speaking, is a sales comparison approach. Value is established by analyzing market transactions involving companies or partnerships that are similar to the subject. According to this approach, transaction prices (whole company or minority stock sales) are typically reduced to a pricing multiple of a selected economic measure such as earnings or revenues, and the resulting multiple is applied to the subject to arrive at an indication of value.

The data for applying this approach are normally derived from trades of minority shares in public companies or partnerships, and the value is a minority-marketable value. Data on transfers of entire holding companies may also be used to obtain a value of the whole, but these transactions are hard to find since transfers usually involve the sale of assets, not the holding entity. Data concerning transfers of fractional interests in pri-

---

9. Revenue Ruling 59-60, § 5 (b).

vate partnerships are even more difficult to find because no reporting mechanism or no organized market exists for them. Variations of the comparative company approach are guideline company methods and direct sales of private interests.

Guideline company methods. Guideline company methods are most appropriate for operating entities, including partnerships that, in addition to holding assets, have ongoing business operations. For example, a subject partnership that actively manages or buys and sells properties is a good candidate for the application of these methods because a reasonable case might be made for comparing its performance with publicly traded companies for which financial and other data are readily available. The comparable investment would be a reasonable alternative for the potential buyer. Guideline company methods are less appropriate for valuing interests in small, relatively passive real estate holding companies or partnerships whose assets represent all or nearly all their value.

The case study, valuing Suburban Office Partners, II, uses the net asset value approach to develop the value of the partnership as a whole, followed by a guideline/comparative company method to discount NAV to obtain the minority-marketable level value. This method relies on transactions that involve minority interests in public real estate limited partnerships. Although the comparison to public companies is difficult, it is used only to complete the step of moving from net asset value to minority-marketable value and incorporates less uncertainty than if the entire valuation were developed from public market data sources.

Direct sale of private interests. Direct sales of private interests would be ideal for valuing a limited partnership interest if they could be reasonably compared to the subject interest. Direct sales would allow the valuer to skip the two-step discounting process altogether. However, such data are hard to find, the conditions of sale would be difficult to understand, and the asset values would be difficult to develop. Public partnership trading data are practical because a great number of transactions are involved, regressing conditions of sales to a mean. Further, public partnerships often undergo annual asset appraisals and report their net asset values, enabling the discount to be calculated. However, sales of interests in the subject partnership should always be analyzed and may provide useful value indications.

Income Approach
The income approach to establish levels of value can be based on discounted future returns and capitalized returns. The next year's expected returns, typically net cash flow, may be capitalized using a single (overall) capitalization rate developed

from the market. A single rate is appropriate if operations are expected to remain reasonably stable for the expected holding period. If irregular or unstabilized returns are expected, then a discounted cash flow model (DCF) may be required.[10]

> *Values developed using data from publicly traded entities are generally (but not always) minority-marketable values, eliminating the need to develop a separate discount for lack of control.*

Either of the two ways of applying the income approach is appropriate when the partnership is engaged in buying, selling, and the active management activities typical of real estate companies, and when the partnership holds real property assets but also performs operations unrelated to real estate.

Capitalization rates typically are developed from public real estate company market trading data, not from real property sources. Equity risk adjustments are extracted from risk premiums observed for real estate investment trusts (REITs), public real estate companies, and public limited partnerships. Build-up methods generally involve adding incrementally to a risk-free or safe rate to arrive at a discount rate that represents risk for the particular income stream under consideration. Values developed using data from publicly traded entities are generally (but not always) minority-marketable values, eliminating the need to develop a separate discount for lack of control.

These applications of the income method are appropriate when a significant enterprise value exists in addition to the partnership's real property holdings, or in any situation in which the buyer of the interest anticipates the liquidation of specific assets as a component of his or her return.

Mixed Valuation Methods

The methods of valuing a limited partnership are usually mixed. The typical alternatives are shown in Figure 1.1, Comparing Valuation Methods.

The bold arrows show the principal valuation methods used for the case study; other methods are shown for illustrative purposes. The use of several methods together is helpful in valuing a partnership or other business, as long as the methods are reasonable. Mixed valuation methods can also be used at different levels of value to capitalize on superior data sources, which may be most appropriate for the particular value level.

---

10. In a DCF model, a discount rate is applied to a set of projected income streams and a reversion. The analyst specifies the quantity and timing of the reversion and discounts each to its present value at a specified yield rate. *The Dictionary of Real Estate Appraisal*, 4th ed. (Chicago: Appraisal Institute, 2002).

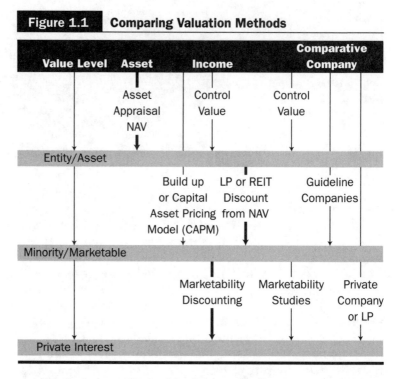

Figure 1.1 **Comparing Valuation Methods**

Value Level	Asset	Income	Comparative Company
	Asset Appraisal NAV	Control Value	Control Value
Entity/Asset			
		Build up or Capital Asset Pricing Model (CAPM)	LP or REIT Discount from NAV	Guideline Companies
Minority/Marketable			
		Marketability Discounting	Marketability Studies	Private Company or LP
Private Interest			

For the case study in this chapter, the first two steps—valuation of the whole partnership followed by the discount for lack of control—could be checked using the income approach and by answering the question: Is the yield to the minority-marketable level reasonable when considering investment alternatives?

In instances in which an income or comparative company approach is preferred, an asset approach can be used to verify whether the results make sense. In such an instance, the valuer would ask the questions: Is the minority purchaser paying more than net asset value for his or her interest and, if so, is it justified by an unusually high cash flow that would not be obtainable at a similar risk with other investments?

When using multiple methods at the same level, the valuer should place weight on the quantity, quality, and appropriateness of each method, often choosing the one that best mirrors the actions of buyers and sellers in the marketplace. Based on these criteria

- An asset approach would be preferred if the buyer would be attracted to, and evaluate, the investment based on its specific asset holdings and also expect to realize its pro rata value on their eventual sale.

- A comparative company approach would be preferred if transactions involving directly comparable interests were available and could be appropriately analyzed. (Transactions involving subject partnership interests should always be considered.)

* The income approach would be preferred if the buyer expects to look to cash flow from the investment (and eventual sale of the interest), comparing the yield to other investment alternatives.

In any case, the valuer should consider how well the selected approach conforms with the buyer's decision-making process when buying an interest in a small real estate limited partnership. The valuer should also consider whether the same buyer would purchase an interest in a publicly held real estate entity and whether the buyer's perception of risk is appropriately represented by the market-observed risks (discount rates) associated with public companies.

Partnership Description

Valuing a limited partnership involves not only understanding the required components of the valuation report, but also taking into account its history and the relationships of the partners. This may include the nature and history of the business and its distributions, the real estate assets held, past sales of interests in the partnership, distribution of ownership, and partnership and other agreements. In short, the valuer must consider all the material facts relative to the partnership that a typical buyer of an interest in the partnership would deem important in making an informed decision.

History of the Business

The history of the business entity being valued includes basic facts such as the formation date, the circumstances pertaining to its formation, and relevant transfers of interests. The valuer is not expected to know the entire history of the business and may not have full supporting documentation; nevertheless, he or she should describe significant events and circumstances, as well as summarize key elements of the partnership agreement to provide a basic orientation for the reader.

Distribution History

A history of the payments made to limited partners is important to the valuation report because it can establish a pattern of payments and an expectation of future payments for the potential buyer of an interest. Payment of distributions is most likely tied to the cash flow generated by the partnership's assets, but it can also demonstrate the general partner's desire to accumulate cash flow for investment, capital improvements, or other uses.

Real Estate Assets Held

This section of the valuation report is a summary of the real property appraisal that highlights key attributes of the property. (These attributes are analyzed in greater detail in later sections of the appraisal report.) It is a good practice to summarize the important facts from the real estate appraisal that directly affect the analysis of the limited partner's interest.

Past Sales of Interests in the Partnership

Sales of capital stock or other ownership interests in the business should be disclosed but not analyzed at this point. The relevance of these transactions to the valuation can be revisited after the entire process has been completed.

Distribution of Ownership

The distribution of ownership lists percentage interests in the partnership as of the date of value. Minority status can be compromised by the distribution of ownership in the event that the subject interest could be combined with another interest to achieve a significant increase in the degree of control over the enterprise. The ability to exercise control may also be modified by concerns over any practical legal hurdles that exist.[11]

The Partnership Agreement and Other Agreements

A partnership valuation should summarize the limited partnership agreement and all of its amendments. The summary includes basic information such as its name, relevant dates, and purpose. The valuer should identify the terms and conditions of the agreement that can affect value, listing provisions that are likely to influence the subject interest's degree of control, impediments to selling the interest, and allocations of cash flow and proceeds from sales, which affect the degree of control and marketability.

Many provisions of the agreement are unrelated to the value of the limited partner's interest. Some may affect control or marketability but may be difficult to tie to value (e.g., capital call provisions), and others always affect control (e.g., voting percentages related to the swing vote potential for the subject interest) and marketability (e.g., buy-back provisions).

A summary of the partnership agreement helps the reader and analyst to focus only on the terms in the agreement that affect value and to compare the various provisions within the agreement with each other. For instance, there could be vot-

---

11. These concerns are expressed in the following questions: Even for a general partnership in which the partner has the right to cause liquidation of the partnership's assets and distribution of the proceeds, or in limited partnerships in which a high percentage interest has the right to do the same, would a buyer be able to successfully cause liquidation? Would the other partners and the general partner be likely to challenge these attempts by the newcomer? Would the buyer price the interest based on the ability to liquidate the assets at will, and is such a right transferable to the buyer?

ing provisions that overlap in which one voting threshold can override another. By grouping related provisions from the agreement in the summary together, the appraiser can convey a more accurate assessment of the agreement.

Other agreements. The valuer should review any loan agreements. The terms and conditions of private promissory notes and evidence of their payment or nonpayment can be important to assessing the market value of the partnership's assets and liabilities. The terms of mortgage loans and bank notes are also important because they could include constraints on the partnership's actions with respect to tenancy in ways that might not have been considered in the real estate appraisal,[12] refinancing, and other matters. Moreover, all documents associated with loans should be reviewed.

Leases typically lie within the domain of the real estate appraisal, but such an appraisal may include only a summary of terms that are relevant to a fee value analysis, and other issues important to a valuation might be ignored. The business valuer, therefore, should review complete copies of all leases.

Management agreements, and any other documents concerning the use or operation of the property, should also be reviewed because the objectives of the business valuer and the real estate appraiser differ, and all relevant conditions pertaining to a valuation may not have been addressed in the real estate appraisal. The relevant terms and conditions of all other agreements should be summarized in the report as well.

Potential Legal Concerns

When advising clients on matters that involve the interpretation of partnership agreements, business valuers risk practicing law; typically only members of the state bar may practice law. Therefore, they should become reasonably knowledgeable about the statutes in the states in which they work, and at a minimum, develop a working familiarity with the Uniform Limited Partnership Act (ULPA) on which most state laws concerning limited partnerships are based.

The recommendations in this section are intended to familiarize real estate appraisers with valuation issues, and not to suggest that the appraiser should interpret the provisions of the agreement. Material issues that involve interpretations should always be referred to the client's counsel. Indeed, the valuer may require the counsel's written opinions on many issues that are key to establishing value (e.g., whether the interest transferred is an assignee or limited partner interest, whether an apparent right to force sale of the property or ter-

---

12. For example, a long-term net lease with a credit tenant may underlie repayment of a real estate loan, and rent assignments may have been executed for this purpose.

mination of the partnership is enforceable or could be successfully contested). Practical legal issues, even with apparent de jure voting powers, may be affected by de facto circumstances, and aspects of the valuation can hinge on counsel's advice about the practicality of enforcing agreement provisions.

Much of the valuation report will be based on experience and common sense. However, when specific issues or circumstances arise that are difficult to understand, or where there are apparent conflicts, the valuer should consider asking for an opinion of counsel and rely on that opinion in the report. Moreover, business valuers should be sufficiently familiar with legal issues to recognize when they are dealing with issues or interpretations that are beyond their competency and should seek the client's counsel's support when in doubt. The valuer should be competent in the basics, but if such agreements have provisions that are arguable, or that may conflict with statute, it is proper for the valuer to obtain guidance, or even an opinion, from counsel.

CASE STUDY APPLICATION

Facts, Circumstances, and History of Suburban Office Partners, II

This assignment involves the valuation of a family limited partnership, Suburban Office Partners II, L.P. The decedent, John Builder, developed office buildings in Southern California for 35 years and accumulated a sizable estate. He owned many of the buildings outright and some with his longtime partner Ed Helper. After Builder's wife's death in 1992, he formed several limited partnerships for holding various types of assets to provide stability and management succession, and to create a vehicle for transferring wealth to his children, Billy and Sara. Billy is the executor of the estate.

Suburban Office Partners, II, is a California-based limited partnership that owns and operates a 33,000-sq.ft. suburban multitenant office building located in Tustin, California.

Builder was the sole stockholder of the general partner, JB Management, Inc., which held the 1% GP interest. Builder held a 49% interest as a limited partner and Helper held the remaining 50%. Builder donated 3% of his interest to Boy's Home, an orphanage. When Helper needed cash for an operation in 1995, Builder bought 10% of his share for $120,000, reducing Helper's share to 40%. Helper told Billy later that his dad had paid a ridiculously high price because he was a very generous man (and Ed had sufficient capital losses to offset any gains at this point).

In later years, Builder assigned interests to Billy and Sara. When he died on January 17, 1997, each child held 18%. Before his death Builder transferred the stock in JB Management to a trust, naming Billy and Sara trustees and Builder the beneficiary. Upon his death, Builder's limited partnership interest and JB Management stock passed to the two children. Billy had been groomed to assume the management of the Suburban Office Partners, II, and a number of his father's other properties, but had only been involved directly in management for two years before his father's death. Although Sara trusted her older brother, her husband, Harold Morganstern, became increasingly involved in her financial affairs, particularly since she stood to inherit a large amount of money and property. Nothing is known about the relationship between Harold and Billy. Helper is now in his 80s and lives out of state. The family owns 15 other income-producing properties and has never sold one, despite having debated the issue. The estate has substantial liquid assets and does not need to sell any properties to pay taxes.

The appraisal assignment is to value, for estate tax purposes, the limited partner interest that John Builder held as of the date of his death. The valuer has been instructed to ignore any interest in JB Management because the interest is small and the benefit for taking any discount approximates the cost of valuing that interest.

The limited partnership interest that John Builder held as of the date of his death is calculated as follows

Original interest	49%
Less Builder's Boy's Home donation	– 3%
Plus interest purchased from Ed	10%
Less gifts to Billy	–18%
Less gifts to Sara	–18%
Net percentage interest to be valued	20%

The components of the valuation report for Suburban Office Partners, II, are listed below. Additional facts and circumstances pertaining to the partnership that affect value are presented next.

Introduction to the Valuation Report

Partnership Name and Type of Organization
Suburban Office Partners, II, a California limited partnership

Purpose or Business of the Partnership
To own and manage real property as detailed in the partnership agreement

Real Estate (and Any Other Assets) Held
A 33,000-sq. ft. office building located in Tustin, California

Type and Percentage Interest Being Valued
The 20% limited partnership interest held by John Builder before his death

Definition of the Interest
A minority interest

Definition of Value
Fair market value: The price at which the property would change hands between a willing buyer and willing seller, neither being under any compulsion to buy or sell and both having reasonable knowledge of the relevant facts. [Internal Revenue Service Regulations §20.2031-11b]

Purpose, Client, and Intended Use
To develop an opinion of the fair market value of the limited partnership interest on the effective date of the valuation for estate tax use. The client is William Builder, executor of the estate of John Builder. The intended users are the estate and its agents, and the Internal Revenue Service.
(See Standards Rule 9-2, Standards Rule 10-2, and SMT-9.)

Date of Value and Date of Report
The effective date of this valuation, the date for which value is concluded, is January 17, 1997, the date of death of John Builder. The date of the report is June 18, 1997.

Standards Compliance

This report and valuation were performed in compliance with the Code of Professional Ethics and the Standards of Professional Appraisal Practice of the Appraisal Institute (or other appraisal association), and the report has been prepared in conformity with these standards.

Partnership Description

Distribution History

Suburban Office Partners, II pays nearly all of its cash flow to its partners each year. Cash flows are increasing slowly because of the escalation clauses in the leases. However, some circumstances may reduce cash flows in the near future. (See the discussion of the real estate appraisal, Chapter 2)

Real Estate Assets

The partnership owns a 33,000-sq.ft. office building that John Builder built in 1987. It is occupied by 10 tenants and currently has one vacancy. The tenants are on three-to-10-year leases, five of which are coming due in 2000. These are mostly the longer-term tenants, and their leases are currently set about 20% above market rent.

Past Sales of Interests

John Builder purchased a 10% interest from Ed Helper in 1995 for $120,000.

Distribution of Ownership

General Partner

JB Management, Inc.	1.0 %

Limited Partners

John Builder (subject)	20.0 %
Edward Helper	40.0 %
Billy Builder	18.0 %
Sara Builder Morganstern	18.0 %
Boy's Home	3.0 %
Total	100.0%

For estate tax purposes, ownership is calculated as of the instant before death. Thus, the 20% interest that John Builder held before his death is the subject interest. Valuation of the 1% general partner interest has been excluded from this assignment.

Loans and Guarantees

The partnership's mortgage is a nonrecourse loan, and there are no personal loan guarantees.

Salient Elements of the Partnership Agreement

This section is a summary of the Agreement of Limited Partnership of Suburban Office Partners II, L.P., included in Appendix B, and references to the document are identified by the symbol §. The appraiser should identify the terms and conditions that are likely to affect value.

General Provisions

Name	Suburban Office Partners II, L.P. §1
Beginning date	July 24, 1993 (end of document) [Because a specific beginning date is not always stated, the date of signing is used, but the exact date is of no material importance for valuation purposes.]
Ending date	December 31, 2050 §5

Extensions	None
	May be continued by majority vote (§15.3.1), but since a limited partner may withdraw at that time, it does not affect value and would not necessarily be noted in the valuation
Purpose/scope of business	List §4.1/ Any lawful business §4.2
	[This means the general partner can engage in virtually whatever activity it wishes, limited only by its fiduciary obligations.]

Allocations[13]

Net cash flow:	In proportion to percentage interests §7.2, unless required for investment/business purposes
Profit and loss:	In proportion to percentage interests §7.1
Proceeds of sale:	In proportion to percentage interests §15.6.5. (See also net cash flow.)
Dissolution:	Generally, in proportion to capital accounts and then in proportion to respective percentage interests §15.6.5, §15.6.5
Additional capital:	The general partner has the power to make capital calls. Partners who choose not to participate in capital calls are penalized by the adjustment of all capital accounts, giving credit at the rate of 150% for amounts contributed §6.5. This provision is unusual but is illustrative of the surprises that some partnership agreements may contain.
Compensation of GP:	To be reasonable §8.17
Capital gains/basis:	IRC §754 election §10
	Adjusting the basis of the partnership's assets is done at the absolute discretion of the general partner

Matters of Control

Vote to terminate:	GP and 100% of limited partners §15.2.2, and indirectly §15.1
Vote to sell all assets:	GP and 75% of limited partners §8.15.2, but does not necessarily cause termination or distribution of proceeds §15.2.5
Vote to require distribution:	Majority can force GP to distribute rather than accumulate net cash flow §7.2. (Net cash flow also includes proceeds of sale §20.18)
Vote to remove GP:	None. GP cannot withdraw without the consent of all other partners §16.1
Vote to amend:	Unanimous consent of all partners required §8.15.5
Right to withdraw:	None §8.2.1. Can withdraw on dissolution based on inference (see Vote to terminate)

13. These allocations are typical of family limited partnerships, but in other partnerships the splits can be complex, with preferred payments, allocation of tax benefits to one class of partner, and other provisions. It is important to read the agreement in each case.

Matters of Marketability

Repurchase agreement:	None
Can transfer interest to:	Any partner, issue of a partner, charitable organization §11.10. (GP interest not transferable without unanimous consent of partners §11.12)
Right of first refusal:	None
	Usually refers to right to purchase at terms and conditions offered by an outside buyer
Right to purchase:	At fair market value §11.3.2 but financed at favorable terms §11.4.3
Admission as limited partner:	Unanimous written consent of all partners §11.2, §11.6.1
Transfer/assignment fee:	Reasonable expenses, not to exceed $2,000 §11.6.6

Other Items

Confidentiality:	No partner may disclose information identified as confidential §9.3.

This is not an exhaustive list, and it is relevant only for family limited partnerships and other relatively simple limited partnerships. Valuing more complex partnerships may require knowledge that is beyond the scope of this book. It should be noted in the valuation report that this summary does not address all elements of the partnership agreement and is to be used for valuation purposes only.

CHAPTER 2

Appraising the Real Property

Asset appraisal is a special case of the generalized business valuation process.[1] This chapter outlines the appraisal process from the report user's point of view, which includes the partnership valuer.[2] Its goal is twofold:

- To help valuers understand the process and scope of real estate appraisers' work so that they can evaluate the assignment to determine whether an existing appraisal is suitable to value the partnership
- To help the real estate appraiser define the scope of work needed to support the partnership valuation

For the sake of brevity, this case study addresses only the elements of a real estate appraisal that are directly pertinent to valuing a limited partnership. Aspects of the appraisal that have no direct bearing on the development of a valuation report have been excluded. The appraisal need not be as detailed in all respects as it is for this case study. However, the real estate appraiser and the business valuer will have to discuss important information omitted from the appraisal report. To the greatest extent possible, it is recommended that real estate appraisers address the appropriate topics described in this chapter when valuing an asset holding

1. The real estate appraisal process is generally consistent with Revenue Ruling 59-60, although the foundation of real estate appraisal predates the ruling, and it is not referenced as such in real estate appraisal literature.
2. This book makes distinctions between the asset appraisal/appraiser and the business appraisal/appraiser, since both are being discussed together throughout the work. "Appraisal" and "appraiser" are retained for reference to the former, but "valuation" and "valuer" are used in most instances when referring to the latter. This is done for the sole purpose of clarity in this presentation, and not to redefine word usage in the business valuation discipline. Although references to valuation, valuer and even "valuator" are not uncommon in the literature, the technically correct terms remain business appraisal and appraiser.

CASE STUDY APPLICATION

Subject Multitenant
Office Building, 200 S.
Main Street, Tustin, CA

Table 2.1	Summary of Important Data and Conclusions

Property type:	multitenant office
Location:	200 South Main Street, Tustin, CA 92680
Map reference:	830-A3 Thomas Guide
Assessor's parcel no:	3190-240-07,12,13
Zoning:	C3-2, neighborhood commercial
Highest and best use:	current multitenant office use
Building area:	36,300 sq. ft. gross
	33,000 sq. ft. rentable
Number of stories:	3
Land area:	47,916 sq. ft. gross
Definition of value:	market value
Date of value:	January 17, 1997
Date of report:	June 15, 1997
Value indications:	
Cost approach:	$3,750,000
Sales comparison:	$3,270,000
Income approach: direct capitalization	$3,335,000
yield capitalization	$3,211,000
Value conclusion:	$3,250,000

company. The adjustments discussed in this chapter are part of the business valuation, not the real estate appraisal, and are also covered in Chapter 3, Developing the Partnership's Net Asset Value.

Definition of Problem and Scope of Work

The scope of work is particularly important for short valuation reports that summarize the data and analysis and also for retaining important information in the appraiser's work file. The user of the real property appraisal should know what the appraiser did and did not do, and what information was relied upon in developing the value conclusion.

Purpose and Use of the Appraisal

The purpose of the appraisal is the stated reason for the assignment: to develop an opinion of the defined value of the specified real property interest. The purpose of the report is to develop an opinion of the fair market value of the leased fee estate of the subject property, Suburban Office Partners, II, a California limited partnership, as of the effective date of the appraisal—in this instance, January 17, 1997—the date of John Builder's death. It is to be used for estate tax reporting as part of a valuation of an interest in the property. The intended users are the client and at least the appraiser performing the valuation. The appraisal was performed in compliance with the Uniform Standards of Professional Appraisal Practice of the Appraisal Institute (the "Standards").

Definition of Value

The definition of value for the subject property is fair market value, defined as "the price at which the property would change hands between a willing buyer and a willing seller, neither being under any compulsion to buy or to sell and both having reasonable knowledge of the relevant facts." (IRC §20.2031-1(b))

When specifying the real estate appraisal assignment to the real estate appraiser, the business valuer should use the same definition of value used in the valuation. This is true especially when using appraisals that were prepared for another purpose. For instance, appraisals prepared for use in eminent domain proceedings may apply a different definition of fair market value than those prepared for other purposes.

Property Rights Appraised

The property right appraised is a leased fee interest, defined as "an ownership interest held by a landlord with the rights of use and occupancy conveyed by lease to others. The rights of lessor (the leased fee owner) and lessee are specified by contract terms contained within the lease."[3]

3. *The Dictionary of Real Estate Appraisal*, 4th ed. (Chicago: Appraisal Institute, 2002).

Relying on an appraisal prepared for a different use and for different users can raise tricky questions.

Effective Date of Value, Date of the Appraisal Report

Date of value should be the same for the appraisal and for the valuation. This can be an issue when the client wants to use an appraisal prepared at an earlier time and usually for a different intended use. In the absence of a new or updated appraisal (if no change in value has occurred between the two dates), the real estate appraiser could supply a statement for the valuation report that market conditions are stable, or that a further analysis of later data would not likely result in a changed opinion of value. If the asset value has changed as part of the valuation, however, the real estate appraisal must be reviewed, and the appraisal process is subject to the requirements of USPAP Standard 3. (This applies only when an appraiser qualified to appraise the subject property prepares the valuation.) A business valuer or accountant who changes the real estate value, for any reason, might want to consider competency provisions in their governing standards.

Client, Intended Users, and Intended Use

The client, intended users, and intended use for the real property appraisal should be compatible with the corresponding elements presented in the business valuation. Relying on an appraisal prepared for a different use and for different users can raise tricky questions. For example, if the intended user as stated in the appraisal is the client but not the business valuer does the latter have the right to rely on the value conclusion? If an error or omission occurred that affected the property value conclusion and, consequently, the value conclusion of the partnership interest, must the business valuer assume liability? Does the valuer properly disclose any extraordinary assumptions regarding the credibility of the real property appraisal he is relying upon in performing his assignment?

The most prudent course of action, according to these scenarios, is to have the real property appraiser acknowledge the business valuer along with the client as an intended user, or at least acknowledge the business valuer on behalf of the client. The intended use should then be the same as the intended use of the partnership/business valuation report. This can be specified when the appraisal is ordered.

Another problem can arise when a client wants to use an existing appraisal that specifies a different intended user. Under USPAP, a valuation service is applicable only for the identified use and users based on an agreement between the appraiser and the client. If the real property appraiser prepares a report for intended use A, the appraiser has no responsibility to the client or any other third party if the client decides to employ it for use B.

Using an Appraisal for a Second Set of Clients

An assignment is a valuation service provided as a consequence of an agreement between an appraiser and a client. Therefore, if a new party wishes to be identified as a client, by definition, there must be a new assignment. Further, because intended users are identified at the time of the assignment, if additional parties wish to become intended users, there must be a new assignment. Because a report constitutes the communication of the results upon completion of an assignment, a new assignment requires a new report. When developing the new assignment under such circumstances, an appraiser, in the interest of saving a client money, might rely on work performed for a previous assignment, but that does not alter the fact that it is a new assignment and a new client/user/use. Because the date of value, relevant property characteristics, or assignment conditions (extraordinary assumptions, hypothetical conditions, supplemental standards) might be different, the new client/user/use may or may not result in the same value conclusion.

This is not to say that an older appraisal, prepared for another use, absolutely cannot be used for a business valuation report, but only that if it is used, the real property appraiser is not responsible for the unintended use (assuming the original client and use was stated clearly in the original report).

Other Problems Related to Intended Use

Problems can occur when a business valuer uses a real estate appraisal that was prepared for another intended use. Suppose, for instance, that the intended use in the prior appraisal assignment was financing, the appraisal was performed before one of the owners died, and the business valuer uses the existing real property appraisal as is rather than performing a new assignment. Suppose further that distribution of the estate results in a division of assets and one of the heirs contests the equitability of the division and has the property reappraised as of the date of death. Finally, suppose that the new appraised value differs significantly from the value opinion in the appraisal for lending, which later is found to be flawed, and the heirs look to the original appraiser to make them financially whole. (The real property appraiser noted that his work was performed for the lender so the estate was not an intended user.) Based on this hypothetical situation, the real estate appraiser would not be responsible, but the question arises as to whether the business valuer who used the flawed value in his valuation report could also escape responsibility. Of course, this situation might be obviated if the

Particularly important to valuing a business such as a partnership are growth rates and trends and the time frame for any anticipated events (i.e., changes in supply and demand relationships, zoning, nearby development, and rental market trends).

business valuer properly disclosed any extraordinary assumptions regarding the use of the real property appraisal and properly disclosed his/her scope of work.

As is obvious from the scenario described, the client and valuation stand to benefit by having a real property appraisal intended specifically for use in the valuation, even if the valuer can offer an opinion of value for the real estate.[4]

Assumptions, Hypothetical Conditions, and Limiting Conditions

Assumptions, hypothetical conditions, and limiting conditions should be reviewed for incompatible conditions and limitations. Of particular concern are hypothetical conditions that were relevant for the real property as a whole but not for a noncontrolling interest in the partnership, or the failure to apply the appropriate valuation methodology that might not be needed for the appraisal, but is required for the valuation (i.e., an income approach is almost always needed for the valuation). Statements concerning conformance with standards and impartiality should be consistent with the requirements for the preparer of the valuation.

Market Area Data and Analysis

The appraisal of real property includes both broad and local views of economic and other conditions and trends that affect value. It begins with an analysis of the geographic region in which the property is located. For properties that are marketed nationally, it may begin with an analysis of national conditions and trends. The analysis addresses characteristics of the specific jurisdiction (city or county), district, or neighborhood. Generally, these attributes are external to the property.[5] Particularly important to valuing a business such as a

4. Some states, Colorado among them, allow CPAs to express opinions on real estate values. If the business appraiser is also a real estate appraiser, he or she could conclude real estate value, a solution that is not necessarily advantageous since the work is being done by someone else. [Under USPAP, the reviewer can provide his or her own opinion of value, which might differ from the appraiser's and would require conforming to Standard 3, Appraisal Review. It may also involve Standard 1. The reviewer would report his or her alternate value conclusion in the review report under Standards Rule 3-2]. An appraisal for a new intended use always results in a new appraisal assignment under USPAP.

5. An analysis of market data satisfies Revenue Ruling §4.01(b), which requires the appraiser to consider "the economic outlook in general and the condition and outlook of the specific industry in particular." The term *specific industry* means both the real estate industry in general and the market for the particular property type. Interpreting the revenue ruling for real property application requires some conversion of terminology.

partnership are growth rates and trends and the time frame for any anticipated events (i.e., changes in supply and demand relationships, zoning, nearby development, and rental market trends). Often, trends are not quantified in the property appraisal, but a real estate appraiser who is aware of how the report will be used may be able to anticipate the need to present more detail on future expectations. It is more likely, however, that the business valuer will need to develop the necessary information in an interview with the appraiser.

CASE STUDY APPLICATION

Market Area Data and Analysis Summary

Market conditions in Orange County, California, continued to improve in 1996 and exceeded conditions in the rest of the five-county area. Unemployment averaged 4.1% in 1996, and job growth averaged 2.3%, compared to a 1.9% rate for the nation. The office market trend was also positive; it indicated a 2% decline in vacancy rates in 1996. The subject district exhibited a vacancy rate just below 10%, the lowest vacancy rate in the market area. Low vacancy rates have triggered some of the first speculative development in the county, and plans have been announced for at least one large project in South County and several smaller office projects in the district. New space that will become available in the next few years will likely cause an increase in vacancy rates for Class B buildings such as the subject property.

The effective lease rate has been increasing since late 1993, and the rate of increase through 1996 has been more than 6%, but the data tend to be weighted toward larger Class A office space. The lease rate for Class B office space appears to be lower. This rate has increased from a low point reached during the four-year recession and has been fueled by a lack of new construction. Over the next five to seven years, the market expects that the rate of increase will slow and will average from 3% to 4% per year for Class A office space, and 2% to 3% for Class B office space.

Property Data and Analysis

The property data and analysis covers the specific characteristics of the land and improvements, including personal property, and specific zoning requirements and sources of depreciation such as physical deterioration and functional obsolescence. Specific repair needs and instances of deferred maintenance, if any, are identified, and the subject is compared to competing properties.

This step in the appraisal process partly satisfies Revenue Ruling §4.01(a), which requires analysis of "the nature of the business and the history of the enterprise from its inception." The nature of the business in the case study is related to the specific real estate held by the partnership (as well as the historic activities of the partnership).

This section of the report is often short on necessary detail. For example, it is often assumed that the buyer of a property will make needed upgrades, and if the property is compared with similar properties that need upgrades or if the analysis is based solely on lease income, the cost of upgrading may not be explicitly considered. However, these costs may be an important consideration for the partners for whom the interest in the property is being valued during the expected holding period, and this cost information may be important. Moreover, the business valuation may call for a specific equipment replacement schedule to develop a realistic cash flow over the selected holding period, whereas the appraisal may provide only a market-derived allowance for replacement.

Zoning regulations and other information presented in this section may lead to obvious conclusions as to whether the property can be partitioned if the business "entity" is common tenancy ownership. However, it is more likely that, when partition is a real possibility, an additional analysis of the feasibility and costs associated with the partition process will be needed (see Chapter 8).

The real estate appraiser's basic responsibility in performing the property data analysis is to include sufficient detail to accurately replicate the actions of market participants. The business valuation often requires more detailed information to properly analyze the cash flows and events expected by the partners or cotenants over the holding period.

CASE STUDY APPLICATION

Property Data and Analysis Summary

The subject 47,916-sq.-ft. site is located at the southeast corner of Main and Second Streets and has 260 feet of frontage on Main St. and 184 frontage feet on Second St. The improvements are located against the east lot line. Parking is available along both frontages and at the north end of the site. There are 102 surface parking spaces, with adequate access from Main and via Second through a nonexclusive easement to the east (see Figure 2.1).

There are similar, conforming office buildings to the north and east of the subject. Small apartment buildings and single-family residences are located to the east and south. A church is located directly across Main Street, and an older office park is located to the north. Main Street to the south of Second Street is residential. Several newer shopping centers are located three blocks north, at Main and Euclid.

The subject improvements consist of a three-story, wood-frame, multitenant office building with a stucco and glass facade. The first floor has a small lobby and three office suites. The second and third floors each have four office suites. Rentable area varies from 1,200 to 4,650 square feet per suite. Interior spaces have suspended t-bar ceiling grids with acoustic, ventilation, and fluorescent lighting panels. Interior clearance under the ceiling grid is eight feet. Two elevators serve all floors. The interior spaces are equipped with air conditioning.

The improvements appear to be in good condition overall. Interior surfaces vary from good to average condition. The roof covering appears to be fairly new and no deferred maintenance is noted.

The remaining economic life of the improvements is estimated to be 45 years based on the life expectancy guidelines for commercial structures published by Marshall and Swift, and on the building's estimated effective age, which is 10 years—the same as its actual age.

The subject improvements conform to market standards in all respects, except that the interior ceiling clearance is at least one foot lower than would be typical for new construction. This may put the subject property at a competitive disadvantage and may be a source of functional obsolescence when competing buildings are completed in the next few years.

The quality of the improvements is average to good. Functional limitations are typical of many buildings of the same age in the district, and the overall market appeal of the property is average.

Figure 2.1 Site Plan for Appraised Property

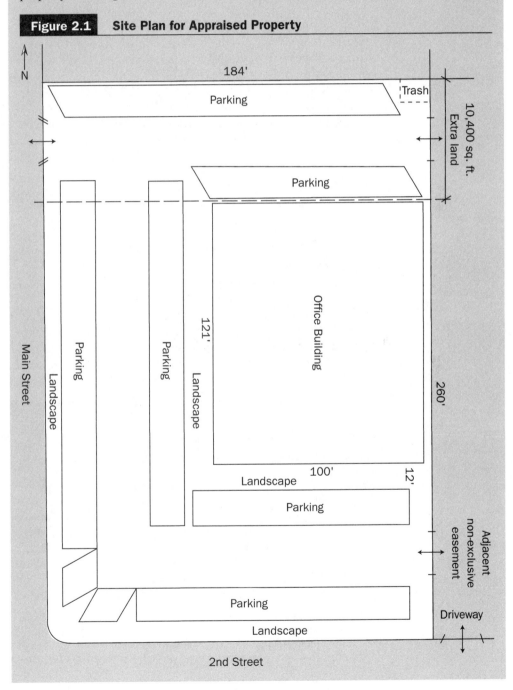

> *There are many instances when a detailed highest and best use analysis is needed for the business valuation report.*

Highest and Best Use

Highest and best use is defined as that reasonably probable and legal use of vacant land or an improved property, which is physically possible, appropriately supported, financially feasible, and that results in the highest value.[6] This section of the appraisal report provides the basis for the selection of comparables and the analysis that will be presented in the approaches to value.

The four criteria of highest and best use must be met sequentially; i.e., only uses that are legally permissible and physically possible will be considered for the productivity tests. All uses that produce a positive economic return are considered financially feasible, and, finally, those that produce the highest return are highest and best.

This section of the appraisal report is often given short shrift, and the four elements are not explicitly discussed. This may be appropriate when the existing use of the land is permissible and feasible and when no one expects to replace the improvements with another use in the foreseeable future. However, there are many instances when a detailed highest and best use analysis is needed for the valuation report.

It is not unusual, particularly in down markets, for the highest and best use of an underdeveloped property to be to hold it for future development, which is what a hypothetical buyer might do in such a market. The business valuer, in valuing a partnership interest, however, needs to consider the following questions:

- When will it be feasible to develop the property based on market trends?
- Would the current owners redevelop the property?
- What if the property only needs a facelift?

In another instance, suppose a poorly performing retail center is valued assuming capital expenditures and an increased revenue stream. The general partner might not be willing to make such expenditures because future cash flows under his or her management may be very different than the income expected by a typical buyer of the 100% fee interest. This would not change the concluded value, which is based on a hypothetical sale of the whole property, but it would change the expected cash flows, which would affect the valuation.

Highest and best use is also the key to the value analysis. When ownership issues, time constraints, and other business entity-level restrictions are imposed, the meaning of highest

6. *The Dictionary of Real Estate Appraisal*, 4th ed.

CASE STUDY APPLICATION

Highest and Best Use Analysis

As If Vacant

The site is larger than most commercial sites in the district and can accommodate office and commercial structures typical for the area. Commercial C3-2 zoning allows both office and retail uses. Retail is concentrated at principal intersections, and restaurants, several bank branches, and local stores are located within three blocks of the subject. The local office building's employee population would likely be inadequate to support retail space at the subject location, and the existing nearby retail outlets appear to be sufficient.

Office use would be the most conforming use of the subject in the short term; however, new construction nearing completion may affect office occupancy. As noted in the market data analysis, a few projects are in development, and vacancy is low. New construction would compete effectively with older space, and the conclusion is that additional new office space would be supported; therefore, the highest and best use of the subject site as though vacant is mid-rise office. The market is equally divided between owner/users and investors, but prices are greater for owner/user buildings, and a newly constructed building would likely be built for a single user.

Building area is limited by parking requirements. To allow for surface parking, the improvements would likely be 45,000 square feet built in three stories (at 2 spaces/1,000 sq. ft.); improved area would be reduced to approximately 38,000 square feet, for a parking ratio of 2.5/1,000).

As Improved

The existing use of the property conforms to current zoning regulations. The improvements are in good condition and are satisfactorily adapted to their multitenant, general office use. The building could be adapted for single-tenant use, and it is possible that the conversion costs would be offset by an equal increase in market value.

The current parking ratio, at 2.8 spaces/1,000 square feet, is more than the legal requirement of 2.0. Many older buildings were constructed with a 2.0 ratio, but new construction generally provides 3.0 spaces/1,000 square feet. To be competitive, a building should have at least 2.5/1,000, but preferably a ratio of 3.0. Approximately 37,500 square feet are required to support the improvements at the 2.0 ratio, giving a surplus site area of more than 10,400 square feet that could be developed under current zoning regulations.

Management has been discussing the possibility of constructing additional improvements because of this excess parking space. At a ratio of 2.0 for the office improvements and 3.0 for new retail improvements, the site would support an additional 4,500 square feet of retail space. (The site is too small for competitive office and other uses, such as bank branches and health clubs, which usually require more parking than can be accommodated.) However, the highest and best use as though vacant analysis indicates that retail space is not likely to be the highest and best use of the site anyway, since there is competing retail space nearby. Further, reducing the office-parking ratio to 2.0 instead of the existing 2.8 may limit the ability of the subject property to compete with new construction.

The subject property's improvements contribute value in such a way that the improved value of the land is greater improved than it would be if the land were vacant. The current use is the same as the property's highest and best use as improved, and the conclusion is that the highest and best use of the subject property as improved is its current use as office space.

> *Highest and best use may have to be considered further in common tenancy ownership, in which the feasibility of dividing the property can become an issue.*

and best use can be affected. Thus, careful consideration of the highest and best use concept is often needed to fully understand the position of the minority interest holder in a property.

Highest and best use may have to be considered further in common tenancy ownership, in which the feasibility of dividing the property can become an issue prompting the following questions: If the property is divisible, then what is the highest and best use of each part? Is it the same, or is it changed? For example, the highest and best use for a 10-acre agricultural parcel that borders a suburban development may be to develop it with a single-family residence. If zoning regulations mandate a five-acre minimum lot area for residential use, however, a two-acre parcel (20% of the whole) would not be developable, and its highest and best use may be the agricultural purpose for which is it currently being used. Thus, the highest and best use analysis provides the key to understanding feasibility of partitioning the property.

Cost Approach

The cost approach is a technique for developing an opinion of value based the cost of constructing a similar property that exhibits the same condition and utility as the subject property. It is founded primarily on the economic principle of substitution, which states "a prudent buyer would pay no more for a property than the cost to acquire a similar site and construct improvements of equivalent desirability and utility without undue delay."[7] The cost approach to value is applied in four steps:

1. Conclude the value of the site as though vacant.
2. Estimate the cost of reproducing or replacing the existing improvements.
3. Estimate and deduct depreciation from all causes.
4. Add the value of the site to the depreciated value of the improvements.

This approach is used most often by market participants when valuing new construction or special-purpose properties. Its usefulness is diminished if

- Differences between the subject and comparable sites are great

---

7.   *The Appraisal of Real Estate*, 12th ed. (Chicago; Appraisal Institute, 2001), 350.

- The value of the site is difficult to determine
- The improvements are old and/or obsolete (with conditions that result in significant deductions for accrued depreciation)
- Data to measure depreciation are inadequate
- The site is not developed to its highest and best use as though vacant

Thorough appraisals may contain highly detailed cost-to-cure and depreciation schedules for short-lived building components. Repair costs should be considered in the improvement analysis if they cannot be made explicit in the cost approach, and they may appear in the other approaches as well.

The cost approach also includes an analysis of land value; however, this can also be set apart as a separate section of the appraisal. Land value may be also estimated independently for use in the sales comparison approach or the income approach.

CASE STUDY APPLICATION
Cost Approach Conclusions

The subject site was valued using a sales comparison approach. The sales of parcels sold for the development of commercial improvements were compared with the subject and their adjusted value indications were reconciled to obtain an indicated price per square foot for the site. The concluded site value is:

$$47{,}916 \text{ sq. ft.} \times \$22.00/\text{sq. ft.} = \$1{,}054{,}152$$
$$(\text{rounded}) \ \$1{,}054{,}000$$

The cost approach was used in appraising Suburban Office Partners, II, because competing buildings are under construction in the district. The subject exhibits little physical deterioration and no external obsolescence, but does show functional obsolescence because of the low ceiling. This obsolescence has not been measured separately but could account for the difference in the value indications of the cost and sales comparison approaches. A value opinion is derived as follows:

Replacement cost new of improvements	$3,295,000
Less physical deterioration	− 599,000
Depreciated value of improvements	$2,696,000
Concluded value of land	1,054,000
Value indicated by the cost approach	$3,750,000

Sales Comparison Approach

To apply the sales comparison approach, the appraiser analyzes sales of properties that are similar to the subject to derive an opinion of value. The approach is based primarily on the economic principle that the value of a property tends to be set by the price that would be paid to acquire a substitute property of similar utility and desirability within a reasonable amount of time.[8, 9]

In the sales comparison approach, sale prices are adjusted for elements of comparison, or particular differences, between the subject and individual comparables. Elements of comparison are the characteristics of properties and of sale transactions that cause prices to vary. They include the real property rights conveyed, financing terms, conditions of sale, market conditions, location, physical and economic characteristics, use, and other elements not directly related to the real estate. Prices are reduced to generally accepted units of comparison. After adjustments have been applied to the comparable prices, the most indicative units of comparison, i.e., those that are most suitable for determining value such as price per square foot, price per unit, or gross income, are applied to the subject to arrive at a value conclusion.

The sales comparison approach is often used to value smaller properties and in owner/user markets because data for its application can be obtained and applied relatively easily by market participants. The reliability of the approach is diminished if

- The differences between the subject and the comparables are great
- Sufficient market transactions are not available, or
- Significant imbalances exist between the land and its improvements, the property and its environment, or the supply of and demand for similar properties

Data from real estate transactions and general market data derived from surveys and interviews form the basis for the appraiser's estimate of the market exposure time linked to the value opinion.[10] The data may be presented in this section or after the reconciliation and conclusions section of the report. When valuing a real estate holding company, exposure time may be important if the conditions encountered when analyzing the fractional interest dictate a shortened marketing period or a forced sale.

---

8. *The Appraisal of Real Estate*, 418.
9. The approach was once called the *market approach*, but all approaches are market approaches, so the more specific name was adopted.
10. *Exposure time*, as defined by *The Dictionary of Real Estate Appraisal*, "is the estimated length of time the property interest being appraised would have been on the market prior to the hypothetical consummation of a sale at market value on the effective date of the appraisal."

Sales Comparison Approach Summary

The site and its improvements were valued by comparing it to similar office properties that were sold the previous year. Comparables were selected for their size, age, location, and quality. Investors purchased a few of these properties, but most were purchased for owner occupancy.

The sale prices were adjusted for financing terms, conditions of sale, and market conditions. Each comparable's adjusted price per square foot was further adjusted for location, land-to-building ratio, and other physical elements.

Although the subject property is a multitenant building, it would be possible to convert it to single-tenant use. No cost to convert was considered in the analysis because it would depend on the particular purchaser's business, and any conversion would take place only if the existing tenants were removed. The comparables that were purchased for use, rather than investment, also required interior alterations. The value concluded by the sales comparison approach is:

$$36{,}300 \text{ sq. ft.} \times \$90.00/\text{sq. ft.} = \$3{,}267{,}000$$
$$\text{(rounded)} \ \$3{,}270{,}000$$

Income Approach

The most important step in the appraisal process for the entity valuation is the income approach. Even if it is not relevant for appraising the fee simple estate, it is still needed because minority interests are financial interests, and the market for minority interests is typically an investor market. The income approach is based on the premise that the value of a property is represented by the present worth of its anticipated net income. It is based on the premise that "...value is created by the expectation of benefits to be derived in the future," and "change is the result of the cause-and-effect relationship among the forces that influence real property value."[11]

An investor in real estate expects to derive net income and other future benefits from a property and values these benefits based on the likelihood that they will be realized as forecast. The greater the perceived risk or uncertainty of receiving a particular future benefit, the less an investor will pay today for the right to receive it later.

In the income approach, income and expenses are forecast for the subject property, and the quality, quantity, and durability of this net income stream is analyzed.[12] The resulting net income is capitalized into an indication of value using a capitalization rate developed from the marketplace or by some other acceptable method. The income and expense analysis, capitalization rates, growth rates, and other information developed in the income approach are required for valuing the business entity and minority interests.

---

11. *The Dictionary of Real Estate Appraisal.*

12. In real estate appraisal, the use of the word *income* in this context refers to cash flow, not a tax-affected earnings stream as it would in valuation of a corporate entity.

> *Owner-users often anticipate personal business-related benefits of occupancy that cannot be quantified.*

The reliability of the income approach to value is diminished if the future benefits that typical buyers expect to receive cannot be measured directly. In owner/user markets, for example, property owners are not investors, and their properties do not generate measurable rental income. Owner-users often anticipate personal business-related benefits of occupancy that cannot be quantified. If the subject property has characteristics for which rent cannot be supported with available market data, its income-generating capacity cannot be predicted with confidence. When appraising an owner/user property, the appraiser may, therefore, ignore an income approach entirely, because it often has nothing to do with the actions of buyers and sellers of the particular property. However, if the same report is being prepared for the purpose of a business valuation, major elements of the income approach will be needed. The real estate appraiser would then provide at least a rent survey and an income analysis, which partially fulfills the requirements of the approach.

The income approach satisfies Revenue Ruling §4.01 (d) and (e) in part. The ruling requires the appraiser to consider "the earning and dividend-paying capacity of the company." For a real estate holding company, the earning capacity is tied directly to the income-generating capacity of its holdings. The company's earning and dividend-paying capacity is also affected by financing and other activities and investments of the partnership.

The income approach section of the appraisal includes a forecast of gross rental income, a lease analysis, an expense analysis, and the application of capitalization rates in direct or yield capitalization. The application of capitalization rates to net operating income (*NOI*) gives the value conclusion.

Forecast of Gross Income

The initial step in determining the income-generating capacity of the subject property is to forecast the potential gross income of the property. This figure is based on fair market rental rates and/or scheduled rental income from leases and may include income from other sources (e.g., laundry income in an apartment building). If the property is leased, the actual rental income and the probability of receiving this level of income in the future is considered and compared to the fair rental value of the property. Potential rental income is then forecast for the year that follows the date of value.

If the property is not rented, a market rental rate is imputed and rent forecast. This can be done even if the property would most likely be occupied by an owner/user (e.g., a small office, or an industrial building, and other property types).

Lease Analysis

If the subject property is leased, the rent level, lease terms, and current market rents and terms become important. The appraiser must ask: Is rent above or below current market rents? Or, based on the lease terms, will it be above or below market levels in the future? For example, the market may expect annual increases of 3% based on the Consumer Price Index, but the lease may provide for a 5%-per-year increase, or the rent may be level for the remaining term.

If a mismatch exists between the lease rents and market rents, the appraiser should determine if the lease is likely to be renegotiated (if rents are too high) or whether rents can be increased to market levels on lease termination (if they are too low). To estimate the effect on value, the appraiser may adjust the (single period) capitalization rate plus or minus from the concluded rate, adjust the value conclusion for the present value of excess or lost rent, or show annual rental income explicitly with a discounted cash flow (DCF) model.

The appraiser must also forecast expected vacancy and collection losses as well as any expense reimbursements due under the terms of the lease. Although management may have the right to charge tenants for certain expenses, it may not have done so in the past for a variety of reasons, and the likelihood of receiving agreed-upon future reimbursements may be impaired. Potential gross income less vacancy and collection loss equals effective gross income *(EGI)*.

Expense Analysis

The next step in determining the income-generating capacity of the subject property is to examine its current and historical operating expenses and forecast the operating expenses that a market participant would expect the property to incur during the year after the date of value. A 12-month income forecast is used with direct capitalization, but a multiperiod forecast may be needed for yield capitalization.

Expenses are usually divided into three groups: fixed expenses, variable expenses, and replacement reserves. Fixed expenses are incurred regardless of whether the property is occupied. Variable expenses pertain to the operation of the property and generally vary with occupancy. Replacement reserves allow for the replacement of short-lived items on an annualized cost basis. The income and expense statement is typically constructed to show actual expenses at the date of value in one

> *Management fees are usually set at a market-supported percentage of EGI since the fee interest holder can change offsite managers and would presumably seek to maximize its return.*

column for reference, and forecast expenses (for the 12 months following the date of value) in another column.[13] Actual expenses are generally provided by the owner.

Adjustment of expenses. The forecast is usually developed by the appraiser and is intended to reflect the income and expenses after the property is transferred based on typical and competent management, which is what a new owner would expect. Expenses are forecast based on historical patterns, market survey data, and/or projections of current cost items. Some items, such as ad valorem taxes, may be based on the purchase price, and other taxes and management fees might be recalculated based on the forecast *EGI*. The income and expense statement is important for the business valuation because some of the expenses may have to be adjusted to develop the likely income stream that would be realized within the partnership after transfer of the minority interest. Thus, it is important to have the rationale for each expense stated in the real estate appraisal. If a summary report is prepared, it may be necessary for the business valuer to discuss some items with the appraiser to determine whether adjustments are needed.

Some expense items that might need adjusting are ad valorem taxes, management fees, and reserves. Adjustments for property taxes may be required in states where property is reassessed on transfer if the appraisal assumes that the new buyer will be taxed based on a reassessment at the appraised value. In that event, the property transfer would not be an assumption of the business valuation, and the actual property taxes expected for the coming year should be substituted for the appraiser's forecast taxes.[14]

Management fees are usually set at a market-supported percentage of *EGI* since the fee interest holder can change offsite managers and would presumably seek to maximize its return. However, with the agreement of the other partners, a general partner or affiliate might charge a higher rate. Because the minority holder cannot change the management arrangement, the actual expense amount should be used in the valuation.

13. The reference column may include expense information from the previous reporting period, at the date of value, or for another defined and meaningful period.

14. In California, for example, reassessment is triggered if more than 50% of the property interest is transferred. If the interest is above this threshold, increased taxes would have to be considered, and the new partner might have to bear the entire increase following some agreed-upon formula.

It is also possible that some of the management fee might have been for partnership management services but allocated to the property. In this instance, the business valuation should show a portion of the fee reallocated to partnership management as a normalization adjustment.

Immediate repair requirements are often explicitly identified, and an annual reserve is deducted in the appraisal. More often though, the real estate appraiser, guided by the market's method of addressing this issue, may not explicitly consider a potential expenditure that might not be required until several years later. If such expenditures would be expected during the valuation's holding period, an additional reserve for these items may be needed in the valuation.

The need to make adjustments in expenses does not affect valuation of the 100% fee simple interest because the appraisal's forecast is projected to conform to the expectation of a buyer who will control the entire property. Adjustments to the partnership-level income forecast are discussed further in Chapter 3, Developing the Partnership's Net Asset Value.

Capitalization

Capitalization is generally defined as a process used to convert expected future benefits into a present value. In business valuation terms, however, it is a conversion of a single period of economic benefits into value.[15] Whereas the single-period rate is commonly referred to as the "cap rate," real estate appraisers refer to it as the "overall rate." In direct capitalization, a capitalization rate is applied to a single year's expected income. Yield capitalization may include a detailed analysis of the income stream, typified by analyzing explicit annual cash flows in a DCF model.

Direct capitalization. Direct capitalization is often preferred as a means of converting expected future benefits into a present value because of its simplicity and its capacity to reflect market behavior in many circumstances. However, it only provides part of the picture: the capitalization rate includes an implicit growth rate, and the two must be separated for business value analysis.

Yield capitalization is typically performed for larger properties. It is the norm for institutional and other sophisticated investors and for properties whose income stream is not stabilized, such as shopping centers, office buildings undergoing renovation, and properties that have nonmarket rent levels under short-term leases. Yield capitalization is ideal for

---

15. From *International Glossary of Business Valuation Terms*, 2d ed., a joint effort of the American Institute of Certified Public Accountants (AICPA), the American Society of Appraisers (ASA), the Canadian Institute of Chartered Business Valuators (CICBV), the National Association of Certified Valuation Analysts (NACVA), and the Institute of Business Appraisers (IBA). By contrast, *The Dictionary of Real Estate Appraisal* defines *capitalization* in more general terms as the conversion of income into value.

developing the valuation since growth and yield rates are made explicit, as are future cash flow-influencing events.

Direct capitalization converts a single year's income expectancy into an indication of value in one direct step—usually by dividing the net income estimate by an appropriate overall capitalization rate (OAR, R_O, or "going-in" rate). Although only one year's income is used, a satisfactory return for the investor and the recapture of the capital invested is implicit in the overall rate.

The overall rate can be derived from real estate market transactions or investor survey data, or it can be developed using other methods. After an appropriate rate is determined, *NOI* is divided by the rate selected to derive property value.

Obtaining overall rates from transactions is a reliable method as long as the appraiser has enough dependable comparable information on sale prices, terms of sale, and net annual income. Comparable transactions should be similar to the subject in property type, use, and property rights conveyed, and net income should reflect stabilized operating conditions.

Investor survey data[16] can be used directly when the market for the property is adequately described by the investors being surveyed. The data are also used in the absence of good local market data or to support the results developed from actual sale transactions.

CASE STUDY APPLICATION

Direct Capitalization

The cash flow forecast for Year 1 of Suburban Office Partners II, is summarized in Table 2.2. The summary of individual lease rates and terms is not shown. The overall capitalization rate (R_O) is developed largely from local investor purchases of similar leased office buildings. However, because only a few of these transactions occurred, national survey data for suburban office properties in Los Angeles (the nearest and most directly comparable market reported by the survey) were also used. The indicated range was 8.0% to 11.5%, and the selected rate was 9.50%. The value concluded by direct capitalization is:

$$\$316,800 \ NOI \ / \ 0.0950 = \$3,334,737$$
$$\text{(rounded)} \ \$3,335,000$$

---

16. Includes PriceWaterhouseCoopers, *The Korpacz Real Estate Investor Survey*; CB Commercial, *National Investor Survey*; Realty rates. com, *Quarterly Investor Survey*; and *RERC Real Estate Report*, Real Estate Research Corporation.

Table 2.2	Property Income Statement Summary	
Income	**Actual**	**Forecast**
Scheduled rent*	$495,000	$509,900
Less vacancy†	(49,500)	(76,500)
Gross rental income	$445,500	$433,400
Other income‡	1,850	1,800
Reimbursements§	30,272	58,000
Effective gross income	$477,622	$493,200
Expenses		
Real estate taxes	$18,420	$32,500
Insurance	2,512	2,600
Utilities	26,311	27,100
Maintenance and repair‖	18,480	23,100
Building services	31,078	31,700
Management#	33,413	19,500
Other administrative	35,882	36,600
Reserves**	0	3,300
Total expenses and reserves	$166,096	$176,400
Net operating income	$311,526	$316,800

* Rent expected under current leases for 1997. This rent is approximately 10% above market for 15,500 sq. ft., and at market for 12,870 sq. ft.; 3,630 sq. ft. are vacant. The above-market leases are due in 1999 and 2000.

† Current vacancy is approximately 10%, and the forecast is 15% to account for the condition described in (*) above.

‡ Other income covers late fees and parking, including short-term agreements for parking on the excess portion of the site.

§ Reimbursements are for common area maintenance (CAM) only, and have not been collected from some tenants for the past few years. The market has changed, and it is expected that new management will be able to collect increased but not full reimbursements.

‖ Maintenance was down for 1996 and is forecast at a more normal $0.70/sq. ft.

An affiliate of the owner currently charges a management fee of 7.5% of gross rental receipts. We forecast a market rate of 4.5%.

** Reserves for replacement are not currently maintained, and reserve funds would not pass from seller to buyer. Reserves are forecast at $0.10/sq. ft., and are at the low end of the market survey range.

Yield Capitalization

Yield capitalization, or the discounted cash flow method, is used to convert future benefits over a specified holding period into present value by applying an appropriate yield or discount rate.[17] This method entails three steps:

1. Project all future cash flows or cash flow patterns and analyze the relationship between present and future cash flows for a specified holding period.

2. Select an appropriate yield (discount) rate.[18]

3. Convert future benefits into present value by discounting each annual future benefit.

Yield capitalization uses a discounted cash flow model in which the annual patterns for income and expense items are made explicit. The advantage of such a model is that it leaves nothing to the imagination. Annual rental income can be shown to vary with lease turnover if the pattern for rental income is expected to be unusual. Vacancy and collection loss and expense reimbursements can also change from year to year. Expenses that are a function of income (e.g., management fees) are shown to vary with *EGI*. Reserves for major repairs or capital replacements can also be made explicit, although it is more typical to show a constant annual amount for this item. Growth rates are applied for individual items, and expected growth for both cash flows and value can be calculated directly from the DCF model.

The DCF model assumes termination of the investment at the end of the selected holding period (the reversion of the property), usually by applying an overall rate (termed a *terminal rate* or *going-out rate*) to the expected *NOI* for the year following the period (year $n + 1$ for a holding period of n years). The terminal rate usually bears a relationship to the overall, or going-in, rate and can be developed from local market or from investor survey data.

17. The *discounted cash flow method* is defined in the *International Glossary of Business Valuation Terms* as a method within the income approach by which the present value of future expected net cash flows is calculated using a discount rate. In contrast, *yield capitalization* is defined by *The Dictionary of Real Estate Appraisal* as the capitalization method used to convert future benefits into present value by discounting each future benefit at an appropriate yield rate or by developing an overall rate that explicitly reflects the investments income pattern, value change and yield rate.

18. The *yield rate* (*Y*) is defined in *The Dictionary of Real Estate Appraisal* as a rate or return on capital, usually expressed as a compound annual percentage rate. A yield rate considers all expected property benefits, including the proceeds from sale at termination of the investment. The concept is similar to yield to maturity (YTM), which the *Dictionary of Financial Terms, TIAA-CREF* defines as "the yield on a bond from the current date until the date on which it is scheduled to be retired; it takes into account the gain on a discount or loss on a premium." A yield rate is used here as a general term for a total investment return. For the purpose of this book, it is considered to be the same as a discount rate, although the discount rate may be different depending on how it is extracted from the market. Using the term *discount rate* conflicts with the notion of valuation discounts from net asset value, so the term *yield* is used instead. The term *yield rate* will be used throughout this book when referring to investment return, except in Chapter 4 when the term *yield* refers to the annual dividend payment or dividend yield.

CASE STUDY APPLICATION

Yield Capitalization Summary

Cash flows for the five-year holding period are forecast individually. Income is forecast based on current leases and expected turnover and renewals, and expenses are developed from historical trends and market expectations. The discounted cash flow model and its underlying assumptions are shown in Table 2.3.

Table 2.3   Discounted Cash Flow

		1996 Year 0	1997 Year 1	1998 Year 2	1999 Year 3	2000 Year 4	2001 Year 5	2002 Year 6 Reversion
Income								
Gross revenue*		$495,000	$509,850	$525,146	$540,900	$530,597	$546,515	$562,910
Vacancy rate†		10%	10%	10%	12%	20%	14%	10%
Vacancy		(49,500)	(50,985)	(52,514)	(64,908)	(106,119)	(76,512)	(56,291)
Gross rental income		$445,500	$458,865	$472,631	$475,992	$424,478	$470,003	$506,619
Other income‡ 0.4% of gross		1,850	1,800	1,854	1,867	1,665	1,844	1,987
Reimbursements§		30,272	61,449	62,273	62,974	61,199	65,234	68,549
Effective gross income		$477,622	$522,114	$536,759	$540,833	$487,342	$537,081	$577,156
Expenses								
Real estate taxes	2.0%	$18,420	$32,500	$33,150	$33,813	$34,489	$35,179	$35,883
Insurance	3.5%	2,512	2,600	2,691	2,785	2,883	2,984	3,088
Utilities	3.0%	26,311	27,100	27,913	28,750	29,613	30,501	31,416
Maintenance and repair‖	2.0%	18,480	23,100	23,562	24,033	24,514	25,004	25,504
Building services	2.0%	31,078	31,700	32,334	32,981	33,640	34,313	34,999
Management# 4.5% of gross		33,413	20,649	21,268	21,420	19,101	21,150	22,798
Other administrative expenses	2.0%	35,882	36,600	37,332	38,079	38,840	39,617	40,409
Reserves**		0	3,300	3,300	3,300	3,300	3,300	3,300
Total expenses and reserves		$166,096	$177,549	$181,550	$185,161	$186,381	$192,048	$197,398
Net operating income		$311,526	$344,565	$355,208	$355,672	$300,961	$345,033	$379,758
Reversion								
Sale price @	10.5%							$3,616,742
Less cost of sale	3.5%							(126,586)
Net reversion								3,490,156
Conclusions								
Cash flows			$344,565	$355,208	$355,672	$300,961	$3,835,189	
Value by yield capitalization	12.0%	$3,211,433	$307,648	$283,170	$253,160	$191,266	$2,176,189	
Rounded		$3,211,000						

* Rent expected under current leases for 1997. This rent is approximately 10% above market for 15,500 sq. ft., and at market for 12,870 sq. ft.; 3,630 sq. ft. are vacant. The above-market leases are due in 1999 and 2000.

† Current vacancy is approximately 10%, and the forecast is 15% to account for the condition described in (*) above.

‡ Other income covers late fees and parking, including short-term agreements for parking on the excess portion of the site.

§ Reimbursements are for common area maintenance (CAM) only, and have not been collected from some tenants for the past few years. The market has changed, and it is expected that new management will be able to collect increased but not full reimbursements.

‖ Maintenance was down for 1996 and is forecast at a more normal $0.70/sq ft.

An affiliate of the owner currently charges a management fee of 7.5% of gross rental receipts. We forecast a market rate of 4.5%.

** Reserves for replacement are not currently maintained, and reserve funds would not pass from seller to buyer. Reserves are forecast at $0.10/sq. ft., and are at the low end of the market survey range.

The yield, or discount, rate (Y) was developed from the same local market transactions as the R_O developed for direct capitalization. Because the data available are not adequate to compute the buyer's yield rate (buyers generally use direct capitalization for stabilized properties in this market), yield rates are imputed by adding the net market-expected growth rate for *NOI*. This expected growth rate is 2.5% over the five-year holding period. Investor survey data for Y and growth rates are consistent with and support the local observations. The concluded yield rate is calculated as

$$R_o + \Delta a = Y$$
$$9.5\% + 2.5\% = 12.0\%$$

Because the terminal (residual or going-out) capitalization rate is not supported by local market data, it is derived from investor survey data, which show an average premium of 0.4% to 1.5% over the overall (going-in) rate. Increased premiums are associated with lower rates, and because the overall rate of 9.5% was at the lower end of the indicated range, the valuer selected a terminal premium of 1.0%. The concluded terminal capitalization rate is therefore 10.5%.

Value calculations are shown in the discounted cash flow analysis. The income approach conclusions are reconciled and greater weight is given to the value derived by yield capitalization, which includes explicit expectations concerning lease turnover and vacancy. The direct capitalization conclusion is included because market participants use this method, but in this case many appraisers would be expected to also use yield capitalization.

Value derived by direct capitalization	$3,335,000
Value derived by yield capitalization	$3,211,000
Income approach conclusion	$3,250,000

The terminal or reversionary value might be developed differently if, for example, the improvements were expected to be worthless at the end of the holding period and the property sold for its land value to a developer. In that case, the land value would have to be forecast or projected to the end year, and that value would be used directly for the reversion.

In yield capitalization, a yield rate is developed in the same manner as the overall rate for direct capitalization. However, more reliance tends to be placed on investor survey data sources because extracting yield rates from local market transactions is more difficult than extracting overall rates. More than one discount rate may be required, depending on the relative risk of the cash flows involved. (A land value reversion may be more or less risky than reversion for a property in continued use, for example, in which case, one rate would be used for cash flow and another for the reversion.) From multiple rates, an internal rate of return (IRR)[19] could be calculated, providing a single yield rate that represents the risk associated with the real estate asset.

---

19. The *IRR* is a profitability measure similar to the equity yield rate.

Because abundant transaction data are available, rates for calculating the *IRR* are not typically built up from risk-free, or safe, rates in real estate appraisal as they are in business valuation. As a result, yield rates for real estate holding entities that are developed from yields appropriate for the underlying assets can be more reliable (i.e., less subject to the appraiser's judgment) than yields developed using build-up methods. The market-derived rates developed in the real estate appraisal account for the nature of the business, risk, and stability issues for the real property at the asset level of value.

Yield Capitalization and Financing

The use of direct or yield capitalization is typically a real estate appraisal decision based on the property type, how buyers make purchasing decisions, and other factors, but it also depends on the need to develop yield rates at the minority level when financing is present. The declining loan balance and resulting equity buildup obviates the use of simplified methods for calculating minority yields. The business valuation requires a DCF model, regardless of whether the real estate market considers it important.

Developing a DCF model for the partnership without first developing one for the real property requires that the business valuer make many assumptions concerning the property that are better made by the real estate appraiser. The best course of action to take when financing is involved is to require that a yield capitalization be included in the real estate appraisal, even if it is not needed to develop or support the property value conclusion itself.

Holding period selection. Yield capitalization requires an explicit holding period, selected to match the typical holding period for investors in the particular property type and market area. Sometimes the holding period can be adjusted to coincide with some event in the property's future such as expiration of a lease or a license. However, the holding period may not be what the buyer of a minority interest in the partnership would expect because of many other facts and circumstances affecting the minority holder. It may be necessary to change the holding period, depending on the decisions that the valuer of the minority interest has made. This situation may require constructing another DCF model, not to recompute the real property value but to develop accurate yield and growth rates for use in the valuation.

Reconciliation of Overall, Yield, and Growth Rates

The overall rate, yield rate, and growth rate for a business entity may or may not be included in the appraisal, but these rates are often needed for the valuation analysis and should be obtained from the real estate appraiser.

The ideal appraisal, for partnership valuation purposes, includes a discounted cash flow model in which the yield rate (Y) and growth rates (Δa^{20}) are explicitly stated. Of the three rates, direct capitalization with its overall rate (R_O) is the most common. Growth is implicit in this direct model, and the real estate appraiser may have no need to state growth rates. In such a case, the yield rate needed for the valuation can usually be developed from the overall rate by using the constant growth model:[21, 22]

$$Y = R_0 + a$$

Growth rates refer to both distributions $(\Delta_D a)$ and value or reversion $(\Delta_V a)$, and the valuation of the business may require both. In the model above, Δa is a blended rate that reflects the total change or growth in cash flow and value. If the real estate appraisal uses only direct capitalization, all three expressions of Δa (cash flow, reversion, and overall) may have to be obtained. All rates used in the valuation should be appropriate for the period over which a buyer would expect to hold the subject interest.

If the property is not income producing, the rates may have to be imputed. The yield rate Y is intended to be a measure of overall risk associated with the property, so it may be necessary to find a proxy for risk for non-income producing property.

If the appraiser had used only a single-period model, growth and yield rates would have to have been extracted from the facts and developed from the capitalization rate (overall rate) in the appraisal.

When a property has stabilized operating conditions and no mortgage loan, an overall capitalization rate and growth rates for cash flow and value are all that are needed because the constant growth model can be used to calculate the yield. However, if conditions are unstable (as they are for the Suburban Office Partners, II, whose above-market leases end in a few years), or if mortgage financing is a factor (as it is for Suburban Office Partners, II), then the calculations become more complex and DCF analysis is really the best method for developing the needed rates.

---

20. The symbol Δa is an adjustment rate, and the symbol Δ denotes change. This symbol is used in *The Appraisal of Real Estate*, but other sources may use different symbols.

21. *The Appraisal of Real Estate*, 561

22. Shannon P. Pratt, DBA, CFA, FASA, et al. *Valuing a Business, The Analysis and Appraisal of Closely Held Companies*, 4th ed. (Chicago: Irwin Professional Publishing, 2000), 206–208.

Yield and Growth Rates

Table 2.4 shows growth and yield calculations added to the *DCF* model of the appraisal. The table shows the conclusions from the real estate appraisal, which are the inputs for the valuation. These calculations are not needed in the real estate appraisal, but they will be needed for the partnership interest valuation, so it is recommended that the *DCF* model be included in the valuation report but without the property income and expense detail. The business valuer will not be changing these items or taking responsibility for their accuracy. Net operating income, the value conclusion, and the reversion will be the starting point for the valuation.

Table 2.4		**Calculating Yield and Growth Rates for Suburban Office Partners,II**					
		1996	1997	1998	1999	2000	2001
Period		**Year 0**	**Year 1**	**Year 2**	**Year 3**	**Year 4**	**Year 5**
Conclusions from real estate appraisal							
Net operating income		$311,526	$344,565	$355,208	$355,672	$300,961	$345,033
Net reversion							$3,490,156
Yield rate	12.0%						
Concluded value		$3,250,000					
Growth rate calculations							
Value @ year end (approx.)		$3,250,000				$3,490,156	
Annual compounded value growth (i)*	1.4%	$3,250,000	$3,296,671	$3,344,013	$3,392,035	$3,440,746	3,490,156
Net operating income		311,526	344,565	355,208	355,672	300,961	345,033
Cash flow change, annual			10.61%	3.09%	0.13%	-15.38%	14.64%
Annual cash flow during year		$344,565				$345,033	
Annual compounded cash flow growth* (straight-line approximation)	0.03%		$344,565	$344,682	$344,799	$344,916	$345,033

* Values in Years 1–4 are shown to illustrate the compounding process but do not imply intermediate value conclusions.

The compounded value growth rate (i_v) shown in Table 2.4 is calculated using the formula $FV = PV \times (1 + i)^n$, where *PV* is the value of the real estate in Year 0 (at the date of value, the beginning of Year 1), and *FV* is the net reversion at the end of Year 5 (which is based on cash flow in Year 6). The calculation was made using the spreadsheet formula for the rate; annual compounding is shown for checking purposes.

The compounded cash flow growth rate (i_{cf}) is also calculated according to the formula $FV = PV \times (1 + i)^n$, where *PV* is the *NOI* forecast for Year 1, and *FV* is the cash flow forecast for Year 5. (Year 0 is ignored because of the normalizing adjustments made between actual Year 0 and the forecast for Year 1.) The holding period selected is four years.

Note: Calculated value and cash flow figures for intermediate Years 2 to 4 show the process of calculating the average growth rates. They are not meant to imply the expected cash flows or value in those years. There would be no need to show the intermediate figures in the valuation report.

Both rates seem relatively low, considering that annual growth rates of 2% to 3% are expected by the real estate market. However, revenues drop significantly in Years 3 and 4 because of the turnover of leases, and the reversion is a function of revenues from the new leases. Thus, the lower rates appear to be consistent with the facts.

Reconciliation and Value Conclusion

The last step in the appraisal process is to evaluate each of the approaches to value and reconcile their value indications into a final value conclusion. This process is the same for any appraisal or valuation that involves multiple methods. Multiple methods of developing rates or discounts are also recommended as are intermediate conclusions at any level of value.

Each of the approaches is evaluated for its appropriateness, accuracy, and the quantity of evidence on which the value indication is based. Appropriateness is judged by the effectiveness with which the procedures used relate to the purpose of the appraisal, the characteristics of the subject property, and the way in which the market participants make investment decisions. Accuracy refers to the appraiser's confidence in the data, the adjustments required, and the resulting precision of the indicated values derived within the approach. The amount of evidence presented affects the statistical validity of the value indication. A summary real estate appraisal report might not state the process by which the reconciliation is performed, but the approaches should still be evaluated on that basis. The estimated exposure time linked to the value opinion may be presented here or in the sales comparison approach section of the appraisal.

CASE STUDY APPLICATION

Reconciliation and Value Conclusion

All three approaches to value were used in appraising Suburban Office Partners, II. Each approach has been evaluated for its appropriateness, accuracy, and the quantity of evidence on which its value indication is based.

Cost approach	$3,750,000
Sales comparison approach	$3,270,000
Income approach	$3,250,000

Because the subject property is a leased multitenant office building, the purchaser would most likely be an investor. Of the three approaches, the greatest weight was given to the income approach because adequate evidence is available to support it and the data that support the various capitalization rates were consistent.

The sales comparison approach was given little weight because the building is leased, and an owner/user would need to hold it for several years before the current lease would expire. Although the price per square foot was developed partly from investor sales, it is not an indicator that investors typically use. The approach is less appropriate than the income approach, although the accuracy and quantity of evidence were adequate.

The cost approach is given no weight at all because the high value derived may not reflect certain sources of functional obsolescence such as the subject's 8-ft. ceilings in a market in which the standard height is nine feet or more. This obsolescence was accounted for in the sales comparison approach and in the rent comparison, which used comparables of a similar age. It was also considered in the income approach, which was based on lease income, which presumably reflected the market effect of functional problems.

Based on the investigation outlined in this report, it is the opinion that the fair market value of the leased fee estate of the subject property, as of January 17, 1997, is $3,250,000. Transactions included in the sales comparison approach showed market exposure periods of one to 24 months; the older transactions generally show the longer periods. An analysis of current listings, and discussions with active brokers in the subject market suggest that the current exposure period is two to four months. This is supported by transactional data from one to six months ago. The conclusion is that the subject property would have had a market exposure period of two to four months before the date of value. It is also the concluded that the marketing time (the time required to sell the property following the date of value) would have been two to four months.

Types of Reports

The appraisal process can result in a self-contained report, or a summary report, or a restricted use report. A self-contained report should give the user all the data that support the reasoning that led to the value conclusions. For a summary or restricted report, however, the specific limitations must be identified. USPAP allows the appraiser considerable latitude in producing a summary report, but it is possible—even likely—that key information needed for the partnership valuation will be lost in the summarization. The details of many of the internal steps of the appraisal process described in this chapter must be understood. If they are not included in the real estate appraisal, the business valuer often will have to fill in the missing information by obtaining it from the real estate appraiser. Omissions such as these could violate Standard Rule 2-1(b), which states that each report must "contain sufficient information to enable the intended users of the appraisal to understand the report properly."

Form reports are almost always summary reports and are typically used for residential and some small commercial properties. The forms were not designed for the valuation of business entities, however, and such reports almost always are short on information such as growth rates.

Restricted use reports are intended for specific users, who are familiar with one or more topics that would normally be included in a summary or self-contained report. Information can be omitted from these reports, often at a significant savings for the client but, like summary reports, they are generally not suitable for use with business valuations.[23]

---

23. The valuation report may be restricted, however, depending on its purpose and use, under Standards Rule 10-2(b). A restricted report would not be suitable for the case study.

CHAPTER 3

Developing the Partnership's Net Asset Value

Three approaches are followed to obtain a value for John Builder's interest in Suburban Office Partners, II. They include the asset approach, used to obtain a value for the partnership as a whole; the comparative company approach, used to develop the discount for lack of control; and the income approach, used to develop the discount for lack of marketability. This chapter describes the balance sheet analysis of the partnership's assets in arriving at a value for the entire partnership. Chapter 4 will discuss developing the discount for lack of control, and Chapter 5 will cover developing the discount for lack of marketability. This chapter also includes adjustments to the partnership statement that are needed in Chapters 4 and 5.

Using the asset approach, the partnership's assets and liabilities will be adjusted to current fair market value to establish the partnership's net asset value as the sum of its assets less the sum of its liabilities. The difference between the normalized and adjusted assets and liabilities of the partnership is the partners' equity, or *NAV* of the partnership.

Elements of the Real Property Appraisal

The business valuation report should restate the salient elements of the real estate appraisal, which may be incorporated into the report or referenced as an appendix item. (See the summary of important data and conclusions in Chapter 2.) The valuation contains a description of the property, a description of the partnership's assets, and any facts, assumptions, and hypothetical or limiting conditions that can affect expected future cash flows. These include lease terms and conditions, e.g., the relationship between rent level and market

> *The property appraisal assumes that a transfer of the entire property will occur, but the valuation report assumes that only a transfer of a noncontrolling minority interest will take place.*

rents, expected repairs, and other items that may generate costs or require decisions during the holding period. If these conditions are customary but have not been addressed in detail in the appraisal, the valuer should have access to copies of the leases, schedules for major repairs or renovations planned by management, and information on other significant expenses.

Assumptions Related to Control and Holding Time

The property appraisal assumes that a transfer of the entire property will occur, but the valuation report assumes that only a transfer of a noncontrolling minority interest will take place. Thus, some assumptions that the real estate appraiser has made based on a hypothetical real property transfer may have to be reconsidered. These assumptions are related to control and holding time. Assumptions related to control often involve competent management and highest and best use. For example, an appraisal of the 100% fee interest generally assumes typical or competent management, but a minority partner is stuck with the partnership's chosen management, for better or worse, and the valuer must consider the need to make adjustments for any differences related to control.

In addition, an analysis of highest and best use may lead the valuer to the assumption that a prudent owner, intent on maximizing the property's economic potential, would make certain improvements. However, the current management may have no intention of making the changes, or the partners may be reluctant to submit to the required calls for capital. Thus, differences in highest and best use may require adjustments when valuing the minority interest.

Perhaps the most important single issue facing a buyer of any undivided interest is the length of time that he or she can expect to hold the interest before the underlying, pro rata value of the partnership (and property) can be realized. This concern has a profound effect on value, and the business valuation would have to consider whether there are any circumstances associated with the property that would encourage its sale at some point in the future.

Assumptions Related to Control and Holding Time for Suburban Office Partners, II

The site on which Suburban Office Partners, II, is located has in excess of 10,400 square feet of surplus land, and Billy Builder is interested in developing a one-story concrete block building that would be leased to office service companies such as sandwich and coffee shops, small printers, and suppliers. The nearest office services are three blocks away. If the land were to be developed, a sale might occur after its occupancy is stabilized. The land is currently used to provide monthly permit parking for a few of the building's tenants and for tenants from office buildings nearby. John Builder did not support his son's development idea and put if off, but Billy plans to pursue it.

In valuing Suburban Office Partners, II, the business valuer must take into account all of the material facts that would influence a potential buyer's decision to purchase an interest in the property. The case study thus far has included several conditions that would affect the timing of the property's sale, and it is important that the valuer identify as many circumstances related to timing as possible. Circumstances that pertain to Suburban Office Partners, II, include a loan agreement, lease agreements, and holding periods.

The original mortgage loan on the property was made in February 1987 with an initial principal amount of $1,973,000. The interest rate was 10.75% and was fully amortized over 30 years, with a balloon payment due in 15 years (2002), which is about five years after the date of value. Loan information is included in Appendix A. Because the interest rate was so high, it would have been prudent to refinance the mortgage loan to obtain a lower rate. However, either a capital call or the sale of the property might have been required to make the balloon payment due in 2002.

Leases on a large portion of the rentable area are due in 2000, and rents are above market level. This is typical of the market area following the recession during which market rents declined but actual rents continued to rise under the terms of the lease. A footnote from the Property and Income Statement (Table 2.2, Chapter 2) indicated that management had stopped collecting CAM reimbursements for some tenants. However, the real estate appraiser assumed that new management would be able to increase collections significantly. This suggests that a sale is likely when income is still high or after the situation stabilizes (probably late in 2000), if management is disposed to sell.

The real estate appraiser established that the typical holding period for buyers of three-story multitenant office buildings is five to 15 years, but most often 10 years.

Financial Statements

Financial statements communicate a business's financial position at a point in time and its operational results for a stated period. These statements include the income statement, balance sheet, cash flow analysis, ratio of stockholders' equity to partners' capital, and other information that may be audited, reviewed, or compiled.[1] In some instances, the business valuer, without the oversight of an accountant, may need to work with statements prepared by management. In others, the valuer may need to reconstruct financial statements from the partnership's federal tax returns.[2] Entities that have signifi-

---

1. An *audited statement* is a statement in which the auditor expresses an opinion in accordance with generally accepted accounting principles (GAAP). A *reviewed statement* is one for which no material modifications are required to conform to GAAP, but it does not provide the level of assurance that an audit does. A *compiled statement* presents financial information from management expressed in the form of a statement but without assurance.

2. See "Extracting the Necessary Data from Financial Statements and Tax Forms," by Lari Masten in Appendix E.

cant intangibles or business activities are not considered asset holding companies, and their analysis is outside the scope of this book.

Because of the limited scope of activities that are typical for real estate partnerships, the accounting demands for a small real estate partnership are limited. Operating activities generally include only normal property management (often by fee managers), if that, and sometimes a small proportion of securities or other assets.

The financial performance of an asset holding company is closely tied to the economic performance of its assets, and the cash flow forecast will be based largely on the forecasts for its individual assets. Its distributions may not always match its operating cash flows, so its distribution history should be stated separately, and any differences should be reconciled. The volatility of historical distributions may also be of interest to the buyer of a minority interest, apart from historic cash flows.

To understand business operations, a valuer would normally review historical statements for a five-year period. However, apart from showing a relationship between operating cash flow and distributions, this history is not particularly useful. For example, the real estate appraiser will base line item forecasts on a partnership's past history to ascertain patterns for maintenance expenditures and utility usage, but other costs such as taxes and insurance are generally forecast on a forward basis. The real property appraiser provides these forecasts, and the business valuer's task is to adjust the line items for the changed premise of the valuation and add a forecast for business-level items.

The historical performance of the business pertaining to distributions also may be meaningless if it has recently purchased a major asset. However, if the previous owner has provided information about the partnership's historical operations, it can be used to see how the property has performed over time, and the relationship of distributions to cash flow can be determined. If the partnership has been formed recently and its assets held previously under a different ownership structure, its historical operations can be extrapolated from real estate operating statements if necessary, but the activities of the general partner in making distributions or capital accumulations, for example, can only be inferred. Off-balance sheet items, such as awards or liabilities related to tenant or environmental litigation, may also need to be considered during the partnership valuation.

Income Statement

Partnerships, LLCs, and S corporations are all tax pass-through entities taxed at the shareholder level, not the business level. Because business-level financial statements do not include income taxes, there is little difference between income and cash flow statements. The only differences are changes in working capital and borrowings because noncash items (largely depreciation and amortization) can be ignored.[3] Real estate appraisals generally show income statements, which are really statements of operating cash flows generated by the property, not income statements as defined by the accounting profession.

The analysis of historical operations primarily involves analyzing the performance of the real estate asset to arrive at a forecast. The analysis of past operations is largely an analysis of the performance of the real estate assets, and the forecast for valuation purposes is based on the real estate appraiser's projection of revenue from leases, vacancy and collection losses, and expense line items and reserves, which most often are based on the property's current and expected performance. A forecast of cash flows for the partnership will also include revenues from other sources, partnership expenses, anticipated borrowings, loan repayment and interest expenses (principal and interest lumped together as debt service, because tax deductibility of interest is not a consideration), capital accumulation plans, if any, and other items.

Adjustments to the income statement. Non-real estate-related items are relatively minor, and their forecasts can be based on the real estate income statement. Business-level items must be added, and some of the real estate expenses may have to be adjusted to forecast the cash flows and distributions that a reasonable buyer of the subject interest would expect. Items that the partnership valuer should include in this analysis are

- Net operating income from the real estate appraisal
- Reserve allowance, if needed
- Any other real property items not included in *NOI*
- Interest and income from other sources
- Adjustments for property taxes
- Accounting, legal, and general and administrative costs
- Other taxes, if any
- Debt service
- Income must be adjusted further for any expected changes in working capital

The last item is important for operating companies but less so for holding companies. Generally, a real estate partnership does not anticipate new borrowings, and debt service includes the repayment of principal, so no financing adjustments are required; nor would it anticipate any new invest-

---

3. This is true when working from a tax basis income statement by adding back depreciation and amortization.

ments or other investment transactions.[4] Cash balances should be reconciled, however. The partnership should have adequate cash reserves to manage its building operations. Management might also accumulate cash for reinvestment.

Differences may also be due to payment timing. Many partnerships report on a cash basis, recognizing revenue and expenses when they are received or paid rather than according to the accrual method required by generally accepted accounting principles (GAAP). The valuer should determine from management or its accountants whether the books were prepared according to GAAP. If they were not, the valuer should inquire about any significant departures. If such departures exist, the books should be adjusted.

If the partnership has an accumulation program, the IRS has ruled that income is to be imputed to the partners, whether it is received or reinvested. In light of this, a good basis exists for assuming that all cash flow will be distributed. As with any unusual legal or accounting problem, the valuer's best course of action is to seek the advice of the client's counsel and accountants to fully understand all agreements and statements.

Finally, the income statement should be normalized.[5] Other noneconomic, nonrecurring cash flows or other unusual items should be adjusted as needed. (Normalization adjustments are more typical of operating companies than asset-holding partnerships.)

CASE STUDY APPLICATION
Income Statement Analysis

The data for the income statement or cash flow analysis for Suburban Office Partners, II, are derived from Table 2.2, Chapter 2. The partnership financials include the 1996 Federal Tax Form 1065, U.S. Partnership Return of Income, as well as the bank statement and distribution history provided in Appendix B.

The cash flow forecast has been prepared considering the minority status of the subject interest. The real estate appraiser's income statement contains several items that must be adjusted. The tax return includes all the financial activities of the partnership, both real property-related and business-related.

A property tax adjustment is included, but this is an effect of California property tax laws, which assess properties only at the time of transfer (of more than a 50% interest). Great discrepancies may develop between the taxes to be paid by a new owner (an assumption of the real estate appraisal) and the current owner (the partnership). This type of adjustment may not apply in states where properties are reassessed at market values. The case study points out the potential need to consider such an adjustment.

The appraisal's single-period statement for direct capitalization is used for simplicity. The case study includes both single- and multi-period models. The multi-period models will be addressed in Chapter 5.

---

4. If it did, it would be more complex than the case study envisions and should always be handled by a business valuer. Historic income statements may need to be adjusted for these items to obtain accurate cash flows if a controlling interest were being valued.

5. The *International Glossary of Business Valuation Terms* defines normalized earnings as the economic benefits adjusted for nonrecurring, noneconomic, or other unusual items to eliminate anomalies and/or facilitate comparison.

Table 3.1 — Partnership Income Statement (Cash Flow) Analysis

Suburban Office Partners, II

Income	1996	Forecast
Net operating income*	$311,526	$316,800
Adjustments		
Add back forecast management fee[†]		19,500
Less fee at current rate		(32,500)
Add back forecast real estate taxes[‡]		32,500
Less taxes for past year		(18,420)
Less forecast increase		(370)
Adjusted net operating income	$311,526	$317,510
Interest income[§]	3,154	3,046
Total partnership income	$314,680	$320,556
Other partnership expenses [‖]		
General and administrative	$273	$280
Insurance	1,414	1,440
Legal and professional	1,638	1,670
Franchise tax	800	800
Debit service	221,011	221,011
Total partnership expenses	$225,136	$225,201
Partnership net income	$89,544	$95,355
Adjustments	(57,350)	0
Net cash flow available for distribution**	$32,194	$95,355

*   Net operating income is taken directly from the property income statement in the real estate appraisal.

†   The management fee is forecast at a market rate of 4.5%, but JB Management has been charging 7.5%, and there is no reason to believe that the rate will change. The amount forecast is added back to *NOI*, and an amount calculated at the new rate is subtracted.

‡   Real estate taxes are forecast based on the property's reassessment at the appraised value. However, the property will not be transferred. Because the percentage of the interest is below the threshold for reassessment in California, taxes will increase from their current level by the allowed annual amount (2%). Changes in direct assessments may also occur and should be considered if they have been addressed in the real estate appraisal. The forecast taxes are added back, and then the previous year's taxes and the expected increase for the forecast year are deducted.

§   Interest income is taken directly from Form 1065. This is money market interest on the partnership's investment checking account. Because this was a small amount, it would be reasonable to apply the same percentage rate (developed by dividing the interest amount by the 1996 average cash balance) to the expected cash balance for 1997. The cash balances are taken from the Form 1065 balance sheet (Schedule L):

$$\$3,154 / (\$74,250 - \$16,900) = 5.5\%$$
$$\$55,382 \times 0.055 = \$3,046$$

Cash is discussed in the balance sheet analysis.

‖   Other partnership expenses are taken directly from Form 1065 items, except for debt service, which is taken from the mortgage statement. Ideally, the forecast for general and administrative, insurance, and legal and professional categories should be made by management or its accountants. The valuer should talk with them to determine whether there were any extraordinary expenses for 1996 and expectations over the long term. The forecast should represent a long-term, stabilized condition.

     Reserves could have been increased because the appraiser used the low end of the survey range (i.e., $0.10/sq.ft. when the range is $0.10 to $0.25). An allowance should be deducted from any reserve items or any expected, extraordinary items that will need to be replaced during the holding period. In this case study, there are no such identified items, so no allowance was made.

**   Cash flow adjustments for 1996 include only the change in working capital. The increase from $16,900 to $74,250 is taken from the balance sheet, Schedule L. There is no reason to expect that this accumulation will continue, and it is not clear what it is for. No reduction is taken for the next year. This is considered further as part of the balance sheet analysis. The forecast shows all cash flow distributed. The risk that it will be accumulated instead will be incorporated later in the valuation analysis.

Balance Sheet

The balance sheet for Suburban Office Partners, II, is actually Schedule L of Form 1065 in Appendix B. It is reproduced in another format in Table 3.2 to facilitate application of the concepts that are key to using the asset approach to value. Typical balance sheet items included for valuing real estate limited partnerships are

- Current assets, including cash and equivalents; accounts receivable; and security deposits held. This may also include advances to partners.
- Fixed assets, including real property. Nonoperating assets could include automobiles and other personal property.
- Intangible assets, if present, which may include loan fees less amortization. The meaning of any such items should be verified with the accountants.
- Current liabilities, which may also include the current portion of long-term debt
- Long-term liabilities, including mortgage debt, other notes, and security deposit liability
- Partners' capital accounts

Balance Sheet Adjustments

When valuing a business entity such as a partnership, the valuer, using historical results, normalizes adjustments to approximate the partnership's operations under normal conditions to project a buyer's expectations. This process involves nonoperating assets, surplus assets, asset (inventory) shortages, and related income items. Some of these assets may be liquidated, depending on the ability of the buyer of the subject interest to do so. If such an asset is removed, the expenses related to it should be removed also. Generally, a minority interest could not cause the general partner to sell an item that might be owned by the partnership (e.g., a condo at a ski resort), and the item may have to be included at its current market value. The following also may require adjusting when the asset approach is used to value a partnership such as Suburban Office Partners, II:

- Loans to affiliated parties, which may require reclassification as long-term debt or equity
- The date of value for the assets and liabilities according to their market values. The balance sheet should reflect conditions at the date of value, not the date that the accounting period ends.
- Cash and small amounts of marketable securities may be included at their value as of the date of value, but if bank balances have changed significantly, they should be ad-

justed. Receivables should not be significant, but if back rent payments are due, the likelihood of receiving them should be weighed and the amount adjusted to market, if necessary.

- Loans or advances. If there is no expectation of repayment, the amount might be reduced to zero. If the borrower is a general partner who has a fiduciary responsibility to the other partners, it would be difficult to argue that the obligation is worth less than its face amount.

- The real estate, adjusted to the appraised amount

- Intangible assets, such as loan fees, which may still be carried on the books, but generally have no current value, other than generating annual amortization deductions. Therefore, they would be adjusted to zero.

- Liabilities, adjusted for the date of value. For example, if loan payments are made between the reporting date and the date of value, the new principal balance should be reflected in the normalized statement.

- Long-term debt, which is often split between the portion due in the coming year as a current liability item and the remaining portion included as a long-term liability. (It is

CASE STUDY APPLICATION

Balance Sheet

Table 3.2	Partnership Balance Sheet for Suburban Office Partners, II		
Assets	**1995**	**1996**	**Normalized adjusted**
Current assets			
Cash and equivalents	$16,900	$74,250	$55,382
Accounts receivable:			
Skipper Strickland	6,000	6,000	0
Builder Construction, Inc.	40,000	40,000	40,000
Total current assets	$62,900	$120,250	$95,382
Fixed assets			
Real property	2,500,000	2,500,000	3,250,000
Other	0	0	0
Accumulated depreciation			
Real property	(136,730)	(191,746)	
Other	0	0	0
Total fixed assets	$2,363,270	$2,308,254	$3,250,000
Total assets	$2,426,170	$2,428,504	$3,345,382
Liabilities and capital			
Current liabilities			
Accounts payable	0	325	325
Current portion of long-term debt	24,106	26,829	24,701
Other			
Total current liabilities	$24,106	$27,154	$25,026
Long-term debt			
First mortgage	1,818,406	1,791,577	1,791,577
Notes payable	0	0	0
Security deposits	16,500	16,500	16,500
Total long-term liabilities	$1,834,906	$1,808,077	$1,808,077
Partners' equity	567,158	593,273	1,512,279
Total liabilities and capital	$2,426,170	$2,428,504	$3,345,382

Cash and equivalents for Suburban Office Partners, II, include only checking and investment checking accounts. The February 7 bank statement showed a balance of $74,250. The year-end amount was reduced by a mortgage payment made on January 14 and payments totaling $450 that were made on January 15. This was the only interim period adjustment required because the period ended December 31, 1996, and the date of value is January 17, 1997. (For longer periods, an interim statement may be required.)

The amount of cash is high but not unreasonable when the likelihood of turnover and the possibility of losses in rental income in a few years are considered. Nonetheless, it would be prudent to account for the high amount of cash, since it was so low at the beginning of the year. Management does not have a stated plan for building reserves or accumulating cash for investment. In the absence of such a plan, the current cash balance is also considered to be the expected average annual balance and will be used for computing the forecast interest income for the previous statement. The question of whether cash is being accumulated for investment has not been addressed, and it creates uncertainty that will affect the discounts, which will be applied later in the analysis.

Accounts receivable include an advance that Builder made to a cousin, Skipper Strickland, in 1994. Strickland has no apparent means of support, and the likelihood of collecting the money is remote. The other receivable is the advance made to Builder Construction that was supposed to be paid back in 1996. Management says it will be paid soon, so the amount is left in.

Fixed assets include only the office building. Its basis at the time it was transferred to the partnership may have been increased by capital improvements, and its book value is decreased by accumulated depreciation. In this valuation, it is adjusted to the appraised value.

Current liabilities include a few small bills that were not paid in December, the current portion of long-term debt, and the mortgage, which was decreased by the payment made in January. The cash balance and mortgage loan balance have both been reduced.

Long-term liabilities include the portion of the mortgage that was due after 1997, which is unchanged. A liability for security deposits exists and was booked. It is possible that this item won't appear on the partnership's statement, particularly if a reserve account has not been established. If not, is important to check with management or the real estate appraiser to obtain a statement of the security deposit obligations.

Partners' capital accounts, which appear in the normalized adjusted column, are net partners' equity (the net asset value of the partnership).

unnecessary to make the distinction for this case study.) Long-term debt may be adjusted if the interest being valued has the power to cause an adjustment in the partnership's capital structure.[6]

Built-in Capital Gains

The depreciated book value has no direct effect on the value conclusions, but there may be an indirect effect if book value is low. In that case, built-in capital gain could be taxed upon the

---

6. When valuing controlling interests, business valuers generally assume that the buyer can adjust the company's capital structure and refinance mortgage debt if current rates or other terms are unfavorable. There may be other barriers to this, however, and a clear understanding of debt obligations is important. For noncontrolling interests, the valuer considers the debt structure as it is, regardless of terms. The assets of holding companies would not generally be purchased when mortgage debt exists, so the only issue would be minority positions, which is the case for this case study, in which the subject interest cannot influence debt carried by the partnership.

sale of the assets, and the gains would be taxable to the partners. This can occur if the partnership's assets have appreciated substantially, and if the assets are real estate, securities, or any other asset that has a market outside the partnership.

Normally, the general partner would make an election under IRC §754 that raises the tax basis of the partnership's assets to match the transferee's cost basis in the interest for the benefit of the transferee. Such an adjustment might be made if there is reason to believe that the election is in doubt, but it would be unusual and would require a strong argument that an election would not be beneficial to the other partners. There may also be an election already in force, most likely if there had been built-in gains and an interest had been transferred previously.

Other questions that the valuer should address include whether:

- A seller of the interest would accept a price based on a discount for built-in gains
- The willing seller, being a partner, would influence the general partner to make the §754 election
- The buyer would require assurance that the election would be made, and
- The election would be beneficial to the other partners

This is another example of an issue that requires the valuer to consult the partnership's counsel and accountants. Methods of making adjustments to built-in gains, usually using a discounted cash flow model to determine the present value of future lost tax savings, are explained in the literature for C corporations. These methods can be adapted for partnerships.[7]

Alternative Net Asset Value Calculation

A valuer might wish to show the balance sheet in a slightly different form, i.e., by adjusting the value of the partnership's principal asset. (See Table 3.3, Alternative *NAV* Calculation for Suburban Office Partners, II.) This is only useful if the balance sheet is fairly simple, as it is in this case.

The net asset value corresponds to the top level of value–the value of the partnership as a whole, or the entity level (see Figure I.2, Levels of Value). For this partnership valuation it is a hypothetical, intermediate value conclusion.

Other Tangible Assets

Suburban Office Partners, II, is a single-asset partnership with accumulated cash as its only other significant asset. When the accumulation of cash begins to exceed the amount nor-

---

7. John R. Cooper and Richard Gore, "Built-in Gains Discount Calculation," *Valuation Strategies* (Jan/Feb 2001): 5–13, 44. Because §754 is not available, most of the adjustments can be made for potential capital gains liability for a C corporation.

CASE STUDY APPLICATION

Table 3.3 Alternative *NAV* Calculation for Suburban Office Partners, II	
Real estate	$3,250,000
Adjustments for partnership equity	
Current assets	95,382
Current liabilities	(325)
Long-term liabilities	
Mortgage current portion	$24,701
Mortgage long-term portion	1,791,577
Balance due	(1,816,278)
Security deposits	(16,500)
Total adjustments	(1,737,721)
Net asset value of partnership	$1,512,279
Cash flow available for distribution	$95,355
Return on net asset value	6.3%

mally required for the partnership's real estate operations, valuing the cash as a separate asset must become part of the entity valuation. This cash may be substantial, depending on the level of tenancy risk, potential improvements in the quality of tenants, repair and renovation, and other real property requirements. Partnerships often hold other cash-equivalent assets, such as marketable securities, bonds, and other partnership interests, and can hold virtually any other fixed asset or investment vehicle. A common method of valuing portfolios that contain such assets is to develop discounts using the asset approach, or yield rates (using an income approach) separately, and then take a weighted average to arrive at a single discount for the whole portfolio. This is generally a control issue that would affect the discount developed in Chapter 4. The valuer should consider the following questions when applying this method:

- Will the asset mix remain the same for the expected holding period of the investment?
- Would the hypothetical buyer invest in a particular asset mix?
- Would the buyer consider portfolio diversification to have an effect on value apart from the effect of the individual assets?

Because limited partnership agreements typically allow the general partner considerable latitude in choosing investments, the asset mix as of the date of value may not remain the same throughout the life of an investment in the partnership. The valuer then should ask whether the general partner has a history of changing the asset portfolio, and whether the hypothetical buyer of the interest, after performing due diligence, would conclude that there is assurance that the asset mix will remain as it is or there is a risk that the portfolio will change.

If the assets being valued today are not the same as the assets the partnership may hold tomorrow, a potential future trend of asset change should be considered when the valuation is performed. The risk that assets may change is a control issue, and may emerge as a management competency issue as well.

For valuation purposes, business valuers often remove excess cash and equivalents from net asset value, returning it after discounts are applied. However, if the limited partners cannot effect distribution, the valuer must consider whether it should be left as part of net asset value and then discounted based on its likely use, e.g., the possibility of its being used to purchase another asset.

Mixed assets can create another problem, to the extent that an investor in one might not want the particular mix that is offered.[8] Investors who seek participation in a particular property type (say, residential) can be less enthusiastic about an interest in an entity that owns an odd mix (say, residential, retail, and office park). This might also be a problem for a potential buyer looking for a real estate-related investment, if the entity also holds securities.

Conclusion

Portfolio considerations may reduce the discount if the partnership holds similar properties and can effectively manage them, but discounts may also be increased as a penalty for exacerbating the effects of lack of control. Any portfolio adjustment should have good common-sense support; the specific reasons the mix is undesirable should be made clear and compelling. If the portfolio does mitigate risk and is within the management capability of the general partner, then it may be desirable, a condition that should also be addressed and supported.

---

8. See Pratt, page 251. The "portfolio effect" is identified as a discount for a company that owns dissimilar operations and/or assets that do not necessarily fit well together. Discounts are observed in the market by comparing prices of conglomerate companies with their breakup value. Part of the reason for the discount may be that buyers invest with the intent of participating in a particular industry, and prefer to control the industry mix rather than having a manager choose for them. Management may also be an issue in this instance.

CHAPTER 4

Developing the Discount for Lack of Control

A discount for lack of control is typically required when asset methods are used to value a partnership as a whole. Deriving the discount for lack of control from limited partnership data is the step between obtaining the 100% value of the partnership and its hypothetical minority-marketable value. This value applies only for a certain percentage ownership (or range of percentages) and includes some underlying assumptions pertaining to the size of the ownership interest. The assumptions pertaining to value-influencing elements other than size that led to the discount conclusion will be discussed later in this chapter.

The flow diagram of Figure 4.1, Minority Interest Discounting Process, equates the control value of equities (referring to stock corporations) and net asset value (real estate partnerships). Exchange-traded interests represent the minority-marketable level, and the benchmark of full liquidity is exchange-traded shares.

Data taken from markets other than the major exchanges exhibit an additional discount for lack of marketability, shown in the figure as the trading market discount. In order to develop the net minority interest (control) discount, it is necessary to subtract the trading market discount from the discount indication developed from these "less liquid" markets.

Market Data for Developing the Discount

After reviewing the characteristics of different types of data to establish minority values, it has been determined that trades of public real estate limited partnership interests are the most appropriate and accessible data for developing the discount for lack of control for real estate limited partnership interests.

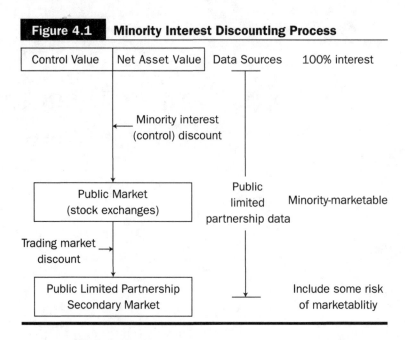

Figure 4.1	Minority Interest Discounting Process

Data on REITs and other investments can be used, but their differences are more difficult to accommodate using a comparative company approach.

As much as possible, market data from stock exchanges should be selected in conformance with the requirements of Revenue Ruling 59-60 §4.01(h) and Standards Rule 9-4(b)(v), both of which state that the business valuer should consider sales of publicly traded interests in companies (or partnerships) whose line of business is similar to the subject being valued.

The term *similar* is not clearly defined. However, the revenue ruling states that "...care should be taken to use only comparable companies. Although the only restrictive requirement, as to comparable corporations specified in the statute, is that their lines of business be the same or similar, yet it is obvious that consideration must be given to other relevant factors in order that the most valid comparison possible will be obtained."[1] The valuer, therefore, must identify the criteria that contribute to a valid comparison. These criteria are referred to as *value-influencing elements.* For the purpose of the valuation of Suburban Office Partners, II, the general line of business is real estate holding. Publicly traded real estate holding companies and limited partnerships typically perform the following activities:

- Hold real property such as apartments, office buildings, or shopping centers for the production of income
- Buy and sell real property

---

1. Revenue Ruling 59-60 §4.01 (h).

- Actively manage real property
- Develop new properties or renovate existing properties
- Manage real property assets for others

Criteria for Selecting Similar Partnerships

The criteria for selecting partnerships to be compared to the subject, Suburban Office Partners, II, generally embody those set forth in Revenue Ruling 59-60 for valuing the partnership. Thus the following criteria for comparable partnerships should generally be considered

- Economic influences
- Property type
- Diversification and geographic location
- Size (e.g., assets, revenues, or other appropriate measures)
- Historical business trends
- Prospects for growth
- Capital structure and financial statement
- Management depth
- Dividend-paying capacity
- Actual payment of dividends or distribution history
- Expectations for future dividends
- Expected liquidation date (remaining term)

Although many of these criteria apply to businesses in general, only those that are relevant to partnerships that hold real estate assets are selected for comparative purposes. These are described in more detail below.

Property type. Property type refers to the underlying asset base of the partnerships. The criterion of property type is selected to meet the requirement of Revenue Ruling 59-60 §4.01(h) concerning the comparable's engagement in the same or a similar line of business. If the asset method has been used to develop the underlying value, the market factors that affect the values of different property types would have been accounted for during the valuation of the properties themselves, which would largely satisfy Revenue Ruling 59-60 §4.01(b).

Another possible influence on value of partnership units is related to property type; buyers sometimes apply an additional discount for property types that are perceived to be more stable (e.g., those that have triple-net leases) or more risky (e.g., undeveloped land). This influence may not necessarily have been reflected in the valuation of the underlying real estate.

Holding assets for the production of income should be the principal activity of the business being compared because buying, selling, developing, and managing activities generate significantly greater growth and increase the level of risk.

Geographic diversification. Geographic diversification refers to the geographical location and the number of properties the partnership owns. The fewer the properties owned, or the more localized they are, the more susceptible operations may be to the vagaries of markets and local economies, which may result in potentially greater perceived risk.

Portfolio diversification tends to reduce risk, but other issues that preclude diversification may be involved. For example, partnerships that hold properties at numerous locations require adequate management expertise, which may not always be available. Moreover, it can be less efficient and less effective to manage geographically dispersed shopping centers than local ones. It is also possible that combinations of assets may be less attractive if investors for one property type would not be interested in the others that are part of the asset mix.

Size. Comparability in size based on net asset value, revenues, and other measures is an obvious value-influencing element when selecting comparables from market data. The influence of size on value has been demonstrated conclusively for operating companies. Smaller companies generally exhibit greater risk than larger companies.[2] However, this relationship does not necessarily apply to asset-holding partnerships, except at the extremes. Adjustments for size should be developed from the data specific to limited partnerships and not inferred from data on operating companies in general.

Capital structure. Capital structure, or leverage, affects distributions and can also be a variable with which to compare the subject partnership with publicly traded real estate holding company partnerships when simple methods of extracting discounts are used, such as the discounts derived from averages method described later in this chapter.

Management depth. Management depth is a variable that is more applicable to operating companies, but it could also be one that affects larger partnerships that are diversified according to their asset portfolio or the geographic location of the properties held. For example, if a partnership holds properties in three states but has a management presence in only one, or its managers are familiar with only one of the three markets, there may be insufficient management depth, especially when it is compared to professionally managed partnerships. The same holds true for partnerships that hold differing property types.

2. Roger Grabowski and David King, "New Evidence on Size Effects and Equity Returns, *Business Valuation Review* (March 1998) and "Size Effects and Equity Returns: An Update, *Business Valuation Review* (March 1997).

Distribution history. When valuing a minority noncontrolling interest, the history of the actual distributions paid is more important than the partnership's capacity to pay distributions because earnings may be reinvested or accumulated (subject to restrictions under the partnership agreement and fiduciary limitations). Thus, the distribution rate is an important criterion for selecting partnerships for comparison. Minority interest holders have little or no say about how distributions are handled. The distribution history also reflects the degree to which the partnership's ability to distribute cash to the limited partners has been affected by economic instability or operational and management problems. Generally, a less stable distribution trend suggests that a partnership is vulnerable to changes in economic conditions.

Dividend expectations. Extraordinary uses for cash flow might reduce the payment of dividends to partners in the future. These expenses might be for tenant improvements, property renovation, or balloon payments on loans and should be taken into account by the business valuer when selecting comparables.[3]

Remaining term. Although the remaining term of the investment as a criterion for comparison is not addressed specifically in Revenue Ruling 59-60, it is implicit in the §4.01(g) references to degree of control. If the remaining term is short, the probability that the limited partners will realize the pro rata value of their shares is increased.

Expected liquidation date. Partnerships that have announced liquidation dates are selected as comparables if the subject also has a short remaining term or can be terminated by the subject interest holder. If there is no indication that the partnership will liquidate soon, the subject may be compared with partnership transactions that date from years when the general market expectation was similar to the holding period expectation for the subject.

Data Sources

There are three basic types of public companies to be considered when valuing real estate companies generally: real estate operating companies, real estate investment trusts (REITs), and public limited partnerships that hold real property assets. Public limited partnerships conform best with the

---

3. The valuer may have to consider unusual distribution splits between general and limited partners or between classes of limited partners. Most family limited partnerships require that cash flow and proceeds from a sale or liquidation be distributed according to percentage interests, with no preferred or incentive payments. Although most public limited partnerships provide for such payments, the performance thresholds that were required in the 1980s when partnerships were created are not achievable in today's market. Therefore, de facto distribution requirements for most public limited partnerships are generally similar to those of the small partnerships that are the subject of this book.

> *Public real estate limited partnerships were created primarily during the real estate boom of the 1980s.*

foregoing criteria. They range in size from a *NAV* of about $3 million to $200 million, with the median in the $20–$30 million range. Many are well diversified, but some have only one asset. Life is not indefinite, and the expected holding period can be used as an important point for comparison. They are not taxed at the entity level, but pass through profits and losses to the interest holders.

Operating companies are not usually good comparisons for holding companies like Suburban Office Partners, II, because they generate returns from activities other than passive real estate investment. REITs are holding companies, but they are typically very large and have an indefinite life and a unique organizational structure. REIT data can be used successfully in an income approach, but requires a capital market analysis not presented in this book.

Trades of public real state limited partnership interests are by far the most appropriate and convenient data for developing the discount for lack of control, since we are dealing with a real estate limited partnership. REITs and other sources can be used, but their differences are much more difficult to accommodate in a comparative company approach.

Public Limited Partnership Secondary Market

Public real estate limited partnerships were created primarily during the real estate boom of the 1980s. High prices and front-end fees created conditions in which limited partners could only achieve profitability if values continued to climb, which did not happen. During the recession of the early 1990s, partnership asset values dropped substantially. In many cases they dropped to less than half of the proceeds of the offering and never fully recovered. The secondary market was also created in the early 1980s, first with two independent national broker-dealers, and grew to as many as 20 firms by the early 1990s. Although the market had been active through the 1990s, the number of partnerships has been declining, and secondary market activity has been declining along with it.

Partnership Profiles Database

The bimonthly newsletter *Direct Investments Spectrum* is the recognized authority on the secondary market trading activities of public limited partnerships.[4] Its publisher, Partnership

---

4. "Secondary Spectrum," *The Partnership Spectrum* (Dallas: Partnership Profiles, May/June 1992 and later). The newsletter's name was changed to *Direct Investments Spectrum* in 2004.

Profiles, has been tracking discounts for limited partnerships based on net asset value since 1992 and has developed an extensive database that is invaluable for developing discount indications for publicly held minority interests in limited partnerships. (See Appendix C for a table illustrating how the partnership data are presented.) Its annual May/June issue features secondary market discounts. The 1997 issue (the year for which the subject partnership, Suburban Officer Partners, II, is valued) includes transaction data for 167 limited partnerships.

The number of partnerships that *The Partnership Spectrum* covers has been declining as those formed during the heyday of the 1980s have been liquidated, are being absorbed by REITs, or have take other steps to establish liquidity for the partners. The 2003 discount study contained only 77 partnerships. This reduction is due primarily to liquidations.[5]

The market expects shortened holding periods generally, and discounts have been declining as a result of that expectation.[6] The data show that it is these expectations (along with cash flow and the other characteristic elements that are addressed in the case study) and not the transaction year that determine the discount. Under these conditions, older data can more accurately reflect minority discounts than current data, and the Partnership Profiles database can provide discount indications for privately held real estate limited partnerships for many years.[7]

Market data to develop the discount for lack of control can also be obtained from the Partnership Profiles Minority Discount Database.[8] The database includes partnerships listed in the resale discount studies from 1994 and thereafter. They can be queried by property type; liquidation status, i.e., whether liquidation has been announced; cash flow/net asset value; degree of leverage, and year of transaction. Fields of data that can be targeted are:

- Number of properties
- Price/*NAV* (1 – discount)
- *NAV*
- Revenue
- Property types

5. The number of partnerships tracked has fallen from 662 in 1995 to 301 in 2002. Those included in the discount study dropped from 189 in 1995 to 77 in 2003.
6. "Partnership Re-Sale Discounts Take a Dip," *The Partnership Spectrum* (March/April 2002): 1–2.
7. A study of expected yields for partnership transactions from 1994 to 2002 applied market-wide liquidation horizons of 10 years in 1994, 8 years in 1995, 6 years in 1996, 5 years in 1997 through 1999, and 4 years in 2000–2002. (See *2003 Rate of Return Study, Publicly Held Real Estate Limited Partnerships and Real Estate Investment Trusts* (Partnership Profiles, Inc., Dallas, TX, 2003). Based on this analysis, yields remained nearly constant through the entire period, while real estate yields varied by 90 basis points (See *Korpacz Real Estate Survey*, published by PriceWaterhouseCoopers, 2003Q3, p. 75 and 2000Q3, p. 60.)
8. Access is available online at www.dispectrum.com.

- Leverage
- Distribution yields
- Operating surplus
- Gross/net cash flow rates

A query to the database returns results for multiple partnerships in a single year. Multiyear datasheets for specific partnerships can be ordered separately.

Requested partnership data may require support from alternative sources. The public limited partnership data represent transactions that involve very small interests for which the degree of control is negligible. If the subject interest has sufficient control to force near-term liquidation (i.e., in less than four years), the Partnership Profiles Liquidating Partnership Study may be a useful source of data.[9]

Methods for Developing the Discount

Several methods can be used to develop the discount for lack of control. These methods are analytical techniques for extracting market discount indications from the same limited partnership database. They differ largely in their complexity, degree of reliability, and clarity in communicating the analytical process to the reader. Among the methods are extracting the discount from study averages, using a rigorous multiple linear regression model, performing a graphic analysis using the same database, and making a detailed comparison to individual partnerships using a sales comparison grid format. Any one of these methods or a combination of them may be sufficient. The most appropriate method to use in developing the discount depends on the scope of work and the level of reliability required for the value conclusion. Regardless of the valuer's scope, the objective is to find a method that permits a specific application of the market data to the partnership interest being valued.[10]

Extracting Discounts from Averages

To extract discounts from averages the valuer compares the subject partnership with discounts for one or more categories of partnerships and makes the needed adjustments if possible. Because discounts are presented as averages from broad categories, some refinement is advisable when extracting the discount using this method; i.e., the valuer can make a basic adjustment for yield, attempt to make a more careful analysis of it, and then look for as many points of comparison between the subject partnership and the comparable as possible.

9. "Secondary Market Buyers Playing Arbitrage," *The Partnership Spectrum* (March/April 2000): 1–6.

10. Specificity is becoming increasingly important in court cases that concern the valuation of minority interests in property. See Estate of Berg, 91 TCM 1383 (1991).

Selecting the applicable category. Selecting the applicable category is the most important step in applying partnership study averages, and leverage (debt) is a key classifying element as shown in Table 4.1. The data for the study are from the May/June 1997 issue of *The Partnership Spectrum,* which appears in Appendix C.

Table 4.1	Average Discounts and Yields		
Partnership Category	**Number of Partnerships**	**Average Discount**	**Average Yield**
All partnerships	130	30%	
Equity-distributing (no-to-low debt)	48	28%	8.1%
Equity-distributing (moderate-to-high debt)	24	37%	7.2%
Equity-nondistributing	27	42%	0.0%
Triple-net lease (all)	19	16%	10.1%
Insured mortgages	12	20%	10.3%

The discount study's low and high debt indications are intended to separate the partnerships into two categories: those that have borrowed little and are intended to be cash-flow investments (i.e., generally purchased for this reason) and those that have borrowed heavily and are intended to be capital gain investments (i.e., purchased more often for their potential for gain).

A no-to-low debt partnership has less than 30% debt, defined as borrowings divided by *NAV*. High debt is any debt percentage greater than 30%. This categorization works for public partnerships, which usually have higher administrative costs and fees than small family partnerships and often have difficulty paying distributions when leveraged. A family limited partnership, by contrast, usually passes cash flow efficiently to its partners and, like Suburban Office Partners, II, can produce good cash flows despite having significantly higher levels of debt. Cash flows are more consistent for low-debt public partnerships than for high-debt partnerships. Debt moves more of the expected investment return to the end of the holding period, and the hypothetical buyer's objective is consistent with that of a moderate-to-high debt public partnership interest. For small leveraged private partnerships, it may be most appropriate to use both low leverage and high leverage categories separately in the analysis and reconcile the results, depending on the effect of the leverage.

Valuing a no-to-low-leverage partnership poses fewer problems for a partnership valuer than a high-leverage partnership. The nondistributing category dispenses with yields altogether,

> *After a category is selected, adjustments to the data can be made to facilitate comparisons.*

but some partnerships have the potential for resuming distributions.

Data on the triple-net lease category must be applied carefully because the term *triple-net lease* (NNN) has many meanings and may not be applicable for all real estate categorized as such. To make a valid comparison with the subject partnership, it is advisable to review the partnerships that fall into this category. Tenant creditworthiness, the size of the property, diversification, and other aspects of the real estate are important. The fact that the subject partnership has tenants with triple-net leases does not mean that this would be the most appropriate category to select for the purpose of comparison.

The insured mortgage category can be useful for partnerships that hold significant amounts of debt or even securities. Securities holdings are generally valued using closed-end funds rather than public partnerships, but the mortgage partnerships can provide useful insights, nonetheless.

Adjusting elements. After a category is selected, adjustments to the data can be made to facilitate comparisons. Yield is the most important element that can be adjusted when extracting discounts from averages to develop the discount for lack of control. The discount is adjusted downward for a subject's superior return, for example. The result can only be an approximation, however, because the average yield is not mathematically associated with an average discount.

It may not always be clear how to handle the other independent variables such as distribution stability, trend, partnership size, and diversification. The partnership study excludes those that are expected to wind up in a short term, but some short-term situations remain (e.g., a shorter-than-expected holding period than the general market's five years for 1997 transactions) that do affect the averages. A holding period shorter than the general market's five years in 1997 will affect the averages.

A simple method for addressing these independent variables is to characterize the subject partnership using each of the categories listed in the study. The valuer's familiarity with the partnership database would then likely lead to a narrative comparison with the subject partnership. Another method might be for the valuer to develop a regression model (discussed later in this chapter) and examine the interaction between selected independent variables, such as the sensitivity of a moderate-to-high-debt equity-distributing partnership to changes in distribution yield.

CASE STUDY APPLICATION

Extracting Discounts from Partnership Study Averages

Developing the discount necessitates comparing the subject partnership to one or more categories of characteristics and making the required adjustments. The first category of comparison between Suburban Office Partners, II, and a comparable partnership is yield. Using Table 4.2, the cash flow rate is recalculated as a distribution yield by dividing the cash flow by the minority-marketable level value, V_{MP}. The formula for the minority-marketable level value is: $NAV \times 1$ minus the average discount for all partnerships.[11] Value is a dependent variable, so this step is iterative and calculated as:

> Distribution yield = cash flow / minority-marketable value
> Distribution yield = \$95,355 / [\$1,512,279 × (1 – 0.30)]
> Distribution yield = \$95,355 / \$1,058,596 = 9.0%

This yield is provisional since changing the initial discount conclusion (30%) will change the distribution rate or yield.

Table 4.2	**Average Discounts and Yields (Excluding NNN Leases and Insured Mortgages)**		
Partnership Category	**Number of Partnerships**	**Average Discount**	**Average Yield**
All partnerships	130	30%	
Equity-distributing (no-to-low debt)	48	28%	8.1%
Equity-distributing (moderate-to-high debt)	24	37%	7.2%
Equity-nondistributing	27	42%	0.0%

The leverage calculation is debt/NAV. The approximate division between no-to-low and moderate-to-high is 30%, so the subject leverage is recalculated as:

> Leverage = Debt/NAV
> Leverage = \$1,816,268/\$1,512,279 = 1 .20
> Leverage = 120%

This figure seems high until one considers that the partnership's cash flow is 9.0%. A small, closely held partnership can be leveraged and still have the characteristics of a public partnership in the no-to-low debt group, since a substantial portion of the investor's return is in the form of cash flow. It can also have characteristics of the moderate-to-high debt group, with a significant expectation of a return at the end of the holding period. Debt increases risk but also increases the total return. The low-cost operation of a small partnership allows these conditions to coexist. Using both categories and reconciling the results would make the best use of the data. This can be accomplished after adjusting the averages for the elements that clearly influence the discount.

The equity-distributing/moderate-to-high category shows an average discount of 37% and a distribution yield of 7.2%. For a 9.0% yield, the discount would be adjusted downward for the subject partnership's superior return but probably not as low as the 28% average for the no-to-low debt category. The no-to-low debt category shows an average discount of 28% and a distribution yield of 8.1%. If the valuer chooses this category

---

11. This is the minority-marketable level with the trading market discount included, assuming that the subject partnership is being compared to public limited partnerships traded on the secondary market.

for comparison, the discount would also be adjusted downward because of the subject's superior 9.0% return.

The remaining term for the subject partnership is five years—the same as the general market expectation for 1997 partnership transactions. Thus, except for the influence of the few partnerships that demonstrate a shorter term, this variable needs no adjusting. If the subject's holding period were longer, for example, the discount would be adjusted upward. The valuer might make adjustments for distribution trends if the subject's trend is superior or inferior to the category average. In the case of Suburban Office Partners, II, it is probably superior. Thus, a slight downward adjustment would be indicated. An adjustment in size would not be warranted because size was not important for office partnerships from 1995 to 1997.

Based on the categories selected, the following adjustments for value-influencing elements were made for Suburban Office Partners, II:

Leverage classification	No-to-low	Moderate-to-high
Equity-distributing, average discount	28.0%	37.0%
Adjust for superior distribution (yield) rate	-0.5%	-2.5%
Adjust for superior distribution trend	-1.0%	-1.0%
Concluded discount by averages	26.5%	33.5%

The subject has characteristics that correspond to partnerships in both categories, with expectations of return from cash flows (best represented by no-to-low debt) and of a reversion at the end of the holding period (best represented by moderate-to-high debt). Weighting both discounts equally yields a concluded discount of 30% using the discount from averages method. If a discount other than 30% is concluded, the distribution yield should be recalculated and a new comparison made.

Extracting discounts from averages can be rudimentary, imprecise, and unconvincing. With refinement, it can also become a subject-specific analysis, but the chief shortcoming of the method lies in the valuer's need to know average yields, growth rates and trends, diversification, holding periods, and other important points of comparison that may not be readily accessible. This is the method's most serious limitation. The method can be adequate, however, if the scope of work does not require a precise indication of the discount for lack of control.

Multiple Linear Regression

Using a multiple linear regression model is especially effective for analyzing a large database and extracting coefficients for the most important value-influencing independent variables, which the discount from averages method cannot adequately address. The direct application of coefficients to the subject partnership's variables using multiple linear regression results in a highly subject-specific and accurate analysis of the discount for control.

Other advantages of using the multiple linear regression model are that the business valuer can:

- Accumulate a large database with many property types that can be used for different assignments.
- Provide original support for using data from multiple years.
- Deselect the partnerships for which the data are inconsistent.
- Discover the significance of different variables.

The disadvantages of the method are that

- It is complex.
- If used alone, without adequate explanation, it can appear to be an unconvincing "black box" analysis.
- Inputting data can be tedious.
- The process may be conceptually difficult and requires skill to avoid imbedding errors.

To overcome these challenges and to use this method for developing the discount, valuers of partnerships can refer to the many spreadsheet programs available on the market that facilitate the process of constructing multiple linear regression models.

To use the method well, a large number of partnerships should be initially selected for comparison. The minimum number depends on the number of variables to be compared, but using at least 20 partnerships is recommended because it is difficult to know which of the elements of comparison will emerge as the most important.

CASE STUDY APPLICATION

Using a Multiple Linear Regression Model

The linear regression model for comparing Suburban Office Partners, II, with similar partnerships was derived from a database containing 43 different partnerships and 73 partnership/transaction-year combinations. The source was the Partnership Profiles data from the years 1995 through 1997. Narrowing the pool to partnerships that held office properties reduced the number to 21 partnerships and 32 partnership/transaction-year combinations. (See Table 4.3.)

The database shows a total of 343 market trades. The minimum trade per partnership is two, and the median is five. The high/low spread ranges from 1%, representing only two trades, to 59%. The median spread is 14%. Discounts range from 19% to 53%, and the median is 40%.

To produce the best results using the method, it is important that the independent variables for the subject lie within the range of the data selected. This generally works for all variables except asset size. The selected partnerships range in value from $7.4 million to $95 million; the median is $26 million. This exceeds the subject's NAV of $1.5 million. Therefore, the valuer should be careful to avoid projecting conclusions based on the small asset size.

All of the partnerships except three are distributing. The maximum is 10.3%, and the median is 4.5%. Two partnerships hold one property and one holds two, but the median held is five and the greatest number held is 14. Ten of the partnerships have no debt, and the others range from about 3% to 73% debt. A wide range of distribution trends is represented and these can be classified as declining/loss to level/increasing. Most of the

Table 4.3 Selected Partnership Database

Partnership	Year	Total Units 000	Valuation			Trading					Avg. $/Units Weighted	Discount
			$Mil	$/Unit	#	Units	High	Low	Vol. $000	Spread		
Corporate Prop. Associates 9	1996	60	$58.2	$970.00	14	300	$765.00	$700.00	$219	9%	$730.17	24.7%
Damson/Birtcher Realty Inc Fund I	1997	97	35.6	367.00	2	17	247.60	246.00	4	1%	246.64	32.8%
Damson/Birtcher Realty Inc Fund I	1996	97	37.5	387.00	18	336	240.00	187.00	76	24%	224.85	41.9%
Damson/Birtcher Realty Inc Fund I	1995	97	37.9	391.00	14	196	319.00	180.00	46	59%	236.86	39.4%
Dean Witter Real Est Inc Ptr II	1996	177	95.2	538.00	38	943	405.00	324.00	345	22%	366.00	32.0%
First Capital Growth Fnd XIV	1997	145	7.4	51.00	2	250	39.07	38.00	10	3%	38.43	24.6%
First Capital Growth Fnd XIV	1996	145	7.7	53.00	3	440	33.00	32.00	14	3%	32.27	39.1%
First Capital Growth Fnd XIV	1995	145	7.5	52.00	3	900	26.25	24.60	23	7%	25.31	51.3%
First Capital Inc & Growth Fund XII	1997	950	23.7	25.00	8	2,165	15.30	12.80	30	18%	13.91	44.4%
First Capital Inst. Real Estate Ltd 1	1997	60	28.6	477.00	10	95	370.00	335.00	34	11%	325.00	31.9%
First Capital Inst. Real Estate Ltd 1	1996	60	29.0	484.00	11	89	280.00	251.00	24	11%	269.96	44.2%
First Capital Inst. Real Estate Ltd 3	1996	46	25.9	562.00	12	150	498.00	420.00	68	17%	454.67	19.1%
High Equity Partners-86*	1997	588	58.1	98.87	46	2,071	70.00	57.00	133	20%	64.26	35.0%
High Equity Partners-86*	1996	588	61.7	105.00	37	2,545	54.00	43.00	128	22%	50.14	52.2%
Hutton/GSH Comm Props 2	1996	100	26.6	266.00	5	184	168.00	162.00	30	4%	165.48	37.8%
Hutton/GSH Comm Props 3	1996	109	29.4	270.00	11	410	187.00	150.00	65	24%	157.38	41.7%
Hutton/GSH Qual. Props 80	1997	51	19.0	373.00	2	224	295.00	235.00	54	25%	241.43	35.3%
Hutton/GSH Qual. Props 80	1996	51	17.8	349.00	3	200	260.00	245.00	51	6%	252.50	27.7%
Hutton/GSH Qual. Props 80	1995	51	20.4	400.64	2	40	250.00	225.00	9	11%	231.25	42.3%
JMB Income Properties X	1996	150	52.5	350.00	9	296	212.00	150.00	61	30%	205.61	41.3%
Net 2 LP	1997	477	37.2	78.09	8	1,749	61.00	55.00	100	11%	56.98	27.0%
Net 2 LP	1996	477	33.4	70.00	12	2,765	50.00	45.00	137	11%	45.81	34.6%
Net 2 LP	1995	477	34.2	71.69	7	2,530	46.00	42.00	111	9%	43.86	38.8%
Paine/Webber Equity Partners 2	1996	134,426	48.4	0.36	10	263,881	0.18	0.15	45	18%	0.17	52.8%
Paine/Webber Equity Partners 3	1996	50	22.0	439.00	11	242	260.00	230.00	60	12%	247.43	43.6%
Paine/Webber Growth Props 2	1997	33	24.0	720.00	4	55	430.00	401.00	23	7%	420.43	41.6%
Pru-Bache Watson/Taylor - 3	1996	54	10.5	195.00	7	86	120.00	100.00	9	18%	112.02	42.6%
Pru-Bache Watson/Taylor - 4	1996	66	13.3	202.00	10	194	127.00	95.00	23	27%	117.69	41.7%
Pru-Bache Watson/Taylor - 4	1995	66	12.5	190.00	7	69	108.00	95.00	7	13%	102.93	45.8%
Prudential Acquisition Fnd I	1996	70	21.7	310.00	7	68	300.00	185.00	15	52%	221.29	28.6%
Rancon Realty Fund IV	1997	79	25.2	317.00	2	19	195.00	165.00	4	16%	190.79	39.8%
Rancon Realty Fund V	1997	100	33.9	340.00	8	45	212.00	175.00	9	19%	189.99	44.1%

Table 4.3 Selected Partnership Database (continued)

Partnership	Distributions			Assets			Debt Ratio Pct.	Comments
	$/Unit	Rate Gross	Rate Effective	Type	#	Regions		
Corporate Prop. Associates 9	$84.72	8.7%	11.6%	NNN Indust/Office	14	South, West	58	Increasing dist, temp decr mgt fees.
Damson/Birtcher Realty Inc Fund I	10.40	2.8%	4.2%	Bus Park/Office/Retail	6	IL, WA, AZ, CO, NM	8	Dist were declining, now increasing.
Damson/Birtcher Realty Inc Fund I	10.40	2.7%	4.6%	Bus Park/Office/Retail	7	IL, WA, AZ, CO, NM	4	Distribution from sale proceeds, 1996.
Damson/Birtcher Realty Inc Fund I	10.40	2.7%	4.4%	Bus Park/Office/Retail	7	IL, WA, AZ, CO, NM	0	Distributions declining after 1994.
Dean Witter Real Est Inc Ptr II	33.00	6.1%	9.0%	Office/Retail/Bus Park	6	South, West	0	Dist sl declining w/o dist from sale '96.
First Capital Growth Fnd XIV	3.20	6.3%	8.3%	Office	1	IL	0	Distributions stabilizing.
First Capital Growth Fnd XIV	3.20	6.0%	9.9%	Office	1	IL	0	Distributions irregular, stabilizing.
First Capital Growth Fnd XIV	2.08	4.0%	8.2%	Office	1	IL	0	Distributions irregular, none in 1993.
First Capital Inc & Growth Fund XII	0.00	0.0%	0.0%	Office/Retail	5	FL, KY, CO	56	No distributions.
First Capital Inst. Real Estate Ltd 1	28.00	5.9%	8.6%	Office	2	DC, TX	0	Distributions increasing to level since '94
First Capital Inst. Real Estate Ltd 1	28.00	5.8%	10.4%	Retail/Office	4	DC, TX, CA, GA	0	Dist. irregular; increasing since '93.
First Capital Inst. Real Estate Ltd 3	56.00	10.0%	12.3%	Office	4	FL, MI, TX	0	Dist. increasing since '93 but uncertain.
High Equity Partners -86*	3.08	3.1%	4.8%	Office/Retail/Indust	10	CA and all US	0	Dist. level to increasing, litigation.
High Equity Partners -86*	2.48	2.4%	4.9%	Office/Retail/Indust	10	CA and all US	0	Declining distributions, litigation.
Hutton/GSH Comm Props 2	17.00	6.4%	10.3%	Bus Park/Office	4	FL, CA, TX, AR, MD	0	50% special distribution.
Hutton/GSH Comm Props 3	12.00	4.4%	7.6%	Office/Other	4	South, FL, AR, TX	0	Dist. declining, loss from operations.
Hutton/GSH Qual. Props 80	16.00	4.3%	6.6%	Office/Bus Park	4	TN, CA	16	Declining due to capital improvements.
Hutton/GSH Qual. Props 80	26.00	7.4%	10.3%	Office/Bus Park	4	TN, CA	16	Slightly irregular distributions.
Hutton/GSH Qual. Props 80	23.50	5.9%	10.2%	Office/Bus Park	4	TN, CA	15	Distributions irregular.
JMB Income Properties X	12.00	3.4%	5.8%	Retail/Office	3	TX, NY	30	Declining distributions, sales in '91-95.
Net 2 LP	5.00	6.4%	8.8%	NNN Indust/Retail/Office	9	OH, WI, MD, WA, AZ, CT	32	Distributions level since 1994.
Net 2 LP	5.00	7.1%	10.9%	NNN Indust/Retail/Office	9	OH, WI, MD, WA, AZ, CT	28	Distributions level since 1994.
Net 2 LP	5.00	7.0%	11.4%	NNN Indust/Retail/Office	9	OH, WI, MD, WA, AZ, CT	30	Distributions declining 1991-94, level
Paine/Webber Equity Partners 2	0.01	2.5%	5.3%	Office/Retail/Res	6	KS, CA, SC, VA, WA	26	Declining distributions, sales in 1995.
Paine/Webber Equity Partners 3	20.00	4.6%	8.1%	Retail/Office/Res	4	NM, OR, VA, GA	35	Declining distributions.
Paine/Webber Growth Props 2	15.40	2.1%	3.7%	Residential/Office	1	OR	73	Distributions began 1995, irregular.
Pru-Bache Watson/Taylor - 3	5.00	2.6%	4.5%	Mini-Whse/Office/Land	8	TX, OK, AK, NJ	3	Declining distributions, has vacant land.
Pru-Bache Watson/Taylor - 4	5.00	2.5%	4.2%	Mini-Whse/Office/Land	5	TX, TN	0	Irregular distributions, has vacant land.
Pru-Bache Watson/Taylor - 4	8.72	4.6%	8.5%	Mini-Whse/Office/Land	5	TX, TN	0	Irregular/decl dist., has vacant land.
Prudential Acquisition Fnd I	32.00	10.3%	14.5%	Retail/Office/Indust	5	FL, MN, CA	0	Intend to list for sale in '95; dist sl irregular.
Rancon Realty Fund IV	0.00	0.0%	0.0%	Office/Ret/Res/Res Land	9	So Calif.	26	No distributions (began 1998).
Rancon Realty Fund V	0.00	0.0%	0.0%	Office/Industrial/Res Land	9	So Calif.	27	No distributions (began 1999).

partnerships are assumed to have a holding period that matches the general market expectation, although nine expect to be liquidated in one to two years.

The basic equation for multiple linear regression is

$$y = a + b_1x_1 + b_2x_2 + b_3x_3 + b_4x_4 + \ldots + b_nx_n,$$

where y is the discount for lack of control, a is the constant, and b_1 is the coefficient for the independent variable, x_1. Detailed explanations of the mathematics can be found in a number of references.[12]

The x-variables include distribution rate and trend and the remaining term. Size, degree of asset diversification, leverage, triple-net leases, and other property types can be examined as part of the regression analysis to determine whether they also influence the discount. For the database selected for this case study, none of the variables were significant, so they have been excluded from the regression analysis.

Three of the potential x-variables are numerical and may be used directly. These variables are distribution rate, size,[13] and leverage. The other variables must be expressed using dummy variables. In this instance, the valuer must exercise judgment when interpreting the conditions that the variables represent. The following system is a method for interpreting four of the variables that influence value: distribution rate, distribution trend, remaining term, diversification, and property type.

Distribution trend: The case study model uses the number 1 for a stable or increasing trend, and 0 for a declining trend.

Remaining term: Determining this variable requires interpreting management's statements (usually published in Form 10K and reported in a special addendum to the Partnership Profiles) to ascertain whether a short-term sale of assets and distribution of proceeds occurred. This is expressed as a one- or two-year hold in some instances, which is a "soft" numerical conclusion. The holding period corresponds with the per-year market-expected holds from the 2003 rate of return study, which are eight years for the 1995 transactions, six years for 1996 transactions, and five years for those that occurred in 1997.

Diversification: Combinations that varied in the number of properties and number of regions were tested, e.g., more than three properties, or properties located in more than two regions. But none were significant for the database selected for this case study.

Property type: Individual property types were assigned the dummy variables 1/0 for the category retail/not-retail, and NNN/not-NNN for triple-net leases and non-triple-net leases. The regression for these types then was examined to determine whether the dummy had a significant influence on the output. None were significant for this database, which included partnerships that held some office properties.

The regression model yields several important statistics that show the significance of each variable, the magnitude of its influence, and the validity of the analysis. Regression data and output for this case study are shown in Table 4.4.

---

12. Abrams; *Quantitative Business Valuation: A Mathematical Approach for Today's Professionals.* Microsoft Excel's help feature also explains how to use the formula.

13. Size is generally expressed as a logarithmic transformation of NAV ($x = \ln(NAV)$). A linear function requires that a $5 million change in size would produce the same change for a $10 million partnership as it would for a $70 million partnership, so a logarithmic transformation would make more sense. This can be tested when size is introduced as an independent variable. The transformed variable will be more significant and produce a better fit with the data (i.e., greater R^2).

Table 4.4	Regression Data and Output

Regression Output

Constant	0.408
Standard error of Y (Est.)	0.048
R^2	0.693
No. of observations	32
Degrees of freedom	28

	x1	x2	x3
X-coefficient(s)	-1.775	1.53%	-5.98%
Standard error of coef.	0.333	0.37%	2.05%
t-statistic	5.33	4.17	2.92

Subject:	6.3%	5.0	1.0			
	Base	Dist.	Term	Trend	Predict y	% Error
Rancon Realty Fund IV	39.8%	0.0%	5.0	0.0	48.4%	22%
First Capital Inst. Real Estate Ltd. 1	31.9%	5.9%	5.0	1.0	32.0%	0%
First Capital Inc. & Growth Fund XII	44.4%	0.0%	5.0	0.0	48.4%	9%
Hutton/GSH Qual. Props 80	35.3%	4.3%	5.0	0.0	40.8%	16%
Paine/Webber Growth Props 2	41.6%	2.1%	5.0	1.0	38.7%	-7%
First Capital Growth Fund XIV	24.6%	6.3%	5.0	1.0	31.3%	27%
Net 2 LP	27.0%	6.4%	5.0	1.0	31.1%	15%
High Equity Partners -86*	35.0%	3.1%	5.0	1.0	36.9%	6%
Damson/Birtcher Realty Inc. Fund 1	32.8%	2.8%	2.0	0.0	38.8%	18%
Rancon Realty Fund V	44.1%	0.0%	5.0	0.0	48.4%	10%
Corporate Prop. Associates 9	24.7%	8.7%	6.0	1.0	28.5%	15%
Damson/Birtcher Realty Inc. Fund 1	41.9%	2.7%	1.0	0.0	37.6%	-10%
Dean Witter Real Est Inc. Ptr II	32.0%	6.1%	1.0	0.0	31.4%	-2%
First Capital Growth Fnd XIV	39.1%	6.0%	6.0	0.0	39.3%	0%
First Capital Inst. Real Estate Ltd. 1	44.2%	5.8%	6.0	1.0	33.7%	-24%
First Capital Inst. Real Estate Ltd. 3	19.1%	10.0%	1.0	0.0	24.6%	29%
High Equity Partners -86*	52.2%	2.4%	6.0	0.0	45.8%	-12%
Hutton/GSH Comm Props 2	37.8%	6.4%	6.0	0.0	38.6%	2%
Hutton/GSH Comm Props 3	41.7%	4.4%	6.0	0.0	42.1%	1%
Hutton/GSH Qual. Props 80	27.7%	7.4%	1.0	0.0	29.1%	5%
JMB Income Properties X	41.3%	3.4%	6.0	0.0	43.9%	6%
Pru-Bache Watson/Taylor -4	45.8%	4.6%	8.0	0.0	44.9%	-2%

The coefficient of determination, R^2, indicates that the regression explains about 69% of the variation in y (the discount) for the database used for this analysis. The x-coefficients indicate the change in y as a function of x; i.e., an increase in the distribution rate of 1% will reduce the discount by about 1.8%. The t-statistics for each x-variable are calculated by dividing each coefficient by its standard deviation. Coefficients with t-statistics greater than 2.0 usually indicate a high level of confidence. The most significant x-variables are distribution rate, which has a t-statistic of 5.33, and remaining term, which has a t-statistic of 4.17. Distribution trend is next at 2.92. A number of independent variables were tested, but size, diversification and several property type selections were not significant for this dataset, and thus were deleted.

The regression model identifies the variables that are most important. The predicted y for each partnership is calculated along with its variation in percentage from the transaction discount. A discrepancy in the result can point to an error in inputting data or a missed fact or condition; some errors may be discoverable, while others may not.

The regression formula can then be used to calculate the discount for the subject interest directly by substituting the x-terms and the a and b coefficients.

$$\text{Discount} = y = a + b_1 x_1 + b_2 x_2 + b_3 x_3$$
$$\text{Discount} = 0.408 - 1.775 \times 6.3\% + 1.53\% \times 5 - 5.98\% \times 1 = 31.3\%$$

The x-terms for the distribution rate and remaining term are straightforward, but the x-term for distribution stability/trend is not. Either 0 or 1 could be selected as the dummy variable for the partnerships in the database, depending on whether distributions were level or increasing (1) or declining (0). Distributions were generally increasing with cash flow for the subject partnership, which is largely controlled by the terms of the lease. However, rents were above market, and a step downward in rental revenues would be expected in a few years. Performance did not trend downward, but a drop in distributions could be expected during the holding period.

The distribution trend is an influential element of value that produced a change in almost 6%, depending on whether the dummy variable was 1 or 0. The subject did not appear to increase (1) overall, but was not declining (0). The latter would have implied that the properties held were problematic or would have raised other issues that could cause declines for the partnerships. The case study selected 0.8 as the x-term for the distribution trend, a subjective choice, creating a source of uncertainty for the regression process. Because 1 or 0 was used as the dummy variable, an adjustment should be made to the result.

The discounting effect of the distribution trend for Suburban Office Partners, II, is

$$-5.98\% \times (0.8 - 1) = 1.2\%$$

The concluded discount increased for its trend impairment is:

$$31.3\% + 1.2\% = 32.5\%$$

The case study conclusion, given the limitations of its inputs, has been developed based on a rigorous methodology characteristic of the multiple linear regression approach, but it may be difficult to explain to a user who is not well versed in the method. Therefore, supplemental methods might be needed to augment the multiple linear regression method when it is presented in the final report.

Graphic Analysis

Graphic analysis is another method that can be used to obtain a discount for lack of control using public guideline company data. The method often uses a ranking process to obtain value indications from a small group of comparable public companies (or partnerships). This process is limited to analysis of one variable at a time because of the two-dimensional character of a chart or list. However, if all significant variables can be selected for in developing the database, the process is subject-specific and can be reliable. It can be applied for any ratio, multiple, or other variable that can be extracted from the public company financial statements.[14] The method reveals the relative position of the subject partnership, and the discount indications can be interpolated or reconciled among the indications selected for comparison.

A disadvantage of this method is that reconciliation of the various indications can be highly subjective. While the method reveals relationships between comparable variables, multiple interactions among them cannot be understood or resolved easily. If the public partnerships are chosen well, however, the range of the indications may be minimized and the result will be adequately supported and convincing.

Commercial spreadsheet software programs such as Microsoft Excel and Lotus 123 feature simple graphing capabilities that facilitate the use of graphic analysis. Both feature trending functions that enable the relationships between data to be plotted as a curve based on linear, exponential, logarithmic, or power transfer functions. The resulting curve can be described as the influence of the sum of all the data points on the discount based on their distribution rate (or some other significant variable).

Using only a few data points, ranking is the simplest method for demonstrating relationships and is usually an adequate method for extracting indications for the subject partnership. Graphic analysis is a somewhat more rigorous method, since it can be used with more data. This method has the added advantage of being easily illustrated as an exhibit in the valuation report.

The application of the graphic analysis method for Suburban Office Partners, II, is dependent, in part, on data derived from the multiple linear regression model, which demonstrated that a few of the available independent variables significantly influence the discount for lack of control. Thus, it is a simple matter to chart the relationship between a single independent variable and the discount, demonstrating its comparability with the subject partnership. If the data can be adequately selected to control for the other significant, non-

---

14. Various multiples (e.g., price divided by earnings, cash flow, revenue, or net asset value) are typically used as indicators for public guideline companies. The discount used in this case study is based on the price/net asset value multiple.

charted independent variables, the single-variable method of analysis could produce a discount indication that would be adequate for the purpose of the valuation. Specific public partnerships could also have been selected manually from the discount study, as discussed on page 105.

The distribution rate is the independent variable of choice in applying this method, which will also control for the holding period variable, after which the results will be reconciled.

After the distribution rate is selected as the independent variable and the discount as the dependent variable, a scatter diagram is developed to represent the relationship between the two visually. The greater the scattering, the less reliable is the predictive ability of the function.

CASE STUDY APPLICATION

Using the Graphic Analysis Method

Figure 4.2 shows the 32 data points derived from the regression analysis database. The trend line that corresponds with the data best (greatest R^2) is an exponential function. Its equation is shown in the lower right-hand corner of the chart. The discount can be interpreted from the curve, as shown by the broken lines, and is calculated as:

$$Y = 0.494\ e^{-6.14x}$$
$$\text{Discount} = 0.494 \times e^{-6.14 \times .063} = 0.335$$
$$\text{Discount} = 33.5\%$$

The curve explains nearly 50% of the variation in the discount ($R^2 = 0.48$), and the result is different than the regression model's result, which explained nearly 70% of the variation. The database only controls for property type, so perhaps controlling for one of the other variables will improve the accuracy of this method.

Figure 4.2 Discount vs. Distribution Rate for the Selected Database

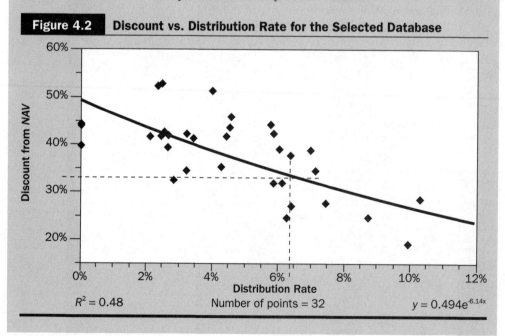

$R^2 = 0.48$ Number of points = 32 $y = 0.494e^{-6.14x}$

Figure 4.3 shows the eight data points from the regression database that had a five-year hold. The trend line that corresponds the closest with the data is also an exponential function. The discount, read from the curve, is calculated as:

$$Y = 0.433 \ e^{-6.91x}$$
$$\text{Discount} = 0.494 \times e^{-6.91 \times .063} = 0.280$$
$$\text{Discount} = 28\%$$

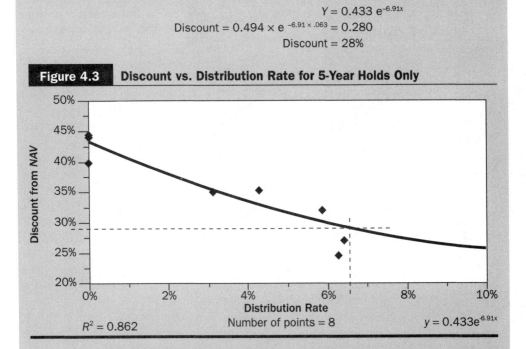

Figure 4.3 **Discount vs. Distribution Rate for 5-Year Holds Only**

$R^2 = 0.862$ Number of points = 8 $y = 0.433e^{-6.91x}$

The curve in Figure 4.3 corresponds better with the data because it explains 86% of the variation in the discount. The data set is smaller than the one used in Figure 4.2, and it controls for property type and holding period. The remaining term and distribution trend also could be controlled, but because these variables were less significant than distribution rate and holding period according to the regression model, they were not considered.

The graphic analysis method for developing the discount for lack of control for Suburban Office Partners, II produced two results based on two different data sets:

Entire transaction database	32 data points	$R^2 = 0.48$	Discount = 33.5%
Five-year holds only	8 data points	$R^2 = 0.86$	Discount = 28.0%

On the surface it appears that the first data set should have yielded the most reliable results because it contains more data points. However, the curve does not correspond with the data as well as it does with the second set. Giving a slightly greater weight to the graphic analysis method using five-year holds, the concluded discount is 30%.

A fourth method for developing the discount, the adjustment grid format, can be presented in a format familiar to real estate appraisers.

Adjustment Grid Format

Of the three methods for obtaining the discount for lack of control described thus far, the regression model has yielded the most reliable discount indication, but it does not necessarily make for a clear and convincing presentation in the valuation report. The graphic analysis method can be presented simply, but it is less rigorous than the regression model. Developing discounts from averages yields only an approximate value.

A fourth method for developing the discount, the adjustment grid format, can be presented in a format familiar to real estate appraisers. The use of a regression model enables the partnership valuer to easily select partnerships that are most similar to the subject and to identify the independent variables that have a significant effect on the discount. These partnerships' discount indications can then be adjusted. The elements that are compared with the subject and their x-coefficients are extracted from the regression and shown as quantitative adjustments to the discounts in the grid. The indicated discounts are then reconciled into a discount for the subject. The format features side-by-side columns that compare specific data elements for the subject limited partnership and a few comparables (guideline partnerships).

The only value indicator used for this method is the discount percentage, which is selected because of its consistency with the data from the Partnership Profiles. The percentage is calculated as follows:

Discount = 1 − [weighted average price per unit] / [*NAV* per unit]

It would also be possible to use price/*NAV* directly as the unit of comparison. The variables included in the grid are the same as those found to be significant in the regression analysis. The layout of the report facilitates qualitative comparisons in reconciling the adjusted discount indications for the subject partnership.

CASE STUDY APPLICATION
Using the Adjustment Grid Format

Table 4.5 shows five partnerships that were selected from the regression model database and used in constructing the adjustment grid format for developing the discount.[15] The selection criteria and other data are listed in the top three sections of the grid, and adjustments are shown in the fourth section. The indicated discounts are reconciled in the bottom, or fifth, section.

The grid's line items are points of comparison between the partnerships and are criteria for interpreting the reliability of the data used to reconcile the resulting discount indications. Most of them are taken directly from the published data. The subject property's leverage (56%) is calculated based on the market value of the real estate, but if it were based on book value net of depreciation, the denominator would change from $3,500,000 to $2,500,000, and the percentage would increase to 73%. The high/low spread is calculated as:

$$\text{High trading price} - \text{low trading price} / \text{weighted average trade}$$

This variable is a useful indicator for the reconciliation, since a wide range combined with a few trades would suggest a less reliable discount indication than many trades in a narrow range.

Table 4.5	Comparable Partnership Grid					
Item	**Subject**	**Comp # 1**	**Comp # 2**	**Comp #3**	**Comp # 4**	**Comp # 5**
Name	Suburban Office Partners II	Damson/ Birtcher Realty Inc I	High Equity Partners - 86*	Net 2 LP	First Capital Growth XIV	Paine/ Webber Growth Props 2
Property types	Office	Bus Park Office Retail	Office Retail Indust	NNN Indust Retail Office	Office	Residential Office
No. of properties	1	6	10	9	1	1
Regions						
Size (*NAV*, $m)	$1.5/$7.4*	$36	$58	$37	$7	$24
Unit value	N/A	367	98.87	78.09	51	720
Leverage	56%/73%	8%	0%	32%	0%	73%
Liquidation announced	No	About 2 Years	No	No	No	Partial
Distributions						
1997/$ unit	-	$10.40	$3.08	$5.00	$3.20	$15.40
Distribution rate	6.3%	2.8%	3.1%	6.4%	6.3%	2.1%
Stability/trend	St decline?	Down to increasing	Level/ Litigation	Level	Incr./decr.?	Increasing
Trading						
No. of trades	0	2	46	8	2	4
High/low spread	-	0.6%	20.2%	10.5%	2.8%	6.9%
Weighted average trade	-	$247	$64	$57	$38	$420
Base discount %	-	32.8%	35.0%	27.0%	24.6%	41.6%
Adjustments to discount						
Distribution rate		-6.2%	-5.7%	0.2%	-0.1%	-7.4%
Remaining term		4.6%	-0.0%	-0.0%	-0.0%	-0.0%
Distribution stabilty/trend		-4.8%	1.2%	1.2%	1.2%	1.2%
Total adjustment		-6.4%	-4.5%	1.4%	1.1%	-6.2%
Indicated discount		26.4%	30.5%	28.4%	25.7%	35.4%
Reconciliation:						
Gross adj, absolute		15.6%	6.9%	1.4%	1.3%	8.6%
Gross adj - % of base		47.6%	19.7%	5.2%	5.3%	20.7%
Weight		1	2	7	3	3
Reconciled discount	29.0%					

* See text

15. These partnerships have been selected to illustrate problems that can arise when the choices are few and hidden influences must be uncovered and explained.

As in the sales comparison approach for appraising real estate, the comparable base discounts must be adjusted to the subject partnership, Suburban Office Partners, II. The adjustments are calculated from the regression output by multiplying the difference between the subject values and comparables for each x-variable by its b-coefficient. For example, Comparable 1 has a distribution rate of 2.8%, so its adjustment to the subject for this element is: $(2.8\% - 6.3\%) \times (-1.775) = -6.2\%$.[16]

Remaining term and distribution stability/trend are the only other variables that were shown to be significant in the regression analysis. Other variables may be adjusted as long as their influence can be reliably extracted from the market. Asset size was tested using the office building regression database and was shown to have an insignificant influence on the discount for the data set used to value Suburban Office Partners, II.[17]

The distribution trend was adjusted separately in the multiple linear regression method because the goal was to limit the regression model to either a 1 or 0; in this study, 0.8 was selected as the x-term for this variable. For the grid, the adjustment can be calculated using the 0.8 instead of 1.0. This is not faithful to the regression method but is consistent with the comparable sales adjustment process.

Other, more subjective elements of comparison between Suburban Office Partners, II, and the five comparables that cannot be reasonably quantified might lead the valuer to place more weight on one discount indication over another, or to consider one indication to be high or low. Because five comparables rather than 32 are the dataset from which a conclusion will be drawn, some of the mathematical precision provided by the regression method is lost. However, considering how the partnerships compare with the subject partnership can capture more influences and result in a more accurate comparison overall.

Narrative descriptions of the comparable partnerships should be included in the valuation report to supply information that does not appear in the grid, to highlight differences and similarities between the comparables and the subject partnership, and to support the reconciliation of the discount indications. The five comparable partnerships are described below.

Comparable 1.   Damson/Birtcher Realty Income Fund I is sponsored by Birtcher/ Liquidity Properties. The partnership holds two office buildings, two retail centers, a technical business park, and an industrial distribution center located in the West and Midwest. Distributions have been declining and bottomed out in 1996. Operations have produced a net loss since 1992 but showed a small gain in 1996. A 1993 amendment to the partnership agreement mandated that properties be sold and that the general partner use an expectation of a 1999 liquidation in its valuation analysis. It appears that the market believes this partnership will be liquidated in 1999.

Comparable 2.   High Equity Partners L.P. Series 86 was sponsored by Integrated Resources, Inc., and is managed by Presidio Capital Corp. Its holdings primarily include office buildings, several shopping centers, and a

---

16. Selecting a discount percentage reverses the normal relationship between the subject and its comparables and can cause confusion. A superior comparable element, such as a greater distribution rate, will decrease the discount indication for that comparable element and require a positive adjustment (unlike a superior real property adjustment, which increases the price indication). Because the value indicator is a percentage, the partnership valuer should avoid using percentages of the base discount. To eliminate confusion, the price/*NAV* could also serve as the unit of comparison. The adjustments would be decimals, and the adjustment direction would also be reversed. (The discount indication for the subject would be calculated separately, after the reconciliation.) If quantitative adjustments have not been developed, then superior/similar/inferior, or +/– entries would be appropriate. Because of this potential for confusion, the valuer should recap, in a short paragraph, the adjustments that were made for each comparable.

17. Size had a significant influence on the discount for the larger database. Partnership size was measured as ln (*NAV*) and had a t-statistic greater than 2.

warehouse. Two of its properties are in located in California, and the others are located throughout the United States. Distributions have been level since 1994 but started to pick up in 1997. The partnership's net asset value was estimated by the general partner–not by an independent appraisal–so the weight for *NAV* is reduced. Integrated Resources filed for bankruptcy in 1990 and was succeeded by Presidio. A class-action lawsuit was filed in 1993 on behalf of the limited partners alleging self-dealing on the part of management. A preliminary settlement was made in 1996 that would, among other things, reorganize the partnership into an REIT to increase cash distributions and the marketability of partners' interests. A small group of limited partners is still challenging the settlement, and the outcome is uncertain. The partnership has paid more than $800,000 in costs associated with defending the general partner and preparing settlement materials, and future costs are uncertain. The possibility of near-term liquidity for this partnership exists but the discount does not reflect it. The stigma of the bankruptcy and lawsuit may override any perceived benefit, or the perceived risk may be high.

Comparable 3. Net 2 L. P. is sponsored by Lepercq Capital Partners. Its holdings are triple-net leased and mainly include warehouse/distribution facilities and some office/warehouse and retail properties in various regions. The partnership is partially leveraged, but leverage has been increasing with new purchases and refinancings. Notes are maturing each year through 2001, but the partnership is in good financial condition and distributions are stable.

Comparable 4. First Capital Growth Fund Series XIV is sponsored by First Capital Financial Corporation. The partnership holds an office building located in Evanston, Illinois. A second office building was foreclosed on in 1993. Distributions have increased from a low point (zero) in 1993 and currently show a growth trend. The general partner commented that increased competition in the office market may cause a reduction in rents, but this condition apparently has not impacted the discount required by the market. This is the smallest of the five comparables and is nearest in size to the subject.

Comparable 5. Paine/Webber Growth Properties 2 L.P. is sponsored by Paine/Webber Properties. It holds a majority joint-venture interest in a single mixed-use, residential/office property in Portland, Oregon. Distributions had been zero because of its high leverage and adverse economic conditions until 1994 but have increased to a stable point this year. The partnership sold two other apartment projects in 1995 and 1996 and has announced plans to begin marketing the remaining property at the end of 1997. A sale and liquidation is possible within the next two years, but it is not reflected in the trading discount.

The next step in applying the adjustment grid method is to reconcile the discount indications based on the quantity of data, the accuracy of the analysis, and their appropriateness to the subject. The five discount indications are weighted as follows, in descending order:

- Comparable 3 is given the most weight because of its similar distribution rate and low gross adjustment despite its being more diverse and having a more stable distribution history than the subject.

- Comparable 5 is weighted second because its holds a single property and has greater leverage. Its weight is mitigated by the possibility that it will liquidate in the next few years and by its low distribution rate.

- Comparable 4 is weighted third. It also holds a single property, has a distribution rate and trend similar to Suburban Office Partners, II, required the least gross adjustment, and is the smallest of the comparables. However, its trading price is based on only two transactions and its discount indication is less valid than the others. Furthermore, its units traded at a discount of 39.1% in 1996 and 24.6% in 1997. In 1998, the general partner announced that it was evaluating the market for potential sale of its remaining property, and the discount declined to 18.2%. Thus, it appears possible that the transactions in 1997 may have been influenced by an unapparent expectation of near-term liquidation, which would have reduced the discount.

- Comparable 2 is weighted fourth because of its large number of trades. Its weight is reduced because the trades have been widespread, possibly indicating that conditions involving the litigation are interpreted differently by buyers.

- Comparable 1 is given the least weight because the market believes that it will liquidate in the near term, it has a low distribution rate, and it required the greatest gross adjustment.

The reconciliation should address differences that have not been captured in the regression analysis, but conditions for reconciliation can be interpreted in many ways and weighting for this group is highly subjective. Other than for Comparable 4, the range of discount indications is not wide, and a variety of reconciliation schemes would produce a similar result. There are many differences between comparables, and an ideal set of comparables will not often be found.

Sometimes matters related to control are not represented in the limited partnership database and cannot be readily quantified. If the subject interest has sufficient control to force a near-term liquidation or block detrimental management decisions, this should be considered in the comparable partnership analysis and supported with data from the Partnership Profiles Liquidating Partnership Study, if necessary.

It is possible to incorporate facts or circumstances into the market data analysis that are more onerous than those that a typical investor in a public limited partnership would face. Although logic might support raising the discount because the interest has no voting rights (e.g., an assignee interest), the discount should not be reconciled outside the indicated range without solid support. These variables can exhibit strong nonlinear characteristics, which could not be understood without supporting data. Most of the influences can be quantified, and there is no need to go outside the range of available data. The best way to resolve matters such as these is to carefully review the provisions of Revenue Ruling 59-60 and make sure that all relevant factors are addressed in the valuation report.

The subject influences have been substantially quantified for this case study, and no further adjustments are needed. Based on value indications weighted according to the list above, the concluded discount is 29%. This reconciled discount is rounded so that its precision is not overstated.

This method can also be applied without benefit of the regression analysis, but the results would be substantially more subjective, and the process is not illustrated for the case study. Nonetheless, manual selection can be made to work, and its results would be much preferred to extracting discounts from averages. The presentation and discussion of comparable transactions would be similar to the next case study application.

The Partnership Spectrum studies include partnership averages by category with a commentary for each entity. Among the variables that can be compared are the value per unit, average trade price, average discount, regularity of distributions, type of real estate, debt level, and distribution rate. The last column of the table includes comments about the specific partnership. These data permit a simple comparison with the subject partnership. Text that accompanies the data presents a detailed discussion of the relationships that can be observed from the data and conclusions that can be drawn based on the author of the study's experience in evaluating partnerships.

Selecting the partnerships for comparison. In the first round of data selection, the partnership valuer's objective is to obtain the names of as many partnerships as possible.[18] Some will be rejected when narrowing the list to include only the best comparables for analysis. If the valuer is able to analyze a significant amount of data, any partnership with a valid discount indication could be included among the pool. This can be advantageous because the valuer can use the database as a source for future valuation assignments.

The most useful selection criteria for partnerships to include in the discount study are distribution rate, remaining term (generally related to transaction year), type of real estate, and comments on the expected liquidation date. Annotated comments about the partnership are also helpful in choosing comparable partnerships for the analysis.

Narrowing the list of comparable partnerships. The most common reasons for eliminating partnerships from the analysis are adjustments made to the unit value, which may be difficult to interpret, and unusual conditions recorded in the comments column. Examples of the latter might be "resumed distributions this year after lengthy suspension," and "quarterly distributions often fluctuate significantly." Of course, these red flags might indicate useful comparables if the subject partnership also exhibits such problems. Another reason to exclude a partnership might be a discrepancy between the GP-estimated value per unit and the value indicated by an inde-

18. The selection process described is different from the generalized process used to select public guideline companies because it relies entirely on data published by Partnership Profiles. The liquidity, activity/turnover, leverage, and profitability ratios normally used for selection and comparison are replaced by indicators specific to real estate holding partnerships.

pendent appraisal, although the estimated values appear to be generally accurate. Data should be selected based on comparable elements and reliable indicators, not to support a desired outcome.

Including other types of partnerships in the discount study may be useful, depending on the subject. For example, if the subject partnership holds securities or mortgages, such partnerships could be included in the database.

Reconciling Discount Indications

Four methods of developing a discount for lack of control were demonstrated in this chapter. Three of the methods used 1997 public partnership trading data, and one included 1995 and 1996 data. The discount indications derived from the four methods are:

- Discounts from averages   30%
- Multiple linear regression   32%
- Graphic analysis   30%
- Adjustment grid format   29%

It is certainly not required that all of these methods be presented in the final valuation report. However, it might be a good idea to present more than one method, since each leads to a different interpretation of the comparison of the subject and public partnerships.

The multiple linear regression model produces the most reliable discount indication because it is based on a specific analysis of the greatest quantity of data and captures the greatest number of variables that influence value. The adjustment grid format is most effective when used in conjunction with the regression model because the variables can be quantified and the format in which the findings are presented is understandable to appraisers. Graphic analysis is also effective when it is used with the regression model because the elements that have a significant influence on value can be identified. Although the first method described, extracting discounts from averages, relies on the most data, the resulting analysis is limited. Therefore, it would not normally be used as a primary method for developing the discount. It would especially be inadequate when the scope of work requires a more carefully considered opinion of value. After reviewing the discount indications from each method, the reconciled discount is 30%.

The Trading Market Discount

Because the secondary market where partnership interests are traded is not as efficient as the New York stock exchange, the benchmark of full liquidity for securities transactions, the discount for lack of control must incorporate an additional marketability discount. The loss of efficiency in trading limited partnership interests is most appropriately measured by how long it takes to consummate a transaction. The results of a 1999 study by the American Partnership Board (the leading secondary market firm based on trading volume) found that the average time required to find a buyer for a partnership is 60 days. The period can be compared to the same-day transaction period on the New York Stock Exchange, assuming reasonable trading volume.[19]

This 60-day illiquidity for partnership trading exposes the transaction to the risk that a significant event will occur during the period such as an announcement concerning partnership liquidation, a sale of partnership assets, a tenant bankruptcy, say, or other unexpected event. Barring such an event, prices are primarily tied to the value of the underlying real property, which will typically exhibit low volatility and would be expected to change little in 60 days. One technique for developing the effect of short-term delays on value based on risk and holding period is to construct a present value model that considers growth, if any, that is expected during the period and distributions, if any, to be received. This produces a small discount using a 60-day hold.

Analysis for a short-term hold can also be considered similar to an analysis for "blockage," which occurs when the market for a certain stock (or any other financial asset) cannot absorb the block being offered at one time without depressing the price.[20] The stock (or other security) must be sold over time, exposing its holder to risk that the price will change in that period.[21, 22] An empirical put option model can be used to analyze the market's interpretation of risk and discounting for short-hold situations.[23]

Short-term delays may also be analyzed using partnership data for transactions for which the buyer anticipated liquidation of the partnership's underlying assets and distribution of the proceeds in a similarly short period. The Partnership Profiles Liquidating Partnership Study is helpful in this respect.[24] This analysis may produce an overstated trading market discount when applied for very short periods, however, since the actual payout expectation (following asset liquidation) can be long with respect to the 60-day assumption.

19. Bruce A. Johnson, ASA, Spencer J. Jefferies, and James R. Park, ASA, *Comprehensive Guide for the Valuation of Family Limited Partnerships*, 2d ed. (Dallas: Partnership Profiles, Inc., 2003), 95–96.

20. Shannon P. Pratt, DBA, CFA, FASA, et al, *Valuing a Business, The Analysis and Appraisal of Closely Held Companies*, 4th ed. (Chicago: Irwin Professional Publishing, 2000), 432–433.

21. Robert F. Reilly, CFA, ASA, CPA, CBA and Robert P. Schweihs, ASA, *Handbook of Advanced Business Valuation* (New York: McGraw-Hill, 2000), Chapter 7.

22. Jay B. Abrams, ASA, CPA, MBA, *Quantitative Business Valuation: A Mathematical Approach for Today's Professionals* (New York: McGraw-Hill, 2000), Chapter 7.

23. The Black-Scholes option-trading model discussed briefly in Chapter 5 can be used with a volatility proxy for public limited partnerships taken from REIT or other public real estate company trading data.

24. "Secondary Market Buyers Playing Arbitrage," *The Partnership Spectrum* (March/April 2000): 1–6.

The discount for market impairment is a small portion of the total discount from *NAV* measured for public limited partnerships,[25] termed the *trading market discount* (D_{TM}). Obtaining this discount will be discussed further in Chapter 5, Developing the Discount for Lack of Marketability.

Calculating the Minority-Marketable Value

The hypothetical minority-marketable value of the partnership is calculated by its net asset value reduced by the gross discount and then increased by backing out the trading market discount. Multiplying by the subject interest's percentage gives its value at this level. Minority-marketable value is considered hypothetical for two reasons: first, it presumes the lack of control associated with the subject interest but shows the value of the entire partnership. Second, interests in the subject partnership are not registered securities, and are not publicly tradable. The value applies only for a certain percentage ownership (or range of percentages) that underlie the reasoning that led to the discount conclusion. Identifying the value as hypothetical may help to avoid its misuse.

The result should also be expressed in a manner consistent with any other valuation approaches, such as guideline company or income methods, that are used in the report. Both methods can produce the hypothetical minority-marketable value directly, and reconciliation of the methods would be simplified if the asset approach also produced a minority-marketable value.

This discussion applies for a partnership holding real estate as its principal asset base, with the value of cash and other minor assets and liabilities adjusted in arriving at net asset value. If the partnership holds significant other assets, such as securities, machinery and equipment, or nonoperating assets, an additional market data analysis may be required to develop discounts associated with these additional assets. A weighted discount indication can then be applied to the total net asset value of the partnership. If significant intangible assets are involved, it becomes a business valuation problem and should be approached differently (see Chapter 3, Other Intangible Assets).

---

25. Johnson, Jeffries, and Park, *Comprehensive Guide for the Valuation of Family Limited Partnerships*, 2nd ed., 95.

CASE STUDY APPLICATION

Concluding the Minority Value and the Net Discount for Lack of Control

The hypothetical minority-marketable value of the partnership, and the subject interest, are then calculated as follows:

Net asset value (from balance sheet)		$1,512,279
Less gross discount for lack of control (from discount from averages method)	× 30.0% =	− 453,684
Impaired minority-marketable value		$1,058,595
Add back trading market discount[25]	@ 8.0% =	+ 92,052
Concluded hypothetical minority-marketable value of Suburban Office Partners, II		$1,150,647
Interest held by John Builder	× 20.0% =	$230,129

The net discount for lack of control–to the minority-marketable level only, not incorporating any component of marketability impairment–can be calculated as the net reduction from *NAV* divided by *NAV*:

Net asset value	$1,512,279
Minority-marketable value	− 1,150,647
Net value reduction	$361,692
Value reduction divided by NAV, or discount for lack of control	23.9%
(Rounded)	24.0%

---

25. The amount of the discount is calculated as:

$$V_{MM} - V_{PM} = V_{MP}\,[1/(1 - D_{TM}) - 1] = \$1{,}058{,}595 \times [1/(1 - 0.08) - 1] = \$92{,}052$$

CHAPTER 5

Developing the Discount for Lack of Marketability

The third step in valuing a partnership using the net asset value method involves developing the discount for lack of marketability. A discount for lack of marketability is developed for interests in all privately held businesses such as corporations, partnerships, and limited liability companies (LLCs) and is an adjustment to value based on the subject interest's impaired marketability; i.e., it cannot be traded in the public marketplace.

Impaired marketability is always associated with a particular holding period during which the investor is exposed to a variety of risks. The investor cannot respond to these risks because the interest cannot be sold at will. A discounted price is required to compensate for this lack of marketability, which relates to the holding period, the specific level of risk, the likelihood that price changes will occur during the holding period, and the economic benefits of holding the interest. Marketability analysis investigates both market efficiency and uncertainty such as the risk that a significant event will occur, e.g., an announcement concerning partnership liquidation, tenant bankruptcy, or another unexpected change. Developing the discount for lack of marketability deals directly with markets, and not as directly with the specifics of a business or its assets.

The analysis for lack of marketability is relevant as long as similarities and differences between the markets for the subject interest and for the data used to derive discount indications are adequately reconciled. This discounting process is shown in Figure 5.1, which is an expansion of the bottom half of the levels of value diagram introduced in Chapter 1 as Figure 1.2.

The minority-marketable level is critical for analyzing partnerships (and equity securities, generally) because the process shifts from a reliance on limited partnership-based

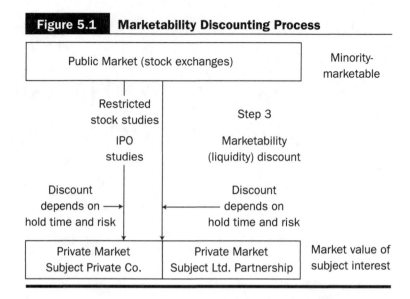

Figure 5.1   Marketability Discounting Process

data (used to develop the discount for lack of control) to equities-based data. The data developed to analyze corporate equities can legitimately be used to analyze limited partnerships because the behavior of markets are being observed, not specific businesses or industries.

The empirical data that support the validity of a discount for lack of marketability are developed by studying transactions that involve restricted stocks and from studies of transactions both before and after initial public offerings (IPOs). The discounts observed in these studies are affected principally by the expected holding time and the risk associated with the securities involved. They are shown on the left side of Figure 5.1.

Risk and holding time are also key elements that underlie the income approach to value, which will be the basis for the case study analysis of the partnership, Suburban Office Partners, II. Thus, the left side of the figure (Private Market/Subject Private Co.) serves as a proxy for the right side (Private Market/Subject Ltd. Partnership) insofar as marketability impairment is concerned.

Using Market Data to Develop the Discount

Two types of market data studies provide direct empirical evidence of marketability discounts: restricted stock studies and pre-IPO studies. Restricted stock studies examine sales of restricted shares of exchange-traded public companies and primarily consider the effects of short-term restrictions on the securities of public companies. Pre-IPO studies examine a company's sales of unregistered shares before and after an initial public offering.

Restricted Stock Studies

Restricted stocks are unregistered shares of exchange-traded companies that cannot be resold for a fixed period (the holding period). Until it was changed in 1997 to one to two years, the law had established a minimum holding period of two to three years as the period covered by most of the studies. Transactions that comprise the studies are private placements that are exempt from registration. The restricted stock study data measure the difference between the privately transacted price and the price of the company's registered shares on that same day. These are effectively paired sales for which the only meaningful difference is the marketability of the shares. Studying paired sales transactions is effective for measuring market efficiency in isolation from other conditions.

Numerous studies of restricted stock transfers have been performed over a 30-year period and show discounts that are similar and generally in agreement with each other. This section is not a comprehensive treatment of these studies, which may be cited in many references. It is intended only to highlight the points that are most relevant and useful for valuation analysis.[1] The results of studies typically referenced in observing marketability discounts are shown in Table 5.1. Three studies that are particularly useful for measuring mar-

Table 5.1	Summary of Restricted Stock Studies	
Study[2]	**Period of Study**	**Discount[3]**
SEC, adjusted	1966–1969	27.5%
SEC, updated	1969 only	33.2%
Gelman	1968–1970	33.0%
Trout	1968–1972	33.5%
Moroney	1969–1972	35.6%
Maher	1969–1973	35.4%
Silber	1981–1988	33.8%
Willamette	1981–1984	31.2%
Management Planning	1980–1995	31.1%
FMV (fair market value) Opinions	1979–1992	23.0%
Johnson[4,5]	1991–1992	20.0%
Columbia Financial Advisors[6]	1991–1995	21.0%
Columbia Financial Advisors	1997–1998	13.0%

Note: Data after 1990 reflect reduced market restrictions under SEC Rule 144Ac (1990) and shortened holding time under Rule 144 (1997).

1. Shannon P. Pratt, DBA, CFA, FASA, et al, *Valuing a Business, The Analysis and Appraisal of Closely Held Companies*, 4th ed. (Chicago: Irwin Professional Publishing, 2000), 395-403; Z. Christopher Mercer, ASA, CFA. *Quantifying Marketability Discounts* (Memphis: Peabody Publishing, 1997), Chapter 2.
2. Pratt, *Valuing a Business, The Analysis and Appraisal of Closely Held Companies*, 404.
3. Discounts are expressed variously as means or medians.
4. Bruce Johnson, ASA, "Restricted Stock Discounts 1991-95," *Shannon Pratt's Business Valuation Update* (March 1999): 1-3.
5. Bruce Johnson, ASA,"Quantitative Support for Discounts for Lack of Marketability," *Business Valuation Review* (December 1999): 152-155.
6. Kathryn F. Aschwald, "Restricted Stock Discounts Decline as Result of One-Year Holding Period," *Shannon Pratt's Business Valuation Update* (May 2000): 1-5.

ket efficiency are the SEC Institutional Investor Study, the Management Planning Study, and the Columbia Financial Advisors Study.

SEC Institutional Investor Study. The SEC Institutional Investor Study is particularly useful for analysis because of its size and the way in which it isolates discounts.[7] Despite its datedness, it is an often-cited seminal work in the field because of its level of detail and strong framework for analysis. Its conclusions have been supported consistently by the later studies.

The SEC study presents numerous data sets that allow interesting conclusions to be extracted. The overall average is the data set cited most often, but it is more meaningful if it is adjusted to eliminate extremes.[8] Also, data from the later years of the study appear to be more consistent with later work.[9] The effects of the study support the notion that greater discounts are associated with smaller transactions and larger companies. Larger companies are, on the whole, more diversified and mature, and consequently less risky because their trading prices are more stable. The study also demonstrates a strong correlation between discount and risk.

Discounts are much greater for companies in the over-the-counter (OTC) category, which generally includes smaller companies, both reporting and nonreporting.[10] Also, the OTC market was a relatively inefficient one before the introduction of the NASDAQ in the early 1970s. The difference between the New York Stock Exchange/American Stock Exchange category and the over-the-counter category is 6.4%, including all the data, or 5.7% adjusted, reflecting these conditions.[11]

---

7. U.S. Congress. House. *Institutional Investor Study Report of the Securities and Exchange Commission*, 92nd Congress, 1st sess., 1971, H.R. Doc. No. 92-64 part 5, 2412–2475.

8. The SEC study includes exchange-traded shares analyzed in various groups of 278 to 391 transactions. The average discount for all transactions in the study and all years covered is 25.4%. The data show a wide range of discounts, which the study presents in 10% bands from 0% to 50%, with extreme bands of -15% to 0% (premiums) and a very wide 50% to 80% high end. If one postulates that the extremes represent unusual conditions, then the adjusted average of discounts for the 94% of transactions that remain is 27.5%. The average was calculated assuming that all transactions were at the midpoint of each discount band except for the extremes. The premiums were disregarded because conditions are likely to be unusual; also, this band is not included for all the study's data groups, and those in the 50% to 80% band were assumed to occur at 60%. This is not a rigorous method but should be accurate within ± 2%, and is most likely accurate between -½% and +1%.

9. Data are from 1966 to early 1969, and the discount increased substantially during this period. The ending discount rate is most consistent with later studies. An updating factor can be extracted from the study and applied to the overall averages to reflect 1969 conditions; the overall average noted above then increases from 27.5% to 33.2%. This is not presented as a rigorous analysis, but a clarification of the discount indications for comparison with the later restricted stock studies.

10. A nonreporting company is not required to submit the same detailed reports to the SEC as is required of the reporting companies. Nonreporting status generally requires that total assets be valued at less than $1 million, or that the company have fewer than 500 stockholders.

11. The adjustment is made by eliminating the tails of the distribution.

**Management Planning
Study.** The restricted
stock study performed by
Management Planning
includes 49 transactions
that were selected from
more than 200 available
private placements from
the years 1980 to 1995.[12,13]

> *The most important influences on the
> discount were earnings stability and price
> stability, both of which are inversely related
> to risk and holding time.*

Its results generally support the conclusions of the other studies
and clarify the relationship between discount and size (the latter
based on revenues, earnings, and market capitalization).

The study is helpful because of the usefulness of its published data. The numerous data points include date, revenues,
earnings, market capitalization, number of shares sold, percentage of company, annual trading volume, price/sales, price/
earnings, and many others. This is in contrast to a number of
studies that publish only a portion of the data and at least one
that published no data at all.

The most important influences on the discount, in addition to size based on revenue and earnings (also confirmed as
influences in the SEC study and others), were earnings stability and price stability, both of which are inversely related
to risk and holding time.[14] Valuers may wish to run their own
regression models and investigate the magnitude of these influences and others such as the price/earnings ratio, also inversely related to risk. A published regression analysis of the
Management Planning study data is included in Abrams, *Quantitative Business Valuation.*[15]

The results from the Management Planning study strongly
support the ideas that risk is the principal influencing variable and that earnings tend to mitigate the magnitude of its
effects. The study spans 15 years but reveals no association
between the discount and date or general market trends (except that the expected holding period is apparently shorter
for transactions that occurred after the Rule 144A-holding

---

12. Mercer, *Quantifying Marketability Discounts*, 19.

13. Daniel L. McConaughy, et al, "Factors Affecting Discounts on Restricted Stock," *Valuation Strategies* (Nov/Dec 2000): 14–24, 46.

14. A multiple linear regression analysis of the Management Planning, Inc., data has been performed to determine the quantitative significance of various influences on value. The most significant influences on the discount were the holding period, defined as 24 months but reduced to 20 months after 1990, and the length of time needed to sell the stock (presented in the study as the number of quarters required to "dribble out" the block into the market under provisions of the SEC rule). Also important were earnings stability and price stability (for the latter, the standard deviation of stock prices was divided by the mean, based on month-end prices for the 12 months prior to the transaction date, directly related to price volatility and risk). The next in significance was a measure of company size (revenues). Certain variables also were shown to have little or no significance. These include general market conditions (increasing or decreasing trend), transaction date, block size, and 10-year historic growth in revenues and earnings.

15. Jay B. Abrams, ASA, CPA, MBA, *Quantitative Busienss Valuation: A Mathematical Approach for Today' s Professionals* (New York: McGraw-Hill, 2000).

period restrictions were relaxed in 1990).[16] This suggests that other influences are more important and that data from the older studies should not be discounted because of their age.

Columbia Financial Advisors Study. Results from a study performed by the Columbia Financial Advisors (CFAI) are included in Table 5.1 and provide more recent data on restricted stocks. An article about the study that was published in 2000 suggested that less restrictive SEC regulations for restricted stock followed by a reduction in the holding period to one year in 1997 caused discounts to decline. Study results before 1990 showed discounts in the 33% to 35% range, dropping to the 21% range after 1990, and to 13% after 1997–the year for which Suburban Office Partners, II is valued.[17] These studies show that discounts declined as a result of relaxed restrictions and a shortened holding time, indicating the sensitivity of the discount to the holding period.

Pre-IPO Studies

The second type of market data studies considered in measuring the marketability of securities of closely held companies analyzes the trading price of a company's stock before and after its initial public offering. The pre-offering price is for a private transfer of a nonmarketable security, and the post-offering price is for an exchange-traded security from the same company.

IPO studies incorporate several conditions that increase the observed discount above that noted in the restricted stock studies. First, there is no guarantee that the offering will be successful, or even that an offering will occur. Thus, the shares may never become liquid. Second, the shares would still be restricted under SEC Rule 144A after the offering, and an additional delay would be required before they could be sold in the public marketplace.

One series of pre-IPO studies was performed under the direction of John Emory at the investment banking firm Robert W. Baird & Company, and another by Willamette Management Associates; both are reported and analyzed in detail.[18, 19] The studies span the years 1975 to 1997 and, with the exception of very high discounts for a few years, produced similar results overall, with discounts roughly in the 40% to 50% range. A post-1997 study that covered the period May 1997 through December 2000 showed a mean discount of 48% and a median of 44%.[20] The most generally accepted discount indication from these studies is 45%.

16. Ibid.

17. Aschwald, "Restricted Stock Discounts Decline as a Result of One-Year Holding Period," 1-5.

18. Pratt, *Valuing a Business, The Analysis and Appraisal of Closely Held Companies*, 407–411.

19. Mercer, *Quantifying Marketability Discounts*, 77–93.

20. John D. Emory, Sr., ASA, and John D. Emory, Jr., "The Value of Marketability as Illustrated in IPOs: May 1997–Dec. 2000," *Shannon Pratt's Business Valuation Update* (October 2001): 1,3.

The transactions from these two studies took place from one to 36 months before the anticipated completion of the offering, and at least a two-year restriction would have to be added. This increases the effective holding time to three to five years, plus any "dribble-out" period after the lapse of the restriction. The discount is not too sensitive to the Rule 144A restriction period since the post-1997 studies showed no reduction for the shorter holding time restriction as was observed for the restricted stock studies. These conditions suggest that the discount would be higher than for the restricted stock studies for which holding time was limited to about two years.

The circumstances under which the pre-IPO studies were performed are reasonably similar to those that affect private securities because a buyer of a private interest would not anticipate having later access to any liquid trading market. However, pre-IPO studies are more difficult for the analyst to use, and the debate over their use is complex and unsettled. This book makes no use of the pre-IPO study data beyond their general support for the direct correlation between the holding period and the discount for lack of marketability.

Estimating the Trading Market Discount

Liquidity impairment present in public limited partnership secondary market data was addressed in Chapter 4, and termed the *trading market discount*. Application of the discount is shown in Figure 4.1. The amount of the discount developed in this case is taken from the illiquidity data discussed so far in this chapter; other methods were discussed in Chapter 4, but are not applied. This section is a continuation of the discussion that was begun on page 106.

The method of applying the trading market discount depends on whether the discount is developed from the control side (i.e., from public company data showing discounts from *NAV*, such as the comparison of REITS and RELPs [real estate limited partnership]), or from the marketability side (restricted stock studies or holding period delay.) In the first instance, it would be additive and could be calculated separately or developed as an adjustment to produce a net discount from *NAV* for lack of control. In the second instance, it would be a sequential discount, similar to the marketability component of Figure 1.2. For this case study, the trading market discount is developed using the sequential method.

Restricted stock studies can provide some support for the trading market discount, e.g., if the discount for a 2-year hold is 20% to 40%, what would the discount be for a 60-day hold?[21]

---

21. Other methods were referenced in Chapter 4, but they are complex, and are not used for the case study. A simpler approximation of market liquidity is taken from the above restricted stock studies.

The restricted stock study performed by Robert R. Trout[22] and the SEC Study[23] demonstrate discount differentials between the OTC and the NYSE and AMEX exchanges; the differential is 8.2% for Trout and 5.7% to 6.4% for the SEC Study. For the purposes of this case study, the OTC will be taken as a rough proxy for the limited partnership secondary market. Reducing the holding period of restricted stock studies, from a nominal two years down to one year, produced an 8.0% reduction in marketability for the approximately one-year change.[24] The OTC proxy is for a short period, but the shortened restriction period is longer. In the absence of a more rigorous analysis, 8.0% is applied in the case study application that concludes Chapter 4.

The trading market discount is not a wholly resolved component of the analysis. It is up to the appraiser to select one or more techniques or studies to support the selected discount, and then to ensure that the process of applying the discount is consistent with its source.

Value-Influencing Elements

Chapter 1 introduced a number of facts and circumstances associated with Suburban Office Partners, II, which may affect the concluded value. The possible influences associated with the real estate were considered in Chapter 2 in the discussion of the real estate appraisal. These value-influencing elements must be tracked throughout the valuation process if the concluded value is to be accurate and credible. Many business valuation reports result in conclusions that are unconvincing because the valuers fail to systematically apply the analytical process to the specific facts and circumstances of the case.

Value-influencing elements fall into two categories: those that affect the expected holding period and those that affect risk exposure. Although other elements may have some effect on the concluded value, these two apply regardless of the methods used to develop the marketability discount.[25]

The business valuer must carefully consider the facts and circumstances of the case that would potentially affect the

22. Robert R. Trout, "Estimation of the Discount Associated with the Transfer of Restricted Securities," *Taxes* (June 1977), published by Commerce Clearing House, Chicago. The regression model showed a coefficient for the exchanged-listed securities of -8.19, meaning that 8.19% of the marketability discount was attributable to the efficiency difference between the NYSE and AMEX exchanges on the one hand, and no listing on the other (presumably the OTC).

23. The difference between the overall average marketability discount and the discount for only those companies in the OTC nonreporting category was 6.8%–the same range as the other observations.

24. See the Columbia Financial Advisors study averages.

25. Concluding a holding period is controversial for operating companies, particularly when an income approach is used for discount valuation. An asset approach is used overall in valuing the partnership in this case study, which assumes that the buyer of the interest will realize its pro rata share of the asset(s) at the end of an expected period. Thus, developing a holding period estimate, even if it is uncertain, is an implicit requirement of an asset-based approach to value and entirely appropriate for a real estate-holding limited partnership.

buyer's perception of a likely holding period. There is no right answer, but the valuer should be able to muster reasonable support for a holding period estimate based on facts. A very long holding period dramatically increases the discount for marketability, which is why a long period should be justified.

CASE STUDY APPLICATION

Analyzing Facts and Circumstances for Suburban Office Partners, II to Estimate the Holding Period

Real Property

Leases Due	Leases on a large portion of the rentable area are coming due in 2000, and rents are above market level. This suggests that a sale is likely when income is still high or after the situation stabilizes three to four years after the date of value (probably late in 2000), if management wishes to sell.
Developable Land	If the extra land were to be developed, a sale would probably occur after its occupancy is stabilized.
Holding Period	The real estate appraiser established that the typical holding period for buyers of three-story multitenant office buildings is five to 15 years, but most often 10 years.
Loan Agreement	The loan is due (in 2002) approximately five years from the date of value. It would make sense to refinance anyway, since the interest rate is high. If the balloon needs to be paid, then it might require a voluntary contribution of capital or sale of the property.

Partnership and Ownership

Termination of Partnership	The partnership terminates on December 31, 2050.
Interest's Degree of Control	John Builder's interest does not have sufficient control to cause termination of the partnership or sale of any of its assets.
Sales History	The family has never sold a property. Since John's death, family members have been debating whether selling properties would be a good idea.
Management	The partnership has new management, and Billy appears to want to develop the extra land. Billy's intentions are beyond that are not clear.
Ownership Control	It is not clear what Sara's husband might want to do. This is important because Sara controls half of the stock in the general partner.
Liquid Assets	The estate has substantial liquid assets and does not need to sell any properties to pay taxes.

Analysis and Conclusions

The partnership is scheduled to terminate in 54 years, far longer than the typical market-holding period of 10 years. Because the leases are expected to turn over in three years, it is not expected that a sale, if intended, would occur until the property is re-leased, new tenants are in place, or the old tenants renew their lease in four to five years.

The loan is due in five years. Refinancing would have to be negotiated by the general partner–in this case Billy and Sara. Presumably, this would be accomplished, since the interest rate is significantly higher than the current market rate. If the property could not be refinanced, it might have to be sold to pay off the $1.82 million balloon.

Billy may have his way with the construction project on the extra land, but it seems like the family, and possibly Sara's husband, would wish to discourage it because, economically, it does not look like a good idea. It appears unreasonable that the family would approve of retaining the property that is a potential development problem. (After all, the family holds 14 additional properties.) On balance, it appears that the leasing would be completed and pressure to sell would build, so a holding period of five years will be concluded.

Identifying Value-Influencing Elements Using Revenue Ruling 59-60

Many value-influencing elements were incorporated into the analysis at the asset and minority-marketable levels. If the business valuer is not careful, he or she can risk double-counting influences by making additional adjustments. It is therefore important that the valuer understand these influences to make a clear and convincing presentation of the analysis and to be able to defend it by showing why elements used more than once are not double-counted. To that end, the valuer should review all influences that are to be considered in the business valuation. A useful format for doing so is to use the sections of Revenue Ruling 59-60 as a checklist. First, the value-influencing elements that pertain to the case study must be selected.

The following list recaps the elements involved in the case study Suburban Office Partners, II, organized in the order of the sections of Revenue Ruling 59-60 introduced in Chapter 1. Some elements only influence the underlying asset value, some were used to develop the discount for lack of control, and some have not yet been addressed. The valuation level at which each item has been considered is indicated by the checked boxes. General comments are also intended to have specific application to the case study.

Identifying Value-Influencing Elements

Value Level:	Asset (*NAV*)	Minority	Marketability	Other

§4.0 1 (a): The nature of the business and the history of the enterprise from its inception

	Asset (*NAV*)	Minority	Marketability	Other
Property type	☑	☑	☐	☐

The market data determine whether the property type influences the minority-level discount and also shows whether an additional adjustment is needed.

	Asset (*NAV*)	Minority	Marketability	Other
Asset diversification	☐	☑	☐	☐

This element appears only after the asset appraisals since they separately address each property. It might appear as a marketability influence if it can be demonstrated that the portfolio is so unusual that the combination of properties or other assets would limit the market for the interest.

	Asset (*NAV*)	Minority	Marketability	Other
History of real estate	☑	☐	☐	☐
History of cash flow (*NOI*)	☑	☐	☐	☐

The performance history of the property itself is addressed in the asset appraisal. (If an income method of developing the minority-marketable value were used, then these elements would be considered in developing the discount or capitalization rate.)

	Asset (*NAV*)	Minority	Marketability	Other
History of distributions	☐	☑	☐	☐

The prospective minority interest holder would be concerned about the distribution history since this interest does not control the property.

§4.0 1 (b): The economic outlook in general and the condition and outlook of the specific industry in particular

	Asset (*NAV*)	Minority	Marketability	Other
General economic conditions	☑	☐	☐	☐
Real estate market conditions	☑	☐	☐	☐

Both are usually covered in the asset appraisal. These influences might be included at lower levels if an independent effect can be demonstrated.

	Asset (*NAV*)	Minority	Marketability	Other
Long-term growth	☑	☐	☐	☐

Growth is implicit in the asset value and may have been made explicit if a discounted cash flow model was used. The marketability analysis considers growth over the expected holding period regardless of how asset value was developed and requires growth expectations for that specific period. Cash flow growth may be dictated partly by lease terms, but also by the expectations of market participants (unless the lease term will extend beyond the holding period). Value growth applies for the value of the asset at the end of the term.

§4.0 1 (c): The book value of the (stock) and the financial condition of the partnership

	Asset (*NAV*)	Minority	Marketability	Other
Value of real estate	☑	☑	☐	☐

Net asset value was arrived at by adjusting the balance sheet, largely for the market value of the partnership's assets. Book value can also mean relative size, and this was supported as a separate element influencing the control discount.

	Asset (*NAV*)	Minority	Marketability	Other
Leverage	☐	☑	☐	☐

The partnership's mortgage debt and its non-real estate assets and liabilities play no part in valuation of the assets because the appraisals assume new ownership, and their purpose is to value real estate, not equity. Also, in arriving at net asset value, the effect of debt on financial condition was not addressed.

The minority interest holder cannot choose to adjust the capital structure or sell assets, so financial condition shows up at this level first as it affects distributions (below) and perhaps as a separate item if market data show the discount affected by a partnership's financial standing.

For real estate holding partnerships, cash flow after debt service is the principal determinant of financial condition. (Partnerships or companies having ongoing operations will have a much more complex financial statement, and other indicators of financial condition will be much more important.)

Leverage might have an additional effect at the marketability level if the debt ratio is unusually high, or there are high prepayment costs or other onerous conditions that have not been captured in the minority discount.

Value Level:	Asset (*NAV*)	Minority	Marketability	Other
§4.0 1 (d) (e): The earning and dividend-paying capacity of the partnership				
Current and future *NOI*	☑	❑	❑	❑
Earnings growth	☑	❑	❑	❑

Earning capacity and growth were considered in the asset appraisal (*NOI*), and at the equity level (earnings).

Current and future distributions	❑	☑	☑	❑
Distribution growth	❑	☑	☑	❑

Minority holders are interested in distributions rather than earnings since they do not control the property. Growth is related to *NOI* and may be increased by leverage, as it was for the case study. This may not be true if there are pending activities, such as additional development that may use cash flow that would otherwise be distributed.

Growth should be adjusted to the time horizon expected for the nonmarketable interest, which may require different assumptions than those used in the real estate appraisal.

Billy's development project is uncertain, but it may affect these elements in the area of development costs, loss of parking revenue, and earnings from the new rentable area.

Suburban Office Partners, II does not present an orderly picture of distribution growth. How would a buyer of the interest with limited or no control weight the various influences? Judgment must be exercised in interpreting this situation.

§4.0 1 (g) The sales (of partnership interests) and size of the block to be valued (control associated with the interest)

Sales of partnership interests	❑	❑	❑	☑

Historical sales should be disclosed and analyzed. The case study considered John's purchase of a 10% interest from Ed in 1995 and concluded that it was at a deliberately high price. If the transaction provided a useful value indication under the appropriate definition of value, then it would be reconciled with the final value conclusion.

Degree of control	❑	☑	☑	❑

The degree of control is an issue insofar as the interest can influence meaningful decisions. The minority discount assumed that there is no influence. If the interest holder can force sale of assets, cause termination, or block pending decisions (such as Billy's development idea), then risk and discount are reduced. This would require an adjustment at the minority-marketable level–perhaps for a shortened holding period–and would also be reflected in the risk associated with the lack of liquidity, expressed as a shortened holding time or as a risk adjustment, or both, depending on the attributes of control.

The interest holder in Suburban Office Partners, II, has no meaningful control.

Value Level:	Asset (*NAV*)	Minority	Marketability	Other
Size of the block[26]	❏	❏	☑	☑

Since subject partnership interests are not publicly traded, blockage issues (the ability of the market to absorb a large block of shares) do not apply. However, the size of the block may apply for a portfolio of properties of which the partnership owns a large market share. For example, if the partnership owns 80% of all the apartment buildings in a small town, the buildings would have to be sold over a number of months or years to avoid depressing the market.

This would be a separate adjustment for the partnership's portfolio value and may be introduced as a separate discount to *NAV*. It can be analyzed within the scope of the income method used for development of the marketability discount. This is essentially a marketability problem, but, realized at the asset level, it applies for all levels of ownership.

§4.0 1 (h): The market price of stocks of corporations engaged in the same or a similar line of business having their stocks actively traded in a free and open market, either on an exchange, or over the counter

Secondary market	❏	☑	❏	❏

The minority discount analysis used comparable public limited partnerships to develop the discount for lack of control. (This would also apply for income methods for which the value at that level is developed directly, using guideline companies or partnerships.)

Restrictive Agreements

Due diligence	❏	❏	☑	❏

The agreement's provision against disclosure of any information identified as confidential may be an impediment to a buyer's due diligence efforts. This information might include documents or statements required by a buyer for its due diligence efforts if designated confidential by the general partners. The effect of this provision would be in addition to any costs associated with due diligence efforts.

Purchase financing	❏	❏	☑	❏

The agreement provides that other partners may purchase another's interest at fair market value, but at favorable terms. This may be interpreted two ways:

1. It may be perceived as a discount to the most likely buyer–another partner–making it easier for that buyer and possibly enhancing its marketability.

2. It could be discouraging for an outsider whose offer may stimulate interest by others that have a financing advantage. (The terms are identified in §1.4.3 of the Agreement.)

§4.0 1 (h): The market price of stocks of corporations engaged in the same or a similar line of business having their stocks actively traded in a free and open market, either on an exchange, or over the counter

Transferability	❏	☑	☑	❏

Although interests are assignable, the assignee cannot become a limited partner without the consent of a managing general partner. It has been assumed so far that a buyer of the subject interest would be admitted as a full limited partner. However, it is likely that an outsider would not be granted such status. The buyer would be entitled to the interest's economic benefits but would not have the ability to influence the affairs of the partnership in any way.

26. Size of the block has another meaning for public market transactions, e.g., shares of restricted stock. It may take a long time to place a block that is large in trading volume. It could take years in some cases. In such an instance, the size of the block leads to an increased holding period expectation. This is important in understanding and using restricted stock studies but is not applicable in the same way for a privately held limited partnership.

If the distinction in status is material, it should be included at the minority-marketable level as a control adjustment. If it is not, then it may be interpreted as a risk factor affecting marketability.

Value Level:	Asset (*NAV*)	Minority	Marketability	Other
Capital calls	☐	☐	☑	☐

The capital call enforcement provision is onerous, and any limited partner who is unable or unwilling to contribute could have his interest diluted. This condition may place the subject interest at a significant competitive disadvantage.

<u>Unclassified Elements</u>

Holding period uncertainty	☐	☐	☑	☐

Holding period uncertainty generally affects only the risk for impaired marketability, since the notion of a forced hold is a liquidity issue.

What is the reasonable upper limit for the period? How certain is the estimate? It appears that the five-year estimate could be a year shorter, but it could conceivably be longer. If Billy develops the extra land, it might be another three to six years before it would be reasonable to sell the property. (He might also incur additional costs trying to remove an unsuccessful building.) The range would then be four, nine, or twelve years, but most likely five years or a little more. This is a difficult issue, but it is one that must be addressed in detail in the valuation.

Due diligence requirement	☐	☐	☑	☐

A hypothetical investor must put considerable effort into properly analyzing and understanding the terms of a limited partnership investment. This is particularly problematic for private limited partnerships, which have no public reporting requirement. Appraisal, building inspection, legal, and (forensic) accounting efforts all require experts, and costs can easily add up.

Even sophisticated investors would have internal costs associated with these expenses. Some costs would have to be borne by a buyer of the fee interest in the real estate as well, but the partnership structure adds to the problem. The value of the 100% fee interest in the real estate is high enough that the cost is proportionately low, but the market value of the subject interest is much lower, and costs can be significant. A cost adjustment can be made, as long as it does not double-count any allowance for due diligence that is implicit in valuation of the underlying assets. Alternatively, participants can assume there is no due diligence investigation, or a limited one at best, and make an adjustment for the resulting uncertainty.

Business/management risk	☐	☐	☑	☐

Business/management risk is normally a factor when the subject has complex holdings that require intensive, ongoing management, or when there are potential management problems related to the business of the partnership. This would not have been considered during the asset valuation because a control-level value assumes new management. Management's ability to control the use of cash flow and thereby reduce distributions would have been considered part of the distribution element and should not be counted again here.

In Suburban Office Partners, II, the minority interest is stuck with inexperienced management and heading for negotiations with tenants and a potential development project. Furthermore, the sale of the property, particularly at the end of the lease term, may require expertise that may not be available from the general partners. If these issues have not been taken into account when developing the discount for lack of control, they should be adjusted for in the marketability discount analysis.

Finally, there is nothing to prevent the general partner from accumulating funds and purchasing other assets without the knowledge or permission of the limited partners. (The effects of possible funds accumulation would have been reflected in the distribution forecast.) Managing these unknown assets may require expertise outside the ability of the general partner, which would introduce yet another element of management risk.

Value Level:	Asset (*NAV*)	Minority	Marketability	Other
Other conditions	❏	❏	☑	❏

Adjustments for other conditions are reserved for partnerships exhibiting onerous conditions to an investor beyond the value-influencing elements identified above. This category can include pending or probable lawsuits and the chance that more, unknown partners will materialize when Ed dies and his estate is distributed to his heirs. If the business valuer can reasonably demonstrate that these or any other unusual conditions would hamper marketability—to the current partners as well as outside interested buyers—and that the holder of the subject interest would not be in a position to respond to such situations if they occur, then adjusting the marketability discount might be appropriate.

Selecting Value-Influencing Elements

The application to the case study was general, including value-influencing elements that were resolved earlier in the analytical process. The next step in developing the discount for lack of marketability isolates the elements required for obtaining the marketability discount for Suburban Office Partners, II. The selected elements in their order of importance for application to this case study are:

- Current and future distributions
- Business/management risk
- Holding period uncertainty
- Due diligence requirement
- Restrictive agreement
  - Due diligence (confidential information)
  - Transferability
  - Capital calls
- Distribution growth
- Long-term growth
- Other conditions
- Leverage (included in the holding period analysis)

Approaches to Developing the Discount

The approaches available for developing the marketability discount vary greatly in their ability to capture the characteristics of the subject ownership interest in the concluded discount, but they all rely on a key underlying principle: The discount is always related to expected holding time and perceived exposure to risk until the interest can be sold and marketability realized. These approaches include the direct application of study data, the use of models, and the income approach.

Direct Application of Study Data

The restricted stock marketability discount study data described earlier can be applied directly to the subject interest being valued using a process similar to that used to develop the discount for lack of control. The principal difference between the two processes is that the marketability study data available are not as detailed as the data published by Partnership Profiles. As a result, the application to the subject interest is less precise. Nonetheless, data from restricted stock transactions can be applied in many ways. For example, averages may be adjusted based on comparative characteristics, or a database of restricted stock transactions may be applied directly, if the transactions contain sufficient data points to allow comparison with the subject.

The simplest application relies on adjusted averages and is, in effect, a sales comparison approach. It is probably the method most commonly used in developing the discount for lack of marketability. In court cases, however, the testimony offered to support the use of this method tends to be more conceptual than analytical, which is a source of annoyance to jurists. Specific shortcomings associated with using adjusted averages include a perception that they are superficial reports that lack depth and are disconnected from the subject.[27] Other difficulties with direct application have been documented based on several recent court cases.[28]

Two sources that allow for a more precise application of restricted stock data are Management Planning data, which allow a valuer to construct his or her own regression model or select specific transactions,[29, 30] and FMV Opinions, which offer an extensive database of restricted stock transactions that permits the easy selection of comparable subgroups for direct application to the subject.

The direct application of study data has been described in various forms in the appraisal literature, but it took on the quality of a method when it was used in the case *Mandelbaum v. Commissioner*, when Judge Laro was dissatisfied with the evidence that the valuation experts presented in the case.[31]

---

27. Robert T. Willis, Jr., CPA, CFA, "Preparing Valuation Reports to Withstand Judicial Challenge," *Estate Planning* (December 1998): 455–462. The article details specific objections to expert testimony that have been raised in numerous cases, based on lack of depth, disconnectedness, and a hypothetical buyer/seller as applied to family limited partnerships.

28. Z. Christopher Mercer, "Developing Marketability Discounts," *Valuation Strategies*, (March/April 2001): 12–21, 46. This article includes reviews of Branson's and Knight's objections to the use of restricted stock studies, Janda's marketability discount studies, and the "QMDM" (income approach to developing marketability discounts).

29. Mercer, *Quantifying Marketbility Discounts*, Chapter 12.

30. McConaughy, et al, "Factors Affecting Discounts and Restricted Stock," 14–24, 46.

31. Mandelbaum v. Commissioner, TC Memo 1995-255.

This ad hoc method has since been adopted by some valuers.

In the Mandelbaum opinion, Judge Laro referred to the discount averages of 35% and 45%, respectively, in the restricted stock and IPO studies and used them as benchmarks for calculating the marketability discount for the property interest in question. Then he developed his own discount analysis, applying adjustments to the discount for the subject company's financial condition, dividend policy, management, restrictions on transferability, holding period for the stock, and other elements. These categories follow Revenue Ruling 59-60 almost exactly. The application was not rigorous and, according to some, the analysis in the opinion contains notable flaws.[32] However, valuers are applying the method, so its use should be understood.

> *The difficulty in this process lies in determining which elements are significant and the size of the adjustment to make.*

Using the "Mandelbaum Method." Before the method can be applied, a through understanding of the data that comprise the restricted stock and IPO studies is necessary. Studies that publish information on restricted stock, such as the Management Planning Study cited earlier, could be sources from which reference levels for the following variables can be extracted:

- Price-earnings ratios or other market multiples
- Price and earnings stability
- Growth history or expectations
- Dividend yields
- Industry classification
- Other variables

Holding time estimates are generally fixed at approximately two years (statutory period plus dribble-out) for the restricted stock studies (before 1997), and three to six years for the IPO studies.

Beginning with the selected discount norm (e.g., 35% from the restricted stock studies), adjustments are made for differences between the subject partnership's characteristics and the elements of comparison that have been extracted from the study data. Additions or subtractions for the various elements are made from the base discount, or the overall effect of the adjustment elements combined is estimated. The difficulty in this process lies in determining which elements are significant and the size of the adjustment to make. The adjusted discount is then applied to the subject minority-marketable

32. Mercer, *Quantifying Marketability Discounts*, 126-136.

value, resulting in a value for the nonmarketable interest. This is an improvement over using discounts from court cases or applying restricted stock and IPO study data based on general assumptions—both of which are all-too-common practices. Still, it is less rigorous than the other available, but more complex methods. Because the supporting data have not been adequately developed, a quantitative illustration of the process cannot be shown in the case study application that follows. However, the apparent influences can be listed to provide a starting point for the application of this process.

Restricted Stock Analysis—FMV Study. Many of the problems associated with the "Mandelbaum Method" for developing the marketability discount can be obviated by using a structured database. The most extensive and easiest to apply is the FMV Restricted Stock Study.[33] It is licensed with a search program and is available directly or through Business Valuation Resources. The published database includes 243 transactions dated from 1980 through April 1997 and has 34 data fields. By inputting parameters into the fields, the valuer can select a comparable group of transactions. The most important fields for valuing Suburban Office Partners, II, are:

- Discount
    Obtained by subtracting the transaction price from the trading price
- Market value
    A base from which to calculate a dividend or earnings rate. The valuer can also use book value, total assets, or tangible assets (total assets less intangible assets).
- Dividends or net income
- Market-to-book ratio
    A method of selecting asset-heavy companies, which function as an approximate comparison for a real estate holding company, since very few real estate companies are contained in the database
- Percentage shares placed
    A field used to select for subject holding periods longer than two years. Transactions that involve 10% or more of a company's shares outstanding are likely to be subject to blockage. Thus, the block would have to be dribbled-out into the market over time, and the effective holding period would exceed the nominal two-year restriction period.[34] (Supplemental calculations would be required to obtain an estimate of the actual

33. FMV Opinions, Inc., Irvine, California [www.fmvopinions.com].

34. There is no indication as to whether the transaction was also subject to the dribble-out provisions of Rule 144A.

holding period. The field is meant only to allow the analyst to select a period of more than two years as the holding time criterion.)

- Registration rights

   For longer holding periods, transactions are normally deselected if the issuer had agreed to register the stock at a future date or by request. Conversely, for holding periods shorter than two years, only transactions that had such rights attached are selected.

A group of selected comparable transactions will show a distribution of discounts from the actively traded stock price, and an additional adjustment can then be made to select a point in the distribution applicable to the subject interest. The result is not a precise sales comparison analysis, however, and individual transactions should not be treated as comparables, as was the case for public limited partnership transactions in Chapter 4. The FMV Study is a substantially refined restricted stock analysis and a significant improvement over the "Mandelbaum Method" and other ways to use restricted stock data to develop discounts for privately held stock or partnership interests.

CASE STUDY APPLICATION

Applying Study Data to Develop the Discount

A number of elements that influence the marketability discount for Suburban Office Partners, II, are listed below. They are provided only to show how the direct application of study data might be used in a partnership valuation report and not for developing the actual discount for lack of marketability for Suburban Office Partners, II, which will be derived later using the income method. The increase or decrease is made to the mean discount.

Item/Description	Subject Comparison to Study Mean	Adjustment to Discount
Size A smaller partnership such as Suburban Office Partners, II, should have a greater discount than a larger company, but only if the adjustment is supported by adequate data	smaller	increase
Price stability Price stability is generally greater for asset-holding companies than operating companies. Suburban Office Partners, II, would be more stable than the study median or average, so its discount should be adjusted downward.	more stable	decrease
Growth Asset-holding companies often experience slower growth, which would increase the discount. (This is not always the case, however, particularly if the real estate holdings are leveraged.)	slower	increase
Dividend yield A greater dividend yield would decrease the discount.	greater	decrease
Restrictive agreement The provisions of the partnership agreement are more restrictive than those that would apply to a buyer of restricted stock (given that the limited partner could not cause near-term liquidation, as has been assumed for the Suburban Office Partners, II). This increases the discount.	more restrictive	increase
Holding period The holding period for Suburban Office Partners, II, is longer than two years, which would increase the discount.	longer hold	increase

The size of the adjustment will be determined by analyzing the magnitude of the value influences in the restricted stock study data. The direct application of restricted stock trading data to the subject raises difficult conceptual issues that will be addressed in the discussion of risk and holding time.

Using Option Models to Develop the Discount

Another approach to developing the discount for marketability involves examining the cost of put options to measure discounts for lack of market-

> *...just as restricted stock is used as a proxy for private company discounts, publicly traded securities can also be used as proxies for volatility.*

ability.[35, 36, 37] Option models forecast put option prices of public securities as a function of the time to exercise the option, the volatility of the underlying stock, and the current stock price. The idea is that a "put" option allows the holder to sell specified shares (the underlying stock) at a specified price (the strike price) at a certain time in the future, effectively purchasing marketability. The premium paid for the option divided by the current price of the shares is, in effect, the discount for lack of marketability. If the buyer of a limited partnership interest could also purchase the option to sell the interest at a particular date in the future, then the cost of such an option would represent the discount for lack of marketability. (This is an oversimplification, meant only to introduce the topic. A reader interested in pursuing this method is urged to make extensive use of the references.) The Black-Scholes option-pricing model provides strong theoretical support for the observation that risk, i.e., the expected volatility of a security interest, has a direct effect on the magnitude of its marketability discount.

The important inputs for using this model for discount analysis are the risk-free rate, the holding period (i.e., remaining term of the option), and the volatility[38] of the underlying security. The present value of any dividend stream can be accommodated with simple additions to the formula. Historical volatility can be measured for actively traded issues, but the principal shortcoming in applying this method to privately held companies is that volatility cannot be measured directly if the interests are not traded. Mercer and others have raised this as an objection to using the Black-Scholes option-pricing model.[39] However, just as restricted stock is used as a proxy for private company discounts, publicly traded securities can also be used as proxies for volatility. One can also track asset volatility as a proxy for the expected volatility of an asset holding company.

35. David B. H. Chaffe III, "Option Pricing as a Proxy for Discount for Lack of Marketability in Private Company Valuations," *Business Valuation Review* (December 1993): 182-188.

36. Francis A. Longstaff, "How Much Can Marketability Affect Security Values?" *The Journal of Finance* (December 1996): 1767-1774.

37. Reynolds Griffith, Ph.D., "Valuation of Restricted Stocks: An Option Theory Approach," *ASA Valuation* (February 1988): 96-102.

38. The standard deviation of annualized returns. (See references below.)

39. Mercer, *Quantifying Marketability Discounts*, 404-414.

There is no shortage of literature on the implementation of the Black-Scholes option model for public securities since these models underlie the entire derivatives market. [40, 41] One excellent reference demonstrates how to use the Black-Scholes model to calculate the restricted stock discount, and it provides a good explanation of how the model is applied to discounting. [42]

The model is based on an empirical formula designed to mimic market behavior, which is directly concerned with liquidity and the value of a security at the end of the holding period. As such, it appears to be a highly appropriate model for deriving marketability discounts in situations in which the holder of the interest being valued is unable to respond to vagaries of the marketplace during the holding period. The model is also appropriate for investment situations in which liquidity at the end of the holding period is considered a major component of return. To some extent, the modeled behavior is more speculative than behavior observed in investment markets where yield comparisons are the basis for decision making. It is aligned more with short-term behavior since financial assets held for a long term eventually become investments. [43]

Income Approach

Of the three suggested approaches for developing the discount for lack of marketability, the income approach is the most appropriate because it makes explicit use of holding time and risk, both of which can be developed for the subject. It is also the most familiar of the applicable approaches. For a privately held limited partnership interest, the buyer's expectation of the holding period may be affected by a variety of facts and circumstances. The holder of the interest is compensated for the greater risk in two ways: by receiving distributions during the period and by obtaining a cash return in the form of price appreciation at the end of the holding period.

Before the income approach can be used to develop the discount for lack of marketability, the distribution rate must be developed at the minority level.

Real estate appraisals for income properties almost always include direct capitalization in the income approach and may also include a yield analysis (DCF). More is better in this instance because development of the marketability discount by the income approach requires growth and yield rates that are typical of a DCF model. If only a single-period model was used by

---

40. Espen Gaarder Haug, *The Complete Guide to Option Pricing Formulas* (New York: McGraw-Hill, 1998).

41. Les Clewlow and Chris Strickland, *Implementing Derivatives Models* (New York: Wiley, 1998).

42. Abrams, *Qualitative Business Valuation: A Mathematical Approach for Today's Professionals*, 243-248.

43. Short term in this context is fewer than two to five years. For short periods the model can be the most effective predictor of discounts.

the appraiser, then growth and yield rates may have to be extracted from the facts and developed from the capitalization rate (overall rate) in the appraisal, as was discussed in Chapter 2.

For stabilized operating conditions and no loan, an overall capitalization rate and growth rates for cash flow and value are all that are needed since the constant growth model can be used to calculate the yield. However, if conditions are unstable (as they are in the case study, with above-market leases ending in a few years), or if there is mortgage financing (as there is in the case study), then calculations become more complex and a DCF is needed.

Cash Flow/Distribution Rate

The equity cash flow rate at the minority level is:

$$R_{EQUITY} = CF_{EQUITY}/NAV$$

The rate increases at the minority-marketable level since the denominator (NAV) is now discounted for lack of control (D_C), but distributions are not discounted. This gives a new distribution rate, as follows:

$$R_{MINORITY} = CF_{EQUITY}/[NAV \times (1 - D_C)]$$

Or, substituting for CF_{EQUITY} (where $CF_{EQUITY} = R_{EQUITY} \times NAV$) and simplifying:

$$R_{MINORITY} = R_{EQUITY}/(1 - D_C)$$

An alternative is to simply divide cash flow at the minority level by net asset value. The result is the same:

$$R_{MINORITY} = CF_{EQUITY}/V_{MINORITY-MARKETABLE}$$

Distribution Growth

The growth rate for cash flow at the equity level is approximately the same as the growth rate for cash flow expected for the real property if there is no debt, if other assets and liabilities are not significant, and if other income and expense items which exhibit their own growth patterns are also not significant. Under these conditions:

$$G_{CF\ APPROX} = G_{NOI}$$

If there are other significant line items in the income statement, then the approximate rate of annual increase at the equity level is changed by the ratio of NOI to cash flow:

$$G_{CF\ APPROX} = G_{NOI} \times NOI / CF_{EQUITY}$$

Notice that *NAV* does not appear in this formula. Distribution growth is not adjusted by the discount for lack of control since all distributions flow to the interest holder regardless of level, and the year-to-year change rate remains the same.

The growth rates for the case study (both G_{NOI} and G_{CF}) will be calculated directly from the DCF model to account for the irregular expected rental income and the effect of the fairly large, but constant, debt service amount.

Value Growth

Real estate value growth can usually be obtained from the market, considering general and local real estate trends as well as any expected changes in capital market conditions (increases in the terminal capitalization rate, for example). Irregular cash flows would not be a factor so long as the relationship of *NOI* in the year following the terminal year to the first years' *NOI* was known. This information can be obtained from the real estate appraiser (see Chapter 2), and is shown in the DCF model.

As for distribution growth, equity value growth will not be much different than real estate value growth if there is no debt, if other assets and liabilities are not significant, and if other income and expense items which exhibit their own growth patterns are also not significant. Under these conditions:

$$G_{\text{EQUITY APPROX}} = G_{RE}$$

If there are other significant line items, then the approximate rate of annual increase at the equity level is changed by the ratio of *NOI* to cash flow, plus growth from other sources (in this case, from paying down debt):

$$G_{\text{EQUITY APPROX}} = G_{RE} \times V_{RE} / NAV + G_{\text{DEBT}}$$

The rate increases at the minority-marketable level since the denominator (*NAV*) is now discounted for lack of control (D_c), but the terminal value is not discounted. (Distribution of each partner's pro rata share of the whole is assumed for the terminal year. The calculation is the same as for the distribution rate.) This gives a new value growth rate, as:

$$G_{\text{MINORITY VALUE APPROX}} = G_{\text{EQUITY}} / (1 - D_c)$$

This simplified calculation does not capture the effect of all the items affecting value growth, so such a calculation is *only an approximation.*[44] With significant debt involved, errors are potentially large, and it is much better to prepare at least a simple DCF model and develop the rates directly and explicitly. The case incorporates a large mortgage loan, so these rates will be taken entirely from an explicit DCF model in the next case study application.

Yields

We took a brief look at extracting various capitalization rates from the real estate appraisal in Chapter 2. As for the growth rates above, the income approach in this chapter needs a yield rate for equity at the minority-marketable level, not for the asset alone. The asset-level (real property) rate is the base, but it must be adjusted first for equity and then for the minority discount.

The yield rate at the equity level is approximately the same as the yield rate at the asset level if there is no debt, if other assets and liabilities are not significant, and if other income and expense items that exhibit their own growth patterns are also not significant. (This is not true for the case, but is often true for family limited partnerships.) Under these conditions, equity and asset yields are similar.

If there is debt or other classes of ownership, then the yield to all invested capital must be divided between equity and debt and/or any other classes. This is often done using a mortgage equity or band-of-investment technique, or weighted average cost of capital (WACC).[45]

Mortgage Financing

This technique is generally applicable for single-period (direct capitalization) rates, but should NOT be used to calculate an equity yield where debt exhibits a declining balance over time, as for a mortgage loan. (Business purchase financing and other types of debt can also exhibit the same problem.) The most appropriate method in this case is to use a DCF

---

44. Why consider approximations? Because many family limited partnerships are quite simple, and in these cases the error is not too great. Also, the analysis for marketability discount contains many approximations so depending on the level of rigor brought to the process, such approximations may be more than adequate. The problem with approximations is knowing how much of an error is introduced. The valuer would be well advised to test such calculations for typical partnership assignments until some familiarity is reached, and the report can be communicated with confidence.

45. Methods for computing yields for debt and equity are described generally as mortgage/ equity or band-of-investment techniques in the real estate discipline (See *The Appraisal of Real Estate*, 12th ed., pp. 490 and 534) and as the weighted-average cost of capital (*WACC*) in the business valuation discipline. (See also Pratt, page 190.)

$$Y_A = [Y_E \times E / (D + E)] + [Y_D \times D / (D + E)]$$

where Y_A is the yield for the real estate, E is partner's equity, D is debt (from the balance sheet), and Y_D is the debt yield taken as the loan's interest rate. Y_A is known and Y_E is unknown so the formula must be altered to solve for the latter. *This formula should NOT be applied for mortgage debt with a declining balance.*

$$Y_E = [Y_A - Y_D \times D / (D + E)] / [E / (D + E)]$$

(The cost of debt can also be tax-affected, as $Y_D \times (1 - t)$ where t is the applicable income tax rate (since interest is a before-tax cost). This adjustment is only appropriate where the equity yield is stated on an after-tax basis. The partnership is a tax pass-through entity, and no tax rate adjustments are appropriate.)

model, and calculate the internal rate of return (*IRR*) to equity as the yield to equity. It is then a simple matter to substitute *NAV* discounted for lack of control and recalculate the *IRR* at the minority-marketable level. This is the process demonstrated in the next case study application.

If there is no loan, yield at the minority-marketable level can be approximated in a manner similar to value growth:

$$Y_{\text{MINORITY VALUE APPROX}} = Y_{\text{EQUITY}} / (1 - D_c)$$

If an income approach is used to develop the minority-marketable value of the partnership, then the yield rate can be taken directly from that approach but may suffer from the same debt-related issues.

CASE STUDY APPLICATION

Calculating Distribution, Yield, and Growth Rates

Cash flow/distribution rate. The following formula may be used for calculating the cash flow/distribution rate:

Minority-marketable level distribution rate =
$$R_{\text{MINORITY}} = R_{\text{EQUITY}} / (1 - D_c)$$
$$R_{\text{MINORITY}} = 6.3\% / (1 - 24.0\%) = 8.3\%$$

An alternate calculation for the distribution rate is:

Cash flow available minority-marketable value =
$$R_{\text{MINORITY}} = \$95,355 / \$1,149,332 = 8.3\%$$

Growth rates for both value and cash flow at the asset level. Calculations for growth rates and cash flow at the asset level are shown for Suburban Office Partners, II, in Table 5.2. The compounded value growth rate (*i*) is calculated using the formula $FV = PV \times (1 + i)^n$, where *PV* is the value of the real estate in Year 0 (at the date of value, the beginning of Year 1), and *FV* is the net reversion at the end of Year 5, based on the cash flow in Year 6. (The calculation was made using the spreadsheet formula for the rate, and then annual compounding is shown for checking purposes.)

The compounded cash flow growth rate is calculated similarly, except that *PV* is the *NOI* forecast for Year 1, and *FV* is the cash flow forecast for Year 5. (Year 0 is ignored because of the normalizing adjustments made between actual Year 0 and the forecast Year 1.) The term is selected as $5 - 1 = 4$ years. Both rates seem relatively low, considering that annual growth rates of 2–3% are expected by the real estate market. However, revenues drop significantly in Year 3 and 4 due to lease turnover, and the reversion is a function of revenues from the new leases, so the lower rates appear to be consistent with the facts.

Equity yield (*IRR*) for the partnership. The equity yield, or investor's required rate (*IRR*), is calculated based on cash flows, assuming that they are received at the end of each period. The concluded equity yield rate of 12.2% from the partnership DCF model is greater than the valuer's asset "discount" rate of 12.0% because the debt yield (interest) rate is 10.75% (leverage increases yield). If the interest rate were reduced to 9.25%, for example, cash flow to the equity position would be greater, and the *IRR* would increase to 13.6%.

Table 5.2 Partnership Discounted Cash Flow

Period		1996	1997	1998	1999	2000	2001	2002
Real Estate Appraisal		Year 0	Year 1	Year 2	Year 3	Year 4	Year 5	Year 6
NOI		$311,526	$344,565	$355,208	$355,672	$300,961	$345,033	$379,758
Reversion								$3,490,156
Adjustments								
Add back forecast management fee			$20,649	$21,268	$21,420	$19,101	$21,150	
Less fee at current rate	7.5%		(34,415)	(35,477)	(35,699)	(31,836)	(35,250)	
Add back forecast real estate taxes*			32,500	33,150	33,813	34,489	35,179	
Less taxes for past year	2.0%		(18,420)	(18,788)	(19,164)	(19,547)	(19,938)	
Less forecast increase	2.0%		(370)	(377)	(385)	(393)	(400)	
Adjusted net operating income			344,509	355,014	355,656	302,776	345,773	
Interest income			3,046	3,046	3,046	3,046	3,046	
Total partnership income			$347,555	$358,060	$358,702	$305,822	$348,819	
Other Partnership Expenses								
General and administrative	2.0%		280	286	291	297	303	
Insurance	2.0%		1,440	1,469	1,498	1,528	1,559	
Legal and professional	2.0%		1,670	1,703	1,737	1,772	1,808	
Franchise tax			800	800	800	800	800	
Debt service			221,011	221,011	221,011	221,011	221,011	
Replacement reserves			0					
Total partnership expenses			225,201	225,269	225,338	225,409	225,480	
Partnership net income			$122,354	$132,791	$133,364	$80,414	$123,338	
Reversion								
Real property								$3,490,156
Loan balance			(1,816,278)					(1,646,703)
Assets-liabilities								78,557
Net asset value (present/future)			$1,512,279					$1,922,011
Conclusions								
Cash flows		($1,512,279)	$122,354	$132,791	$133,364	$80,414	$2,045,349	
IRR	12.2%							
Minority Level								
Discount for lack of control	24.0%							
Cash flows		($1,149,332)	$122,354	$132,791	$133,364	$80,414	$2,045,349	
IRR	19.6%							
Growth Rate Calculations								
Value @ year end (approx.)		$1,512,279					$1,922,011	
Annual compounded value growth	4.9%	$1,512,279	$1,586,561	$1,664,491	$1,746,250	$1,832,024	$1,922,011	
Partnership net income			$122,354	$132,791	$133,364	$80,414	$123,338	
Cash flow change, annual				8.53%	0.43%	-39.70%	53.38%	
Annual cash flow during year			$122,354				$123,338	
Annual compounded cash flow growth (straight-line approximation)	0.2%		$122,354	$122,600	$122,845	$123,092	$123,338	
Minority Level								
Discount for lack of control	24.0%							
Value @ year end (approx.)		$1,149,332					$1,922,011	
Annual compounded value growth	10.8%	$1,149,332	$1,273,819	$1,411,789	$1,564,702	$1,734,179	$1,922,011	

* Real estate taxes are forecast based on the property's reassessment at the appraised value. However, the property will not be transferred. Because the percentage of the interest is below the threshold for reassessment in California, taxes will increase from their current level by the allowed annual amount (2%). Changes in direct assessments may also occur and should be considered if they have been addressed in the real estate appraisal. The forecast taxes are added back, and the previous year's taxes and the expected increase for the forecast year are deducted.

Equity yield for the partnership at the minority level. This minority-marketable level yield should be the rate that would be developed by the income approach, which will be detailed later in this chapter.

Growth rates for both value and cash flow at the equity and minority levels. Growth rates are calculated in the same way as for the asset level. Cash flow growth is increased largely because debt service remains constant while increases in *NOI* flow to equity holders. Cash flow (assumed to equal distribution) growth is unchanged at the minority level, since all distributions flow to the interest holder regardless of level, and the year-to-year change rate remains the same.

Value growth is increased by both capitalized (increased) *NOI* and by the declining loan balance. At the minority level, *PV* is lower, but the reversion remains the same. Growth rates are an important point of comparison when selecting public companies or partnerships for comparison if the data are available. The concluded yield and growth rates from the asset approach are summarized in Table 5.3.

Table 5.3	Yield and Growth Rates		
Level	Asset	Equity	Minority
Value	$3,250,000	$1,512,279	$1,149,332
Distribution rate	9.5%	6.3%	8.3%
Yield	12.0%	12.2%	19.6%
Value growth	1.4%	4.9%	10.8%
Cash flow growth	0.03%	0.20%	0.20%

Using the Build-Up Method to Calculate the Yield Rate and Required Rate of Return

Total risk is expressed as an adjusted yield rate and can also be termed a *required rate of return*, which directly addresses the position of the buyer and seller. An investor would be neutral toward alternative investment choices that exhibit an equal relationship of risk to return.

The yield rate applies for risk at the minority-marketable level of value. This rate must be adjusted to get the investor's required rate of return (R_J) to be used in the cash flow model. Adjustments are made for those elements that increase risk for the holder of the illiquid interest. Using build-up methods to adjust for risk premium elements is well established in business valuation practice, but less common in real estate appraisal.[46, 47] The amount of the adjustment cannot be determined from market sources, except to the extent that the valuer can rationalize the magnitude of a particular increment.

The valuer should identify elements that are not incorporated explicitly in the model (e.g., holding time, distribution rate, and growth), explain why each affects risk, and provide a rationale to support the magnitude of the adjustment. A quantitative analysis should be provided whenever possible. Ad-

46. Pratt, *Valuing a Business, The Analysis and Appraisal of Closely Held Companies*, 159-171.
47. Mercer, *Quantifying Marketability Discounts*, 260-267.

justments are added to or subtracted from the yield rate to obtain the investor's required rate of return. Typically, the incremental addition to the yield rate will be in the range of 20% to 30% of the required rate of return. Some of the adjustment will be supported quantitatively and some will not.

One criticism of the income approach for obtaining the discount for marketability is that it is too sensitive to its inputs (i.e., discount rate and growth rates). This criticism underscores the fact that rates need to be considered carefully, a requirement that extends to all uses of this approach to value. The advantage of this approach is that it relies on quantitative inputs, and influences on the discount can be attributed to something objective, unlike the highly subjective alternatives that are commonly used in practice.

CASE STUDY APPLICATION

Using the Build-up Method to Obtain the Investor's Required Rate

The minority-marketable level yield rate is concluded in the partnership discounted cash flow (see Table 5.2), but adjustments must be made for the value-influencing elements that increase risks. These risks are holding period uncertainty and the business/management risk, which decreases the marketability of the interest in Suburban Office Partners, II.

Minority-marketable level yield rate	19.6%
Holding period uncertainty	+ 1.5%

A holding period of five years was selected, but the number could vary from four to eight years. The shorter period would reduce risk, but three more years would increase it. A valuation spreadsheet model could be used to develop the risk premium that would be required to produce the same discount as increasing the holding period to eight years. In this case, it turns out to be 5.0%. Decreasing it to four years is equivalent to –1.7%. Of course, five years are assumed rather than eight. A one-third probability of each reduces the range from –0.6% to 1.7%. The conclusion +1.5% is based on these ranges, which are within reasonable boundaries.

Business/management risk	+ 2.5%

The risk related to business management is primarily a real estate question that revolves around the question of how much trouble Billy can cause. Other facts to consider are whether Sara or her husband can rein in Billy's ambitions. (The matter very well could end in a lawsuit.) A number of issues require expertise that may not be available.

Would an investor necessarily foresee this? It depends on the relationships between the parties. A risk increment might be developed based on observed differences between poorly and normally managed properties, and a probability applied to the result. The risk to business management appears to be a more important problem than the other risks, so the adjustment is estimated accordingly.

Due diligence requirement	+ 1.0%

This value-influencing element might lend itself better to quantitative analysis. For example, if the buyer's cost to investigate the partnership and all the circumstances that have been considered in the case was $10,000, then the spreadsheet model could be used to test the risk/yield increment necessary to reduce the value conclusion by the same amount. For the Suburban Office Partners, II, this would be about 1.7%. There is always a chance that the buyer would already be a partner, and this risk factor would not apply, so the amount should be reduced. Alternatively, the valuer could assume that no investigation has occurred and adjust for the increased risk that would result.

Restrictive agreement	+ 1.0%

The restrictive agreement comprised a number of the influences—among them due diligence, transferability, and capital calls. They could be separated if each is judged to be sufficiently significant.

Due diligence. (confidential information). This provision could block entirely the ability of a partner to assist an outsider with due diligence, but it would not affect a current partner.

Transferability. This is not necessarily an issue, since the level of control assumed for Suburban Office Partners, II, is not substantially different from that of an assignee.

Capital calls. The potential for the dilution of interests resulting from a capital call affects current partners and outsiders, and it would place the subject at a competitive disadvantage. There appears to be increased risk, but it is partly mitigated by the possibility that the buyer might be a current partner.

Other potential conditions	+ 0.5%

Other conditions that can influence the value of the subject interest include the chance that the number of partners will increase when Ed Helper dies, but since neither they nor the subject would have control, it may not matter. It could complicate things for Billy, who could be heading for a lawsuit over future management decisions. There is no evidence that this would happen, but a potential buyer could not be certain that it wouldn't, so a small adjustment could be made for this possibility.

Concluded investor's required rate, R_I	26.1%

The income approach can be applied to calculate the marketability discount using:

- A discounted cash flow model
- The Quantitative Marketability Discount Model (QMDM)[48]
- Direct application of the partnership's DCF model

Cash Flow Model

Figure 5.2 is a generalized illustration of the process for developing the discount for lack of marketability using an explicit discounted cash flow model.[49-51] It will be used with the

48. Mercer, *Quanitfying Marketability Discounts,* Chapter 8.

49. Pratt, *Valuing a Business, The Analysis and Appraisal of Closely Held Companies,* Chapter 9.

50. *The Appraisal of Real Estate,* 12th ed. (Chicago: Appraisal Insitute, 2001), Chapter 23.

51. Mercer, *Quantitative Marketability Discounts,* Chapter 8.

Figure 5.2	**Cash Flow Diagram**

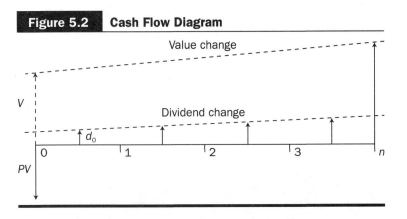

build-up method to obtain a marketability discount conclusion for Suburban Office Partners, II. The process requires a yield rate and distribution and growth rates appropriate for this level of value. These rates may be developed using the formula that follows the figure.

- The initial pro rata value of the interest (V) grows at annual rate $\Delta_V a$ to *FV*. The formula for the present value of the reversion (*FV*), discounted at (R_I), is:

$$PV_V = FV / (1 + R_I)^n$$

- The first years' annual distribution (d_0) increases at a constant rate ($\Delta_D a$), or whatever pattern is expected for distributions to limited partners.[52] The present value of the dividend stream is:

$$PV_D = d_0 \times x [(1 + \Delta_D a)^{(1-x)} / (1 + R_I)^1 + (1 + \Delta_D a)^{(2-x)} / (1 + R_I)^2 + \ldots \\ + (1 + \Delta_D a)^{(n-x)} / (1 + R_I)^n]^*$$

* For payments at year-end, $x = 0$. For midyear convention, $x = 0.5$.

The present value of the interest is the sum of the present values of dividends and reversion:

$$PV = PV_V + PV_D$$

- The yield rate used to discount the cash flows to the present time is the investor's required rate of return (R_I).
- The present value (*PV*) of the income stream is the sum of the present values of the annual cash flows during the term, or holding period, of *n* years and the reversion (*FV*). The full pro rata value of the interest is realized at the end of the term.

---

52. This diagram shows mid-year discounting, but the convention used should conform to the real estate appraisal and/or data used to develop base yield rates.

The marketability discount can be calculated for comparison with study data and expressed as a percentage:

$$\text{Discount} = [1 - (PV / V)] \times 100$$

Alternatively, the discount can be developed directly, by setting $V = \$1$. The discount is then calculated as:

$$\text{Discount} = (1 - PV)$$

CASE STUDY APPLICATION

Calculating the Discount Using Formulas

Suburban Office Partners, II, has an estimated holding period of five years, and its annual cash flow is 8.3%, growing at the concluded rate of 0.2% per year; the value of the partnership's equity is growing at a rate of 10.8% per year. The discount for marketability is calculated using formulas as shown for the cash flow diagram in Figure 5.3.

Figure 5.3	Cash Flow Diagram

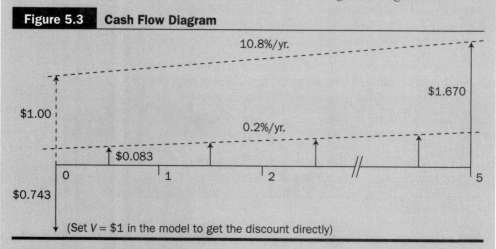

(Set $V = \$1$ in the model to get the discount directly)

	Present Values
FV of $1.00 @ 10.8%/year for 5.0 years =	$1.670
$1.670 discounted to present at 26.1%	$0.524
Dividend stream growing at 0.2% per year, discounted to present value at 26.1%	0.219
Sum of present values	$0.743
Concluded discount	(1 – 0.743) = 0.257
Rounded	0.260
Expressed as a percentage	26.0%

The Quantitative Marketability Discount Model (QMDM)

Mercer's Quantitative Marketability Discount Model (QMDM) is a conventional cash flow model based on an income approach but presented in the style characteristic of the discipline of finance. It is presented as a tabular display of information from which discounts can be estimated by inspection. The table is generated using the formulas from the cash flow diagram. The advantages of this method are that calculations are not required and a range of discounts can be observed, enabling the valuer to understand the sensitivity of the model to the holding period and required return. The disadvantage of this model (and of income models in general) is that it tends to break down under extreme conditions.

The method has met with difficulty in court cases (e.g., *Janda v. Commissioner*) possibly because it can be seen as a "black box" analysis separated from the everyday investment world. While it is actually a mirror of the everyday investment world, clear presentation and a conventional understanding of the analysis are critically important. This book acknowledges the relevance of Mercer's model, which can be presented in numerous ways, all faithful to the basics of the income approach.

CASE STUDY APPLICATION

Calculating the Discount Using the QMDM Model

Suburban Office Partners, II, has an estimated holding period of five years; its annual cash flow is 8.3%, growing at a concluded 0.2% per year; the value of the partnership's equity is growing at 10.8% per year; the required return is 26.1%. The tables used for calculating the marketability discount based on this method are constructed for discrete inputs, and interpolation may be required. However, in this instance, the table in Figure 5.4 was constructed so that its variables are close to actual, and the conclusion is a marketability discount of 26%.

This type of presentation is helpful for showing how sensitive the conclusion is to changes in the required return and the holding period. Sensitivities to dividend yields and growth rates can only be judged by examining multiple tables. Under the conditions described in the Suburban Office Partners, II, case study, this model shows a 4% increase in the discount for a one-year increase in holding period, interpolating halfway between 26%, at 5 years, and 34%, at 7 years (see Table 5.4).

| **Table 5.4** | **Mercer's Quantitative Marketability Discount Model** |

Expected Growth Rate of Value: 11.00%   **Expected Growth Rate of Dividend: 0.00%**

Dividend	Required	Assumed Holding Periods in Years							
		1	3	5	7	10	15	20	30
Yield	Return	Implied Marketability Discount							
8%	12.0%	-6%	-17%	-24%	-30%	-37%	-42%	-43%	-41%
	14.0%	-4%	-11%	-15%	-17%	-18%	-16%	-12%	-1%
	16.0%	-3%	-6%	-6%	-6%	-3%	4%	11%	24%
	18.0%	-1%	-1%	1%	4%	10%	19%	28%	40%
	20.0%	1%	4%	8%	13%	21%	32%	40%	51%
	22.0%	2%	8%	15%	21%	30%	41%	49%	58%
	24.0%	4%	12%	21%	28%	38%	49%	56%	63%
	26.0%	6%	16%	26%	34%	44%	55%	62%	67%
	28.0%	7%	20%	31%	40%	50%	60%	66%	70%
	30.0%	8%	23%	35%	44%	55%	65%	69%	72%

The QMDM model based on the table is constructed mathematically and presents hypothetical combinations of variables that may not occur in practice. In the case of Suburban Office Partners, II, for example, the value growth rate is high because of leverage. For low required returns, discounts are negative. This is an unlikely scenario because high growth rates and leverage lead to higher required returns; high growth and low returns are unlikely.[53] The DCF method that follows exhibits different sensitivities because of the effects of financing, which the simpler models do not capture.

53. Another unusual situation, which is not shown, can arise with long holding periods and high required returns. Such conditions produce very high discounts, which would arguably be invalid under the definition of fair market value, since a willing seller is also required. The willing seller is discussed in some detail in the Mercer and Willis references.

CASE STUDY APPLICATION

Calculating the Discount and Concluded Value Using the Partnership DCF

Many assignments do not involve discounted cash flow models, and the foregoing calculation methods are sufficient. The case study used a DCF for several reasons, the most important of which was incorporating the effect of mortgage financing on growth and yield conclusions. Because the model has already been constructed, it would also make sense to use it directly.

Table 5.5		Calculating the Discount Using the Partnership DCF Model						
Period		**1996** **Year 0**	**1997** **Year 1**	**1998** **Year 2**	**1999** **Year 3**	**2000** **Year 4**	**2001** **Year 5**	**2002** **Year 6**
Partnership net income			$122,354	$132,791	$133,364	$80,414	$123,338	
Net asset value (present/future)		$1,512,279						$1,922,011
Cash flows		($1,512,279)	$122,354	$132,791	$133,364	$80,414	$2,045,349	
Minority Level								
Discount for lack of control	24.0%							
Minority cash flows		($1,149,332)	$122,354	$132,791	$133,364	$80,414	$2,045,349	
Subject interest								
Pro rata value	20.0%	$229,866						
Cash flows			$24,471	$26,558	$26,673	$16,083	$409,070	
Present value using investor's required rate	26.1%	$184,069	$19,406	$16,702	$13,302	$6,361	$128,299	
Concluded value (rounded)		$184,000						
Discount for lack of marketability [1 – concluded value / pro rata value]	20.0%							

Reconciling the Methods

The approaches for discounting marketability are frequently debated despite the fact that all marketability discount predictors for privately held companies are relatively imprecise–part of the nature of the problem. Each is a different way of interpreting the market, and each has its strengths and limitations as noted below. Within each approach, an effort should be made to connect the analysis with the subject. The reconciliation allows a further connection with the subject interest's market.

The direct application of study data isolates influences on value, but it is far less able to accommodate the range of value influences that income models allow. Application of the Management Planning Study data or other data using a regression model would be one way to circumvent the problem and bring rigor to the analysis. Option-pricing models, such as Black-Scholes, are more indirect in their expression of risk than income models since a volatility proxy must be used as an intermediary (as a transfer function or interpretation of equity risk). However, they also

> *In general, it is a good idea to use several analytical methods in a partnership valuation because none can be said to be a truly faithful representation of the market for its nonmarketable interests.*

represent a largely speculative market. The subject interest may attract a speculative buyer if there is an expectation of a short holding period, an investor if cash flows are stable and the holding period is longer, or some buyer in between.

Moreover, the value-influencing elements are identified, quantified, and broken down into a small fraction of the total risk they express. High sensitivity to input variables and assumptions (holding period, dividend rate, growth rates) would be problematic for a model being used to value the company directly.

Mercer's QMDM model has been criticized because the result is sensitive to the assumptions made about the subject interest. The same is true for the income approach in general. However, it is important to keep in mind that the income approach has only been applied for the marketability discount portion of the total value analysis. When it was used at the asset level, its key assumptions were very well supported by real estate market data. The discount for lack of control was supported by partnership market data. Thus, the effect of any such sensitivity is limited to only a portion of the analysis. By reducing most of the assumptions to yield rate adjustments, the model provides a framework for considering how each influences the discount. The analysis can be rebutted by questioning individual adjustments and the interpretation of the facts and other objective components, and differences can be resolved.

Such an income model represents the actions of buyers who consider the partnership interest an investment, comparing its yield with investment market alternatives. The model may be less applicable to short-term holds (i.e., fewer than one or two years), because the behavior of this market may be inconsistent with the investment model. Its use should also be limited to normal ranges of investment yields and growth. Models should always be used within the range of variables demonstrated by their underlying empirical database where validity has been established.[54]

In general, it is a good idea to use several analytical methods in a partnership valuation because none can be said to be a truly faithful representation of the market for its nonmarketable in-

---

54. The extension of any model beyond such supporting data, in this case for very high growth or yield rates or very short or long holding periods, may result in unsupported conclusions.

terests. All rely to one degree or another on proxies, either proxy data, proxy markets, or both. Unlike investor models for business or real estate valuation, it cannot be said that buyers of non-marketable undivided interests in real property rely on any one particular method. Therefore, each method for calculating the discount for lack of control is a way of interpreting behavior in observable markets and applying it to the subject.

Another reason for using more than one analytical method is that each has limitations that might not be revealed if used alone. Through the application of multiple methods, however, the valuer's reconciliation of differences among the approaches can result in a clearer understanding of the hypothetical market dynamics affecting the subject interest, provide a more subject-specific analysis, and heighten confidence in the conclusion.

Because the theoretical foundation is well established for the income approach, however, and because it applies to most real estate partnership situations, it was used to develop the discount for lack of marketability for this case study.

CASE STUDY APPLICATION

Reconciliation and Conclusions

The principal difference between the three methods of the income approach applied to calculate the marketability discount is that the partnership discounted cash flow model uses an explicit series of cash flows, but the formula-based cash flow model and Mercer's Quantitative Marketability Discount Model begin with the cash flow rate from the single-period (direct capitalization) analysis as illustrated here.

Method	Formulas	QMDM	DCF
Cash flow (year 1)	95,355	95,355	122,354
Cash flow rate	8.0%	8.3%	10.6%
Concluded discount	26.0%	26.0%	20.0%

First-year cash flow is lower for the single-period analysis using the formula-based cash flow and the QMDM model because the appraisal included an increased vacancy rate to account for the expected future rent loss, which is an approximation. The discounted cash flow makes explicit annual cash flow assumptions, but its first year's cash flow (of the multiperiod model) viewed alone is too high. This is why the single-period rate was used in Chapter 4 as the most appropriate way to compare the subject to public partnerships.

The formula-based model and the QMDM model use the same growth rates; only the expression for cash flow varies. The discounted cash flow produces a higher value conclusion (and lower discount) because the higher cash flows occur in Years 1 to 3 before leases begin to come due. The other models assume constant growth. If it were not for the short-term above-market leases, the results of all three models would be very close or identical.

Which of the three income methods of calculating the marketability discount is the best representation of the market? One value-influencing element that has been indirectly incorporated into the analysis is the possibility that Billy will continue to accumulate funds for developing the extra land as he had in the year before the date of value. If he does, then the impact could be greatest on the cash flows for Years 1 to 3 since this would still allow reasonable distributions to be paid. After the leases begin to terminate, this would be more difficult.

Another source of uncertainty pertaining to cash flow might be the above-market rent and the likelihood that tenants would demand (and get) rent concessions or a break on CAM reimbursements during the lease term. Billy is now the manager, and the partners do not know how he will respond when faced with such decisions.

These problems were accounted for by increasing the investor's required rate. However, because the DCF indicates a higher value (lower discount) due to the relatively higher cash flows in Years 1 to 3 (the cash flows that are most vulnerable to Billy's plan), perhaps the required rate increase should have been greater for the DCF.

These issues could be expressed better as probabilities, and a range of value indications may be the most appropriate solution. Mercer's table allows for such a range to be selected by inspection, and the analyst may find this an easier way to present these kinds of issues. On the other hand, a value range without some notion of the statistical level of confidence in the result can be difficult to understand. Considering the results in this case study, the greatest weight is given to the single-period (formula-based cash flow and Mercer) models, and slightly less weight to the explicit partnership discounted cash flow model.

Concluded discount for lack of marketability	23.0%

Value Conclusion

The final step in valuing a partnership using a net asset value method is applying the marketability discount to the subject interest's pro rata share of the partnership's minority-marketable value as outlined below.

Net asset value		$_____
Less discount for lack of control	× ____ % =	$_____
Concluded hypothetical minority-marketable value		$_____
Subject Interest	× ____ % =	$_____
Less discount for lack of marketability	× ____ % =	$_____
Concluded market value		$_____

The control discount is usually taken first, and then the marketability discount is applied. However, the math can be performed in any sequence and the same result will be obtained. It is common to see the subject pro rata percentage applied first, then the two discounts; or, the two discounts can be applied to the net asset value and the subject percentage applied last. The above sequence shows the discount for lack of control applied to net asset value because the discount applies for any minority interest (as long as a swing vote or other control element is not involved), and the minority-marketable level can be obtained using other approaches to value.

Thus, the hypothetical minority-marketable value of the whole can be reconciled between approaches.

The marketability discount, on the other hand, is partly dependent on the pro rata size of the interest, so the pro rata portion of the minority-marketable level is calculated first and the marketability discount is applied to the result. The chosen sequence should make sense, given the process developed in the valuation report.

Historical Sales as Evidence of Value

The partnership history section should have discussed any past transactions that involve partnership interests. These may be evidence of value and, if so, should be reconciled with the above conclusion developed from market analysis. Such transactions are not often arms'-length and are made for reasons that are inconsistent with the definition of market value; it should also be understood that one transaction does not constitute a market. Any transfer for consideration should be discussed to make it clear to the reader that value implications have been fully considered.

Overall Discount

The client may require an overall discount, rather than a value, if the amount of an interest is a gift, i.e., an interest transferred, for estate planning purposes—typically from parent to child—and the pro rata percentage is unknown. In that case, the valuer would determine a range of percentage gift interests for which the analysis would apply and then conclude a discount, with this range as a limiting condition. The overall discounts are sequential, and the following formula may be used to calculate a combined, effective, discount:[55]

$$(1 - D_E) = (1 - D_C) \times (1 - D_M)$$

Where D_C is the discount for lack of control, D_M is the discount for lack of marketability, and D_E is the effective, overall discount.

The result should be rounded.

Sensitivity Analysis

The concluded discount can vary greatly, depending on the subject's particulars. A sensitivity analysis is often presented as part of a discounted cash flow analysis so that the reader can understand the significance of the underlying assumptions to the value conclusion.

---

55. The unsubscripted D variable is used in Part II to indicate debt; here it is used with appropriate subscripts to indicate discount.

Precision of the Result

The precision of the result is the compound product of the precision of its components: real estate value, the discount for lack of control, and the discount for lack of marketability. As the case study has demonstrated, the accuracy of the analysis declines as one descends the levels-of-value diagram; the real estate value is the most accurate, and the marketability discount the least accurate. The case study has yielded results rounded at each step to avoid the implication that the analysis is more accurate than it is; however, it is clear from following the case study that a range could be a more appropriate expression of many of the adjustments, rather than a point value.

This is particularly true for the marketability discount, where high and low columns are shown throughout the analysis.[56] If the conclusion is presented as a range, it might create the perception of guaranteeing that the market value lies within the range, unless a probability analysis is provided describing the meaning of the range. It is most important to present the conclusion of value in a manner that is not misleading.

Final Checklist

All conclusions should be checked against a common-sense yardstick to confirm that extreme conditions have not compromised the valuation process and produced an unrealistic result. One strategy for doing this is to use a different method for obtaining the discount; e.g., if an income approach has not been used, examine the dividend yield in relationship to that particular share of the partnership in the subject interest to determine whether the figure makes sense in relation to the interest holder's other investment alternatives.

Another check on the result might be to consider the position of the willing seller. The focus of this exercise has primarily been on a willing buyer of the interest, but the valuer also should consider whether the owner of the interest would be willing to part with it at the concluded discount. The literature addresses reasoning from the seller's perspective and discusses the concept of the willing buyer/seller at length. [57, 58] In the court case cited earlier in the chapter, the judge chided the valuer for focusing only on the willing buyer and neglecting the position of the willing seller, who was expected to part with his shares at a 70% discount.[59]

---

56. Mercer prefers this approach, which is facilitated by the tabular method of computing the discount.

57. Willis, "Preparing Valuation Reports to Withstand Judicial Challenge," 458, 460.

58. Mercer, *Quantifying Marketability Discounts*, Chapter 6.

59. Mandelbaum [opinion 1d.]

CASE STUDY APPLICATION

Concluding Value for Suburban Office Partners, II*

Net asset value		$1,512,279
Less discount for lack of control	× 24.0% =	− 362,947
Concluded hypothetical minority-marketable value of Suburban Office Partners, II		$1,149,332
Interest held by John Builder	× 20.0% =	$229,866
Less discount for lack of marketability	× 23.0% =	− 52,869
Concluded market value estimate		$176,997
(rounded)		$177,000

The overall discount can be applied more simply as follows,

$$D_E = 1 - [(1 - 24.0\%) \times (1 - 23.0\%)] = 41.5\%$$

However, these calculations should not be used to the exclusion of the discount-explicit presentation above.

Net asset value		$1,512,279
Interest held by John Builder	× 20.0% =	$302,456
Less combined discount	× 41.5% =	− 125,519
Concluded fair market value		$176,937
(rounded)		$177,000

Reconciliation to Sale of Partnership Interest

John had purchased 20% of Ed's 50% share in 1995 for $120,000 to provide the cash Ed needed for an operation. This is 10% of the whole, and its pro rata share two years later was $151,228. The partnership net asset value can be approximated as of the end of 1995 from the balance sheet provided and by deflating the market value of the property to $2,950,000. This results in a pro rata net asset value of just over $115,000, so the amount paid was actually a 4% premium. The facts and circumstances indicate that Ed told Billy later that his dad had paid a ridiculously high price because he was a very generous man and that Ed had sufficient capital losses to offset any gains. These nonmarket conditions provide a reasonable justification for the transacted amount, which does not influence the value conclusion.

Sensitivity Analysis

A ± one-year change in holding time would produce an approximate ±2.0% change in the discount, based on the conclusions from the suggested solutions. (A longer hold increases the discount.)

A ±2% change in the cash flow rate (at the asset level) would produce an approximate ±2.5% change in the discount, based on the conclusions from the suggested solutions. (A higher rate decreases the discount.)

A ±2% change in the required rate (at the private level) would produce an approximate +5.0%–3.0% change in the overall discount. (A greater rate increases the discount.)

The remaining influences affect the discount to varying degrees. It is not unusual to conclude an overall discount of 25% or less for a partnership with a high distribution rate and low-risk assets. A high-risk situation with no distributions can produce greater discounts, but the willing seller component of the definition of value becomes an important issue as recommended in the final checklist.

* Note: These conclusions apply only to the case Suburban Office Partners, II, and should not be taken as a baseline for application to other situations.

Part II

Valuing Common
Tenancy Interests

CHAPTER 6

Beginning the Common Tenancy Valuation

Common tenancy is another means of implementing the fractional ownership of real estate. It represents a third organizational form that is amenable to the same valuation process that applies to corporate holding companies and partnerships. The limited partnership analysis addressed in Part I of this book follows a well-established process because the partnership is a business with an operating agreement, comparable transactions are available, and the valuation can rely upon a large body of business valuation knowledge. However, even though common tenancy is a simple form of ownership, its valuation is not a straightforward process. Much of the legal and accounting information concerning the ownership and operations of assets held in common tenancy may be ad hoc, requiring reconstruction and interpretation. Moreover, there are more options for the interest holder to consider and several pathways for the valuer to follow. Thus, valuers of such interests need to have additional analytical tools at their disposal.

The valuation of common tenancy interests increases in complexity when financing, which is under reasonable control within the partnership structure, is present. Financing arrangements among co-owners are a direct and sometimes personal obligation, and can create significant problems.

Agreements may also be used, causing the relationship between cotenants to rise to the level of a partnership for analytical purposes, or the cotenants may create a business arrangement that is less than a partnership but more than simple cotenancy. As a result, the scope of the business valuation cannot be known until the implications of ownership, management, and financing agreements are understood.

Under a common tenancy scenario, the valuer is interpreting the market and not just applying a formularized process to valuation, which raises questions such as:

- Who is the hypothetical buyer?
- What is the typical decision-making process in the market, given the facts and circumstances of the interests being appraised?
- What analytical tools can be used to best model the process for a buyer?

This chapter parallels Chapter 1, Beginning the Limited Partnership Valuation. The valuation of common tenancy interests is based on the partnership model described earlier. The special considerations that the common tenancy creates—primarily its increased level of control—are presented here as modifications and exceptions to the partnership valuation process detailed in Part I.

Applicable Definitions

A number of definitions were introduced in Chapter 1. The definitions applicable to valuing common tenancy interests that are presented here address exceptions to those definitions and issues that are particular to common tenancy. These definitions are tenancy in common, value, and minority interest.

Tenancy in Common

Tenancy in common is an estate held by two or more persons, each of whom has an undivided interest.[1] No one interest controls the property, and a similar interest of any size can block important decisions concerning the property. Common tenancy is defined entirely by common law and statute and varies from state to state.[2] However, the basic character of a tenancy in common is relatively uniform and is identified by the rights pertaining to possession, repairs and capital improvements, leases, agreements, transfer of interest, and partition.

Right of possession. Cotenants enjoy an equal right of possession. Each may occupy the entire property but may not exclude the others. When one cotenant is in possession of the property, he or she is not liable to the other cotenants for its rental value[3] or the value of his labor (e.g., crops). However, he or she must give an accounting to the cotenant(s) for a share of any rents and profits received from third persons and for profits derived from the use of the land that may involve removing a natural resource such as oil or minerals.

1. *Dictionary of Real Estate Appraisal*, 4th ed. (Chicago: Appraisal Institute, 2002).
2. This chapter is general, and its assumptions may need to be modified according to statutory provisions. Appraisers and other practitioners should check the provisions of the law applicable in the state that governs the property rights being valued.
3. This is true unless the cotenants agree on another arrangement.

Repairs and capital improvements. A cotenant generally has a right of contribution if he or she pays taxes or other liens or for necessary repairs. Such expenses may be deducted from income.[4] No corresponding right of contribution regarding capital improvements exists unless the other cotenants have agreed to the improvements.

Leases. A cotenant cannot execute a lease for the whole property or a specific portion that will bind the other cotenants and confer exclusive possession to the lessee,[5] but a cotenant may execute a lease for its undivided portion. A lease that gives a third-party tenant the right to occupy the entire property would have to be signed by all cotenants.

Agreements. The cotenants may make an agreement among themselves as to right of possession, payment of rental value in lieu of possession, or virtually any other terms they deem appropriate.

Transfer of interest. A common tenancy interest may be transferred voluntarily or by the operation of law, without any restriction and without notice to the other cotenants.

Partition. A cotenant has the absolute right to sue for partition; that is, to ask the court to divide the property between other cotenants or to require a sale if such a division is not possible. However, a cotenant may restrict or give up this right by agreement.[6] If the property cannot be partitioned in kind (physically divided), then the court can order sale of the property and division of the proceeds.[7]

Value

As is the case for the partnership valuation, the definition of value should be consistent with the real estate appraisal, particularly since a common tenancy interest generally has an absolute right under state law to cause partition or sale of the property. A valuation based on market value or fair market value may still be appropriate for the common tenancy valuation if the property interest can be sold within a reasonably short marketing time. If the interest has a very limited market, or if the marketing time is expected to be long, the real estate appraiser may also have to consider a forced sale under a liquidation premise for the asset appraisal. Whether liquidation value must be considered depends on the likelihood that a suit will be brought to cause partition or sale, and if a sale is ordered by the court, the likelihood that the property would have limited market exposure.

4. These provisions, as well as many others, vary by state.
5. This right also varies by state and may be blurred.
6. Without clear authority to give up this right, it is unlikely that a lending institution would grant that no partition is allowed.
7. California courts generally prefer partition in kind when possible, for example.

> *Minority interest is a term that is not applicable to common tenancy because the degree of control is mixed.*

Minority Interest

This interest was defined earlier as an ownership position that is less than 50% of the voting interest in an enterprise, but it was also noted that that might be compromised by distribution of ownership (a swing vote). *Minority interest* is a term that is not applicable to common tenancy because the degree of control is mixed. For example, all cotenants must agree and any one can block important decisions. The notion of control is a complex one that will be examined in detail.

The Valuation Process and Scope of Work

The overall valuation process involves two steps:

- Develop the value for the real property and the owners' equity
- Develop the discount for its lack of control and lack of marketability

The first step is an asset approach and largely consists of the real estate appraisal, which, in turn, contains its own approaches to value. The second step may employ one or more of the traditional approaches including sales comparison (comparison with fractional interest sales involving similar properties), and income (partition time and cost).

The approaches to value that are used in the common tenancy valuation, as well as those that are not used, should be discussed and the reason for the selection explained. An asset approach is the method that is clearly preferred because it involves, by definition, a single asset. No other business attributes are associated with ownership, and the pro rata share of the value of the underlying property is expected to be realized by the hypothetical buyer of the interest. If any of these conditions do not apply in a particular case, other approaches would be indicated, but it would no longer be a strictly common tenancy valuation assignment.

Description of the Ownership Interest

A full description of a common tenancy ownership interest begins with its history and, in addition to the basic common law characteristics listed above, includes any modifications and additions to these rights created by operating and financing agreements.

History

Organizational history includes basic information such as the initial owners, the circumstances under which they purchased the property, and transfers of interest, if relevant. When there is no written agreement, understanding the original purpose of the association between the parties may be significant since the objectives of the owners can change over time and usually do.

Distributions

A partnership valuation requires an analysis of the business's distribution history, since it is not controlled by the limited partners. Common tenancy ownership requires distribution under state law when there is no agreement or ongoing and unanimous consent to the contrary, so the distribution history should match the historical cash flow produced by the real property, minus any debt service and expenses (usually minimal). The expectation of future payments would be tied closely to the real property's performance.

Real Estate Asset

This section of the valuation report summarizes the real property appraisal, highlighting important features of the real property. The entire real estate appraisal should be attached to the valuation report, but the valuer should call attention to items that will be most important in the valuation.

Past Sales of Interest

In keeping with Standards Rule 9-4(b)(iv), sales, facts, and circumstances are disclosed but not analyzed at this point. The relevance of these transactions can be revisited after the valuation process has been completed.

Distribution of Ownership

The distribution of ownership enumerates the percentage interests in the real property as of the date of value.

Operating Agreements

Operating agreements might provide for the management of the property, set forth various policies concerning the investment objectives, establish fees for services, and provide for many other functions. Cotenants, for example, may give up their right to sue to partition the property. An agreement may also give them a put option, by which the other cotenants are obligated to buy out a cotenant who wishes to withdraw from the association. The valuer must carefully consider the amount or lack of control established and the effect on marketability.

The agreement could go so far in specifying the rights of owners that it would be tantamount to a partnership agreement, and the interest could be valued as if it were a partnership interest. The case study relating to Suburban Office Partners, II, does not include an agreement, but it would be appropriate to apply the principles and structure described in Chapter 1 in evaluating any agreement and classifying its terms for valuation purposes.

Operating agreements between cotenants are unnecessary, but cotenants generally have the right to enter into them to modify statutory provisions. If valuers of common tenancy interests encounter such agreements, they should be prepared to evaluate them. In nearly all cases, the valuer should obtain advice from the client's counsel regarding the legal position of the subject interest to ensure that the valuation has a reasonable legal foundation and the valuer's interpretation of the agreement does not constitute the practice of law.

Financing Agreements

Loans can greatly complicate the analysis of common tenancy interests, primarily because they can increase the complexity of the problems associated with ownership. Existing loans, in particular, raise many questions for which there can be few general answers. Financing involves multiple agreements and conditions that can vary greatly, but some realities that may arise in the valuation of common tenancy interests are:

- It is unlikely that the buyer will be able to finance its purchase of the interest.

- Cotenants would find it difficult to refinance an existing loan.

- Joint and several liability on a loan may require it to be deducted separately, without discount, for estate tax purposes.[8]

- If a seller cannot be released from a personal guarantee– it could impact the "willing seller" assumption.

- The question of who pays the prepayment penalty if a loan balance is due on transfer becomes an issue–the cotenants who were not involved in the transaction, or the seller or buyer of the interest?

---

8. Mortgage debt may be entered as a separate deduction for estate tax purposes if the decedent was personally liable under the terms of the loan. According to the instructions for Form 706 Schedule K, if the debt (mortgages and liens) is enforceable against other property of the estate not subject to the mortgage or lien, or the decedent was personally liable for the debt, the full value of the property subject to the mortgage or lien must be included in the gross estate under the appropriate schedule, and the mortgage or lien on the property on this schedule may be deducted. However, if the decedent's estate is not liable, only the value of the equity of redemption (or the value of the property less the amount of the debt) can be included in the gross estate, and no portion of the indebtedness on the schedule can be deducted.

   It is possible that the decedent's pro rata share of the loan would be entered on Schedule K without discount. If so, the pro rata discounted amount of the loan would be added back to the concluded value of the interest and the total entered as an asset of the estate. If this condition exists, it is imperative that the appraiser discuss the issue with the preparer of the Form 706 and incorporate any required assumptions and conditions into the valuation.

Given the complexity of questions such as these, it is essential that the valuer have access to and read all the loan documents to understand the issues that might be considered by a hypothetical buyer and seller.

Legal and Practice Issues

Although the basic principles that govern common tenancy interests are relatively uniform from state to state, the business valuer should confirm his knowledge of the law governing the common tenancy interests in the valuation assignment. Advising clients on matters involving the interpretation of the agreement may constitute the practice of law, and only members of the state bar may practice law. When conflicts in any agreement or in the law occur, the valuer should consider requesting an opinion from counsel and should rely on counsel's opinion in the valuation report.[9]

CASE STUDY APPLICATION
Valuing Common Tenancy Interests

The valuation assignment concerns the valuation of an undivided, or concurrent, interest in the same property described in the valuation of the limited partnership interest in Chapter 1. In this scenario, Ed Helper, Billy Builder, and Sara Builder Morganstern are tenants in common. JB Management has managed the property for a fee. There is no existing agreement among the owners or with JBM concerning the property's operation or the management fee; both are based on an informal arrangement that has been in place for 10 years.

John Builder's common tenancy interest and his JB Management stock passed to Billy and Sara upon his death in 1997. The assignment is to value, for estate tax purposes, the common tenancy interest held by John Builder as of the date of his death, January 17, 1997. The items normally included in the introduction to the valuation report are listed below. Additional facts and circumstances that concern the common tenancy interest are presented next.

Introduction to the Valuation Report

Type and Percentage Interest Being Valued
The 20% common tenancy interest held by John Builder before his death

Definition of the Interest
An undivided fractional interest, identified as a tenancy in common

Definition of Value
Fair market value

Purpose, Client, and Intended Use
The purpose of the valuation is to develop, for estate tax use, an opinion of the fair market value of the common tenancy interest that is the subject of this report, as of the effective date of the valuation. (The client and intended users are identified in the cover letter to the report.)

Date of Value and Date of Report
The effective date of this valuation, the date for which value is concluded, is January 17, 1997, the date of death of John Builder. The date of the report is June 18, 1997.

---

9. See also "Working with Attorneys and Other Client Intermediaries," Gerald Lunn, Esq., Appendix E.

Other

This valuation was performed in compliance with, and the report has been prepared in conformity with, the requirements of the Code of Professional Ethics and the Standards of Professional Appraisal Practice of the (Appraisal Institute or other appraisal association).

Cotenancy Description

Distribution History

The cotenants are paid nearly all of the cash flow each year. Cash flows are increasing slowly because of the escalation clauses in the leases. In the near future, however, some circumstances may reduce cash flows, e.g, leases coming due.

Real Estate Assets

The cotenants own the 33,000-sq.-ft. office building that was built in 1987. It is leased by 10 tenants, and currently has one vacancy. The tenants are on three to 10-year leases. Five of the leases come due in 2000. The leases coming due are primarily those of the longer-term tenants whose leases are currently about 10% above market rents.

Past Sales of Interests

John Builder purchased a 10% common tenancy interest from Ed Helper in 1995 for $120,000.

Distribution of Ownership

The distribution of ownership is slightly different than for the partnership case because there is no general partner position, so the former 1% general partner interest is added to the Boy's Home percentage, which makes the subject interest work out to be the same amount–20%.

John Builder (subject)	20.0 %
Edward Helper	40.0 %
William Builder	18.0 %
Sara Builder Morganstern	18.0 %
Boy's Home	4.0 %
Total	100.0%

Operating Agreement

None

Financing

The cotenants have a nonrecourse loan, and there is no due-on-transfer clause, prepayment penalty, or personal guarantee, so the existing loan should not pose a problem. (This is not always the case.) However, refinancing may not be an option as it was for the partnership valuation in Part I, and purchase financing would still be an unlikely option for the buyer because banks are very reluctant to enter into loan agreements with multiple parties, unless the borrowers assume joint and several liability for repayment.

CHAPTER 7

Developing the Common Tenancy Asset-Level Value

The real property for the common tenancy case study is identical to that in the partnership scenario described in Chapter 2 and includes facts and conditions that affect expected future cash flows, holding time, and discount rates. The real property assumptions introduced in Chapter 3 are modified slightly for the common tenancy ownership structure and include appraisal assumptions related to control, holding time, and property taxes. The partnership case "Assumptions Related to Control and Holding Time" from page 66 apply for this section substantially unchanged.

Real Property Assumptions Related to Control

In appraising the real estate, transfer of the entire property is assumed; in the partnership scenario, a transfer of a noncontrolling minority interest only is assumed. Despite the fact that the common tenancy interest has more control than the limited partnership interest, it does not have absolute control. Therefore, assumptions that the real estate appraiser made may need to be reconsidered and adjustments made in the valuation, as they were for the partnership. Assumptions related to control may pertain to management, highest and best use, repairs, and any other issues that are determined to fall in this category.

Management

Although typical or competent management is generally assumed, the cotenant might have been forced to accept the existing management. Consequently, in valuing the common tenancy interest the valuer would need to consider whether a new interest holder would expect to prevail in matters related to

> *The holding period assumed in the real estate appraisal is usually based on a typical market period (explicit or implicit), which may or may not apply to the common tenancy valuation.*

management when any cotenant could block important decisions. If such a situation exists, adjustments might also have to be made for any differences between competent management and the existing management.

Highest and Best Use

The highest and best use analysis may include the assumption that a prudent owner, intent on maximizing the property's economic potential, would make certain changes to realize that goal. The cotenants may have no intention of making the changes and can refuse to contribute the additional capital necessary to do so unless it is required by agreement. Thus, differences between "actual," practices and "prudent," or "typical" may require that adjustments be made when valuing a noncontrolling interest.

Repairs

Owners are obligated to contribute to repairs. Immediate repair requirements may be identified and adjusted for in the appraisal, and future repairs might be expressly considered in the discounted cash flow analysis. However, it is more likely that the real estate appraiser, guided by the market's method of addressing the issue of repairs, may not consider an expenditure that could be required several years in the future. The valuer, therefore, may need to incorporate an adjustment for repairs unless a comprehensive reserve analysis is already included in the real estate appraisal.

Assumptions Related to Holding Time

The holding period assumed in the real estate appraisal is usually based on a typical market period (explicit or implicit), which may or may not apply to the common tenancy valuation. The right of a cotenant to sue for partition may lead to a short holding period, or other facts may argue for a longer period. The question is whether there are any circumstances associated with the property itself that would encourage its sale at a particular point in the future. This is probably the most important single issue facing a buyer of any undivided interest, and it has a profound effect on value.

Financial Statements

The accounting requirements for common tenancy interests are even more limited than they are for small real estate partnerships because such interests include only direct property-related activities. The property owners or managers sometimes prepare financial statements, but often the information has to be extracted from federal tax returns. Because the association between the owners of the real estate holding company may be deemed a partnership for tax purposes, many cotenants report the operating results on the partnership return, Form 1065. In other instances, it may be necessary to construct statements from property management reports, bank statements, and individual tax returns. For guidance, see Appendix E, "Extracting the Necessary Data from Financial Statements and Tax Forms."

The historic relationship between cash flows and distributions should be verified, but it is mostly for the sake of good order, since all net cash flow should be distributed or held in a management account to pay for the property's operation. Capital accumulations and diversion of funds to other investments—a consideration with partnerships—would not normally occur for common tenancy interests. The real estate appraiser's forecast is again the basis for the business forecast. The business appraiser's task is to adjust the line items for the changed premise of the valuation and add a forecast for business-level items.

Income or Cash Flow Statement

The income statement at the common tenancy level is really a cash flow statement based on real estate operating statements. The real estate appraisal usually considers only income and expenses related to real estate operations, but the cotenants may have additional expenses and may also have separate sources of income, although these expenses and income are likely very limited (e.g., interest on an investment checking account). These "entity-level" items must be included, and some of the real estate expenses may require adjusting to develop a forecast of cash flow that a buyer of the subject interest could reasonably expect. Items to include in the analysis are:

- Net operating income (*NOI*) from the real estate appraisal
- Reserve allowance, if needed
- Any other items not included in *NOI*
- Interest and income from other sources
- Adjustments for property taxes
- Accounting, legal, and general and administrative costs
- Other taxes, if any (excluding income taxes)
- Debt service

Generally, cash flow is paid to cotenants because each has a right to a proportionate share of income that the property generates. GAAP adjustments are not required unless the cotenancy associations are more complex e.g., managed under a partnership agreement. In that instance, management would provide the financial statements, and the entity would likely be valued as if it were a partnership, in which case the scenario presented in Chapter 3 would apply.

Owners' Equity Analysis

Because the subject interest represents a fraction of an asset, an asset-based valuation method is the only appropriate way to develop the value of the owner's equity in the property. Using this method, the owners' assets and liabilities are adjusted to current fair market values to determine the value of the owners' equity.

CASE STUDY APPLICATION

Owners' Cash Flow Analysis

The cash flow analysis is nearly identical to the analysis used to value the partnership for Suburban Office Partners, II. The data source documents are from Table 2.2, Chapter 2, the real estate appraisal's property income statement, as well as the Form 1040 Schedule E and bank statement provided in Appendix C.

Table 7.1	Owners' Cash Flow Analysis	
Income	**1996**	**Forecast**
Net operating income*	$311,526	$316,800
Adjustments:		
Add back forecast management fee[†]		19,500
Less fee at current rate		(32,500)
Total owners' income	$311,526	$303,800
Other expenses[§]		
General and Administrative	273	280
Debt service	221,011	221,011
Total owners' expenses	$221,284	$221,291
Cash flow	$90,242	$82,509

Notes:

* Net operating income is taken directly from the property income statement included in the real estate appraisal.

† The management fee is forecast at a market rate of 4.5%, but JB Management has been charging 7.5%, and there is no reason to believe it will change. In the absence of a written agreement, all of the owners must continue to agree, an issue that is addressed further in Chapter 8. The forecast amount is added back to *NOI*, and an amount calculated at the new rate is subtracted.

§ Other expenses, e.g., general and administrative expenses, are taken directly from Form 1040, Schedule E, except for debt service, which is taken from the mortgage statement. This includes only small office expenses that JB Management has been billing back to the owners. The valuer should check to determine whether this practice is representative of long-term stabilized operating conditions, particularly since an operating history was not provided.

The statement makes no adjustment for property taxes. Real estate taxes are forecast based on a reassessment at the appraised value. Unlike the partnership scenario, taxes will be increased for the subject's 20% interest, but not for the other interests. Therefore, the cash flow calculated applies to the subject interest only. The conclusion is referred to as owners' cash flow, but after the transfer, it is a hypothetical amount because actual cash flows to the other owners will be greater based on current, or individual, property tax assessments.[1]

Reserves could have been increased because the valuer used the low end of the survey range ($0.10 per square foot when the range is $0.10 to $0.25). For any reserve items that will need to be replaced during the holding period or any expected extraordinary items, an allowance should be deducted. In this case, there are no such items, so no allowance is made.

No cash flow adjustments are made because the bank account is used only for receiving rent payments, paying expenses, and disbursing the remainder to the cotenants. There should be no accumulation of cash, unless it has been agreed upon separately by all cotenants. There are no other events that affect cash flow.

---

1. This analysis is based on California law. Tax-related adjustments are highly state-specific, and the valuer should check with the real estate appraiser or counsel familiar with the specific jurisdiction.

Reconstructed Balance Sheet

The process begins with an analysis of the historical balance sheet, assuming that the owners filed a Form 1065 or prepared financial statements. If this were not the case, the valuer would need to construct a balance sheet. Assets and liabilities would then be adjusted to their current market values. The difference between the market values of the assets and liabilities is the owners' net equity shown in the normalized adjusted column in Table 7.2.

The historical balance sheet is derived from William Builder's Form 1040, Schedule E (Appendix D) and from other data supplied by management and included in Appendix C. Typical items that might be available for common tenancy asset ownership are listed as follows:

- Current assets, usually a bank account, although for a property with a triple-net lease there may be none because the tenant may distribute the rents directly to the various owners. The valuer should ask if there are other accounts.

- Fixed assets, likely only real property, since it would be unusual for cotenants to have other co-owned assets.

- Current liabilities are any amounts owed as of the date of value that are due within 12 months. Because cash accounting is likely, it may not make sense to accrue these liabilities. (Payment of these liabilities may come out of future distributions that would be owed to a new interest holder.)

- Long-term liabilities include mortgage debt, other notes, and security deposit liability. The existence of mortgage debt should be obvious, but it is also important to ask whether there are any other long-term obligations. If the owners are not aware of a security deposit liability, the appraiser should contact the property manager to confirm the existence of any such liability and may need to review copies of the leases to make such a determination.[2, 3]

CASE STUDY APPLICATION

Table 7.2	Owners' Balance Sheet	
Assets	**1996**	**Normalized Adjusted**
Current assets		
Cash and equivalents*	$29,250	$10,832
Accounts receivable	0	0
Total current assets	$29,250	$10,832
Fixed assets[†]		
Real property	2,500,000	3,250,000
Accumulated depreciation	(191,746)	0
Total fixed assets	$2,308,524	$3,250,000
Total assets	$2,337,504	$3,260,832
Liabilities and equity		
Current liabilities	0	0
Accounts payable	0	0
Other	0	0
Total current liabilities	$0	$0
Long-term debt		
First mortgage	$1,818,406	$1,816,278
Notes payable	0	0
Security deposits	16,500	16,500
Long-term liabilities[†]	$1,834,906	$1,832,778
Net owners' equity	502,598	1,428,054
Total liabilities and equity	$2,337,504	$3,260,832

* Cash and equivalents include only a checking account that JB Management maintains for the owners. (The February 7 bank statement shows the balance; the year-end amount was reduced by a mortgage payment made on January 14.)

† Fixed assets include only the Tustin office building. Its original basis may have been increased by capital improvements, and book value is reduced by accumulated depreciation, as shown on the depreciation tables attached to the 1040 Schedule E. Book value is adjusted to the appraised value. Intangible assets might be present for tax purposes (loan fees less amortization, for example), but these would have no effect on the transferable assets.

‡ *Long-term liabilities* include the mortgage, which was taken from the monthly statement. Security deposit liability exists, as revealed in the lease and confirmed with management.

2. Security deposits might cover cleaning expenses upon turnover, and if the real estate appraiser has included such expenses in the income forecast, this reserve could constitute double counting. In that event, it is possible to back out the turnover cost from operating expenses to the extent it is covered by deposits, since the security deposit would pass from buyer to seller upon sale of the interest.

3. Security deposits will not have necessarily been investigated by the real estate appraiser because these amounts would pass from seller to buyer on transfer, and would not affect the value of the fee interest. They do affect the cotenant's balance sheet, however, and the valuer may have to handle the investigation.

Balance Sheet Adjustments

Normalization adjustments will probably not be needed when valuing common tenancy interests because nonoperating assets would not have been added in. Data should be current as of the date of value, so items taken from the previous year's tax return will require updating. The period from the end of the reporting year to the date of value is December 31, 1996 to January 17, 1997, so the adjustments required should be minimal.

Real estate and other assets and liabilities should be shown at their market value as of the date of value. The real estate is valued at the appraised amount. Loans may present special problems for common tenancy ownership since the original owners are often co-guarantors, and the bank may have loan assumption requirements for new owners. The difference between the normalized and adjusted assets and liabilities is the owners' equity.

Alternative Owners' Equity Calculation

The balance sheet format is sufficient to develop owners' equity. However, the data can be shown in an abbreviated form when there are so few items that a balance sheet would be trivial.

Owners' equity corresponds to the top level of value–the value of equity held by the owner from Figure I.2, Levels of Value. It bears repeating that, for purposes of this valuation, owner's equity is a hypothetical, intermediate value; net cash flow is also hypothetical.[4]

CASE STUDY APPLICATION

Table 7.3	Alternative Owners' Equity Calculation
Real estate	$3,250,000
Adjustments for owners' equity	
Current assets	$10,832
Current liabilities	0
Long-term liabilities	0
Mortgage balance due	(1,816,278)
Security deposits	(16,500)
Total adjustments	(1,821,946)
Net owners' equity	$1,428,054
Net cash flow	$82.509
Return on net asset value	5.8%

4. This is because of the differing allocation of property tax liability between the cotenants.

CHAPTER 8

Developing the Discount for Cotenancy Interests

A variety of circumstances create common tenancy ownership in real property. For example, investors can choose to pool funds to invest in a property, an individual can receive cotenant property rights through a gift or inheritance, or the relationship can be created by the operation of law (e.g., conversion of joint tenancy to common tenancy). An investor might purchase a common tenancy interest in real property to own a share of the property, participate with the other parties in owning and managing it, use the property (in cooperation with the other parties) for his or her own purposes, and share in the cash flow from the property. Typically, the specific circumstances that initially led the parties into common tenancy ownership no longer exist by the time a valuer is asked to value one of the interests.

Risks in Purchasing an Interest

An investor faces a number of risks in purchasing an interest in real property held in common tenancy. These risks are directly related to the following questions, which the prospective buyer of a cotenancy interest will need to resolve before making a final decision to purchase:

- How will management decisions be made, both now and in the future, and will these decisions be made competently?

- Who will be the cotenant's "partners" in the future, and how do I feel about these future, unknown cotenants having the same degree of control as I do?

- If joint and several liability exists for the payment of mortgages or liens, would I be exposed to the full burden of liability (e.g., personal injury, toxic contamination) associated with the property?

- How would I be affected by situations in which the cotenants disagree and possibly withhold approval for capital expenditures, financing, lease agreements, or any other action requiring owner approval?

- How long would I be likely to hold the interest, and will I have difficulty selling it if necessary? What if I change my viewpoint regarding future market conditions, which might require sale of the property—a decision with which the cotenants may not agree?

Cotenants can always sue to partition, which raises even more questions:

- Do I have the temperament for bringing a lawsuit?

- Would one or more of the other cotenants mount a strong opposition?

- How long would a lawsuit take, and what effect would its potential cost have on the price I am willing to pay?

There are few options for addressing risks such as these, which can arise from disagreements between cotenants. Thus, the successful operation of the investment requires continuous agreement at many levels. The limited options for addressing these risks include:

- Entering into an agreement with the cotenants concerning operation of the property

- Counting on the full cooperation of all cotenants in the operation of the property

- Perfecting the interest in the property by assembling the other cotenants into an entity, such as a partnership, that sets forth how the property will be operated and the association controlled

- Bringing an action in court to partition the property, either in-kind or to force a sale and the division of proceeds

Why a Cotenant Might Want to Sell an Interest

A cotenant might wish to sell an interest independently of the other cotenants because of personal financial issues, to pay estate taxes, because of conflicts with other cotenants, because one or more cotenants may have sole possession of the property and the others may consider the arrangement to be unfair, or because of various intra-family conflicts. A cotenant might need to offer the interest for sale to an outside party because the remaining cotenants may not wish to sell the entire property, and may not have the resources to buy the interest themselves.

Despite a cotenant's willingness to sell his or her undivided interest in a property, a number of obstacles can arise. A seller of a common tenancy interest should be aware of the impediments to selling the interest, namely:

- Undivided interests in real estate do not generally trade in the public marketplace.
- Due diligence efforts can be considerably more difficult for an undivided interest than for a 100% fee interest.
- A buyer cannot necessarily obtain financing for the purchase.

Furthermore, an undivided interest can be defined as a security, and thus cannot be advertised to the general public or sold through the same public channels as a fee interest in real estate (or a publicly registered security). As a result, an undivided interest must be sold privately, and a seller who wishes to liquidate such an interest encounters limited marketability, which must be mitigated by offering a discount to the potential buyer. Lastly, lenders may have a right to call any existing loan, may not release the seller from guarantees, or may require new guarantees from the buyer, all of which constitute deterrents for a potential buyer.

The Partition Solution

The cotenant's right to bring a lawsuit to force the partition or sale of the property and distribution of the proceeds can be seen as largely negating any discount for an interest. The discount is reduced (or the price is increased) because a partition action can force a sale of the property and the division of the proceeds. The most conspicuous illustration of this perception is shown in a private letter ruling issued by the Internal Revenue Service.[1] The ruling establishes the cost-to-partition method as the appropriate way to estimate the value of the discount associated with selling an undivided interest in real estate. A variety of possible scenarios illustrate the partition process:

- The cotenants could agree to sell, eliminating the need for a lawsuit.
- A partition-in-kind could be effected, depending on the physical attributes of the property. For example:
  - Vacant land might be divided equitably, but costs will be incurred to subdivide it, and a change in highest and best use between the larger parcel and the resulting two smaller parcels could occur. (A larger parcel can often be more densely developed than two smaller parcels.) The resulting division may reduce the total value and increase the difficulty of establishing an equitable solution through the court.

1. IRS Private Letter Ruling 9336002.

> *The general assumption about partitioning property is that the process is available to cure any impairment to marketability or control.*

- A retail or apartment development may comprise multiple parcels for subdivision. However, dividing parking lots may require cross agreements, which could complicate the partition, making it impractical.

- The legal process for dealing with non-partitionable properties (requiring a court-ordered sale) could be simple, requiring less than a year to judgment, and incur nominal fees (i.e., legal fees plus the cost of a court-appointed referee). However, even this simple process becomes more complex when the number of cotenants increases.

- The entire process can be prolonged by other interest holders who may obstruct the effort through delaying strategies or lawsuits of their own, particularly if they do not want to sell. Thus, the process can take many years and incur considerable costs.[2]

- For more complex but partitionable properties, the process can also consume many years and dollars. In a timberland partition case, for example, the court projected four years time to judgment and $1,325,000 in costs (to be divided among the cotenants).[3]

The general assumption about partitioning property is that the process is available to cure any impairment to marketability or control, and that the holding period used for the purpose of concluding a discount should be limited to the partition period. The corollary is that a buyer who purchased the interest with the intention of forcing the sale of the property would quickly capture the discount. Although a "vulture" concept can apply to some participants in the real estate market generally, it has not been shown to characterize the market for common tenancy interests.

For example, assume a buyer acquires a common tenancy interest as an investment and not as the subject of a lawsuit, but that a disagreement (e.g., concerning a desire to sell early in a perceived market down-cycle) later makes partition the only option. In this case, the valuer might consider whether the holding period should be measured from the acquisition

---

2. Ronald M. Seaman, ASA, CBA "Valuation of Undivided Interests in Real Property" *Business Valuation Review* (March 1997): 32-40. This article describes one study by Southland Business Group of Tampa, Florida (the Southland Study), which included 158 partition suits that were closed between 1978 and 1994. The time to judgment ranged from one to 66 months. The article also cites an informal survey of attorneys who estimated costs of $10,000 to $15,000 for each party and time to judgment of about six to 12 months for an uncontested suit. These costs increased to $30,000 to $50,000 for each party and about three years time to judgment for a contested action.

3. Estate of Bonnie L. Barge v. Commissioner (TCM 1997-188).

of the interest or from the beginning of the lawsuit (or from a point somewhere in between).

A potential lawsuit can have a direct effect on the purchasing decision because onerous conditions typically associated with partition lawsuits would likely reduce the size of the possible market for an undivided interest and would also increase the applicable discount. For a relatively low-value interest, the potential cost can constitute such a large portion of its value that the interest holder would be effectively dissuaded from taking any action.

Other issues are also associated with forcing a sale. A sale that occurs less than a year after the interest is acquired would not qualify for long-term capital gains treatment. In most cases, this scenario effectively places a one-year floor on the holding period. Tax on gain achieved in capturing the discount can be effectively avoided by the owner of the 100% fee through exchange. To defer their tax liability, a high percentage of income property investors prefer a tax-free exchange rather than an outright sale. If two or more co-owners hold title as tenants-in-common, the IRS may deem the owners partners in a partnership for tax purposes. If they exchange into different properties, the exchange may then be partially or fully taxable.[4] If an action is brought to force a sale, an exchange may be prevented altogether. This situation suggests that cooperation rather than confrontation is the most likely scenario and that the influence of an interest holder who does not want to sell right away may be great. The decisions that a buyer of a common tenancy interest must make throughout the holding period are driven by the possibility of a need to sell the interest and bring a partition action. These decisions are illustrated graphically in Figure 8.1.

The decision tree summarizes the buyer's decision-making process before and after purchase until the pro rata share of the property is realized. (Letters reference Figure 8.1.)

A. Motivation, i.e., whether to invest in the property to hold for a particular period (T), or maximize profit by exercising the right to partition.

B. The investment period holding loop. No change occurs unless the buyer's circumstances change and he or she wishes to sell.

C. What will it take to realize the pro rata share? If the other cotenants agree, then the holder of the interest can sell. If they do not, is the buyer's share worth enough to make a court action feasible? If not, return to B.

---

4. It may also be taxable on the basis of the recapture of depreciation. Common tenancy is not a partnership by its nature, but it can easily become one. Revenue Procedure 2002-22 specifies the conditions under which the IRS will consider a request for a ruling on the subject. This is a complex area of practice that always requires qualified professional assistance. It is mentioned only to suggest that the exchange issue may be an important investment consideration in acquiring a common tenancy interest.

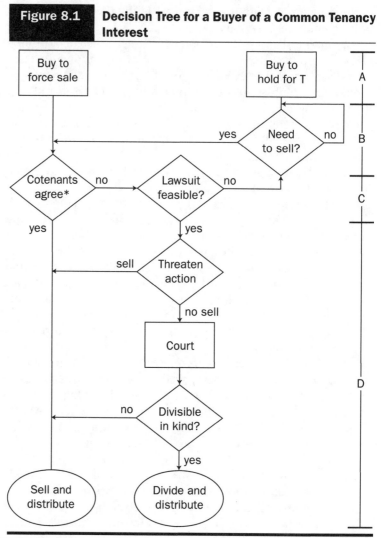

Figure 8.1 Decision Tree for a Buyer of a Common Tenancy Interest

* To sell or buy out subject interest

D. The decisions are directly related to the partition process, showing only the most basic decisions.

A Single Step for Developing the Discount

In the introduction of this book, the Levels of Value diagram (Figure I.2 on page 5) was presented to illustrate a two-step discounting process for closely held corporations and partnerships that are structured to take advantage of transactional data available from public markets in developing the discounts for lack of control and lack of marketability. The challenge in applying this process for common tenancy interest valuation is that the conceptual "minority-marketable" level is not applicable for common tenancy; its minority or control attributes are not directly comparable with the minority attributes of entities traded in public markets.

Because of this limitation, it is most appropriate to analyze only a single step, which entails either:

- Developing a discount for lack of control with a smaller impaired marketability component, or
- Developing a discount for lack of marketability with a smaller impaired control component

While it is possible to develop the discount by applying discounts for each element that influences value, it would not work very well with available market data and would not lead to a useful analysis.

Market Data Sources for Developing the Discount

Although it may seem that skipping the minority-marketable level would reduce the number of data sources that can be applied for developing common tenancy discounts, this is not the case. Possible data sources include direct sales of fractional interests, partition time-and-cost data, restricted stock and pre-IPO study data, option trading data, partnership trading data, and data from sales of private partnership interests.

Direct sales of fractional interests. The discount can be developed by analyzing the sales of fractional interests in comparable properties. Although these are often cited as the most desirable data, the method can be difficult and laborious and is often hampered by insufficient local data to support the analysis. Discount surveys are included in this category and can often be used to support conclusions reached by other methods.

Partition time and cost data. The discount can also be developed from an analysis of the time and cost required to bring legal action to force sale, or subdivide the property. Through this action the interest holder hopes to realize its pro rata share of the whole.

Restricted stock and pre-IPO study data. These data, introduced in the partnership scenario, can be used as a proxy for the circumstances that influence a buyer of the common tenancy interest. Direct comparison is specious since there are so many major differences between public companies' restricted shares and common tenancy interests. However, analysis of the Management Planning Study data and use of the FMV Restricted Stock Study™ would allow for more precise application of the data and might be used as a supplemental method.

Options trading models. Another possibility for developing the discount is to view a common tenancy interest in the context of a hypothetical put option, i.e., today's cost to buy the right to sell the interest at a particular future date for a specified amount.

Partnership trading data. Partnership trading data require the interpretation of the valuation problem as a control issue. The data most directly applicable for this purpose are trades that involve short expected holding periods. For longer holds, the superior control exercisable by the owner of a common tenancy interest becomes a significant problem.

Sales of private partnership interests. Much like private interest sales, sales of private partnership interests allow for direct comparison. The challenge in using this approach to estimate the discount lies in developing points of comparison and making the required adjustments.

For all the market data sources described, the data model a three-step sequence: purchase, hold, and realize pro rata value. The data most illustrative of this process are the restricted stock and pre-IPO studies introduced in Chapter 5. Figure 8.2, shows the comparison between publicly traded interests and common tenancy interests in real estate.[5]

Figure 8.2	Common Tenancy Discounting Process

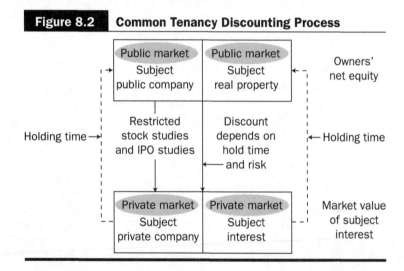

Figure 8.2 shows the marketability discount step on the left, and a parallel step on the right. The top of the figure is the public level, and the bottom is the private level. The discount depends on the holding time and risk for both private securities and private common tenancy interests. In time, both types of private interests carry an expectation that they will realize their pro rata share of the top-level value, either by achieving liquidity, or through sale of the underlying asset or security.

The discounting process for common tenancy interests shown is based, in this case, on marketability. The effects of

5. Figure 8.2 is concerned primarily with liquidity, and its top level collapses the top half of the two-step discounting flow chart of Figure 1.2 into a single level. This is an oversimplification meant to show liquidity issues in isolation, and is not intended to imply equivalency between real property asset value (control level) and the public securities markets (minority level). A cotenancy interest is subject to limited control impairment, addressed as an adjustment in this "marketability-centered" process, rather than as a separate discounting step.

impaired control can be
incorporated within this
step because they are
relatively small, and
showing a minority-mar-
ketable "level" would be
meaningless.[6]

> *The income approach can be applied the same way that it was applied to develop the discount for lack of marketability when valuing the partnership interest.*

Sales Comparison and Related Methods

Most of the methods for developing this discount demonstrate the process of Figure 8.2. Whether direct sales of similar property interests (individual transactions or studies of transactions) or proxy sales (restricted stock and pre-IPO studies), pricing is based on an explicit or implicit holding period and perception of risk. If liquidation is expected, even public partnership interest transactions can be described in the same terms. Options analysis demonstrates this principle as well. Thus, all methods can be used to analyze such a discount, provided that the basis for comparison is clearly stated and properly applied to the subject common tenancy interest.

The Income Approach

The income approach can be applied the same way that it was applied to develop the discount for lack of marketability when valuing the partnership interest. In that scenario, the notion of a discount affected by holding time and risk was analyzed using simple present value analysis, where the interest holder is compensated for assuming the greater risk of receiving a cash return in the form of price appreciation at the end of the holding period and dividends or distributions during the period. This method can model an investor's objectives for partnership interest as well as a common tenancy one. The partition time-and-cost method is also an income approach, which differs only in the process of developing cash flows.

Value-Influencing Elements

Many value-influencing elements have already been incorporated in the analysis at the asset level. However, unlike the limited partnership scenario, no analysis for a discount for lack of control has been performed. To make a clear and convincing presentation of the analysis, it is important to clarify and extract the elements that influence the discount. These value-influencing elements are of two basic types: those that affect the expected holding period and those that affect exposure to risk during the period. Other factors may be relevant, depending on the facts and circumstances concerning the

---

6. It is also possible to adopt the control step as dominant using partnership data to develop the discount, and then adjust for lack of marketability.

subject property. Many of these elements are identical to those of the limited partnership scenario–particularly those that pertain to the real estate property itself. The next two case study applications will pull together and resolve holding period and risk exposure issues.

CASE STUDY APPLICATION

Analyzing Facts and Circumstances to Estimate the Holding Period

A long holding period dramatically increases the discount for impaired marketability. For this reason, the length of a holding period must be justified. The numbered items in the facts and circumstances that follow are repeated from the case study application estimating the holding period section in Chapter 5. To emphasize the differences between partnership interests and common tenancy interests, the text that does not apply to a common tenancy interest appears in strikeout type, and text that was added and applies to a common tenancy interest rather than partnership interests appears in brackets.

Real Property

Leases Due	Leases on a large portion of the rentable area are coming due in 2000, and rents are above market levels. This suggests that a sale is likely when income is still high or after the situation stabilizes three to four years after the date of value (probably late in 2000) if ~~management wishes~~ the cotenants wish to sell.
Developable Land	If the extra land were to be developed, a sale would probably occur after its occupancy is stabilized. [Any interest can effectively block development, so the point of an irrational development may be moot.]
Holding Period	A call to the real estate appraiser established that the typical holding period for buyers of three-story multitenant office buildings is five to 15 years, but most often 10 years.
Loan Agreement	The loan is due (in 2002) approximately five years from the date of value. It would make sense to refinance, since the interest rate is high. If the balloon needs to be paid, then it might require a ~~capital call~~ [voluntary contribution of capital] or sale of the property.
	Additional influences are associated with the ~~Partnership Agreement and the~~ facts and circumstances of the limited partnership scenario.

Ownership

Termination of Partnership	~~The Partnership terminates on July 23, 2043.~~
Interest's Degree of Control	~~John Builder's interest does not have sufficient control to cause termination of the partnership, or sale of any of its assets.~~
Sales History	The family has never sold a property. Since John's death, family members have been debating whether selling properties would be a good idea.

Management	The partnership has new management, and Billy appears to want to develop the extra land. Billy's intentions beyond that are not clear. [We do not know what Billy's intentions or abilities are. He can be blocked, but what would it take for a new cotenant to have an influence on management?]
Ownership Control	It is not clear what Sara's husband might want to do. ~~This is important because Sara controls half of the stock in the General Partnership~~. [We were concerned about the general partner, in particular, in the earlier situation because this partner had control. We are now concerned about everyone's intentions because they all can affect decisions by withholding cooperation.]
Liquid Assets	The estate has substantial liquid assets and does not need to sell any properties to pay taxes.

The following considerations are added for the common tenancy scenario. These are not so much facts as probable occurrences based on the valuer's understanding of the likely market for the interest.

- What would be the initial holding time objective for a buyer of the subject interest?
- Would the subject interest be purchased for liquidation as quickly as possible, or would the buyer have an investment objective? If the latter, what might that objective be?
- What is the chance that all cotenants would be willing to sell the property?
- If it becomes necessary to sue, is a lawsuit likely to be opposed?
- If it is opposed, how much would the suit likely cost? Can the interest holder afford to sue, given the value of the interest? How would this influence the decision to sue and the estimated holding time?

Analysis and Conclusions

Because the leases are expected to turn over in three years, a valuer would not normally expect that a sale, if intended, would occur until it is re-leased in about four or five years.

The loan is due in five years. Refinancing may be difficult, since the cotenants (now several more than the original two) may have to agree to be jointly and severally liable for a new loan, regardless of the size of their interest (unless a nonrecourse loan can be negotiated), or agree to pay off the $1.82 million loan balance. Five years is probably an upper limit for the holding period for this reason.

Billy may still wish to pursue the construction project on the extra land, but it seems like the family, and possibly Sara's husband, would wish to discourage it because it does not appear to be a good idea economically. In any case, a single interest can block capital expenditures.

A new owner could try to convince the others to sell right away, but it is unlikely that Billy would agree since he is the property manager and has development plans. The other cotenants probably would not readily agree either. Given this situation, it might be in the new owner's best interest to hold on for at least the three- to four-year period. Any of the cotenants could initiate a partition suit at any time, but it appears that the family members have sufficient resources to make a lawsuit difficult and expensive, or to counter with a lawsuit of their own, if they chose to do so. A two- to three-year delay in filing a lawsuit would not be unusual, and it would be close to the four-year horizon. Further, a lawsuit could place property management in the hands of a court-appointed referee, who may or may not be competent to handle lease turnover.

Ed's interest has a low tax basis because he was an original owner, and he (or whoever manages his affairs) would be reluctant to allow an outright sale of the property and its recapture because holding the interest until Ed dies would give his heirs a stepped-up basis. Consequently, they may be willing to fight.

A costly legal battle would consume a significant percentage of any discount. The pro rata interest is worth $1,428,000 × 0.20, or $285,600, and a $30,000 to $50,000 fight would consume 10.5% to 17.5% of the value of the interest.

On balance, it appears that the leasing would be completed and the mortgage balloon would increase the pressure on all the cotenants to sell. Thus, a holding period of five years is concluded.

CASE STUDY APPLICATION

Identifying Value-Influencing Elements

As in the partnership application in Chapter 5, some value-influencing elements affect only the underlying asset value, some affect the discount, and some have not been addressed yet. The valuation levels at which each item has been assessed are indicated by the checked boxes. General comments are intended to have specific application to the case study.

Value Level:	Asset (*NAV*)	Discount	Other
§4.0 1 (a): The nature of the business and the history of the enterprise from its inception			
Property type	☑	☑	☐

This element might influence the discount if a sales comparison approach is used to develop it, as would be the case if data were derived from differing property types. Property types might also be an issue in the partition time-and-cost method, but it would not influence the income approach to developing the discount.

	Asset (*NAV*)	Discount	Other
Asset diversification	☐	☑	☐

The subject interest is in a single property, but this element might influence the discount if market data were derived from partnerships that hold multiple properties or other assets.

	Asset (*NAV*)	Discount	Other
History of real estate	☑	☐	☐
History of cash flow (*NOI*)	☑	☐	☐

History of the property itself is addressed in the real estate appraisal.

	Asset (*NAV*)	Discount	Other
History of distributions	☐	☑	☐

Because cash flow cannot be accumulated for other uses without every cotenant's approval, there should be little or no difference between distributions and real estate cash flow (less debt service). Real estate appraisals are typically forward looking, so distribution history will probably not play a part in the interest valuation. However, it could be an issue in comparing the subject interest to other properties or to entities that have substantially different distribution histories. A history of improper withholding of distributions would be an important issue to cotenants.

Value Level:	Asset (*NAV*)	Discount	Other

§4.0 1 (b): The economic outlook in general, and the condition and outlook of the specific industry in particular

	Asset (*NAV*)	Discount	Other
General economic conditions	☑	☐	☐
Real estate market conditions	☑	☐	☐

Both elements are typically covered in the asset appraisal. These influences might be included at other levels if an independent effect can be demonstrated.

	Asset (*NAV*)	Discount	Other
Long-term growth	☑	☑	☐

Growth is implicit in the asset value and may have been made explicit if a discounted cash flow model was used. The discount analysis based on the income approach considers growth over the expected holding period, regardless of how asset value was developed, and requires growth expectations for that specific period. Cash flow growth may be dictated partly by lease terms, but also by the expectations of market participants (unless the lease term will extend beyond the holding period). Value growth applies for the value of the asset at the end of the term. The relative importance of growth depends on the expected holding period.

§4.0 1 (c): Book value of the (stock) and financial condition

	Asset (*NAV*)	Discount	Other
Value of real estate	☑	☑	☐

Owners' equity (*NAV*) was arrived at by adjusting the balance sheet, primarily for the real estate and financing. Book value can also mean relative size, and the size of the interest may be considered in several of the approaches to discount value.

	Asset (*NAV*)	Discount	Other
Leverage	☐	☑	☐

The owners' mortgage debt plays no part in valuation of the property because the appraisal assumes new ownership, and its purpose is to value the real estate, not the equity. The effects of debt on financial condition also were not addressed when determining owners' net equity. (Cash flow after debt service is the principal determinant of financial condition.)

The influence of problem conditions associated with a mortgage loan would usually be considered in the holding time analysis, but a requirement that the new owner also guarantee the loan, for example, could also be included as a risk element in the discount analysis. Issues pertaining to a loan would normally be known before a prospective buyer would purchase such an interest because liability for 100% of the loan, when one owns only 20% of the equity, can be very risky. Whether a loan assumption would be nonrecourse for the buyer of the interest may not be clear to the valuer even after examining all the loan documents because the lender would not have been asked to allow a transfer of the loan to the new interest holder at the time. Whether the seller can be released is another matter that might not be resolved for the valuation. Prepayment penalties might be invoked by a due-on-sale clause, depending on the mortgage provisions. It may be reasonable to retain a financing expert to issue an opinion because of these concerns.

§4.0 1 (e): Earning and dividend-paying capacity

	Asset (*NAV*)	Discount	Other
Current and future *NOI*	☑	☐	☐
Earnings growth	☑	☐	☐

Earning capacity and growth were considered in the asset appraisal (*NOI*), and at the equity level (earnings).

	Asset (*NAV*)	Discount	Other
Current and future distributions	☐	☑	☐

Value Level:	Asset (*NAV*)	Discount	Other
Distribution growth	☐	☑	☐

Earnings and distributions are almost synonymous for common tenancy interests. Growth is related to *NOI* and may be increased for debt leverage. Capital expenditures must be approved by all cotenants.

Growth should be adjusted to the time horizon expected for the common tenancy interest, which may require different assumptions than those used in the real estate appraisal.

§4.0 1 (g): The sales of (common tenancy interests) and size of the block to be valued (control associated with the interest)

Sales of interests	☐	☐	☑

Historical sales should be disclosed and analyzed. The case study considered John Builder's purchase of a 10% interest from Ed Helper in 1995 and concluded that it was bought at a deliberately high price. If the transaction provided a useful value indication under the appropriate definition of value, it would be reconciled with the final value conclusion.

Degree of control	☐	☑	☐

A common tenancy interest can influence meaningful decisions related to control. Such an interest has a substantial degree of negative control because it can block nearly all important decisions. It can also bring a partition lawsuit, potentially shortening the holding time. However, such an interest also exhibits a significant lack of control because cooperation with others is required. The interest in the partnership scenario had no meaningful control, but the interest in the common tenancy does. How much more, and to what extent the control can be meaningfully exercised are important questions that the valuer should consider.

The ability to force a sale exists, but its effect on control is related to the practicality of bringing a partition action. The more feasible the lawsuit option, the more effective the control that accrues to the interest, since threatening to sue is likely to be taken seriously. This condition is largely accounted for in the holding time analysis, but to the extent that it may increase influence with the cotenants, control may be increased.

Management issues are partly covered under business/management risk and primarily concern the managerial abilities of others, not whether the subject interest holder would be managing the property. In this common tenancy case, the ability to block capital expenditures is the most important value-influencing element because Billy plans to undertake a questionable activity, which can be blocked. This represents significantly more control than could be exercised by a minority common stockholder or limited partner.

Although control is gained (compared to the minority-marketable level), it is also lost, since another control issue is the potential for more, unknown cotenants. Common tenancy interests can be transferred, in whole or part, to anyone without notice. A case in point would be a cotenant who tries to persuade others to sell their interests and who is confronted with a list of small interest holders, all of whom would have to be sued to enforce the right to partition. Additionally, when Ed Helper dies, his estate could be distributed to heirs who may or may not be known at the date of value (see due diligence below). The element of control is affected further by whether due diligence efforts concerning Ed's successors have been adequately performed. If they haven't, an adjustment for this element may be necessary.

Partnerships have a process for admitting new limited partners that largely eliminates uncertainty, and the limited partners have little control anyway. In the common tenancy structure, the potential for future transfers to unknown parties is an out-of-control problem.

Value Level:	Asset (*NAV*)	Discount	Other
Size of the block	❏	❏	❏

Fractional interests are not publicly traded, so blockage issues—the ability of the market to absorb a large block of shares—do not apply. This element could apply to a portfolio of properties, but a common tenancy interest concerns only a single property, not a portfolio.

Restrictive agreements

This element is not applicable to the common tenancy scenario because there is no agreement, and common tenancy interests are freely transferable. If there were an agreement between cotenants, any of the elements listed in the case study application identifying value-influencing elements in Chapter 5 might apply, affecting all the other elements in this list.

Unclassified Elements

Holding period uncertainty	❏	☑	❏

Most common tenancy interests are characterized by considerable uncertainty. The right to partition is a powerful tool for forcing one's will and shortening the holding period, but its use can be costly and impractical. Uncertainty should be evaluated based on the facts and always considered as part of the discount analysis. Even assuming a short holding period and the possibility of a partition lawsuit, a small change in the expected holding period can produce a significant change in value.

Due diligence requirement	❏	☑	❏

Due diligence requirements add cost and are normally an increased source of risk. Adequate due diligence is typically undertaken by the buyer of the fee interest, but its value is much greater than the value of a small fraction, and costs can be a significant burden. However, various potential risks (e.g., toxic mold, hidden seismic damage, poor soils, wood-destroying organisms) may not be disclosed for a transfer of fractional interest, and can be difficult to detect.

Because owners may be jointly and severally liable for any consequences (e.g., a serious health problem that can result from undetected toxic mold), liability can be far out of proportion to the value and potential benefits of ownership of a small interest.

Understanding one's cotenants is also more important for common tenancy ownership than for a partnership because each cotenant wields influence, and each would have to be served in a partition action. Useful information may or may not be supplied by the available cotenants, and the cost of investigations could be substantial. Investigations can be forgone, but without knowing the others cotenants, risk is increased, possibly offsetting any cost savings. If cotenants are geographically dispersed, the problem is compounded.

Ownership distribution is known, but if Ed dies, unknown cotenant heirs could become cotenants. Their identities may be known or may require investigation, which would incur additional due diligence costs. (Unknown cotenants were considered under the degree of control section, but this section focuses on known or predictable cotenants, since there would be a way to learn their identities.)

The pro rata value of the subject interest is sufficiently high (about $285,000) that due diligence costs could be insignificant, as long as adequate disclosures are forthcoming. However, a cost adjustment can be made as long as it does not double count any allowances for due diligence implicit in the valuation of the underlying assets. Alternatively, it can be assumed that there would be little or no due diligence investigation, and the valuer can adjust for the resulting uncertainty.

Value Level:	Asset (*NAV*)	Discount	Other
Business/management risk	☐	☑	☐

Unless the cotenants have executed a controlling document, management requires continuous agreement, and the potential for conflicts is ever present. On the one hand, a measure of control is implicit in any interest because of the ability of the interest holder to block undesired decisions; on the other hand, the ability of any interest to exercise that authority can create management impasses and impair the economic performance of the property.

Problems are compounded when significant decisions are pending (such as the expected lease turnover or potential for extra land development). A lawsuit may solve the problem after a judgment is rendered, but management by a court-appointed referee may introduce a new risk. These management issues would not have been considered in the asset valuation because development of a control-level value assumes new management.

Other conditions	☐	☑	☐

This adjustment is reserved for situations that exhibit onerous conditions for an investor beyond those that have been identified above. This category can include pending or probable lawsuits. If the holding period is assumed to be controlled by an expected partition action, an onerous condition would almost certainly exist (unless it can be shown that the market for the interest would be unaffected by the prospect of bringing legal action). Thus, it appears reasonable to consider a lawsuit as prima facie onerous. It is also possible that a cotenant's need to become a nuisance to assert its rights if a lawsuit is not feasible would be viewed as onerous by potential buyers.

Additionally, the real estate may exhibit problems, such as stigma, that might not have been captured in the real estate appraisal due to lack of market support, but that would add to its undesirability for the fractional interest holder in a manner similar to out-of-favor properties for public partnerships. These real estate problems apparently do not apply in this case.

Selecting Value-Influencing Elements

There is sometimes greater potential for double counting value-influencing elements for common tenancy interests than for partnership interests because of the potential for negative control—the power of the cotenant to block important decisions pertaining to the property. Thus, it is important for the valuer to clarify the qualities that are attributed to each element and generate a list for analysis. These elements include only discount-influencing elements, so sales of interests are not included but are considered separately at the end of the valuation analysis. The selected elements in their approximate order of importance for application to this case study are:

- Current and future distributions
- Degree of control:
  - Implicit (negative voting rights)
  - Future/unknown cotenants
- Holding period uncertainty
- Long-term growth

- Business/management risk
- Other conditions–potential lawsuits
- Distribution growth
- Due diligence requirement

The elements that were already considered in the holding period analysis are value of the interest, financing/leverage, and control/ability to force a sale.

Income Approach

The income approach allows direct analysis of holding period and risk and can be applied for developing the discount for the subject common tenancy interest in the same manner in which it was applied to develop the discount for impaired marketability for the partnership. The income approach requires a yield rate for equity, adjusted from the asset-level (real property) base yield. The yield rate at the equity level is approximately the same as the yield rate at the asset level if there is no debt, if other assets and liabilities are insignificant, and if other income and expense items that exhibit their own growth patterns are also insignificant. Under these conditions, equity and asset yields are similar.

If there is debt ownership, the yield to all invested capital must be divided between equity and debt, which is often accomplished using a mortgage equity, or band-of-investment technique, or by calculating the weighted average cost of capital *(WACC)*. Generally, this technique is applicable to single-period (direct capitalization) rates, but should *not* be used to calculate an equity yield where debt exhibits a declining balance over time, as for a mortgage loan. The most appropriate method in this instance is to use a discounted cash flow model (see Table 8.1, Owners' Discounted Cash Flow) and calculate the internal rate of return *(IRR)* to equity as the yield to equity.

CASE STUDY APPLICATION
Calculating Yield and Growth Rates

The *IRR* is calculated on cash flows received at the end of each period. The concluded *IRR* of 12.0% is the same as the valuer's asset "discount" rate of 12.0% (see Table 8.1), first decreased because cash flow is decreased, then increased because the debt yield (interest) rate is 10.75%. (Leverage increases yield, and the two conditions offset each other.) If the interest rate were reduced to 9.25%, for example, cash flow to the equity position would be greater, and the *IRR* would increase to 14.4%.

The holding period must be the same as that concluded for the real estate appraisal of the subject interest. If the real estate appraisal used a different holding period, then the holding period for the discount valuation must be changed accordingly. The concluded yield and growth from the income approach are summarized in Table 8.2.

Table 8.1   Owners' Discounted Cash Flow

Period		1996 Year 0	1997 Year 1	1998 Year 2	1999 Year 3	2000 Year 4	2001 Year 5	2002 Year 6
Real estate appraisal								
NOI		$311,256	$344,565	$355,208	$355,672	$300,961	$345,033	$379,758
Reversion								$3,490,156
Adjustments								
Add back forecast management fee			$20,649	$21,268	$21,420	$19,101	$21,150	
Less fee at current rate	7.5%		(34,415)	(35,447)	(35,699)	(31,836)	(35,250)	
Total owners' income			$330,799	$341,029	$341,392	$288,227	$330,933	
Other expenses								
General and administrative	2.0%		280	286	291	297	303	
Debt service			221,011	221,011	221,011	221,011	221,011	
Total owners' expenses			221,291	221,297	221,302	221,308	221,314	
Cash flow			$109,508	$119,733	$120,090	$66,919	$109,618	
Reversion								
Real property								$3,490,156
Loan balance		$(1,816,278)					(1,646,703)	
Assets-liabilities								(5,668)

Net owners'
  equity (present/
  future)
		$1,428,054						$1,837,786

Conclusions								
Cash flows		$(1,428,054)	$109,508	$119,733	$120,090	$66,919	$1,974,404	
IRR	12.0%							
Growth rate calculations								
Value @ year end (approx.)		$1,428,054					$1,837,786	
Annual compounded value growth*	5.2%	$1,428,054	$1,501,947	$1,579,664	$1,661,402	$1,747,370	$1,837,786	
Cash flow			$109,508	$119,733	$120,090	$66,919	$109,618	
Cash flow change, annual				9.34%	0.30%	-44.28%	63.81%	
Annual cash flow during year			$109,508				$109,618	

Annual compounded
  cash flow growth*
  (straight-line
  approximation)
	0.0%		$109,508	$109,536	$109,563	$109,591	$109,618	

* Values in Years 1 through 4 illustrate the compounding process, but do not imply intermediate value conclusions.

Table 8.2   Yield and Growth Rates

Level	Asset	Equity
Value	$3,250,000	$1,428,054
Yield	12.0%	12.0%
Value growth	1.4%	5.2%
Cash flow growth	0.03%	0.0%

   The preceding discounted cash flow analysis generates growth and yield rates directly. Other income methods can be used for this case, and more simply with other cases that do not include financing, but some of the needed rates must be calculated differently. The cash flow model requires a yield rate, as well as distribution and growth rates, appropriate for this level of value. The partnership version of this topic was presented in Chapter 5. Formulas and commentary for common tenancy are similar, except that they reflect the one-step analytical process rather than the two-step process that was used for the partnership.

Cash Flow/Distribution Rate

The owners' net equity shows forecast equity cash flow and calculates the equity cash flow rate as:

$$R_{EQUITY} = CF_{EQUITY} / V_{EQUITY}$$

Cash Flow/Distribution Growth

The growth rate for cash flow at the equity level is approximately the same as the growth rate for cash flow expected for the real property with no debt, if other assets and liabilities are insignificant and if other income and expense items that exhibit their own growth patterns are also insignificant. (This is not true for the case study, but is often true in common tenancy situations.) Under these conditions:

$$G_{CF \ (APPROX)} = G_{NOI}$$

If there are other significant line items on the income statement, the approximate rate of annual increase at the equity level is changed by the ratio of *NOI* to cash flow:

$$G_{CF \ (APPROX)} = G_{NOI} \times NOI / CF_{EQUITY}$$

The growth rates (both G_{NOI} and G_{CF}) are calculated directly from the owners' discounted cash flow model to account for the irregular expected rental income and the effect of the large, but constant debt service amount. (Without debt and irregular cash flows, G_{CF} could be calculated directly, using the formula.)

Value Growth

Equity value growth will not differ much from real estate value growth if there is no debt, if other assets and liabilities are not significant, and if other income and expense items that exhibit their own growth patterns are also insignificant. (This is not true for this particular case, but is often true in common tenancy situations.) Under these conditions:

$$G_{EQUITY \ APPROX} = G_{RE}$$

If there are other significant line items, the approximate rate of annual increase at the equity level is changed by the ratio of *NOI* to cash flow, plus growth from other sources (in this case, from paying down debt):

$$G_{EQ\,APPROX} = G_{RE} \times V_{RE} / V_{EQUITY} + G_{DEBT}$$

This simplified calculation does not capture the effect of all the items that affect value growth and is only an approximation. When significant debt is involved, errors can be large, and it is better to prepare a simple discounted cash flow model and develop the rates directly and explicitly. This case study incorporates a large mortgage loan, so these rates will be taken entirely from an explicit discounted cash flow model.

The next step is to make adjustments to the yield rate to get R_p the investor's required rate. Adjustments are made for elements that increase risk for the holder of the illiquid interest and should be relatively small, unless support can be found for larger adjustments.

Yield Rate Buildup and Discount Calculations

The remaining analysis follows the same process as in Chapter 5, pages 139–147.

CASE STUDY APPLICATION

Using the Build-up Method to Obtain the Investor's Required Rate

Asset level yield rate for owners' DCF model	12.0%

Adjustments:

Holding period uncertainty	+ 1.0%

A holding period of five years was selected, but actual hold time could vary from four to six years. The shorter period would reduce risk, but another year would increase risk. A valuation spreadsheet model can be used to develop a risk premium necessary to produce the same discount as a holding period increase to six years. In this case, the premium would be 1.5%. Reducing the holding period to four years is equivalent to –1.5%. For the case study, five years are assumed, not four or six. A reduced probability of each decreases the range to ±1.0% or less. The conclusion is based on these ranges–debatable, but within reasonable boundaries.

Due diligence requirement	+ 0.3%

The real estate is relatively simple and requires no more investigation than normal. Thus, an allowance covering due diligence cost is implicit in the real estate value conclusion. There is no indication that undisclosed or undetected toxic mold or hazards are present, and the pro rata value of the subject interest is sufficient to cover the investigation of any such issues.

The attitudes of the cotenants, including Ed Helper's potential successors, should be investigated. (The possibility of additional cotenants depends upon whether Ed dies during the holding period.)

Because some uncertainty remains, a small adjustment to the yield rate is made for added risk. If the due diligence concerns were more complex, it might be worth estimating their costs, adjusting for any amount implicit in the real estate appraisal and deducting the excess directly.

Business/management risk	+ 0.5%

Because all cotenants must approve capital expenditures, the issue of Billy's plans to undertake questionable activities is less important. Expertise would still be needed to manage lease turnover, however, and Billy may be capable. If not, the subject interest-holder may be able to exert some influence.

If a partition action is initiated, potential problems increase. The valuer in this case is assuming only a chance of a lawsuit, however, so the possibility of a court-appointed referee is remote, although it still exists.

Business management risk was the largest adjustment for the partnership valuation, but for the common tenancy valuation it is less important.

Leverage

At a loan-to-value ratio of 56%, leverage is well within the market range; therefore, no added risk would be imputed. However, there would be risk if there were a requirement that the new cotenant guarantee the loan. It has been assumed that the existing loan would allow substitute cotenants, and the loan-related issues discussed in the case study application "Identifying Value-Influencing Elements" would not apply to the common tenancy valuation. An examination of the loan documents, and the engagement of a loan consultant if necessary, may be the best course of action in many cases.

Degree of control	+ 2.5%

There are two aspects to the degree of control. The first is *negative control*, and the second is *potential unknown and/or additional cotenants*. The subject interest has a considerable degree of negative control, which is most meaningful insofar as capital expenditures are concerned. However, the ability of a cotenant to threaten a partition action should also provide some enhanced control. Cooperation among the cotenants is assumed as the most likely outcome for the case study, reducing the potential benefit of a partition action.

An extreme case of control impairment is a typical limited partner in a large public partnership. Impairment of a cotenant's control as great as that of a typical limited partner could require a yield rate increase of 4.0% to 6.5%.[7] The subject interest has significantly

---

7. If this case were a partnership, its discount for lack of control would be between 25% and 35%. (The analysis could use the partnership case, but the valuer would not normally have gone through that analysis, and this instance requires only an order-of-magnitude estimate.) As in Chapter 5, the discount increases the yield rate for the minority interest. The yield rate increase (R_2) for the two control discounts (A and B) can be calculated as follows:

$$R_2 = R_1 / (1 - Dc) - R_1$$
$$R_{2A} = 0.120 / (1 - 0.250) - 0.120 = 0.160 - 0.120 = 0.040$$
$$R_{2B} = 0.120 / (1 - 0.350) - 0.120 = 0.185 - 0.120 = 0.065$$

greater control than a limited partnership interest, but its effective control is limited because the other cotenants also have greater control. (The interest gets a vote, but it is only one of five).

A lawsuit option is somewhat feasible, enhancing the subject interest's control, particularly in relationship to lower-value interests for which a lawsuit would be out of the question. Also, some attributes of control have been accounted for elsewhere. It's important to decide how much control impairment remains of the 4.0% to 6.5% on the yield rate that would represent nearly 100% impairment. In this case it might be as little as one-third, or 1.3% to 2.2%.

The potential for unknown and/or additional cotenants raises uncertainty that is more important to ownership under common tenancy than under the partnership. The known potential transfer of interest to Ed Helper's heirs was considered part of the due diligence adjustment, but the potential for more, unknown, cotenants remains. The prospect of this becoming a problem would increase if relations among the cotenants turn acrimonious and the interest holder expects that the resolution will be a partition action. As a result, an increase in the adjustment for risk is needed to compensate for the uncertainty.

Adjusting for all these elements, some of which offset each other, can be a challenge for the business valuer. One way of zeroing in on such an estimate is to start with obvious upper and lower limits; in this case, no more than the 4.0% to 6.5%, but the increase should be greater than zero. For the case study, a 2.0% adjustment is made for negative control, and a 0.5% adjustment is made for potential unknown and/or additional cotenants, resulting in a total adjustment of 2.5%.[8]

Restrictive agreement	+ 0.0%

The case scenario for common tenancy interests has no agreement, so no adjustment is made.

Other conditions	+ 1.0%

The analysis has demonstrated that purchasing an undivided common tenancy interest in real estate can require a particular temperament on the part of the buyer because of the possibility that he or she would be purchasing a lawsuit. A lawsuit would not necessarily control the expected holding time, but the threat of one might have to be invoked. The possibility of a buyer having to face a lawsuit at all, or even the need to become a nuisance to produce a desired result contributes to a condition for which an adjustment should be made.

Concluded investor's required rate, R_I	17.3%

---

8. This adjustment answers the question that was raised with the original Levels of Value diagram (Figure I.2): What happened to the minority-marketable level, for which control but not marketability is impaired? The answer is not that it disappeared, but that the meaning of using a hypothetical level is lost. The influence of impaired control can be recaptured by adjusting for its effect on risk in the same way as adjustments are made for other elements of comparison.

CASE STUDY APPLICATION

Calculating the Discount Using Formulas

The data used in the cash flow model and the owner's discounted cash flow model were presented earlier in this chapter. The Quantitative Marketability Discount Model was introduced in Chapter 5. Each of the three methods can be applied to derive a discount for the subject common tenancy interest.

The common tenancy case has an estimated holding period of five years. Its annual cash flow is 5.2%, growing at the concluded rate of 0.0% per year. The value of the owner's equity is growing at 5.2% per year. The discount is calculated using the formulas from page 141–142 for the diagram in Figure 8.3.

Figure 8.3	Cash Flow Diagram

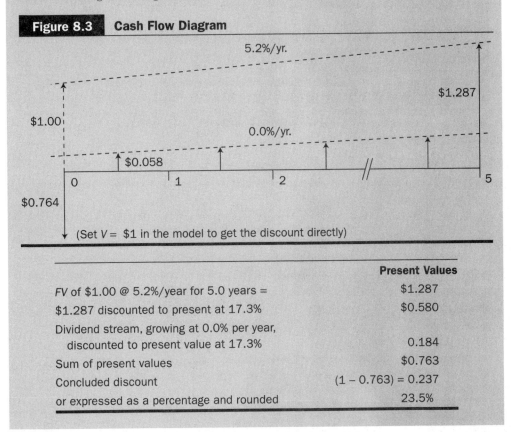

(Set $V = \$1$ in the model to get the discount directly)

	Present Values
FV of $1.00 @ 5.2%/year for 5.0 years =	$1.287
$1.287 discounted to present at 17.3%	$0.580
Dividend stream, growing at 0.0% per year, discounted to present value at 17.3%	0.184
Sum of present values	$0.763
Concluded discount	$(1 - 0.763) = 0.237$
or expressed as a percentage and rounded	23.5%

CASE STUDY APPLICATION

Calculating the Discount Using the Quantitative Marketability Discount Model (QMDM)

The common tenancy case study has an estimated holding period of five years. Its annual cash flow is 5.2% growing at a concluded rate 0.0% per year and the value of the owner's equity is growing at 5.2% per year. The required return is 17.3%. The variables in Table 8.3 are close to actual, with the exception of the required return, and the conclusion is between 21% and 27%, interpolated to 24% or 25%. Value growth is understated in the table, and dividend yield is overstated, so this result is not very accurate as a single point. The table is better suited to generating ranges of discount indications. For the subject, this model shows a 4% increase in the discount for a one-year increase in holding period (interpolating halfway between 21%, at 5 years, and 28%, at 7 years).[9, 10]

Table 8.3	Mercer's Quantitative Marketability Discount Model

Expected Growth Rate of Value: 5.00% **Expected Growth Rate of Dividend: 0.00%**

Dividend Yield	Required Return	1	3	5	7	10	15	20	30
		Assumed Holding Periods in Years							
		Implied Marketability Discount							
5.50%	12.0%	1%	4%	8%	11%	16%	25%	31%	41%
	14.0%	3%	9%	15%	20%	27%	37%	44%	53%
	16.0%	5%	13%	21%	28%	36%	47%	54%	61%
	18.0%	6%	18%	27%	35%	44%	55%	61%	67%
	20.0%	8%	21%	32%	41%	51%	61%	66%	71%
	22.0%	9%	25%	37%	46%	56%	66%	70%	74%
	24.0%	11%	28%	41%	51%	61%	70%	74%	76%
	26.0%	12%	32%	45%	55%	65%	73%	76%	78%
	28.0%	14%	35%	49%	59%	68%	76%	79%	80%
	30.0%	15%	37%	52%	62%	71%	78%	80%	82%

9. Dividend yield and growth rate sensitivities can only be judged by examining multiple tables, which is only slightly less convenient.

10. The table demonstrates that the income approach breaks down under extreme conditions, a problem that was discussed in Chapter 5.

Calculating the Discount Using the Owners' DCF Model

Many assignments do not involve discounted cash flow models, but the case used a DCF for several reasons, the most important of which was incorporating the effect of mortgage financing on growth and yield conclusions. Since the model has been constructed, it would also make sense to use it directly.

Table 8.4 Calculating the Discount Using the Owners' DCF Model

Period		1996 Year 0	1997 Year 1	1998 Year 2	1999 Year 3	2000 Year 4	2001 Year 5	2002 Year 6
Cash flow			$109,508	$119,733	$120,090	$66,919	$109,618	
Net owners' equity (present/future)		$1,428,054					$1,837,786	
Cash flows		(1,428,054)	$109,508	$119,733	$120,090	$66,919	$1,947,404	
Subject interest								
Pro rata value	20.0%	$285,611						
Cash flows			$21,902	$23,947	$24,018	$13,384	$389,481	
Present value using investor's required rate	17.3%	$233,413	$18,671	$17,404	$14,881	$7,069	$175,386	
Concluded value (rounded)		$233,000						
Discount for lack of marketability [1 − concluded value /pro rata value]	18.3%							
(rounded)	18.5%							

CASE STUDY APPLICATION

Reconciliation and Conclusions

The results of the three methods of the income approach applied to calculating the discount are shown below:

Method	Formulas	QMDM	DCF
Cash flow (Year 1)	82,509	82,509	109,508
Cash flow rate	5.8%	5.8%	7.7%
Concluded discount	23.0%	26.0%	18.5%

First-year equity cash flow is lower for the single-period analysis because the real estate appraisal included an increased vacancy rate to account for the expected future rent loss, which is an approximation. The discounted cash flow model makes explicit annual cash flow assumptions, but the first years' cash flow viewed alone is too high.

The formula-based model and the QMDM use the same growth rates; only the expression for cash flow varies. The discounted cash flow model produces a higher value conclusion (and lower discount) because the greater cash flows occur in Years 1 to 3, before leases start coming due. The other models assume constant growth. If it were not for the short-term above-market leases, the results of all models would be very close or identical.

The chance that funds will be diverted for Billy's development plan is reduced, since cotenants are supposed to receive pro rata cash flow. (A potential diversion of funds was an issue under the partnership scenario.) However, uncertainty about cash flow remains because of the above-market rent condition and the likelihood that tenants would demand, and get, rent concessions or a break on CAM reimbursements during the lease term. With Billy as the manager, the other owners do not know how he will respond when he faces such decisions. The power to block decisions may or may not be effective.

This problem was addressed by increasing the investor's required rate. However, because the discounted cash flow model indicates a higher value (but lower discount) because of the relatively higher cash flows in Years 1 to 3 (the cash flows that are most vulnerable to such problems), the increase in the required rate might have been greater for the DCF model than for the single-period models. This would have increased its indicated discount.

These issues could be better expressed as probabilities, and a range of value indications may be the more appropriate solution. The Mercer table in the QMDM analysis allows for such a range to be selected by inspection, and the valuer may find this an easier way to present these issues. On the other hand, a value range without some notion of a level of confidence in the result can be difficult to interpret.

Given the results from the three methods for calculating the discount in this case study application, the greatest weight is given to the simplified single-period discounting model.

Concluded discount	21.0%

Partition Time and Cost Method

The cotenant's absolute right to partition is a unique power. Focus on "cost to partition" as a dominant "approach" to value was advocated by the IRS in a private letter ruling,[11] which attempted to establish the cost to partition, i.e., to physically divide the property, as the appropriate method for developing the value of the

---

11. IRS Private Letter Ruling 9336002, "... the present case, the amount of any discount should be limited to the petitioner's share of the estimated cost of a partition of the property."

discount associated with an undivided interest in real estate. There has been a strong reaction from the valuation community on the appropriateness of such a narrow view.[12, 13] (Another private letter ruling in 1999 softened the IRS's stance and acknowledged that cost to partition was one method of determining the undivided interest discount.)[14] This view may or may not be appropriate, depending on the facts and circumstances of the case, and may produce a wide range of discounts.

A partition time and cost method presupposes a partition action as the dominant influence on value. Although each cotenant has the right to bring such an action, there are many reasons that a buyer would not expect to sue, not the least of which is lack of economic feasibility. Moreover, the onerous conditions typically associated with lawsuits would likely reduce the size of the potential market, and increase the required discount. Nonetheless, a lawsuit is a potential cure for the large number of issues that exist for common tenancy interests, and partition time and cost may be a realistic method for developing the discount. The process requires numerous estimates or opinions of costs, time, and risk.[15] The steps are listed below.

1. Consider a negotiation period to precede the lawsuit based on the facts and circumstances of the case. Estimate the costs and time devoted to the lawsuit, up to and including the judgment, considering:

   - Discovery/due diligence
   - Legal, appraisal, and court costs
   - A referee, if any
   - Any resultant increases in operating costs during the period
   - Out-of-pocket costs
   - Processing time and potential for delays

   Costs and time can vary based on the likelihood of a challenge, countersuits, complexity (greater for partition-in-kind), and the number and geographic location of the cotenants and witnesses.

2. Decide whether the property is partitionable and, if so, develop a plan for equitable division of the property, analyzing the associated costs and time. This process would occur after judgment and would require subdivision, a survey, an appraisal, and legal fees. Estimate time for completion.

---

12. Lance Hall, "Should the IRS Surrender Cost-to-Partition Discounts for Undivided Interests?" *Valuation Strategies* (January/February 1998): 25-27, 46, 48.

13. John A. Bogdanski, *Federal Tax Valuation* (Boston: Warren, Gorham & Lamont, Updated 2003), 15.01[2][e][iii].

14. Private Letter Ruling 199943003, June 7, 1999.

15. Because the subject interest cannot be partitioned, i.e., physically subdivided, no case study application is provided for this approach as was done for the other approaches presented in this book. The approach is presented here merely to acknowledge its existence to valuers who may encounter assignments to which its application would be appropriate.

3. **Estimate additional costs after the judgment for partitionable properties.**

    The value of the resulting property will presumably be the pro-rata share of value decided by the court. However, any changes in highest and best use and the particulars of the property should have been addressed by appraisers as part of the action. Consider whether the sum of the market values of all the divided properties would be less than the value of the original property.

    There may still be some risk that the resulting property will require a longer marketing time or have proportionately less utility than the original, larger property. If marketing time is increased, an additional delay for the buyer's liquidation of the parcel may need to be considered. The period ends when title to the partitioned property is received.

4. **Estimate additional costs after judgment for nonpartitionable properties.**

    The underlying appraisal assumes a typical marketing time. If a shorter period is required, both the real estate appraisal and the business valuation may require a liquidation premise for the reversion, resulting in an additional discount or condition-of-sale adjustment for a short marketing period.

    Determine whether to include the marketing period after judgment in the holding period.[16] The costs of sale may or may not be includable because they might be implicit or explicit in the underlying real estate appraisal.

5. **Prepare a discounted cash flow model.**

    *   Project or forecast cash flows from the property over the period. Maintenance expenses could be included, although they would be incurred regardless of the partition action. They should be shown in the cash flow model if property income and expenses are listed separately. If only *NOI* is shown, the model already incorporates maintenance costs. However, if expenses are increased as a result of the partition process (e.g., management by a receiver), these costs should be added.

    *   Reversion is the expected sale price for the resulting property (forced sale) or the market value of the divided portion received (partition-in-kind). The gross sale price might be reduced by sale costs, including commissions and transaction costs, unless they are implicit or explicit in the real estate appraisal.

---

16. Some appraisers add the selling period after the sale is ordered based on the notion that the period ends when the interest is converted to cash. However, the fact that the underlying real estate was first appraised based on a particular marketing period must be considered. If it is unchanged, the property should be valued at judgment (reversion), rather than upon receipt of cash. Cash flow during the marketing period would still be attributed to the interest.

- Assign calendar times to the cash flow elements.

6. Develop one or more capitalization (discount) rates. Rates should reflect risk and uncertainty for at least two cash flow elements: real property (*NOI* and reversion) and process-related costs. (More divisions can be made if *NOI* and reversion, or the various costs, carry markedly different levels of uncertainty or risk.)

    Risk elements considered earlier in the build-up method for calculating the yield rate may be applied as is, or there may be some differences, depending on the holding period and the circumstances of the partition scenario.

    - The holding period may have been uncertain to some extent, but through the partition process the possible holding period range is reduced. On the other hand, the model covers a shorter period, and uncertainty may be greater in proportion to the shorter period.

    - If the property is managed by a receiver, management risk may be increased.

    - Control issues may be different because of the change in the holding period. The potential for additional unknown cotenants is probably moot, because the period for making such transfers is relatively short.

    - The potential for a lawsuit was previously considered a risk element, but the actuality of the lawsuit may require an increase in yield. The amount would be the yield premium that would be demanded when participation in a lawsuit (in preference to other alternatives) is a condition of realizing the terminal value of the investment.

    Costs may be discounted using a borrowing rate or any other appropriate method. The rate selected should reflect the likelihood of the costs being incurred and whether the buyer would consider only maximum costs. However, returns include the value reversion at the end and must be discounted at a rate that will probably exceed the case's investor-required rate.

    In a well-known partition case, a very low overall discount rate of 10% was used for all cash flows (income and reversion net of expenses) apparently overvaluing the interest.[17]

7. The value of the interest by the cost to partition method is calculated as the present value of the subject interest's share of cash flows and reversion.

---

17. Estate of Bonnie Barge v. Commissioner, TCM 1997-188. Ten percent is a low yield for real property returns generally, so the cash flows were overvalued. The costs of partition, however, were undervalued. Increased positive values and decreased negative values resulted in an overvalued interest. Ten percent appears to have been used for the partition process because it had been used by the real estate appraiser in valuing the underlying property. Further analysis would have produced a more accurate and beneficial result.

CASE STUDY APPLICATION

The Partition Time and Cost Method

The fundamental structure of a discounted cash flow model is its time intervals. The case study assumes a contested action, so the elements include a trial and show the most probable periods in the mind of the buyer. For the sake of illustration, the case assumes an initial period of six months as the earliest time from the date of purchase that the buyer might need to liquidate its position. A negotiation period of three months follows, which is assumed to be unsuccessful. At the end of the period, the holder files a partition action.

After filing, the case assumes a nine-month delay to trial. Countersuits and other delaying tactics could easily influence this interval. Trial to judgment is then shown as two months. The remaining delay is expected to be four months from judgment to sale and distribution of proceeds.[18] The total period from purchase until distribution of proceeds is 28 months. Cash flows for the real estate, owners' equity, and partition process are shown as Tables 8.5, 8.6, and 8.7.

The five-year discounted cash flow model (see Table 8.4) now has to be shortened to two years, with a reversion calculated on Year 3's cash flow (see Table 8.5).[19] It might be advisable for the real estate appraiser to prepare such a model since the terminal rate needs to be developed from market data, based on the quality and durability of the income stream for the two months trailing Year 2, with the lease situation expected to be whatever it is at that time. For the case study, this is significantly different from the situation trailing the end of the five-year period, when occupancy is expected to be stabilized. At two years, the terminal rate is increased from 10.5% to 11.0% because of the uncertainty present in Year 3.

Table 8.5   Partition Cash Flow Model—Real Estate

Period		1996 Year 0	1997 Year 1	1998 Year 2	1999 Year 3
Income					
Gross revenue		$495,000	$509,850	$525,146	$540,900
Vacancy rate		10%	10%	10%	12%
Vacancy		(49,500)	(50,985)	(52,514)	(64,908)
Gross rental income		$445,500	$458,865	$472,631	$475,992
Other income*	0.4% of grs.	1,850	1,800	1,854	1,867
Reimbursements†		30,272	61,449	62,273	62,974
Effective gross income		$477,622	$522,114	$536,759	$540,833
Expenses					
Real estate taxes	2.0%	$18,420	$32,500	$33,150	$33,813
Insurance	3.5%	2,512	2,600	2,691	2,785
Utilities	3.0%	26,311	27,100	27,913	28,750
Maint. and repair‡	2.0%	18,480	23,100	23,562	24,033
Bldg. services	2.0%	31,078	31,700	32,334	32,981
Management§	4.5% of grs.	33,413	20,649	21,268	21,420
Other administrative	2.0%	35,882	36,600	37,332	38,079
Reserves‖		0	3,300	3,300	3,300
Total expenses and reserves		166,096	177,549	181,550	185,161
Net operating income		$311,526	$344,565	$355,208	$355,672
Reversion					
Sale price @ rate	11.0%				$3,233,381
Less cost of sale	3.5%				(113,168)
Net reversion					$3,120,213

*   Other income covers late fees and parking, including short-term agreements for parking on the excess portion of the site.
†   Reimbursements are for common area maintenance (CAM) only, and have not been collected from some tenants for the past few years. The market has changed, and it is expected that new management will be able to collect increased but not full reimbursements.
‡   Maintenance was down for 1996 and is forecast at a more normal $0.70/sq. ft.
§   An affiliate of the owner currently charges a management fee of 7.5% of gross rental receipts. We forecast a market rate of 4.5%.
‖   Reserves for replacement are not currently maintained, and reserve funds would not pass from seller to buyer. Reserves are forecast at $0.10/sq. ft., and are at the low end of the market survey range.

18. The four months includes marketing exposure, the escrow period, and any other delay until the proceeds are distributed to the cotenants. If the property required an unusually long marketing period and the judgment required forcing a sale in a shorter period, the appraised terminal value would have to be developed based on a forced sale or liquidation premise.

19. To be exact, the date of valuation would be selected at the end of the market exposure period (two to four months from the real estate appraisal, about three months for this analysis), based on cash flow for the trailing 12-month period, which would be nine months from Year 3 and three months from Year 4. Because the delays listed above are approximations, making this fine an adjustment would probably be overanalyzing.

Selling before the end of the five-year period is disadvantageous for all of the cotenants, and results in a considerable discount from the five-year period value (see Table 8.6, Partition Cash Flow Model–Owners' Equity). As illustrated in the table, partition can be a risky proposition.[20]

The real property cash flow is adjusted to get cash flow and reversion to the owner's equity position.

Table 8.6	Partition Cash Flow Model—Owners' Equity			
		1996	1997	1998	1999
Period		Year 0	Year 1	Year 2	Year 3
Real estate adjustments					
NOI		$311,526	$344,565	$355,208	$355,672
Reversion					$3,120,213
Add back forecast management fee			$20,649	$21,268	$21,420
Less fee at current rate	7.5%		(34,415)	(35,447)	(35,699)
Total owners' income			$330,799	$341,029	$341,392
Other expenses					
General and administrative	2.0%		280	286	291
Debt service			221,011	221,011	221,011
Total owners' expense			221,291	221,297	221,302
Cash flow			$109,508	$119,733	$120,090
Reversion					
Real property					$3,120,213
Loan balance		(1,816,278)			(1,759,082)
Assets-liabilities					(5,668)
Net owners' equity (present/future)		$1,428,054			$1,355,463

The value of the interest by the partition time and cost method is calculated as the present value of the subject interest's share of cash flows and reversion (see Table 8.6). Costs are highly dependent on the complexity of the case, the extent to which discovery is needed to reveal important ownership, property and management information, the number of cotenants, and whether the property is divisible.

Court costs were put at $10,000/year, a gross approximation.[21] Some fees, such as appraisal and subdivision (for partition-in-kind) might be shared between the parties. Costs may vary over a wide range, depending on the probable response of the existing cotenants, and the analyst may wish to show two models to generate a range of value conclusions.[22]

The fees shown are meant to be illustrative of process only, and should not be used as benchmarks of any type. It is important to review the facts and circumstances with counsel in order to have a reasonable basis for the cost forecast.

20. This brings up a question that may affect the court proceeding because, if the opposing cotenants knew to make this argument, the judgment of the court might be different. Otherwise, the judge might be ordering a loss for all cotenants.

21. Seaman, "Valuation of Undivided Interests in Real Property." The Southland Study reports that legal costs of $10,000 to $15,000 would be reasonable if there were only minor disagreements, but that a contested suit might cost $30,000 to $50,000 in legal fees and run three years.

22. The fees shown are meant to be illustrative of the process only, and should not be used as benchmarks of any type. To have a reasonable basis for the cost forecast, it is important to review the facts and circumstances with counsel.

Table 8.7 Partition Cash Flow Model—Process

Event	Purchase	Need out	File action	Trial	Judgment	Division
Month	0	6	12	21	24	28
Income						
NOI from property		$54,754	$54,754	$89,800	$29,933	$40,030
Present values	17.3%	50,248	46,113	66,486	21,230	26,812
Subject share	20.%	10,050	9,223	13,297	4,246	5,362
Reversion at sale						$1,355,463
Present values	17.3%					$907,881
Subject share	20.0%					$181,576
Costs						
Discovery		$1,500	$1,500			
Legal fees			5,000	$20,000		
Appraisal fees			1,000			
Court costs					2,000	
Out-of-pocket		500	500	500	500	
Subdivision						0
Total costs		(2,000)	(8,000)	(20,500)	(2,500)	0
Present values	8.3%	(1,919)	(7,369)	(17,753)	(2,121)	0
Value by partition time and cost						
Sum of present values	$194,592	$8,130	$1,854	$(4,456)	$2,125	$186,939
Pro rata equity	$285,611					
Discount	31.9%					
(rounded)	32.0%					

The yield rates must be appropriate to the risk associated with the various cash flows. This example uses the same investor's required rate of return that was developed for the income discount model to calculate the present value of the NOI and the reversion. It may be appropriate to make different adjustments in deriving this rate because the holding period is shorter and the circumstances are slightly different.

Partition costs are direct payments, shown discounted at the prime borrowing rate. They are discounted to present value because they occur in the future, but the cash to make the payments is also cash-in-hand, and a borrowing rate is often used for this type of cash flow.[23] The discount conclusion shown in Table 8.7, based on analysis of partition time and cost, is 32%

This method shows a fairly deep discount, which is unusual for such a short holding period. This is largely due to the low reversionary value of the property. If there were no significant increase in risk between Year 6 (original termination) and an earlier termination in Year 3 (Table 8.6), the terminal rate would be unchanged at 10.5%, and the discount would be 25%, down from 32%.

---

23. It might also be reasonable to argue that the amounts could be deducted from real property cash flows, and the net cash flow discounted at the investor's required rate. However, because these are not real estate expenses, the question of the appropriateness of combining them for present value analysis arises. (This change would decrease the discount because the present value of these costs [negative cash flows] would then be discounted at a greater rate, reducing their negative present value and increasing the net present value.) An increased present value for the interest means a decreased discount conclusion. This reasoning works only if there is available cash flow from the property. If there is not, and cash comes from the interest holder's bank, or is borrowed, the question of the appropriateness of a borrowing rate is raised. Overall, a borrowing rate appears to be most appropriate for such cash payments.

Partition is not as simple a process as it is sometimes portrayed. Rather, it is an involved discounted cash flow valuation method that is appropriate for some cases but not others. It requires detailed consideration of cost-and-time elements based on the facts and circumstances of the case.

If partition-in-kind is feasible, it should always be considered. Partition time and cost can prove the feasibility of a partition lawsuit and, if appropriate, generate a convincing and supportable value conclusion. Even when bringing a partition action is apparently feasible, it may produce detrimental consequences that would argue against assuming a successful lawsuit and a consequently short holding period.

The outcome of a lawsuit is uncertain. There is always a chance that the other side could convince the court that a sale would be detrimental.

Sales Comparison Approach

The sales comparison approach was described in considerable detail in Chapter 2, Appraising the Real Property.[24] The approach is used by market participants for its simplicity and intuitive appeal. Its appeal and familiarity lead courts[25] and appraisers alike to look for sales that will provide direct indications for common tenancy discounts. These sales are difficult to find, however, and once found, the analysis is not as simple as one might expect. The advantages of using this approach are its simplicity, its understandability, and its acceptability. The disadvantages are its potential labor intensiveness and its susceptibility to abuse.

The steps of the sales comparison approach entail:

- Selecting and confirming the sales of similar interests in comparable properties (or properties whose differences can be adjusted). Direct participants (i.e., buyer, seller, and broker) should confirm the sales.

- Adjusting sale prices for

    - Any reported conditions of sale, e.g., duress, nonmarket incentives, unusual conditions, and lack of market exposure

---

24. It is used to value fee interests because sales of similar properties can usually be found and confirmed, and market participants often consider alternative properties as part of the decision-making process. The approach is most often used with smaller, non-income-producing properties because deriving a value indication is relatively simple and straightforward and it is often preferred by the market. Investors in larger income properties typically use the income approach, although a sales comparison approach is also valid in an owner/user market.

25. Estate of George W. Youle v. Commissioner, 56 TCM 1989-138. The opinion rendered was that "While sales of fractional interests in real estate would be good indicators of fair market value, in this case there were no comparable arm's-length sales . . . ." Similar comments can be found in other opinions.

- Nonmarket financing (e.g., low or high interest rates, high loan-to-value ratio)

- Changes in market conditions (price movements) between the date of the transaction and the date of value

- Differences between the subject and the comparable (e.g., location, condition, nuisances, and any other relevant elements whose influence can be extracted from the market)

- Calculating a unit price (price per square foot, or some other relevant unit)[26]

- Reconciling the adjusted prices of the comparables into a value indication for the subject

Applying the Approach to Common Tenancy Interests

Applying the sales comparison approach to value common tenancy interests requires additional steps, namely:

- Determining the value of the owners' net equity in the underlying property if the price has been reported and calculating the price discount from the interest's pro rata net equity: Discount = [1 − price/equity]. (This requires knowledge of the loan balance and terms as of the date of the transaction,[27] as well as the underlying fee value of the real estate.)[28]

- If a discount has been reported, the underlying value/equity may be irrelevant because the discount in the mind of the buyer and seller is what was calculated (above). Discounts should be accepted with care, and multiple parties to the transaction may have to be interviewed to ascertain whether the buyer and seller agreed on the amount of the discount. If they believed the pro rata equity to be a certain amount, the actual or appraised value may be unimportant.

- Adjusting the price (and/or discount) for conditions of sale[29] and nonmarket financing. Changes in market conditions between the transaction date and the subject date of value are probably not adjustable.[30]

---

26. This is not generally done for single-family residences (SFR), which are selected to be highly similar to the subject. For a SFR appraisal, the adjusted sale price is the indicated value of the subject.

27. This is irrelevant when a 100% fee interest is involved because, under the definition of value, a transaction is assumed in which existing financing will be paid off, and the buyer will pay cash or its equivalent with a new market-rate loan.

28. The appraiser will likely have to appraise the property separately, unless the parties show reasonable agreement on the value or the discount.

29. Don L. Harris, MAI et al, "The Valuation of Partial Interests in Real Estate," *ASA Valuation* (December 1983): 63-73; Walter H. Humphrey, "Unsyndicated Partial Interest Appraisals," *Valuation Insights and Perspectives* (Third Quarter 1998): 9-12; and Walter H. Humphrey and Bruce B. Humphrey, MAI, "Unsyndicated Partial Interest Discounting," *The Appraisal Journal* (July 1997), 267-274, provide anecdotal information on conditions of sale.

30. Whether the discount is affected by market conditions is an open question; since the market is not sufficiently active, that support can be developed.

- Adjusting the comparable's discounts for differences with the subject interest regarding holding period, the buyer's perception of the risk elements presented as the value-influencing

> *The valuer has to understand much more about each transaction than the appraiser needs to when he or she performs an appraisal of the 100% fee interest.*

elements earlier in this chapter, and any other relevant elements. The physical characteristics of the properties may also be important.

- Reconciling the discount indications to a single discount to be applied to the subject interest.

What is normally a straightforward process increases in complexity because, in addition to real estate differences, issues pertaining to undivided interests are central to its application, and they are not well reported. The valuer has to understand much more about each transaction than the appraiser needs to when he or she performs an appraisal of the 100% fee interest.

The limitations on property rights imposed by the common tenancy ownership structure are complex, and are unlikely to be well understood by a buyer. But the definition of fair market value, "…both [parties] having reasonable knowledge of the relevant facts," requires that both buyer and seller have reasonable knowledge of such limitations. Conditions of sale may, therefore, require adjustment of the sale price based on whether the buyer was fully informed.

Transactional data are the only direct evidence that common tenancy interests in real estate are traded at a discount from owners' equity. Thus, these data can be more convincing than the indirect methods illustrated in this chapter. However, sales of fractional interests are difficult to obtain and apply in the analysis.[31] They are also relatively rare, so a valuer cannot rely on having appropriate transactions for every common tenancy valuation assignment. Further, misuse can create significant vulnerabilities in a valuation report that can be easily attacked by a knowledgeable adversary.

Studies of Transactions Involving Undivided Interests
Some of the difficulties of working with individual transactions on the purchase and sale of fractional interests can be overcome if enough data are assembled. If the information is sufficient, the data can be analyzed to provide good discount

---

31. Ted Israel, CPA/ABV, CVA, "Discounts on Undivided Interests in Real Estate," *Valuation Strategies* (May/June 2003): 14-19, 47. The article discusses the process of accumulating a searchable database of usable transactions.

indications. The following studies contain data on the sale of undivided interests that can assist the valuer in understanding and determining value-influencing elements and in developing the discount.

- Harris: A group of 18 transactions involving undivided interests in agricultural real estate showed value discounts ranging from 15% to 54%; the mean is 32% percent, and the standard deviation is 8.3%.[32]

- Patchin: Two groups of 24 transactions, also agricultural real estate, showed discounts of 44% to 79% and 15.2% to 55%; the standard deviations are relatively low: 11.2% and 8.3%. The mean discounts were 56% and 32%, respectively.[33]

- Hall: In an unreported study, the author indicates an average discount of approximately 34%. It was lower for income-producing properties (27%); for no- or low-income situations, it was 38%.[34] The study was prepared by FMV Opinions, Inc., and includes 40 transactions from 1971 to 1993. The author also notes that value discounts appear to decrease with improving economic conditions and for interests greater than 50%.

- Humphrey: A group of 11 case studies involving a variety of real estate fractional interests showed value discounts ranging from 16% to 67%. Their calculated mean was 46%.[35] This study provided detailed and potentially useful information for the 11 cases that yield discount indications from offers to buy and sell and included a number of actual transactions. However, in nearly every situation, conditions required adjusting the transaction price.

Humphrey concluded the discount by directly adding or subtracting percentages associated with each value-influencing element from a list that included degree of control, financing impairment, increased management cost, cash flow (positive or negative), the liquidation prospect (holding period), potential legal costs, stigma, and uncertainties associated with each. A valuer might benefit from reading the studies to find support for value conclusions reached by other approaches or to develop a more detailed analysis along the lines of Humphrey's process.[36]

Studies of transactions involving undivided interests generally do not provide enough information to support usable discount indications, but they still should be cited in the valuation report.

32. Harris, "The Valuation of Partial Interests in Real Estate," 62-73.

33. Peter J. Patchin, CRE, "Market Discounts for Undivided Minority Interests in Real Estate," *Real Estate Issues* (Fall/Winter 1988):14-16.

34. Hall, "Should the IRS Surrender Cost-to-Partition Discounts for Individual Interests?" 48.

35. Walter H. and Bruce B. Humphrey, "Unsyndicated Partial Interest Discounting," 267-274.

36. Israel, "Discounts on Undivided Interests in Real Estate."

CASE STUDY APPLICATION

Concluding Value Using the Sales Comparison Approach

Sales transactions of three undivided interests in real property involving different property types in widely different locations provide the bases on which the subject property, is compared. The data are represented in an adjustment grid similar to that used for real property sales comparisons in Chapter 4.

Sale 1. This sale is a 25% interest in an office building located in a large city central business district in the adjacent county. The building is a high rise with multiple tenants, but without the prospect of leases turning over in three years, which is the case for the subject. Three of the six cotenants are unrelated. For personal reasons, the seller had to raise funds and tried to market the interest through brokers, offering a 30% discount. The interest was eventually sold to one of the cotenants at a discount of more 45%. Because the property had been appraised for another cotenant two months before, all parties to the transaction agreed on its market value. A relatively small loan balance is outstanding, but information on other assets and liabilities of ownership were not available. The cotenants have an operating agreement that stipulates that management decisions be delegated to one party and that each cotenant give up his or her right to partition.

Sale 2. This sale is a 42% interest in a mixed-use, retail store and single-family residence located in an older urban neighborhood. The buildings are older and in average condition, are suited to the current tenant's use, and conform with other buildings on the street. The cotenants are two heirs and a former investment partner of their mother's. One of the heirs was simply tired of having anything to with the properties and wanted out. The listing generated offers to buy the entire property. The interest was eventually sold to her sister, but for a non-interest-bearing note that required six equal semiannual payments. The sisters relied on the broker's opinion of value as the sale price for the total property. There are no operating agreements, but the local broker manages this property and several other family properties.

Sale 3. This sale is a 15% interest in a large parcel of Mississippi timberland. Two brothers each owned 50% of the property and were not getting along. A neighbor who owns similar timberland (operated under pulpwood management) approached them to buy the property. A local broker provided an estimate of value for the land and timber, which the parties agreed upon. The neighbor offered $0.80 on the dollar; one brother agreed to this price but the other had no interest in selling. It appears that the buyer expects to combine half of the property with his own, if the other brother does not sell. Cash flow is low and is not expected to change very much. Because the holding period is short, the management issue is not expected to pose a significant problem.

Table 8.8 shows the three sales transactions used in the sales comparison approach and the adjustments made to determine common tenancy discount indications for the subject interest.

Adjustments to discounts are relative adjustments, intended to increase the discount for conditions that are superior to the subject and vice versa. By contrast, adjustments to sale prices are related to the transactions, not the subject property. There are many potential adjustments to value-influencing elements for this case study. The following are presented as reasonable possibilities.

Conditions of sale. This adjustment applies only to Sale 1, in which the seller was forced to sell because of personal circumstances. The market effect of such a condition is difficult to quantify, particularly since the parties are likely to have no reference point for a condition-less transaction.[37] Sale 3 involved the purchase of adjoining land by a

---

37. For the 100% fee value, there would be other comparable transactions of which the parties would be aware. A broker active in the sale of partial interests may be a source for determining the effect the condition had on the transaction, but the conclusion will still be an approximation.

Table 8.8	**Sales Comparisons for Valuing a Common Tenancy Interest in Suburban Office Partners, II**			

	Subject	**Sale 1**	**Sale 2**	**Sale 3**
Property address	200 S Main St Tustin, CA	125 Fourth St Los Angeles, CA	1227 Lemon St Torrence, CA	Paradise Rd Pearl, MS
Property				
Type	Suburban Office	CBD Office	Comm + SFR	Timberland
Year built	1987	1972	1953	NA
Building area in sq. ft.	36,300	115,200	1,470	0
Site area in acres	1.1	1.9	0.2	5,125
Income				
Net cash flow rate	5.8%	6.5%	8.9%	0.7%
Expected growth rate	5.2%	3.0%	3.5%	0.0%
Ownership				
Number of owners	5	6	3	2
Interest	20.0%	17.0%	23.0%	50.0%
Transaction				
Sale date	N/A	12/02/1994	06/02/1996	06/02/1962
Purchase price	NA	$950,000	$36,000	$1,850,000
Financing		All cash	3 yrs, no interest	All cash
Holding period	5 years	Indefinite	Indefinite	2 years
Owners' equity				
Property rights	Leased fee	Leased fee	Leased fee	Fee simple
Property value	$3,250,00	$9,450,000	$185,000	$4,615,00
Loan	(1,816,278)	1,200,125	0	0
Other assets/liabilities	(5,668)	N/Av	N/Av	N/Av
Owners' equity	$1,428,054	$10,650,125	$185,000	$4,615,00
Base discount		40.9%	15.4%	19.8%
Adjustments to price				
Purchase price		$950,000	$36,000	$1,850,000
Conditions of sale		95,000	0	(185,000)
Adjusted rights		$1,045,000	$36,000	$1,665,000
Property rights		156,750	0	0
Adjusted price		$1,201,750	$36,000	$1,665,000
Financing		0	(4,800)	0
Adjusted price		$1,201,750	$31,200	$1,665,000
Adjusted discount		25.2%	26.7%	27.8%
Adjustments to discount				
Holding period		-9.0%	-9.0%	-12.0%
Number of owners		2.0%	0.5%	1.0%
Equity cash flow		2.0%	10.0%	-15.05%
Growth prospects		-5.0%	-4.0%	-6.0%
Real estate risk		2.0%	0.0%	1.0%
Management risk		2.0%	0.0%	2.0%
Total adjustment		-6.0%	-2.5%	-5.0%
Indicated discount	21.1%	19.2%	24.2%	22.8%
(rounded)	21.0%			

neighboring landowner who intends to combine at least half of the property with his own. Plottage value is attributed to this combination (which would not change the highest and best use of the property), and a 5% adjustment is made for plottage value.

Property rights. This adjustment refers to any of the bundle of rights that might have been given up, or amplified, usually by agreement. An extreme example of relinquishing rights would be an agreement between cotenants that is as restrictive as a partnership agreement (in which case the interest would be discounted as if it actually were a partnership interest). An adjustment can be made by relating the degree of control to that of a limited partner and proportioning the discount that would be normally applied to a partnership that holds a similar property. The ownership agreement of Sale 1 appears to be limited, but little detail is known, and an adjustment of 15% is concluded.

No adjustments are shown for market conditions because it has not been demonstrated that there is any connection between general market conditions and the discounts required for undivided interests.

Holding period. The parties to Sale 1 have given up the right of partition, so a short holding period could not be forced, unless the validity of the agreement were challenged. No other basis for selecting a holding period is apparent. The adjustment for the holding period is taken as the amount by which the subject discount would change if the holding period were increased from five to 10 years. (The adjustment is based on the subject's facts and circumstances, not the facts and circumstances of the comparable sale, so this adjustment would be an approximation.) Sale 2 represents a low-value interest that, arguably, cannot afford to bring about a partition action, so the adjustment is the same as for Sale 1. The right to partition appears to be important to Sale 3, which is a high-value interest, so a short two-year hold is imputed, and a large upward adjustment, measured in a manner similar to Sale 1, is required.

Number of owners. An adjustment may be required for transactions that involve significantly different numbers of cotenants (which would complicate management). For Sale 1, interaction between owners is largely eliminated by the operating agreement, so, compared to the subject's five cotenants, this would represent a superior position. A small adjustment is made for this condition because the control effect of the agreement has already been considered. Sales 2 and 3 also have few owners, a slightly superior condition to the subject.

Equity cash flow and growth prospects. Equity cash flow has a significant effect on discounts for common tenancy interests at all levels. Adjustments can be made for differences as they were for the holding period–i.e., by changing the subject property's cash flow rate to that of the rate of the comparable sale, and observing the resulting change in the discount. Growth prospects can be adjusted in the same manner as equity cash flow.

Real estate risk. This condition is related to the property itself but contains elements that are not captured in the other categories. Sales 1 and 3 are stabilized and do not face tenancy risk, a superior condition. A single tenant who has been renting for 15 years occupies the subject property in Sale 2. Historical stability for Sale 2 is superior, but if the tenant leaves, vacancy would be 100%. The property might require renovation to suit another tenant, which is an inferior, offsetting condition. No basis for adjustment exists for differentials in property type, but the similarity of the property would be a reason for giving more weight to this particular sale in reconciling discount indications.

Management risk. This condition is reduced for Sale 1, which is managed professionally and is not burdened with the problems associated with developable land, as is the subject property. Sale 2 is also managed professionally, but the interest in the property would be affected if the tenant left; therefore, Sale 2 is equivalent to the subject overall. Sale 3 has a short expected holding period and no known management problems.

Other points of comparison may be appropriate, depending on the subject property type, the amount of the data available, and the valuer's diligence in analyzing each transaction. As the valuer's reliance on the sales comparison approach increases, the need to understand and compare the transactions becomes increasingly important.

Although Sale 1 required the greatest gross adjustment, it is the most similar overall and is given the greatest weight.[38] Sale 2 is weighted second, despite the fact that it is a substantially different property type, because it required the smallest gross adjustment. Sale 3 is given the least weight because it is the least similar overall, and the magnitude of the adjustment for plottage, as a condition of sale, is not well supported.

Comparable Sale 1	19%
Comparable Sale 2	24%
Comparable Sale 3	23%
Concluded discount by sales comparison	20%

38. Gross adjustment is the sum of the absolute value of all adjustments (with dollar adjustments calculated as percentages), divided by the base discount percentages.

Reconciling the Approaches

Three approaches to developing the discount for real estate interests owned in common tenancy have been presented in this chapter: the income approach, the partition time and cost approach, and the direct sales comparison approach. Each is evaluated for its appropriateness, accuracy, and the quantity of evidence on which its value indication is based. Of the three, only the direct sales comparison approach does not rely on proxies, which gives it a major theoretical advantage over the others. However, shortcomings related to the quantity of evidence and the applicability of the data to the subject interest often limit its usefulness. Unless the business valuer has access to a large database that contains wide-ranging property types and other variables to facilitate comparison with the subject property, the other two approaches may prevail as the most important options for developing the discount.

The partition time and cost approach is actually a discounting method, which applies directly to divisible properties. It is more of a feasibility check for those that are not divisible. In many cases, the feasibility of the partition option is not obvious, and a shortened version of the approach presented may be useful in supporting the valuer's conclusion, as it is for this case study.

The income approach is the most appropriate for valuing the common tenancy interest for several reasons. Its theoretical foundation is well established, it offers a rigorous analysis of the value-influencing elements that contribute to risk, it provides sufficient evidence of yield rates, and its well-established holding period more closely corresponds with a potential buyer's objective for purchasing the interest. For short holding periods, however, income methods may be limited in their ability to describe market behavior. Other methods, such as option models or short-term liquidating partnership analysis, may be more appropriate. Restricted stock can work as a direct comparison for holding periods of one to three years.

The valuation tools available for assessing the case-specific facts and circumstances pertaining to common tenancy interests are all interpretations of the market, whether the sales transactions are direct or proxy. Therefore, several methods are often needed to describe a market that trades fractional interests, which is largely uncertain and poorly understood.

CASE STUDY APPLICATION

Reconciling the Approaches

The discount indications derived from the three ways to conclude to value are:

Income approach	21%
Direct sales comparison approach	20%
Partition time and cost method	32%

Of the three, the greatest weight is placed on the income approach because the holding period is long enough that a buyer would purchase the interest for investment, and this approach is appropriate. The quantity of evidence pertaining to yield rates is adequate. The process accounted explicitly for all the important facts and circumstances of the case, and the variables are within the range of the model, so the accuracy of the approach is reasonable.

The sales comparison approach is given less weight than the income approach because the quantity of data and information about each transaction was limited. It might be appropriate as a representation of actual market behavior toward common tenancy interests, but the valuer's ability to adjust the discount indications to the subject was hampered because the quantity of data from which adjustments could be extracted is severely limited. Nonetheless, its conclusion does support the conclusion of the income approach.

The partition time and cost method was given no weight because of the indivisibility of the real property. However, had it produced a low discount, the holding period premise of the case may have had to be reconsidered. The greater discount suggests that an early forced sale is clearly disadvantageous for all parties. Thus, based on the income approach, the concluded discount applicable to the common tenancy interest is 21%.

Support for the Conclusion

Results of some published studies of transactions involving undivided interests were presented earlier in this chapter. The data are inappropriate for direct application to the subject, primarily because the data involve agricultural land, which is generally partitionable, and the conditions of sale are not known. The observed discount range is

15% to 67%, and the mean indications of the three studies are 32%, 46%, and 56%. Because a moderately short 5-year holding period is hypothesized and the common tenancy interest receives a higher cash flow and growth rates than are typical of the transactions that make up the studies, the conclusion should fall well below the mean indications of the studies. The conclusion of 21% is consistent by this measure, and the studies support the concluded discount.

Value Conclusion

The final task in valuing an undivided common tenancy interest in real property is to apply the discount to the subject interest's pro rata share of the owners' equity as shown:

Owners' equity	$_____
Interest held by John Builder × ___% =	$_____
Less discount × ___% =	$_____
Concluded market value	$_____

The computations can be performed in any sequence to obtain the same result. In this example, the discount is partly dependent on the pro rata size of the interest, so the pro rata portion of owners' equity is calculated first, and then the discount is applied to the result.

Historical Sales as Evidence of Value

The history section of the valuation report should have included past transactions that involved undivided interests in the subject property. If these transactions are evidence of the value of the interest, they should be reconciled with the concluded market value that was developed from market analysis.

Sensitivity Analysis

The final discount can vary greatly, depending on the particulars of the situation. A sensitivity analysis is often presented as part of a discounted cash flow analysis (just as it was for the limited partnership scenario) to reveal the significance of the underlying assumptions to the value conclusion.

Precision of the Result

Precision is the compound result of the precision of the component value estimates, the real estate value, and the discount. As both case study scenarios have demonstrated, the accuracy of the analysis declines as one descends the levels-of-value diagram. The real estate value is the most accurate, and the common tenancy discount is the least accurate; however, it is clear from following the case study that a range could be a more appropriate expression for many of the adjustments than a point value. This is particularly true for the discount, in which case it would be important to show high and low columns throughout the analysis. If the conclusion is presented as a range, it may create the perception of guaranteeing that market value lies within the range, so it is most important to present the value conclusion in a way that is not misleading.

Final Checklist

Value conclusions should always be subjected to a sanity check to confirm that extreme conditions have not influenced the valuation process and produced an unrealistic result. One way of checking is to use another method, e.g., if an income approach was not used, to look at the dividend yield to the subject interest to determine whether it makes sense in relation to other investments. Another way of checking the result is to consider the objectives of the willing seller. Granted, most of the attention has been focused on the willing buyer, but the value conclusion must also be reasonable so that the owner of the interest would be willing to part with it at the concluded discount.

CASE STUDY APPLICATION

Concluding Value for Suburban Office Partners, II		
Owners' net equity		$1,428,054
Interest held by John Builder	× 20.0% =	285,611
Less discount	× 21.0% =	– 59,978
Concluded market value		$225,633
(rounded)		$226,000

John Builder had purchased 20% of Ed Helper's 50% share in 1995, for $120,000. This represented 10% of the whole, and his pro rata share two years later was $142,805. The partnership net asset value can be estimated as of the end of 1995 by recalculating the balance sheet for 1995 and deflating the market value of the property to $2,950,000. This results in a pro rata net asset value of just over $115,000, so the amount paid was actually a 4% premium.

The facts of the case indicate that Ed told Billy later that his father had paid an inflated price because of his generosity; the facts also indicate that Ed had sufficient capital losses to offset any gains. These nonmarket conditions provide a reasonable justification for the transacted amount, which does not influence the value conclusion.

A ± one-year change in holding time would produce an approximate ±2.5% change in the discount, based on the conclusions from the suggested solution. (A longer hold increases the discount.) A ± 2% change in the cash flow rate would produce an approximate ±3.5% change in the discount, based on the conclusions from the solution sheets. (A higher rate decreases the discount.) A ± 2% change in the required rate (at the private level) would produce an approximate ±5.0 to 6.0% change in the overall discount. (A higher rate increases the discount.)

The remaining influences on value affect the discount to different degrees. It would not be unexpected for a valuer to conclude a small discount for a large-value interest combined with circumstances that would allow a quick and effective partition action. On the other hand, a high-risk situation for a low-value interest with no distributions can produce discounts nearly as high as for limited partnerships.

Appendixes

Real Property Information

<u>SECURED PROMISSORY NOTE</u>
800364212

$1,973,000.00   February 1, 1987

1.   FOR VALUE RECEIVED, John Builder, as to an undivided 50%
interest and Edward Helper as to an undivided 50% interest, as
"Borrower" ("Borrower" to be construed as "Borrowers" if the
context so requires), hereby promise to pay to the order of FIRST
STEPFORD BANK, an Oklahoma corporation (as "Lender"), having a
principal place of business and post office address at c/o First-
Stepford Management, LLC, PO Box 20514, Oklahoma City OK 73112, or
at such other place as Lender may designate, the principal sum of
One Million Nine Hundred Seventy-three Thousand and 00/100 Dollars
($1,973,000.00) (the "Loan Amount") or so much thereof as shall
from time to time have been advanced, together with interest on the
unpaid balance of said sum from February 1, 1987 (the "Closing
Date"), at the rate of ten and seventy-five one-hundredths percent
(10.75%) per annum, computed by multiplying the actual number of
days elapsed in the period for which interest is being calculated
by a daily rate based on the foregoing annual interest rate and a
360-day year in installments as follows:

     Beginning on February 1, 1987, principal and interest shall
be due and payable in installments of Eighteen Thousand Four
Hundred Seventeen and 59/100 Dollars ($18,417.59), with an install-
ment in a like amount due and payable on the same day of each month
thereafter until said principal and interest are fully paid, except
that all remaining principal, interest and other Indebtedness shall
be due and payable on January 31, 2002 ("Maturity Date"). Each
installment shall be credited first upon interest then accrued and
the remainder upon principal, and interest shall cease to accrue
upon principal so credited. All principal and interest shall be
paid in lawful money of the United States of America by automated
clearing house transfer through such bank or financial institution
as shall be approved in writing by Lender, shall be made to an
account designated by Lender, and shall be initiated by Lender or
shall be made in such other manner as Lender may direct from time
to time.

2.   No privilege is reserved by Borrower to prepay any principal
of this Note prior to the Maturity Date, except in strict accordance with the provisions of the Loan Agreement.

3.   Borrower agrees that if Lender accelerates the whole or any
part of the principal sum evidenced hereby, or applies any proceeds
pursuant to the provisions of the Loan Documents, Borrower waives
any right to prepay said principal sum in whole or in part without
premium and agrees to pay, as yield maintenance protection and not
as a penalty, the Make Whole Premium.

Borrower by adding its initials to the end of this paragraph, (A)
expressly waives any rights it may have under California Civil Code
Section 2954.10 to prepay this Note, in whole or in part, without
penalty, upon acceleration of the Maturity Date of this Note and

-2-

(B) acknowledges and agrees that Borrower has no right of prepayment of this Note, except as provided above; and that, if the maturity of this Note is accelerated by Lender, Borrower specifically agrees to pay as a prepayment premium, the applicable sum specified herein as the Make Whole Premium, specifically including but not limited to the case where the holder of this Note has accelerated the maturity of this note due to Borrower's default of any provision contained in 2(f) of the Deed of Trust. By initialing this provision, Borrower hereby declares that Lender's agreement to make the Loan evidenced by this Note for the interest rate and for the term set forth in this Note constitutes adequate consideration, given individual weight by Borrower, for this waiver and agreement.

Initials:

4.   If any payment of principal, interest, Make Whole Premium, or other Indebtedness is not made when due, damages will be incurred by Lender, including additional expense in handling overdue payments, the amount of which is difficult and impractical to ascertain. Borrower therefore agrees to pay, upon demand, the sum of four cents ($0.04) for each one dollar ($1.00) of each said payment which becomes overdue ("Late Charge") as a reasonable estimate of the amount of said damages, subject, however, to the limitations contained in paragraph 6 hereof.

5.   If any Event of Default has occurred and is continuing under the Loan Documents, the entire principal balance of the Loan, interest then accrued, and Make Whole Premium, and all other Indebtedness whether or not otherwise then due, shall at the option of Lender, become immediately due and payable without demand or notice, and whether or not Lender has exercised said option, interest shall accrue on the entire principal balance, interest then accrued, Make Whole Premium and any other Indebtedness then due, at a rate equal to the lesser of (i) the Default Rate or (ii) the maximum rate allowed by applicable law until fully paid.

6.   Notwithstanding anything herein or in any of the other Loan Documents to the contrary, no provision contained herein or therein which purports to obligate Borrower to pay any amount of interest or any fees, costs or expenses which are in excess of the maximum permitted by applicable law, shall be effective to the extent it calls for the payment of any interest or other amount in excess of such minimum. All agreements between Borrower and Lender, whether now existing or hereafter arising and whether written or oral, are hereby limited so that in no contingency, whether by reason of demand for payment or acceleration of the maturity hereof or otherwise, shall the interest contracted for, charged or received by lender exceed the maximum amount permissible under applicable law. If, from any circumstance whatsoever, interest would otherwise be payable to Lender in excess of the amount permitted under applicable law; and if from any circumstance Lender shall ever receive anything of value deemed interest by applicable law in excess of the maximum lawful amount, an amount equal to any excessive interest shall, at the option of Lender, be refunded to Borrower or be applied to the reduction of the principal hereof and not to the

-3-

payment of interest or, if such excessive interest exceeds the unpaid balance of principal hereof such excess shall be refunded to Borrower. This paragraph shall control all agreements between Borrower and Lender.

7.   Borrower and any endorsers or guarantors waive presentment, protest and demand, notice of protest, demand and dishonor and nonpayment, and agree the Maturity Date of this Note or any installment may be extended without affecting any liability hereunder, and further promise to pay all reasonable costs and expenses, including but not limited to, attorney's fees incurred by Lender in connection with any default or in any proceeding to interpret and/or enforce any provision of the Loan Documents. No release of Borrower from liability hereunder shall release any other maker, endorser or guarantor hereof.

8.   This Note is secured by the Loan Documents creating among other things legal and valid encumbrances on and an assignment of all of Borrower's interest in any Leases of the Premises located in the County of Orange, State of California. Capitalized terms used herein and not otherwise defined shall have those meanings given to them in the Loan Documents. In no event shall such documents be construed inconsistently with the terms of this Note, and in the event of any discrepancy between any such documents and this Note, the terms hereof shall govern. The proceeds of this Note are to be used for business, commercial, investment or other similar purposes, and no portion thereof will be used for any personal, family or household use. This Note shall be governed by and construed in accordance with the laws of the State where the Premises is located, without regard to its conflict of law principles.

9.   Notwithstanding any provision to the contrary in this Note or the Loan Documents and except as otherwise provided for below, the liability of Borrower and any general partner of Borrower under the Loan Documents shall be limited to the interest of Borrower and any general partner of Borrower in the Premises and the Rents. In the event of foreclosure of the liens evidenced by the Loan Documents, no judgment for any deficiency upon the Indebtedness evidenced by the Loan Documents shall be sought or obtained by Lender against Borrower or any general partner of Borrower. Nothing herein shall in any manner limit or impair (i) the lien or enforcement of the Loan Documents pursuant to the terms thereof or (ii) the obliga-tions of any indemnitor or guarantor, if any.

Notwithstanding any provision herein above to the contrary, Borrower and any general partner of Borrower shall be personally liable to Lender for:

(a)   any loss or damage to Lender arising from (i) the sale or forfeiture of the Premises resulting from Borrower's failure to pay any of the taxes, assessments or charges specified in the Loan Documents or (ii) Borrower's failure to insure the Premises in compliance with the provisions of the Loan Documents;

-4-

(b)   any event or circumstance for which Borrower indemnifies Lender under the Environmental Indemnity;

(c)   nonpayment of taxes, assessments, insurance premiums and utilities for the Premises and any penalty or late charge associated with nonpayment thereof;

(d)   failure to manage, operate, and maintain the Premises in a commercially reasonable manner;

(e)   any sums expended by Lender in fulfilling the obligations of Borrower as lessor under any Lease of the Premises prior to a sale of the Premises pursuant to foreclosure or power of sale, a bona fide sale (permitted by the terms of paragraph 2(f) of the Deed of Trust or consented to in writing by Lender) to an unrelated third party or upon conveyance to Lender of the Premises by a deed acceptable to Lender in form and content (each of which shall be referred to as a "Sale" for purposes of this paragraph) or expended by Lender after a Sale of the Premises for obligations of Borrower which arose prior to a Sale of the Premises;

Borrower's personal liability for items specified in (c), (d) and (e) above shall be limited to the amount of rents, issues, proceeds and profits from the Premises ("Rents and Profits") received by Borrower for the twenty-four (24) months preceding an Event of Default and thereafter; but less any such Rents and Profits applied to (A) payment of principal, interest and other charges when due under the Loan Documents or (B) payment of expenses for the operation, maintenance, taxes, assessments, utility charges and insurance of the Premises including sufficient reserves for the same or replacements or renewals thereof ("Operation Expenses") provided that (x) Borrower has furnished Lender with evidence satisfactory to Lender of the Operation Expenses and payment thereof, and (y) any payments to parties related to Borrower shall be considered an Operation Expense only to the extent that the amount expended for the Operation Expense does not exceed the market rate for such Operation Expense.

To the extent Lender is impounding for taxes and insurance and Borrower has fully complied with all terms and conditions regarding such impounds, then Borrower shall not be personally liable for Lender's failure to apply any of said impound amounts held by Lender.

(f)   any rents or other income regardless of type or source of payment (including, but not limited to, common area maintenance charges, lease termination payments, refunds of any type, prepayment of rents, settlements of litigation, or settlements of past due rents) from the Premises which Borrower has received (or could have received using commercially reasonable efforts to collect) after an Event of Default under the Loan Documents which are not applied to (A) payment of principal, interest and other charges when due under the Loan Documents or (B) payment of Operation Expenses provided that (x) Borrower has furnished Lender with evidence satisfactory to Lender of the Operation Expenses and payment thereof, and (y) any payments to parties related to

-5-

Borrower shall be considered an Operation Expense only to the extent that the amount expended for the Operation Expense does not exceed the market rate for such Operation Expense;

(g) any security deposits of tenants, together with any interest on such security deposits required by law or the leases, not turned over to Lender upon conveyance of the Premises to Lender pursuant to foreclosure or power of sale or by a deed acceptable to Lender in form and content;

(h) misapplication or misappropriation of tax reserve accounts, tenant improvement reserve accounts, security deposits, prepaid rents or other similar sums paid to or held by Borrower or any other entity or person in connection with the operation of the Premises;

(i) any insurance or condemnation proceeds or other similar funds or payments applied by Borrower in a manner other than as expressly provided in the Loan Documents; and

(j) any loss or damage to Lender arising from any fraud or willful misrepresentation by or on behalf of Borrower, Interest Owner or any guarantor regarding the Premises, the making or delivery of any of the Loan Documents or in any materials or information provided by or on behalf of Borrower, Interest Owner or any guarantor in connection with the Loan.

Notwithstanding anything contained in paragraphs 9(a)(i) and 9(c) herein above as it relates solely to taxes, assessments and insurance premiums, to the extent Lender is impounding for taxes, assessments and insurance premiums in accordance with the Loan Documents and Borrower has fully complied with all terms and conditions of the Loan Documents relating to impounding for the same, then Borrower shall not be personally liable for Lender's failure to apply any of said impound amounts held by Lender in accordance with the Loan Documents.

Notwithstanding anything to the contrary in the Loan Documents, the limitation on liability contained in the first paragraph of this paragraph 9 SHALL BECOME NULL AND VOID and shall be of no further force and effect in the event:

(k) of any breach or violation of paragraph 2(f) (due on sale or encumbrance) of the Deed of Trust, other than (i) the filing of a nonmaterial mechanic's lien affecting the Premises or a mechanic's lien affecting the Premises for which Borrower has complied with the provisions of paragraph I(e) of the Deed of Trust, or (ii) the granting of any utility or other nonmaterial easement or servitude burdening the Premises, or (iii) any transfer or encumbrance of a nonmaterial economic interest in the Premises not otherwise set forth in (i) or (ii).

(l) of the failure of Borrower to remain a Single-Purpose Entity; or

-6-

(m) of any filing by Borrower of a petition in bankruptcy or insolvency or a petition or answer seeking any reorganization, arrangement, composition, readjustment, liquidation, dissolution or similar relief under the Bankruptcy laws of the United States or under any other applicable federal, state or other statute or law.

10. If more than one, all obligations and agreements of Borrower and of any general partners of Borrower are joint and several.

11. This Note may not be changed or terminated orally, but only by an agreement in writing and signed by the party against whom enforcement of any waiver, change, modification or discharge is sought. All of the rights, privileges and obligations hereunder shall inure to the benefit of the heirs, successors and assigns of Lender and shall bind the heirs and permitted successors and assigns of Borrower.

12. If any provision of this Note shall, for any reason, be held to be invalid or unenforceable, such invalidity or unenforceability shall not affect any other provision hereof, but this Note shall be construed as if such invalid or unenforceable provision had never been contained herein.

13. This Note may be executed in counterparts, each of which shall be deemed an original; and such counterparts when taken together shall constitute but one agreement.

By: John Builder as to a 50% interest

_____
John Builder

By: Edward Helper as to a 50% Interest

_____
Edward Helper

```
                    **PAYMENT DUE NOTICE**
                     FIRST ENTERPRISE BANK
                         PO BOX 20514
                   OAKLAHOMA CITY OK   73112
```

THIS IS NOTIFICATION THAT YOUR PAYMENT WILL SOON BE DUE AS
INDICATED BELOW.

```
                          LOAN NUMBER           800364212
                          PAYMENT DUE DATE        01/01/97
                          PREVIOUS DUE                0.00
                          PRINCIPAL DUE           1,770.09
                          INTEREST DUE           18,904.91
JOHN BUILDER ET AL        ESCROW DUE                  0.00
4715 MAIN STREET     GR;E LATE CHARGES DUE            0.00
ORANGE, CA 92668          TOTAL DUE              20,675.00

                          PRINCIPAL BAL       1,851,908.83
                          ESCROW BALANCE             0.00
```

PLEASE RETURN A COPY OF THIS NOTICE WITH YOUR PAYMENT. THANK YOU.

LOAN AMORTIZATION SCHEDULE

Month	Interest	Principal	Balance
Feb-87			1,973,000
Feb-95	19,274	1,401	1,886,630
Mar-95	19,259	1,416	1,885,214
Apr-95	19,245	1,430	1,883,784
May-95	19,230	1,445	1,882,340
Jun-95	19,216	1,459	1,880,880
Jul-95	19,201	1,474	1,879,406
Aug-95	19,186	1,489	1,877,916
Sep-95	19,170	1,505	1,876,412
Oct-95	19,155	1,520	1,874,892
Nov-95	19,140	1,535	1,873,356
Dec-95	19,124	1,551	1,871,805
Jan-96	19,108	1,567	1,870,238
Feb-96	19,092	1,583	1,868,655
Mar-96	19,076	1,599	1,867,056
Apr-96	19,060	1,615	1,865,441
May-96	19,043	1,632	1,863,809
Jun-96	19,026	1,649	1,862,160
Jul-96	19,010	1,665	1,860,495
Aug-96	18,993	1,682	1,858,812
Sep-96	18,975	1,700	1,857,113
Oct-96	18,958	1,717	1,855,396
Nov-96	18,940	1,735	1,853,661
Dec-96	18,923	1,752	1,851,909
Jan-97	18,905	1,770	1,850,139
Feb-97	18,887	1,788	1,848,351
Mar-97	18,869	1,806	1,846,544
Apr-97	18,850	1,825	1,844,719
May-97	18,832	1,843	1,842,876
Jun-97	18,813	1,862	1,841,013
Jul-97	18,794	1,881	1,839,132
Aug-97	18,774	1,901	1,837,232
Sep-97	18,755	1,920	1,835,312
Oct-97	18,735	1,940	1,833,372
Nov-97	18,716	1,959	1,831,413
Dec-97	18,696	1,979	1,829,434
Jan-98	18,675	2,000	1,827,434
Feb-98	18,655	2,020	1,825,414
Mar-98	18,634	2,041	1,823,374
Apr-98	18,614	2,061	1,821,312
May-98	18,593	2,082	1,819,230
Jun-98	18,571	2,104	1,817,126
Jul-98	18,550	2,125	1,815,001
Aug-98	18,528	2,147	1,812,854
Sep-98	18,506	2,169	1,810,685

LOAN AMORTIZATION SCHEDULE

Month	Interest	Principal	Balance
Oct-98	18,484	2,191	1,808,494
Nov-98	18,462	2,213	1,806,281
Dec-98	18,439	2,236	1,804,045
Jan-99	18,416	2,259	1,801,786
Feb-99	18,393	2,282	1,799,505
Mar-99	18,370	2,305	1,797,200
Apr-99	18,346	2,329	1,794,871
May-99	18,323	2,352	1,792,519
Jun-99	18,299	2,376	1,790,142
Jul-99	18,274	2,401	1,787,742
Aug-99	18,250	2,425	1,785,317
Sep-99	18,225	2,450	1,782,867
Oct-99	18,200	2,475	1,780,392
Nov-99	18,175	2,500	1,777,892
Dec-99	18,149	2,526	1,775,366
Jan-00	18,124	2,551	1,772,814
Feb-00	18,097	2,578	1,770,237
Mar-00	18,071	2,604	1,767,633
Apr-00	18,045	2,630	1,765,003
May-00	18,018	2,657	1,762,345
Jun-00	17,991	2,684	1,759,661
Jul-00	17,963	2,712	1,756,949
Aug-00	17,936	2,739	1,754,210
Sep-00	17,908	2,767	1,751,442
Oct-00	17,879	2,796	1,748,647
Nov-00	17,851	2,824	1,745,822
Dec-00	17,822	2,853	1,742,969
Jan-01	17,793	2,882	1,740,087
Feb-01	17,763	2,912	1,737,176
Mar-01	17,734	2,941	1,734,234
Apr-01	17,704	2,971	1,731,263
May-01	17,673	3,002	1,728,261
Jun-01	17,643	3,032	1,725,229
Jul-01	17,612	3,063	1,722,166
Aug-01	17,580	3,095	1,719,071
Sep-01	17,549	3,126	1,715,945
Oct-01	17,517	3,158	1,712,787
Nov-01	17,485	3,190	1,709,597
Dec-01	17,452	3,223	1,706,374
Jan-02	17,419	3,256	1,703,118

Partnership Case Study

AGREEMENT OF LIMITED PARTNERSHIP OF
SUBURBAN OFFICE PARTNERS II, L.P.

> This Agreement has been prepared solely for instructional purposes. It is not to be used, in whole or in part, for any legal purpose whatsoever.
>
> Some sections, typically included in such documents, have been deleted, because they have no bearing on valuation issues that are the subject of the text for which this document was created.

LAW OFFICES OF GERALD E. LUNN, JR.
1901 AVENUE OF THE STARS
SUITE 1545
LOS ANGELES, CA 90067

TABLE OF CONTENTS

AGREEMENT OF LIMITED PARTNERSHIP
OF
SUBURBAN OFFICE PARTNERS II, L.P.

As of the date that this Agreement has been signed by the General Partner and the Initial Limited Partners listed below, such parties shall have entered into the following limited partnership agreement.

General Partner: JB Management, Inc.

Initial Limited Partners: John Builder
                            Edward Helper

RECITALS:

A. The Partners desire to enter into this agreement (the "Agreement") to establish a limited partnership (the "Partnership") under the California Revised Limited Partnership Act; and

B. The Partners desire that the Partnership transact business and make investments, and that they share in the risks, benefits, profits and losses of such businesses and investments.

NOW, THEREFORE, THE PARTNERS AGREE AS FOLLOWS:

AGREEMENT:

SECTION 1: NAME

The Partnership's official name is "Suburban Office Partners II, L.P."

SECTION 2: DEFINED TERMS

The terms defined in Section 20 below shall have the meanings set forth in such Section.

SECTION 3: PLACE OF BUSINESS, REGISTERED AGENT AND FORMALITIES

3.1   Place of Business.

The Partnership's principal place of business will be 4715 Main Street, Orange, California. The General Partner may from time to time relocate the Partnership's principal place of business upon notice to all Limited Partners.

-1-

3.2   Agent for Service of Process.

The General Partner or its President shall be the Partnership's agent for service of process.

3.3   Formalities.

The Partnership shall hold, operate, and manage its assets and enter into contracts as a limited partnership. A "Certificate of Limited Partnership" under California Corporations Code Section 15621 shall be prepared and signed by the General Partner, and filed in the office of the California Secretary of State. The Partnership shall not conduct any business until such Certificate is filed. The General Partner shall take all steps required for the formation and continuation of the Partnership as a limited partnership under California law, and under the applicable law of any other state.

SECTION 4: PURPOSES AND SCOPE OF BUSINESS

4.1   Purposes.

The Partners desire to make a profit, increase their wealth, and preserve their assets. The Partners intend and hope that the Partnership will accomplish the following:

4.1.1   resolve any disputes that may arise with respect to assets, preserve harmony and avoid (or reduce) litigation expenses and problems;

4.1.2   control assets in a businesslike and productive manner;

4.1.3   consolidate fractional interests and avoid holding such assets as tenants in common;

4.1.4   establish a method by which annual gifts may be made without fractionalizing assets;

4.1.5   increase Partners' wealth;

4.1.7 to 4.1.12   [deleted]

4.1.13 provide possible tax savings with respect to Transfers of Partnership Interests;

4.1.14 provide long-term skilled management of the assets contributed by the Partners for the long-term benefit of the Partners; and

4.1.15 limit the liability of the Limited Partners with respect to obligations of the Partnership and claims against the Partnership.

4.2   Scope of Business.

The Partnership may conduct any lawful business and investment activity permitted under Section 15616 of the Act and other applicable law. If the Partnership qualifies to do business in a foreign jurisdiction, then it may transact all business permitted in that jurisdiction.

The powers of the General Partner conferred by this Agreement and by law shall be construed broadly to implement the intent of the Partners that the Partnership may engage in any legal business, including, without limitation, investment in and management of real estate, stocks, bonds, all other forms of investment and operation of businesses of all types.

SECTION 5: TERM

The Partnership shall begin on the date that this Agreement is signed by all parties and end on December 31, 2050. Termination of this Partnership before December 31, 2050 shall require the written consent of all Partners.

SECTION 6: CAPITAL ACCOUNTS AND PARTNERSHIP INTERESTS

6.1   Classes of Partnership Interests.

For purposes of Sections 15631.5 and 15645 of the Act, the Partnership shall have only one class of Partnership Interests.

6.2   Maintenance of Capital Accounts.

A Capital Account shall be established for each Partner. Capital Accounts shall be maintained in a manner that corresponds with the capital of each Partner in compliance with the Code and the Regulations. Each Partner's Capital Account shall be credited with the value of the Partner's contributions of cash or other property to the Partnership or such capital as may be otherwise acquired by the Partner. Property contributed to the Partnership shall be valued based on its fair market value net of any liabilities that are attached to such property as provided in Section 752 of the Code. Furthermore, each Partner's Capital Account shall be credited or charged annually with that Partner's distributive share of items of income, gain, ordinary loss, capital loss, and credit for federal income tax purposes. Each Partner's Capital Account shall also be charged with that Partner's distributive share of Partnership expenditures as defined in Section 705(a)(2)(B) of the Code. The Partners' Capital Accounts shall not bear interest.

Distributions of cash or other property to a Partner shall be charged against the Partner's Capital Account as withdrawals of capital. Distributions of property shall be valued based on fair market values, adjusted as provided in Section 752 of the Code to account for any associated liabilities.

The federal income tax basis of a Partner's Partnership Interest and all other matters pertaining to the distributive shares and taxation of items of income, gain, loss, deduction and credit may be determined by the General Partner in any manner that is

-3-

permitted by the Code and the Regulations and is consistent with the provisions of this Agreement. It is anticipated that, absent extraordinary circumstances, a Partner's Capital Account shall at all times equal the sum of that Partner's capital contributions plus that Partner's share of profits and capital gains, and reduced by that Partner's share of ordinary and capital losses and by distributions to that Partner, so as to fully comply with Section 704(b) of the Code.

6.3   Initial Capital Contribution.

The amount and nature of each Partner's initial capital contribution is set forth in Schedule A.

6.4   Voluntary Additional Capital Contributions.

Each Partner may voluntarily make additional contributions to the capital of the Partnership (in cash or in kind) with the written consent of the General Partner. Such additional contributions shall be added to that Partner's Capital Account and/or increase that Partner's Percentage Interest in such amounts as may from time to time be reasonably agreed upon with the General Partner. Such additional contributions shall be subject to Section 6.9 below and the other provisions of this Agreement relating to capital contributions.

6.5   Involuntary Capital Calls.

The Partnership, acting by the General Partner, shall have the authority to "call" on the Partners to contribute additional capital when: (1) additional capital is reasonably necessary to pay existing or anticipated expenses of operation and administration and debt service; and, (2) the calls for capital are not discriminatory, that is, when all Partners, both general and limited, are required to contribute capital proportionate to each Partner's Percentage Interest in the Partnership.

A required contribution of capital must be made within sixty (60) days from the date the call is made.

If a Partner cannot, or does not, contribute capital in an amount proportionate to his, her, or its Percentage Interest in the Partnership, other Partners may pay the deficiency as an additional capital contribution. In each such case, the General Partner shall have the authority to reallocate the Percentage Interests of all Partners, increasing the Percentage Interests of those who made full contributions and decreasing the Percentage Interests of those who did not make full contributions. The reallocation of Percentage Interests shall be determined by dividing the balance of each Partner's Capital Account by the total of all of the Capital Accounts of all Partners, but giving credit to amounts paid pursuant to the capital call at the rate of one hundred fifty percent (150%) of the amounts contributed. The reason for such 150% crediting rate is to strongly encourage all Partners to participate in capital calls and to reward any Partners who take up the slack created by Partners who do not so participate. Nothing in this Section 6.5 is intended to create any requirement that any Partner contribute additional capital (except as required to comply with Section 6.10 below).

6.6   <u>Normal Adjustments</u>.

Each Partner's Capital Account shall be adjusted whenever necessary to reflect (1) such Partner's distributive share of profits and losses based on such Partner's Percentage Interest, including capital gains and losses, (2) such Partner's additional capital contributions to the Partnership, (3) distributions made by the Partnership to the Partner, and (4) other adjustments that are necessary or deemed appropriate by the General Partner under the Code and the Regulations. A Partner's loans to the Partnership shall not be added to such Partner's Capital Account.

6.7   <u>Extraordinary Adjustments in Percentage Interests Based on Capital Accounts</u>.

The General Partner, acting with the written consent of a Majority in Interest of the Limited Partners, shall have the authority to adjust the Percentage Interests of all Partners based upon the balance of each Partner's Capital Account in relation to the total of all the Capital Accounts of all Partners. Such reallocation of Percentage Interests ownership shall be determined by dividing the balance of each Partner's Capital Account (including any adjustments pursuant to Section 6.5 above) by the total of all of the Capital Accounts. The General Partner shall also have the authority to make special distributions (without the consent of any other Partner) for the purpose of causing the Capital Accounts of the Partners to be proportionate to their Percentage Interests. Furthermore, the General Partner shall have absolute authority to restate the Partners' Capital Accounts at any time (without the consent of any other Partner) to comply with the requirements of the Regulations under Section 704 of the Code. The provisions of this Section 6.7 are included for purposes of maintaining Capital Accounts and Percentage Interests in accordance with California law and the Code, but it is anticipated that these provisions will not be necessary, absent extraordinary circumstances.

6.8   <u>No Interest</u>.

No Partner shall receive any interest on any capital contributions.

6.9   <u>No Right to Return of Capital Contributions</u>.

A Partner shall not have the right to withdraw or reduce any capital contribution except upon dissolution of the Partnership. A Limited Partner shall look solely to the assets of the Partnership and shall have no claim against the General Partner on account of any contribution. In no event shall a Partner have a right to demand and receive property other than cash in return for any contribution.

6.10   <u>Minimum Percentage Interest of General Partner</u>.

The General Partner(s) may never own a (total) Percentage Interest of less than one percent (1%) as General Partner(s) and shall immediately make whatever capital contributions are required to maintain such Percentage Interest.

6.11   <u>Loans to the Partnership</u>.

-5-

A Partner may make loans to the Partnership on such terms as may be agreed upon between such Partner and the General Partner. If any Partner makes loans to the Partnership or advances money on its behalf, then the amount of any such loan or advance shall be deemed a loan and shall not affect the Percentage Interest or Capital Account of the lending Partner. Other than as expressly agreed, the amount of any such loan, plus accrued interest thereon, computed at the prime rate as charged by the Union Bank of California (or its successor in interest) on the date of the loan, shall be an obligation of the Partnership to such lending Partner. Absent the written consent of the Partner(s) with outstanding loans, such loans (including accrued interest) must be repaid prior to any distribution of Net Cash Flow pursuant to Section 7.2 below. If there are insufficient funds available (in the discretion of the General Partner) to repay all such loans, then the oldest loan(s) shall be repaid first and loans made on the same date shall be repaid on a pro-rata basis.

6.12   Records.

The Partners and their initial Percentage Interests are identified in Schedule A. The General Partner shall maintain correct records of the Percentage Interests of the Partners and of all changes in such Percentage Interests.

SECTION 7: PROFITS, LOSSES AND CASH FLOW

7.1   Profits and Losses.

The Partnership's net profits and losses shall be computed in any reasonable manner determined by the General Partner that is in accordance with applicable provisions of the Code and Regulations. The Partnership's net profits and losses and every item of income, deduction, gain, loss, and credit shall be allocated proportionately among the Partners according to their Percentage Interests. No Partner shall have priority over any other Partner as to Partnership profits or losses. Income, gain, loss, and deductions with respect to property contributed to the Partnership by a Partner shall be shared among the Partners so as to take account of any variation between the basis of the property so contributed and its fair market value at the time of contribution, in accordance with any reasonable methodology permitted under the Regulations.

7.2   Required Distribution of Net Cash Flow.

The General Partner shall cause the Partnership to distribute its Net Cash Flow to the Partners at least annually, except to the extent that the General Partner reasonably determines that an extraordinary accumulation is necessary for the business of the Partnership, for capital reserves for reasonably anticipated expenses or for investment or reinvestment by the Partnership; provided that an accumulation of Net Cash Flow for investment or reinvestment may not occur if a Majority in Interest of the Limited Partners file written objections with the General Partner. All distributions of Partnership Net Cash Flow shall be made to the Partners in proportion to their Percentage Interests; provided that the General Partner may make special distributions to cause the Partners' Capital Accounts to conform with their Percentage Interests as provided in Section 6.7 above. The General Partner shall have a duty of good faith and loyalty to the Limited Partners in exercising reasonable business judgment pursuant to this Section.

-6-

7.3   Assignment or Death.

In the event of an assignment of a Partnership Interest or of a Partner's death, retirement, or expulsion, profits and losses shall be allocated based on the number of days in the particular year during which each Partner (or Assignee) owned his, her or its Partnership Interest (or rights as an Assignee), or on any other reasonable basis determined by the General Partner that is consistent with applicable provisions of the Code and Regulations.

SECTION 8: MANAGEMENT AND OPERATIONS

8.1   Rights and Obligations of Limited Partners.

Except as otherwise expressly provided herein or absolutely required under the Act, the Limited Partners shall take no part in and have no power, authority or vote respecting the Partnership's management and operations; however, the General Partner, in its reasonable discretion, may engage the services of one or more Limited Partners on behalf of the Partnership and cause the Partnership to pay reasonable compensation for such services, or may engage and compensate a Limited Partner as an employee of the General Partner.

A Limited Partner shall not be, or become, liable as a General Partner, nor shall a Limited Partner be liable to creditors of the Partnership, except to the extent absolutely required by applicable law.

8.2   Breaches by Limited Partners.

A Limited Partner shall be liable for all damages to the Partnership arising from any breach by such Limited Partner of this Agreement, including, without limitation:

8.2.1   attempting to withdraw from the Partnership;

8.2.2   interfering in the management of the Partnership;
8.2.3   engaging in conduct that could result in the Partnership losing its tax status as a Partnership;

8.2.4   engaging in conduct that could bring the Partnership into disrepute;

8.2.5   allowing the Partner's Partnership Interest to be subject to a charging order, attachment, or similar legal proceedings; or
8.2.6   breaching any provision of this Agreement or failing to meet any commitment to the Partnership.

The Partnership shall have a first priority right to deduct any such damages from any distributions otherwise payable to a Limited Partner who is liable for such damages, to any Assignee of such Limited Partner, or to any Assignee who so breaches this Agreement.

8.3   Services of General Partner.

The General Partner shall devote whatever time and effort may be reasonably necessary to the business and affairs of the Partnership. The Partnership shall at all times have at least one General Partner and such General Partner(s) shall have (at all times) a (total) Percentage Interest of at least one percent (1%).

8.4   General Partner Not Liable for Good Faith Actions; Indemnification.

The General Partner shall not be liable to the Partnership or to the Limited Partners for any action that the General Partner may take in good faith, and shall not be liable if it is unable to render services as General Partner for causes beyond its control.

Pursuant to the Act, the Partnership shall indemnify, defend and hold harmless the General Partner, its affiliates, officers, directors, partners, employees, and agents from any loss, damage, cause of action, claim, liability, settlement, penalty or award suffered or sustained by the Partnership or any Partner by reason of acts or omissions or alleged acts or omissions by the General Partner, performed (or not performed) by the General Partner on the Partnership's behalf, or in furthering the Partnership's purposes, absent clear and convincing evidence of willful misconduct or gross negligence. This indemnification shall include all rights and benefits that may be granted under the Act, including reasonable attorneys' fees and expenses (whether or not litigation has commenced), and shall be satisfied from Partnership assets only.

8.5   Powers of General Partner.

The General Partner shall have the full and exclusive power on the Partnership's behalf and in its name, to manage, control, and operate its business and affairs and to do or cause to be done anything it deems necessary or appropriate for the Partnership's business and affairs, including (but not limited to) the power and authority to do the following:

8.5.1   General Management of Assets.
Manage, administer, insure, repair, improve, develop, operate, lease, utilize, and defend the Partnership's assets, directly or by employing third parties, and incur any reasonable expense in connection therewith.

8.5.2   Sell or Exchange Property.

Sell or exchange any real or personal property, giving any warranties or assurances deemed appropriate.

8.5.3   Acquire Property.

Purchase, lease, or otherwise acquire real or personal property to conduct the Partnership's business or as an investment.

8.5.4   Permissible Investments.

Invest (and reinvest) in every kind of property and investment, including individual, corporate and governmental bonds and other obligations of every kind (whether purchased at par, at a premium or at a discount); preferred and common stock and warrants to acquire stock; interests in partnerships, limited liability companies and all other forms of business entity; life insurance policies; oil, gas and mineral interests; shares in investment Trusts, money market accounts, market funds, index funds, and mutual funds; interests in real estate and tangible personal property; options to buy or sell stock or other property; and mortgage participations. The General Partner may open one or more brokerage accounts in the name of the Partnership to facilitate the investment and management of Partnership assets.

8.5.5   Risky Investments.

An investment having a high degree of risk and a high potential return shall be proper if the General Partner deems such risk to be justified. The General Partner may invest up to fifty percent (50%) of the Partnership's assets in such risky investments; provided that with the consent of a Majority in Interest of the Limited Partners, the General Partner may invest up to ninety percent (90%) of the Partnership's assets in such risky investments.

8.5.6   Nondiversification.

Retain or acquire any property and make investments without regard to diversification.

8.5.7   Unproductive and Under-Productive Property.

Retain or acquire property that does not produce income, or that produces income below the current market rate.

8.6   Interests in Other Business Enterprises.

The Partnership may serve as the general partner of another limited partnership. The Partnership may form or invest in a trust, partnership, limited liability company, corporation, or other entity in which it will be a shareholder, partner, member, trustee, beneficiary, or owner. Such other entity may be located in any jurisdiction and may facilitate management and/or investment functions.

Whenever an interest in a business (including a proprietorship, partnership, corporation, or other entity) is held by the Partnership, the General Partner may hold, manage, sell or liquidate the business; carry out or contest the provisions of any agreements relating to the business; and directly or indirectly withdraw profits or retain them in the business; provided that the power to retain profits in the business shall be subject to the same limitations as set forth in Section 7.2 above regarding required distribution of Net Cash Flow. Absent actual notice to the contrary, the General Partner may accept financial and other statements rendered by such a business entity as correct.

-9-

8.7   Securities.

The General Partner may exercise all the rights, powers, and privileges of an owner with respect to securities held by the Partnership and may allow such securities to be held in "street name" under a custodial arrangement with an established securities brokerage firm.

8.8   Bank Accounts and Securities Accounts.

The General Partner may open and maintain checking, savings and securities accounts with any bank or savings and loan associations or brokerage or securities firms or mutual funds and deposit any funds into such accounts, whether or not the funds may earn interest. Funds may be withdrawn by check or other instrument signed by the General Partner or any other Person authorized by the General Partner. Any such bank or association or brokerage firm or securities firm or mutual fund is hereby authorized to pay a check or other instrument or receive it for deposit to the credit of the holder when so signed, without inquiry of any kind, and payments and credits so made shall not be subject to objection by any Person.

8.9   Borrowing; Encumbrances.

The General Partner may borrow money on behalf of the Partnership from any Person (including a Partner), and establish margin accounts and purchase securities on margin, all upon such terms as the General Partner deems proper; obligate the Partnership for repayment; and encumber property of the Partnership, by mortgage, deed of Trust, pledge or otherwise for any sole or joint debt of the Partnership; or acquire property subject to existing encumbrances.

8.10   Loans.

The General Partner may loan Partnership funds to any Person (including a Partner); provided that any loan shall bear interest at a commercially reasonable rate and be adequately secured.

8.11   Litigation.

The General Partner may prosecute any claims of the Partnership or defend any claims against the Partnership in any forum and may compromise any claim, except as otherwise expressly provided herein.

8.12   Insurance.

The General Partner may obtain liberal amounts of insurance in all forms against loss and liability with respect to the Partnership's operations and assets, including insurance relating to the Partnership's obligations hereunder or otherwise to indemnify the General Partner and other parties. The General Partner may also obtain insurance on the life of any Partner. All such insurance policies shall be owned by the Partnership.

8.13   Employment of Consultants, Employees, Agents and Others.

The General Partner may employ consultants, accountants, attorneys, investment advisers, corporate fiduciaries, and any other agents, advisers or employees to assist in administering the Partnership, and rely on the advice of these agents and advisers. The General Partner may pay reasonable consideration for services performed by these agents and advisers from Partnership assets as the General Partner may determine. These payments shall be considered in determining the reasonable compensation of the General Partner. A Limited Partner may serve as such an agent or advisor pursuant to an arm's-length agreement between such Limited Partner and the General Partner.

8.14   Incidental Powers.

The General Partner may do anything necessary or useful in exercising its powers and may execute, acknowledge, and deliver any and all instruments to effectuate any of the foregoing powers and carry out the duties of the General Partner. The preceding sentence shall be interpreted in the broadest possible manner and any third party may rely on a written certification of the General Partner that the General Partner is authorized to take any proposed action. No third party shall have any duty to verify that the General Partner is acting in compliance with this Agreement.

8.15   Prohibited Powers.

Notwithstanding the other provisions of this Agreement, the General Partner shall not have authority to:

8.15.1 do anything that would make it impossible to carry on the ordinary business of the Partnership without the consent of at least ninety percent (90%) in Percentage Interests of all Partners.

8.15.2 sell substantially all of the Partnership's investment assets in liquidation or cessation of business without the consent of at least seventy-five percent (75%) in Percentage Interests of all Partners;

8.15.3 compromise any claim or dispute having an amount or value in issue exceeding fifty percent (50%) of the total value of the Partnership's assets without the consent of at least seventy-five percent (75%) in Percentage Interests of all Partners;

8.15.4 personally deal with Partnership property for less than reasonable consideration or directly or indirectly borrow funds of the Partnership without commercially reasonable interest and security or the consent of all other Partners; or

8.15.5 amend this Agreement without the consent of all other Partners, except as otherwise provided in this Agreement.

8.16   Reliance by Third Parties.   [deleted]

8.16.1 Right to Rely on Acts of General Partner.

-11-

Any Person dealing with the Partnership, other than a Partner, may rely on the authority of the General Partner in taking any action in the name of the Partnership without inquiry into the provisions of this Agreement. Any document executed by the General Partner shall be deemed to be the action of the Partnership as to any third parties. No purchaser, tenant, transferee, obligor or other Person shall have any obligation to see to the application of payments made to the General Partner.

8.16.2 <u>Right to Rely on Certificate</u>.

Any Person dealing with the Partnership or the General Partner may rely upon a certificate signed by the General Partner as to:

8.16.2.1   the identities of the Partners;

8.16.2.2   any conditions precedent to acts by the Partnership;

8.16.2.3   the Persons who are authorized to execute any documents and bind the Partnership; and

8.16.2.4   any other matter involving the Partnership or any Partner.

8.17   <u>Compensation of General Partner</u>.

The General Partner shall receive reasonable compensation for managing the Partnership's business. Such compensation shall comply with all federal income tax law requirements pertaining to partnerships in which capital is a material income-producing factor and shall constitute a guaranteed payment and bear interest at the applicable federal rate if it is deferred. Such reasonable compensation shall be measured by the time required in the management and administration of the Partnership, the value of property under the General Partner's administration, the responsibilities assumed, the results achieved and any other relevant factors.

8.18   <u>Reimbursement for Expenses</u>.

All reasonable expenses incurred by the General Partner in managing and conducting the Partnership's business, including (but not limited to) overhead, administrative and travel expenses, and professional, technical, administrative, and other services, shall be reimbursed by the Partnership.

8.19   <u>Tax Matters Partner</u>.

The General Partner shall be solely responsible for representing the Partnership in all dealings with the Internal Revenue Service and any state, local, and foreign tax authorities. The General Partner shall keep the other Partners reasonably informed regarding any problems with any tax authority.

8.20   <u>Waiver of Self-Dealing</u>.   [deleted]

-12-

8.21   Annual Meetings.   [deleted]

8.22   Advisory Committee.   [deleted]

SECTION 9: BOOKS AND RECORDS

9.1   General.

The Partnership's books and records shall be kept on the cash or accrual method of accounting, as the General Partner may determine, and in accordance with generally accepted accounting principles and applicable law, and shall reflect all Partnership transactions. The Partnership books shall be kept based on a calendar year. The Partnership's records shall be maintained at the Partnership's principal place of business. Such records shall include all records required to be maintained pursuant to Section 15615 of the Act.

9.2   Financial Statements.

Within a reasonable period after the close of each fiscal year, the General Partner, at the Partnership's expense, shall give a written report to each other Partner indicating such Partner's share of the Partnership income and expenses. This requirement may be satisfied by giving each Partner a copy of a tax return or form which includes such information. The General Partner shall also provide each other Partner with any other information reasonably necessary to prepare their federal and state income tax returns.

9.3   Confidentiality of Information.

Each Partner shall be entitled to information under the circumstances and subject to the conditions stated in this Agreement and as required by law. The Partners acknowledge that they may receive information regarding the Partnership in the nature of trade secrets or that is otherwise confidential. They also acknowledge that the release of such information might damage the Partnership. Each Partner will hold in strict confidence any information that he, she or it receives regarding the Partnership that is identified as being confidential. The Partners acknowledge that breaching this Section's provisions may cause irreparable injury to the Partnership for which monetary damages are inadequate, difficult to compute, or both. Accordingly, the Partners agree that this Section's provisions may be enforced by specific performance. No Partner may disclose confidential information to any Person other than another Partner, except as required by law; provided that a Partner may disclose such information to the Partner's attorneys or accountants, but only if they have agreed in writing to be bound by this Section's provisions.

SECTION 10: TAX ELECTIONS AND DECISIONS

No election shall be made to exclude the Partnership from the application of the provisions of Subchapter K of the Code or from any similar provisions of state tax laws. If a Partnership Interest is transferred, a Partner dies, or Partnership assets are distributed to a Partner, the General Partner may, in its absolute discretion, elect to cause the basis of the Partnership's assets to be adjusted for federal income tax purposes under Code Sections 734, 743 and 754 and for state income tax purposes under applicable state law. Partners affected by

-13-

this election, if made, shall supply to the Partnership the information that may be required to make the election. The General Partner shall not be liable for making or failing to make any tax election absent clear and convincing evidence of bad faith. Furthermore, the General Partner shall not be liable for any tax reporting position or allocation for tax purposes taken in reliance on advice of an accountant.

SECTION 11: TRANSFER OF PARTNERSHIP INTERESTS

11.1   Reasons for Restricting Transfers.

The Partners do not want Partnership Interests to be made generally available to Persons other than the present Partners.

This Partnership is formed by parties who know and trust one another, who will have surrendered certain management rights in exchange for limited liability (in the case of the Limited Partners) or who will have assumed sole management responsibility and risk (in the case of the General Partner) based upon their relationship and trust. An unauthorized Transfer of a Partnership Interest could create a substantial hardship for the remaining Partner(s), jeopardize the Partnership's capital base, and adversely affect its tax structure. These restrictions upon ownership and Transfer are not intended as a penalty, but as a method to preserve relationships based upon trust and harmony and the Partnership's ability to continue.

11.2   Consent of All Partners Required.

The parties agree that no Partner will Transfer any portion of his, her or its Partnership Interest except in accordance with the terms of this Section 11 and with the prior written consent of all other Partners. No Partner shall be under any obligation to give such consent, it being the understanding of the Partners that each Partner acting alone can prevent any Transfer (other than a Permitted Transfer under Section 11.10 below) in order to preserve the objectives of the Partnership described in Section 4.1 above. An attempted Transfer of any Partnership Interest not in accordance with the terms of this Section 11 or with the prior written consent of all other Partners shall be invalid, except to the extent required by the Act.

11.3   Right to Purchase Upon Transfer of Limited Partner's Interest.

In the event of a voluntary Transfer by a Limited Partner not permitted under this Agreement, or an involuntary Transfer of a Limited Partner's Partnership Interest, whether by Insolvency, Bankruptcy or otherwise, including an assignment for the benefit of creditors or a lawful "charging order," the other Partners shall have the right, within one hundred twenty (120) days following such event, to take one of the following three actions:

11.3.1 unanimously agree to admit such Assignee as a Limited Partner,

11.3.2 purchase the interest of such Limited Partner ("Transferring Limited Partner") at its fair market value.

-14-

11.3.3 allow such Assignee to remain an Assignee under this Agreement if such purchase is not completed as provided in this Section 11.

Such one hundred twenty (120) day period shall not commence until the General Partner has received a written opinion from counsel for the purported Assignee that the Partnership is legally required to recognize the Transfer, and such period shall be tolled if the General Partner or the Transferring Partner seeks a judicial determination regarding the validity of the Transfer (in which event, such period shall commence on the date that a final judicial determination upholding the visibility of the Transfer is no longer appealable). The date on which one or more of the remaining Partners give notice of their intent to purchase the interest of the Transferring Partner is referred to below as the "Notice Date." Except as provided in Section 11.10 below, in no event shall an Assignee become a Limited Partner without the consent of all Partners and full compliance with the provisions of this Section 11. An Assignee who does not become a Limited Partner shall have only those rights granted by law.

Notwithstanding in this Section 11.3 shall be interpreted as precluding or limiting any rights of the Partnership or limiting any rights of the Partnership or any Partner to bring an action (for damages and/or equitable relief) against a Partner for damages resulting from a Transfer or attempted Transfer that violates any provision of this Agreement.

11.4   Terms of Purchase.

The following provisions shall apply with respect to the purchase of a Limited Partner's interest pursuant to Section 11.3 above.

11.4.1 Fair Market Value.

The purchase price shall be determined based on the fair market value of the Limited Partner's Partnership Interest on the Notice Date determined in the same manner as fair market value is determined for federal gift and estate tax purposes, including all appropriate valuation adjustments and valuation adjustments. Such "Fair Market Value" shall be determined by an independent Appraiser approved by each Partner; provided that if the Partners cannot agree on a single Appraiser, then the Transferring Partner or his, her or its duly authorized representative shall nominate one Appraiser and the remaining Partners shall nominate another Appraiser and if such two Appraisers cannot agree on a value, but the lower valuation is at least eighty percent (80%) of the higher valuation, then an average of the valuations shall be used, and if the valuations are not this close, then such two Appraisers shall nominate a third Appraiser and the third Appraiser shall be solely responsible for determining the Fair Market Value of the interest to be Transferred, but such value must be in the range of the values promulgated by the first two Appraisers. If such two appraisers fail to agree on a third appraiser within ten (10) business days after their appraisals are both complete, then any party may file a request with the presiding judge of the Los Angeles County Superior Court to provide the parties with a list of three appraisers who can certify that they are not acquainted with any Partner or Assignee. Upon receipt of such list and such certifications, each side may strike one appraiser from such list and the remaining appraiser shall serve as the third appraiser hereunder, or if both sides strike the same appraiser, and cannot agree as to who they prefer between the remaining two candidates, then the third appraiser shall be chosen by lot from the remaining two candidates. The General Partner shall give notice to all Partners within ten (10) business days after such value is determined pursuant to this Section 11.4.1.

11.4.2 Notice by Partners Who Wish to Buy Interest of Transferring Partner.

Upon the receipt of notice of a determination of value pursuant to Section 11.4.1 above, each Partner (excluding the Transferring Partner) shall have a right to buy a proportionate share of such Partnership Interest and a proportionate share of any share not purchased by the other remaining Partners. Each Partner may buy a share of such Partnership Interest having the same proportion to the whole of such Partnership Interest as his, her or its own Partnership Interest bears to those of all Partners, excluding the Transferring Partner. Each Partner may exercise this right to purchase by giving the General Partner written notice within thirty (30) calendar days after receipt of the General Partner's notice pursuant to Section 11.4.1 and such notice may also exercise a right to purchase a proportionate share of any portion of such Partnership Interest that is not purchased by other Partners. Partners who so desire shall have the right, but not the obligation, to purchase all or any part of the Partnership Interest that would otherwise have been purchased by other Partners.

11.4.3 Terms of Purchase.

In order to reduce the burden on the remaining Partners, the purchase price shall be paid as follows: ten percent (10%) payable in cash at the closing, and the balance in fifteen (15) equal annual principal payments beginning one year after the date of closing, with simple interest added to each installment, computed against the outstanding principal balance at two percent (2%) over the prevailing prime interest rate charged by the Union Bank of California on the date of such closing; provided that if the remaining term of the Partnership is less than fifteen (15) years, then the principal payments shall be made over such term. The purchasing Partner(s) shall give the Transferring Partner and/or any Assignee (to the extent that each is entitled to the benefit of the Partnership Interest in question) a promissory note as evidence of this debt, and the purchasing Partner(s) may prepay all or any part of the principal balance of such note at any time without penalty or premium.

11.5 Closing.

11.5.1 Time.

The purchase of a Partnership Interest pursuant to this Section 11 shall take place at a closing to be held not later than the thirtieth (30th) day after the earlier of: (1) the date on which the Partners' purchase options all have expired; or (2) the earliest date on which the remaining Partners in the aggregate exercise their purchase options, if any, to buy all of the Transferring Partner's Partnership Interest.

11.5.2 Place.

The closing will be held during normal business hours at the Partnership's principal place of business, or at any other place to which the parties agree.

11.5.3 Procedures.

At the closing, the Partnership will change its books to indicate the change of Partnership Interests. If the Transferring Partner or the Assignee is not present at the closing, then the purchasing Partners shall deposit the appropriate portion of the purchase price by check, note, and/or other property as this Section 11 requires, with the General Partner, as escrow holder, to be paid to the Transferring Partner and/or Assignee as soon as is reasonably practicable, less an appropriate fee to the Partnership (not to exceed two thousand dollars ($2,000)) to pay for reasonable administrative costs.

11.6 Conditions Precedent to Admission of Substituted Limited Partner.

Except as expressly provided in Section 11.10 below, no Assignee may become a Limited Partner except upon satisfaction of all of the following conditions:

11.6.1 The General Partner and all Limited Partners agree, in writing, to admit such Assignee as a Limited Partner.

11.6.2 The Assignee accepts and adopts, in a form satisfactory to the General Partner, all of the terms and conditions of this Agreement as if the Assignee were one of the original Partners hereunder.

11.6.3 In the case of a corporate Assignee, a certified copy of a resolution of its Board of Directors authorizing it to become a Limited Partner under the terms and conditions of this Agreement must be delivered to the General Partner.

11.6.4 The Transferring Partner (or his, her or its duly authorized representative) and Assignee execute a statement, in a form satisfactory to the General Partner, specifying the interest being assigned, and that the Assignee is acquiring the Partnership Interest for investment and not for resale.

11.6.5 The Assignee executes, acknowledges, and delivers such other documents or instruments as the General Partner may reasonably require in order to effect the admission of the Assignee as a Limited Partner.

11.6.6 The Assignee pays such reasonable expenses as may be incurred by the Partnership in connection with the admission of that Limited Partner, not to exceed two thousand dollars ($2,000).

11.7 Allocation Upon Transfer of Partnership Interest.

11.7.1 Methodology.

Upon a Transfer of all or any part of the Partnership Interest of a Limited Partner, the net profits, gains, and losses attributable to the Partnership Interest so assigned shall be allocated between the Transferring Partner and the Assignee as provided in Section 7.3 above.

11.7.2 Distributions.

Any distributions of cash or other property shall be made to the owner of record of the Partnership Interest on the date of distribution; provided that such distributions may be made to an Assignee to the extent required by applicable law.

11.8 Limitations Imposed by Federal and State Securities Laws.

Any Assignee shall be informed that the Partnership Interests of the Partnership have not and will not be registered or qualified under any federal or state securities laws. Such Partnership Interests may not be offered for sale, sold, pledged, or otherwise Transferred unless so registered or qualified, or unless an exemption from registration or qualification exists. The availability of any exemption from registration or qualification must be established by a written opinion of counsel for the owner thereof, which opinion must be reasonably satisfactory to the General Partner.

The Partnership will not be subject to the reporting requirements of the Securities Exchange Act of 1934, as amended, and will not file reports, proxy statements and other information with the Securities and Exchange Commission.

11.9 Nonrecognition of an Unauthorized Transfer.

Except to the extent required by the Act, the Partnership shall not be required to recognize the interest of any Assignee who has obtained a purported interest as the result of a Transfer of ownership which is not an authorized Transfer. If the ownership of a Partnership Interest is in doubt, or if there is reasonable doubt as to who is entitled to a distribution of the income realized from a Partnership Interest, the Partnership may accumulate the income until this issue is finally resolved as provided in Section 19 below. Accumulated income shall be credited to the Capital Account of the Partner whose interest is in question.

11.10 Permitted Transfers.

The restrictions of this Section 11 shall not apply to Transfers ("Permitted Transfers") without consideration to any of the following classes of transferees, who shall be called "Permitted Transferees" and who shall be endowed with the rights and obligations of the Limited Partners hereof, except as otherwise provided by this Agreement:

11.10.1   any other Partner;

11.10.2   any Issue of a Partner except that such Issue shall remain an Assignee and not be admitted as a Partner and, accordingly, shall not be permitted any voting or decision-making rights under this Agreement, until such Issue reaches age thirty (30) or there is no other Limited Partner hereunder, whichever shall first occur, at which time such Issue shall be admitted as a Partner and shall acquire said rights previously denied her or him;

11.10.3   the trustee of any trust for the benefit of one (1) or more members of the Family, but only if such trust provides that no one other than one (1) or more members of the Family will be a beneficiary unless and until all such members of the Family

-18-

are deceased. The trustee of said trust shall not have any voting or decision-making rights under this Agreement unless said trustee is already a Partner or a Current Spouse (as that term is defined in Section 11.10.4, below) or until the earlier to occur of the youngest current beneficiary of such Trust reaching age thirty (30) or there being no Limited Partner hereof, at which time such trustee shall be admitted as a Partner and shall acquire said rights previously denied her or him;

   11.10.4   any current spouse of a Partner as of the date of this Agreement ("Current Spouse"), except that such Current Spouse shall not be admitted as Partner, and accordingly, shall not have any voting or decision making rights under this Agreement, and so long as said Current Spouse agrees in writing that at any time said Current Spouse's spouse who is a Partner hereof may on sixty (60) days notice purchase all or any part of the Current Spouse's interest at its fair market value pursuant to Sections 11.4 and 11.5 above;

   11.10.5   the trustee of any trust created as the result of the death of a Partner for the benefit of the Partner's surviving spouse, but only if such trust qualifies for the federal estate tax marital deduction under Section 2056(b)(7) of the Code, such trust prohibits distributions of principal to or for the benefit of such surviving spouse (unless such surviving spouse already holds a Percentage Interest hereunder of at least ten percent (10%), and such trust provides that upon the death of such surviving spouse, the balance of the trust assets after taxes and expenses will pass to or for the benefit of one or more Issue of the deceased Partner or descendant of the grandparents of the deceased Partner;

   11.10.6   any charitable organization described in each of the following sections of the Internal Revenue Code: Section 170(b)(1)(A); Section 170(c); Section 2055(a); and Section 2522(a);

   11.10.7   any charitable remainder trust created under Section 664 of the Internal Revenue Code, but only if the non charitable beneficiaries are all either Partners or Permitted Transferees.

   11.11 Manner of Transfer.

   A Partnership Interest may pass to any Permitted Transferee in any of the following ways:

   11.11.1   under the last Will and Testament of a Limited Partner duly admitted to probate;

   11.11.2   by intestate succession;

   11.11.3   by a signed instrument delivered to the General Partner while the Limited Partner is alive; or

   11.11.4   under a trust in which the Limited Partner has the right, limited or unlimited, determine the beneficiaries of the trust.

Notwithstanding the foregoing, a Permitted Transferee who is not already a Partner may not become a Limited Partner pursuant to Section 11.10 above unless such Permitted Transferee complies with all provisions of Section 11.6, excluding Section 11.6.1. Furthermore, notwithstanding any contrary provision of this Agreement, a Permitted Transferee may not become a Limited Partner if this would cause a termination of the Partnership under Section 708 of the Code or a change in ownership under Section 60 of the California Revenue and Taxation Code of any real property interest or a material violation of any state or federal securities law.

11.12 <u>General Partner's Interest Not Transferable</u>.

Notwithstanding any other provision of this Agreement, the Partnership Interest of the General Partner may not be transferred without the written consent of all Partners. Furthermore, if the ownership of more than ten percent (10%) of the stock of the General Partner passes to any one or more Persons who would not be eligible to be a Permitted Transferee pursuant to Section 11.10 above, then a Majority in Interest of the Limited Partners may designate a new General Partner that so qualifies and such new General Partner may purchase the Partnership Interest of the prior General Partner on the terms set forth in Sections 11.4 and 11.5 above.

11.13 <u>Marital Property Interests</u>. [deleted]

SECTION 12: <u>GENERAL PARTNER'S LIMITED PARTNER INTEREST</u>.

The General Partner shall enjoy all of the rights and be subject to all of the obligations of a Limited Partner to the extent of the General Partner's Limited Partner Interest, if any.

SECTION 13: <u>AMENDMENTS</u>

Except as otherwise expressly provided herein, this Agreement may be amended only with the unanimous written consent of the Partners.

SECTION 14: <u>LIMITED PARTNER'S DEATH, INSANITY, OR INCOMPETENCY</u>

A Limited Partner's death, adjudication of insanity, or incompetence shall not dissolve the Partnership. Rather, the executors or administrators of the estate or successor Trustees of the revocable Trust of a deceased Limited Partner, or the committee or other legal representatives of the estate of an insane or incompetent Limited Partner, shall have the same rights (and be subject to the same obligations and limitations) as the deceased, insane or incompetent Limited Partner, and shall be subject to the provisions of Section 11 regarding assigning the interest of the deceased, insane or incompetent Limited Partner.

SECTION 15: DISSOLUTION

15.1 Unilateral Right to Terminate the Partnership Denied.

No Partner shall have the unilateral right to compel a dissolution of the Partnership or to compel a partition and distribution of the property of the Partnership. Nor will any Partner have any direct ownership interest in the property of the Partnership. All Partnership property shall be held in the name of the Partnership. The Partnership, as an entity for federal income tax purposes and for state law purposes, will not terminate by reason of: (1) the death, disability, dissolution or bankruptcy of a Limited Partner; (2) the removal, resignation, or other inability to continue service of a General Partner or the addition of a General Partner, unless, at the conclusion of one hundred (100) days from the act of withdrawal or termination, the Partnership does not, in fact, have at least one General Partner; (4) a Partner's marital separation or divorce; or, (5) any other act or omission to act, not having the approval or consent of all Partners, which is or may be otherwise construed to be a termination of the Partnership as an entity. To the greatest extent permitted by law, any act or omission to act which is or may otherwise be construed to be a termination or dissolution shall nonetheless be construed as an intended reconstitution or continuation of the Partnership, without the requirement of liquidation and winding-up.

15.2 Causes for Dissolution.

The Partnership shall be dissolved upon the earliest to occur of the following events:

15.2.1 expiration of the term of the Partnership, on December 31, 2050;

15.2.2 the determination by the General Partner, with the unanimous consent of the Limited Partners, that the Partnership should be dissolved;

15.2.3 the dissolution, termination or Bankruptcy of all General Partners, unless a new General Partner is elected within one hundred (100) days after such event;

15.2.4 the Bankruptcy of the Partnership;

15.2.5 the sale of all, or substantially all, of the Partnership's assets and distribution of the proceeds to the Partners; provided that the Partnership shall not be dissolved if the General Partner properly reinvests all or part of the proceeds of such sale; provided further that if such sale is made for consideration payable in whole or in part over a period of time, such distribution shall not be deemed to occur until substantially all payments have been distributed; or

15.2.6 the entry of a decree of judicial dissolution pursuant to Section 15682 of the Act.

15.3 Option to Continue or Reconstitute.

15.3.1 Election to Continue or Reconstitute the Partnership.

-21-

Upon occurrence of any of the events described in Section 15.2, the Limited Partners may either: (a) continue the business of the Partnership or (b) reconstitute the business of the Partnership in a new limited partnership on the terms and conditions of this Agreement. Such continuation or reconstitution shall occur only if, within one hundred (100) days after such event, a Majority in Interest of the Limited Partners shall so elect in writing, provided however that if there is no remaining General Partner, the unanimous written consent of the Limited Partners shall be required to elect a new General Partner and continue the Partnership. If the Limited Partners elect to continue or reconstitute the Partnership with a new General Partner(s), then such new General Partner(s) shall succeed to all of the powers, privileges, and obligations of the former General Partner, and the former General Partner's interest in the Partnership shall become a Limited Partner Interest. Expenses incurred in the reconstitution or attempted reconstitution of the Partnership shall be deemed expenses of the Partnership.

15.3.2 Obligations Not Affected.

No dissolution of the Partnership shall release any of the parties hereto from their contractual obligations under this Agreement.

15.4 Liquidation and Termination.

15.4.1 Liquidator.

15.4.1.1 Liquidation Upon Dissolution.

If the Partnership is dissolved or if the General Partner has withdrawn and no successor has been chosen in accordance with this Section 15 and Section 16 below, a Person (referred to herein as the "Liquidator") shall commence to wind up the Partnership's affairs and to liquidate and sell its non liquid assets. The Partners shall continue to share operating profits and losses and other items of income, gain, loss, and deduction during the liquidation period. The Liquidator shall proceed, as promptly as practicable without undue sacrifice, to liquidate and sell the Partnership's remaining non liquid assets. The Liquidator, in the Liquidator's reasonable discretion, may also distribute property of the Partnership to the creditors of the Partnership or to Partners, in kind. The Liquidator may be required by a Majority in Interest of the Limited Partners to give a bond (at the Partnership's expense) to assure that the Liquidator faithfully performs the Liquidator's duties. The Liquidator shall receive reasonable compensation for services rendered, payable from the Partnership's assets. The Liquidator may resign at any time by giving thirty (30) days' written notice to the Partners. The Liquidator (or any successor Liquidator) may be removed at any time by written notice of removal by unanimous consent of the Partners (for this purpose, if the Liquidator is also a Partner, the Liquidator shall have no vote). Upon the Liquidator's death, dissolution, removal, or resignation, a successor Liquidator shall, within thirty (30) days, be appointed in the same manner as the original Liquidator. Any duly appointed successor Liquidator shall succeed to all the original Liquidator's rights, powers, and duties.

15.4.1.2 Appointing a Liquidator.

The General Partner shall serve as Liquidator if the General Partner is then serving as General Partner. Otherwise, the Limited Partners may unanimously select a person to serve as Liquidator. If, within thirty (30) days following the Partnership's dissolution, no Person is so selected to serve as the Liquidator or if, within thirty (30) days after the need for a successor Liquidator arises, no successor has been appointed and accepted appointment as the successor Liquidator, any interested Partner may make application to a State or Federal District Court Judge to appoint a Liquidator. The Judge, acting in a judicial capacity, shall be fully authorized to appoint a qualified, neutral Person to serve as Liquidator.

15.5 The Liquidator's Powers.

The Liquidator shall have the powers of the General Partner to the extent necessary to carry out the Liquidator's duties and functions, including the following powers:

15.5.1 The power to manage any Partnership business during the liquidation, including the power to enter into contracts that may extend beyond the liquidation.

15.5.2 The power to execute deeds, bills of sale, assignments, and other instruments to convey Partnership property to third parties or to the respective Partners incident to disposing of the remaining Partnership property. The Liquidator may not, however, impose personal liability upon any Partner or his, her or its legal representatives or successors in interest under any warranty of title contained in any instrument.

15.5.3 The power to borrow funds, in the Liquidator's best judgment, reasonably required to pay any Partnership obligations, and to execute security documents encumbering property as security for the Partnership's indebtedness. The Liquidator may not, however, create any personal obligation for any Partner or any Partner's successors in interest to repay indebtedness other than from available proceeds from foreclosure or sales of property of the Partnership as to which a lien is granted.

15.5.4 The power to settle, compromise, or adjust any claim asserted to be owing by or to the Partnership, and the right to file, prosecute, or defend lawsuits and legal proceedings in connection with any matters.

15.6 Liquidating Distributions: Priorities.

The proceeds from liquidation of Partnership assets (subject to such reasonable reserves for anticipated liabilities as the Liquidator may establish) shall be applied as follows:

15.6.1 First, all of the Partnership's debts and liabilities to Persons other than Partners and expenses of dissolution and winding up shall be paid and discharged in the order of priority as provided by law.

15.6.2 Second, the Liquidator may set aside a reasonable reserve for contingent or unforeseen liabilities.

15.6.3 Third, all debts and liabilities to Partners (including amounts due as compensation for services) shall be paid and discharged in the order of priority as provided in this Agreement and by law.

15.6.4 Fourth, distributions shall then be made to the Partners, both General and Limited, in amounts equal to any credit balances in their respective Capital Accounts so that the Capital Account of each Partner shall be brought to zero, and if this is not possible, then such Capital Accounts shall be proportionately reduced. For the purpose of determining and making distributions in liquidation, a negative Capital Account balance shall be considered to be a loan from the Partnership to a Partner, which loan shall be repaid, in cash, by such Partner upon demand, and in no event shall any such loan be payable later than the date required under the Code and applicable Regulations.

15.6.5 Fifth, any remaining assets shall be distributed proportionately among the Partners in the ratios of their respective Percentage Interests.

All of the foregoing distributions may be made in cash or in kind, in the reasonable discretion of the Liquidator. Furthermore, if the Partnership is "liquidated" within the meaning of Treasury Regulations Section 1.704-1(b)(2)(ii)(g), distributions will be made in compliance with Section 1.704-1(b)(2)(ii)(b)(2) of the Regulations.

15.7 Gain or Loss.

Any gain or loss on the disposition of Partnership properties in the process of liquidation shall be credited or charged to the Partners in proportion to their Partnership Interests; provided, however, that gain or loss with respect to property contributed to the Partnership by a Partner shall be shared among the Partners so as to take account of any variation between the basis of the property so contributed and its fair market value at the time of contribution, in accordance with applicable Regulations. Any property distributed in kind in the liquidation shall be valued and treated as though it were sold and the cash proceeds distributed. To the extent required by the Code and Regulations, the difference between the value of property distributed in kind and its book value shall be treated as a gain or loss on the sale of property, and shall be credited or charged to the Partners accordingly or in such manner, consistent with the Code and the Regulations, as the General Partner may determine.

15.8 Partnership Assets Sole Source.

The Partners shall look solely to the Partnership's assets for the payment of any liabilities owed by the Partnership to the Partners and for the return of their capital contributions and liquidation amounts. If the Partnership property remaining after the payment or discharge of all of its debts and liabilities to Persons other than Partners is insufficient to return the Partners' Capital Accounts, then they shall have no recourse hereunder therefor against the Partnership or any other Partners, except to the extent that such other Partners may have outstanding debts or obligations owing to the Partnership.

15.9 Accounting.

Within a reasonable time after completing the liquidation of the Partnership, the Liquidator shall prepare an accounting and may require, as a condition to

-24-

distribution of the Partnership's assets, a signed statement from each proposed distributee that the accounting has been thoroughly examined and accepted as correct; a discharge and release from any loss, liability, claim or question concerning the exercise of due care, skill, and prudence of the Liquidator in the management, investment, retention, and distribution of property during the term of service of the Liquidator (including service as the General Partner), except for any undisclosed error or omission involving fraud or bad faith; and an indemnity in favor of the Liquidator, to include the payment of attorney's fees, from any asserted claim of any taxing agency, governmental authority, or other claimant. Any Partner having a question or potential claim may require an audit of the Partnership's books and records as an expense of administration. Failure to require such audit prior to acceptance of the report, or the acceptance of payment, will operate as a final release and discharge of the Liquidator except as to any error or omission involving fraud or bad faith.

SECTION 16: SUCCESSOR GENERAL PARTNERS

16.1 General Partner Agrees Not to Withdraw.

The General Partner agrees not to withdraw as General Partner without first obtaining the written consent of all other Partners. Any withdrawal shall be effective upon the later of (1) thirty (30) days after the necessary written consent is given, or (2) the date specified in the written consent. If the General Partner withdraws in violation of this Section, the withdrawal will be a breach of this Agreement and the Partnership may recover damages arising from such breach. Furthermore, such improper withdrawal may be treated (by vote of a Majority in Interest of the Limited Partners) as an unauthorized Transfer, with the result that the rights of such former General Partner are reduced to the rights of an Assignee and shall be subject to purchase by the other Partners as provided in Section 11.

16.2 Appointing Successor General Partners.

If the General Partner ceases to serve for any reason, then the remaining Partners acting unanimously may appoint one or more successor General Partners. Each newly appointed General Partner shall purchase the withdrawing General Partner's Partnership Interest in accordance with Section 11, and if there is more than one new General Partner, then such purchase shall be made on a pro rata basis. Each General Partner must at all times hold a Partnership Interest such that the General Partners together represent not less than a one percent (1%) Percentage Interest.

SECTION 17: POWER OF ATTORNEY

17.1 Grant to General Partner.

Each Limited Partner hereby irrevocably makes, constitutes and appoints the General Partner as his, her or its true and lawful attorney-in-fact and agent, in his, her or its name, place and stead to execute, acknowledge, swear to, file, and record documents with respect to the Partnership, including without limitation:

-25-

17.1.1 the Certificate of Limited Partnership and such amended Certificates of Limited Partnership as may be required or appropriate under California law, or the laws of any other state;

17.1.2 statements of fictitious name;

17.1.3 documents to effect Transfers of Limited Partnership Interests when the provisions of this Agreement have been complied with;

17.1.4 all checks made payable to the Partnership; and

17.1.5 any document that may be required or appropriate to effect the continuation of the Partnership, the admission of a Limited Partner, or the dissolution and termination of the Partnership in accordance with the provisions of this Agreement, or any document that may be required to be filed by the Partnership under the laws of the State of California or any other state or by any governmental agency, or any document which the General Partner elects to file that is consistent with the provisions of this Agreement.

17.2 Power Coupled With an Interest.

The power of attorney granted under Section 17.1:

17.2.1 is a power coupled with an interest;

17.2.2 is irrevocable and shall survive the Limited Partner's death, dissolution, incompetency or incapacity and extend to the Limited Partner's heirs, executors, successors and assigns;

17.2.3 may be exercised by any General Partner by a facsimile signature or by listing the names of all of the Limited Partners with a signature of the General Partner as the attorney-in-fact for all of them; and

17.2.4 shall survive the assignment of a Limited Partner's interest, and shall empower the General Partner to act to the same extent for an Assignee or a successor Limited Partner.

17.3 Limitations on Powers of General Partner.

Notwithstanding the provisions of this Section 17, when acting in a representative capacity, the General Partner shall not have the power or authority to amend or modify this Agreement, except to reflect:

17.3.1 a change in the name or principal place of business of the Partnership;

17.3.2 the admission and withdrawal of Limited Partners in accordance with the provisions of this Agreement; or

17.3.3 a change that is advisable in the opinion of the General Partner to ensure that the Partnership will not be treated as an association or a corporation for federal income tax purposes or to ensure that its allocations will satisfy the substantial economic effect test of Section 704(b) of the Code.

17.4   Scope of this Section.

Nothing in this Section shall be construed as enlarging the powers granted to the General Partner under any other Section.

SECTION 18: MISCELLANEOUS   [deleted]

SECTION 19: RESOLUTION OF DISPUTES   [deleted]

SECTION 20: Definitions
When used in this Agreement, the following terms shall have the meanings set forth below.

20.1   Act.

"Act" means the California Revised Limited Partnership Act, as amended, and any successor statute.

20.2   Agreement.

"Agreement" refers to this document and all Schedules referred to herein, as they may be amended from time to time.

20.3   Appraisal.

"Appraisal" means a written valuation report by an Appraiser that analyzes, describes and values the fair market value of a Percentage Interest in the Partnership.

20.4   Appraiser.

"Appraiser" means a person or firm qualified to perform Appraisals of partnerships and ownership interests in partnerships. Unless all interested parties otherwise agree, the Appraiser must be a member of the Appraisal Institute (Chicago, IL) or the American Society of Appraisers (Washington, DC).

20.5   Assignee.

"Assignee" means a Person who has acquired all or a portion of a Partnership Interest by voluntary or involuntary assignment or other Transfer. The assignment of a Partnership Interest shall become effective as of the date on which all requirements for an assignment expressed in this Agreement, particularly Section 11, will have

-27-

been met. An Assignee shall have only the rights granted under Sections 15672 and 15673 of the Act. An Assignee shall not become a partner except as provided in this Agreement.

20.6   Bankruptcy.

The "Bankruptcy" of any Person shall be deemed to occur when such Person (i) voluntarily files a petition in bankruptcy or voluntarily takes advantage of any bankruptcy or insolvency law or (ii) is the subject of a petition or answer proposing adjudication of such Person as a bankrupt, and such individual or entity either consents to such petition or answer, or fails to cause such petition or answer to be discharged or denied within ninety (90) days from the service of such petition or answer upon such Person.

20.7   Capital Account.

A Partner's "Capital Account" shall be maintained in the manner provided in this Agreement.

20.8   Certificate.

"Certificate" refers to the certificate of limited partnership filed on behalf of the Partnership, as amended from time to time.

20.9   Code.

"Code" refers to the United States Internal Revenue Code of 1986, as amended from time to time.

20.10   Family.

"Family" means John Builder, Edward Helper and their "Issue," including future-born Issue. For purposes of the preceding sentence, "Issue" shall be defined as provided in Section 50 of the California Probate Code.

20.11   Family Assets.

"Family Assets" means all Property owned by the Family, individually or in combination with others, that has been contributed to or acquired by the Partnership.

20.12   General Partner.

"General Partner" refers to JB Management, Inc., a California corporation, or any successor general partner(s).

20.13   Including.

The word "including" shall always be deemed to be followed by the words "but not limited to" and the words "include" and "includes" shall be similarly interpreted, except where the context clearly requires a narrower interpretation.

20.14 Issue.

"Issue" shall have the meaning set forth in Section 50 of the California Probate Code.

20.15 Insolvency.

The "Insolvency" of a Person shall be deemed to occur when such Person's assets are insufficient to pay his, her or its liabilities.

20.16 Limited Partner.

The terms "Limited Partner" and "Limited Partners" shall refer to one or more of the persons whose names are listed on Schedule A to this Agreement as Limited Partners and any person who subsequently becomes a Limited Partner pursuant to the provisions of this Agreement.

20.17 Majority in Interest of the Limited Partners.

"Majority in Interest of the Limited Partners" refers to Limited Partners whose Percentage Interests exceed fifty percent (50%) of the Percentage Interests of all Limited Partners.

20.18 Net Cash Flow.

"Net Cash Flow" refers to the Partnership's taxable income, increased by: (1) any depreciation or depletion deductions taken into account in computing taxable income and (2) any nontaxable income or receipts (other than capital contributions and the proceeds of any Partnership financing), and reduced by: (a) expenditures to acquire, preserve or improve Partnership assets and to operate the Partnership to the extent that such expenditures did not reduce taxable income, and (b) proceeds from the sale, exchange, maturity or redemption of Partnership assets.

20.19 Partners.

The terms "Partners" or a "Partner," when used without the words "General" or "Limited," shall refer to both the General and Limited Partners.

20.20 Partnership.

"Partnership" means the limited partnership formed under this Agreement.

20.21 Partnership Interest.

"Partnership Interest" refers to the ownership interest of a Partner in the Partnership.

20.22   Percentage Interests.

The "Percentage Interests" are the relative percentage ownership interests of the individual Partners in the Partnership, as indicated on Schedule A, and as adjusted pursuant to this Agreement. Except as otherwise expressly provided, a Partner's Percentage Interest will be determinative of: (1) a Partner's ownership interest in the Partnership as an entity; (2) a Partner's share of cash available for distribution; (3) a Partner's allocable share of items of income, gain, loss, deduction and credit; and (4) a Partner's distributive share of cash and other property upon dissolution of the Partnership.

20.23   Person.

"Person" means any individual, estate, partnership, corporation, trust, unincorporated association, limited liability company, joint venture or any other entity.

20.24   Regulations.

"Regulations" refers to the applicable Treasury Regulations issued under the Code.

20.25   Transfer.

A "Transfer" of a Partnership Interest includes any sale, pledging, encumbering, giving, bequeathing, or other transferring or disposing of such Partnership Interest; or permitting such Partnership Interest to be sold, encumbered, attached, or otherwise disposed of; or having ownership of a Partnership Interest changed in any manner, whether voluntarily, involuntarily, or by operation of law. The word "Transfer" shall have these meanings whether used as a noun or as a verb.

IN WITNESS WHEREOF, the undersigned have executed this Agreement of Partnership.

JB Management, Inc.
as General Partner

Dated: July 24, 1993   By:_____
                                              President

John Builder
as Limited Partner

Dated: July 24, 1993   By:_____

Edward Helper
as Limited Partner

Dated: July 24, 1993   By:_____

-31-

STATE OF CALIFORNIA _____)
_____) ss.
COUNTY OF LOS ANGELES _____)

On _JULY 24, 1993_____ before me, ___MICHEL SCHTA_____, personally appeared _JOHN BUILDER_____, personally known to me (or proved to me on the basis of satisfactory evidence) to be the person(s) whose name(s) is/are subscribed to the within instrument, and acknowledged to me that he/she/they executed the same in his/her/their authorized capacity(ies), and that by his/her/their signature(s) on the instrument the person(s), or the entity upon behalf of which the person(s) acted, executed the instrument.

WITNESS my hand and official seal.

_____ [SEAL]
Notary's Signature

> MICHEL SCHTA
> Commission # 11506
> Notary Public - California
> Los Angeles County
> My Comm. Expires Aug 9

STATE OF CALIFORNIA _____)
_____) ss.
COUNTY OF LOS ANGELES _____)

On _JULY 24, 1993_____ before me, ___MICHEL SCHTA_____, personally appeared _____, personally known to me (or proved to me on the basis of satisfactory evidence) to be the person(s) whose name(s) is/are subscribed to the within instrument, and acknowledged to me that he/she/they executed the same in his/her/their authorized capacity(ies), and that by his/her/their signature(s) on the instrument the person(s), or the entity upon behalf of which the person(s) acted, executed the instrument.

WITNESS my hand and official seal.

_____ [SEAL]
Notary's Signature

> MICHEL SCHTA
> Commission # 11506
> Notary Public - California
> Los Angeles County
> My Comm. Expires Aug 9.

SCHEDULE A

	Initial Capital Contribution	Percentage Interest
JP Management, Inc. General Partner	$ 5,509	1%
John Builder Limited Partner	$ 269,953	49%
Ed Helper Limited Partner	$ 275,462	50%

Form **1065**		**U. S. Partnership Return of Income**		OMB No. 1545-0099
Department of the Treasury Internal Revenue Service		For calendar year 1996, or tax year beginning _____ ,1996, and ending _____ ,19 ___ . ▶ **See separate instructions.**		**1996**

A Principal business activity REAL ESTATE	Use the IRS label.	SUBURBAN OFFICE PARTNERS II, L.P. 4715 MAIN ST ORANGE, CA 92668	**D** Employer identification number 95-4786646
B Principal product or service RENTALS	Other-wise, please print or type.		**E** Date business started 7/24/93
C Business code number 6520			**F** Total assets (see page 10 of the instructions) $2,428,504

G Check applicable boxes: **(1)** ☐ Initial return **(2)** ☐ Final return **(3)** ☐ Change in address **(4)** ☐ Amended return
H Check accounting method: **(1)** ☒ Cash **(2)** ☐ Accrual **(3)** ☐ Other (specify) ▶
I Number of Schedules K-1. Attach one for each person who was a partner at any time during the tax year.... ▶ 6

Caution: Include **only** trade or business income and expenses on lines 1a through 22 below. See the instructions for more information.

I N C O M E	**1a**	Gross receipts or sales	1a	
	b	Less returns and allowances	1b	1c
	2	Cost of goods sold (Schedule A, line 8)		2
	3	Gross profit. Subtract line 2 from line 1c		3
	4	Ordinary income (loss) from other partnerships, estates and trusts (attach schedule)		4
	5	Net farm profit (loss) (attach Schedule F (Form 1040))		5
	6	Net gain (loss) from Form 4797, Part II, line 20		6
	7	Other income (loss) (attach schedule)		7
	8	**Total income (loss).** Combine lines 3 through 7		8
D E D U C T I O N S (SEE INSTRUCTIONS FOR LIMITATIONS)	**9**	Salaries and wages (other than to partners) (less employment credits)		9
	10	Guaranteed payments to partners		10
	11	Repairs and maintenance		11
	12	Bad debts		12
	13	Rent		13
	14	Taxes and licenses		14 · · · · · 800
	15	Interest		15
	16a	Depreciation (if required, attach Form 4562)	16a	
	b	Less depreciation reported on Schedule A and elsewhere on return	16b	16c
	17	Depletion **(Do not deduct oil and gas depletion.)**		17
	18	Retirement plans, etc		18
	19	Employee benefit programs		19
	20	Other deductions (attach schedule) .... See Statement 1		20 · · · · · 3,325
	21	**Total deductions.** Add the amounts shown in the far right column for lines 9 through 20		21 · · · · · 4,125
	22	**Ordinary income (loss)** from trade or business activities. Subtract line 21 from line 8		22 · · · · · -4,125

Please Sign Here

Under penalties of perjury, I declare that I have examined this return, including accompanying schedules and statements, and to the best of my knowledge and belief, it is true, correct, and complete. Declaration of preparer (other than general partner or limited liability company member) is based on all information of which preparer has any knowledge.

▶ _(signature)_   Signature of general partner or limited liability company member   ▶ 4/13/97   Date

Paid Preparer's Use Only	Preparer's signature ▶ William Johnson, E.A.	Date	Check if self-employed ▶ ☐	Preparer's social security no. -- --
	Firm's name (or yours if self-employed) and address ▶ Manhattan Business Services 324 Manhattan Bch Blvd Ste 202 Manhattan Beach, CA		EIN ▶ ZIP code ▶ 90266	

For Paperwork Reduction Act Notice, see page 1 of separate instructions.

Form **1065** (1996)

KFA

Form 1065 (1996)   SUBURBAN OFFICE PARTNERS II, L.P.   95-4786646   Page **2**

Schedule A   Cost of Goods Sold (see page 13 of the instructions)

1	Inventory at beginning of year	1	
2	Purchases less cost of items withdrawn for personal use	2	
3	Cost of labor	3	
4	Additional section 263A costs (attach schedule)	4	
5	Other costs (attach schedule)	5	
6	**Total.** Add lines 1 through 5	6	
7	Inventory at end of year	7	
8	**Cost of goods sold.** Subtract line 7 from line 6. Enter here and on page 1, line 2	8	

9a Check all methods used for valuing closing inventory:

    (i) ☐ Cost as described in Regulations section 1.471–3

    (ii) ☐ Lower of cost or market as described in Regulations section 1.471–4

    (iii) ☐ Other (specify method used and attach explanation) ▶ _____

  b Check this box there was a writedown of "subnormal" goods as described in Regulations section 1.471–2(c) ▶ ☐

  c Check this box if the LIFO inventory method was adopted this tax year for any goods (if checked, attach Form 970) ▶ ☐

  d Do the rules of section 263A (for property produced or acquired for resale) apply to the partnership? ☐ Yes ☐ No

  e Was there any change in determining quantities, cost, or valuations between opening and closing inventory? ☐ Yes ☐ No

    If "Yes," attach explanation.

Schedule B   Other Information

		Yes	No
1	What type of entity is filing this return? Check the appropriate box:		
a	☐ General partnership b ☒ Limited partnership c ☐ Limited liability company		
d	☐ Other (see page 14 of the instructions) ▶		
2	Are any partners in this partnership also partnerships?		X
3	Is this partnership a partner in another partnership?		X
4	Is this partnership subject to the consolidated audit procedures of sections 6221 through 6233? If "Yes," see **Designation of Tax Matters Partner** below		X
5	Does this partnership meet **ALL THREE** of the following requirements?		
a	The partnership's total receipts for the tax year were less than $250,000;		
b	The partnership's total assets at the end of the tax year were less than $600,000; **AND**		
c	Schedules K–1 are filed with the return and furnished to the partners on or before the due date (including extensions) for the partnership return.		
	If "Yes," the partnership is not required to complete Schedules L, M–1, and M–2; Item F on page 1 of Form 1065; or Item J on Schedule K–1		X
6	Does this partnership have any foreign partners?		X
7	Is this partnership a publicly traded partnership as defined in section 469(k)(2)?		X
8	Has this partnership filed, or is it required to file, **Form 8264**, Application for Registration of a Tax Shelter?		X
9	At any time during calendar year 1996, did the partnership have an interest in or a signature or other authority over a financial account in a foreign country (such as a bank account, securities account, or other financial account)? (See page 14 of the instructions for exceptions and filing requirements for Form TD 90–22.1.) If "Yes," enter the name of the foreign country. ▶ _____		X
10	During the tax year, did the partnership receive a distribution from, or was it the grantor of, or transferor to, a foreign trust? If "Yes," see page 14 of the instructions for other forms the partnership may have to file		X
11	Was there a distribution of property or a transfer (e.g., by sale or death) of a partnership interest during the tax year? If "Yes," you may elect to adjust the basis of the partnership's assets under section 754 by attaching the statement described under **Elections Made By the Partnership** on page 5 of the instructions		X

Designation of Tax Matters Partner (see page 15 of the instructions)

Enter below the general partner designated as the tax matters partner (TMP) for the tax year of this return:

Name of designated TMP	▶ William Builder
	Identifying number of TMP ▶ 547-10-4121
Address of designated TMP	▶ 4715 MAIN ST. GRANTS CA 92668

Form 1065 (1996)   SUBURBAN OFFICE PARTNERS II, L.P.   95-4786646   Page **3**

Schedule K   Partners' Shares of Income, Credits, Deductions, etc.

	(a) Distributive share items		(b) Total amount
Income (Loss)	1 Ordinary income (loss) from trade or business activities (page 1, line 22)	1	-4,125
	2 Net income (loss) from rental real estate activities (attach Form 8825)	2	68,151
	3a Gross income from other rental activities **3a**		
	b Exp. from other rental activities **3b**		
	c Net income (loss) from other rental activities. Subtract line 3b from line 3a	3c	
	4a Portfolio income (loss): a Interest income..............................	4a	3,154
	b Dividend income	4b	
	c Royalty income..	4c	
	d Net short-term capital gain (loss) (attach Schedule D (Form 1065))....................	4d	
	e Net long-term capital gain (loss) (attach Schedule D (Form 1065))	4e	
	f Other portfolio income (loss) (attach schedule)	4f	
	5 Guaranteed payments to partners	5	
	6 Net gain (loss) under section 1231 (other than due to casualty or theft) (attach Form 4797)	6	
	7 Other income (loss) (attach schedule)	7	
Deduc-tions	8 Charitable contributions (attach schedule)	8	
	9 Section 179 expense deduction (attach Form 4562)............................	9	
	10 Deductions related to portfolio income (itemize).............................	10	
	11 Other deductions (attach schedule)......................................	11	
Invest-ment Interest	12a Interest expense on investment debts	12a	
	b (1) Investment income included on lines 4a, 4b, 4c, and 4f above	12b(1)	3,154
	(2) Investment expenses included on line 10 above	12b(2)	
Credits	13a Low-income housing credit:		
	(1) From partnerships to which section 42(j)(5) applies for property placed in service before 1990...	13a(1)	
	(2) Other than on line 13a(1) for property placed in service before 1990.....................	13a(2)	
	(3) From partnerships to which section 42(j)(5) applies for property placed in service after 1989	13a(3)	
	(4) Other than on line 13a(3) for property placed in service after 1989	13a(4)	
	b Qual. rehabilitation expenditures related to rental real estate activities	13b	
	c Credits (other than credits on lines 13a & 13b) related to rental real estate activities................	13c	
	d Credits related to other rental activities....................................	13d	
	14 Other credits	14	
Self-Employ-ment	15a Net earnings (loss) from self-employment	15a	
	b Gross farming or fishing income...	15b	
	c Gross nonfarm income..	15c	
Adjust-ments and Tax Pre-ference Items	16a Depreciation adjustment on property placed in service after 1986	16a	9,875
	b Adjusted gain or loss	16b	
	c Depletion (other than oil and gas)	16c	
	d (1) Gross income from oil, gas, and geothermal properties	16d(1)	
	(2) Deductions allocable to oil, gas, and geothermal properties.....................	16d(2)	
	e Other adjustments and tax preference items (attach schedule)	16e	
Foreign Taxes	17a Type of income ▶ _____ b Foreign country or U.S. possession ▶ _____		
	c Total gross income from sources outside the U.S. (attach schedule).....................	17c	
	d Total applicable deductions and losses (attach schedule)	17d	
	e Total foreign taxes (check one): ▶ ☐ Paid ☐ Accrued	17e	
	f Reduction in taxes available for credit (attach schedule)	17f	
	g Other foreign tax information (attach schedule)	17g	
Other	18 Section 59(e)(2) expenditures: a Type ▶ _____ b Amount ▶	18b	
	19 Tax-exempt interest income..	19	
	20 Other tax-exempt income	20	
	21 Nondeductible expenses	21	
	22 Distributions of money (cash and marketable securities)	22	54,700
	23 Distributions of property other than money..................................	23	
	24 Other items & amounts required to be rptd. separately to partners		

	(a) Distributive share items		(b) Total amount
Ana-lysis	25a Income (loss). Combine lines 1 through 7 in column (b). From the result, subtract the sum of lines 8 through 12a, 17e, and 18b	25a	67,180

b Analysis by type of partner:	(a) Corporate	(b) Individual		(c) Partnership	(d) Exempt organization	(e) Nominee/Other
		i. Active	ii. Passive			
(1) General partners	672					
(2) Limited partners		64,492			2,016	

Form 1065 (1996) SUBURBAN OFFICE PARTNERS II, L.P.   95-4786646   Page **4**

Note: If Question 5 of Schedule B is answered "Yes," the partnership is not required to complete Schedules L, M-1, M-2.

Schedule L Balance Sheets

Assets	Beginning of tax year		End of tax year	
	(a)	(b)	(c)	(d)
1 Cash		16,900		74,250
2a Trade notes and accounts receivable	46,000		46,000	
b Less allowance for bad debts		46,000		46,000
3 Inventories.				
4 U.S. government obligations				
5 Tax-exempt securities				
6 Other current assets (attach schedule)				
7 Mortgage and real estate loans				
8 Other investments (attach schedule)				
9a Buildings and other depreciable assets	2,500,000		2,500,000	
b Less accumulated depreciation	136,730	2,363,270	191,746	2,308,254
10a Depletable assets				
b Less accumulated depletion				
11 Land (net of any amortization)				
12a Intangible assets (amortizable only)				
b Less accumulated amortization				
13 Other assets (attach schedule)				
14 Total assets		2,426,170		2,428,504
Liabilities and Capital				
15 Accounts payable				325
16 Mortgages, notes, bonds payable in less than 1 year				
17 Other current liabilities (attach schedule). See . St . 2 .		24,106		26,829
18 All nonrecourse loans				
19 Mortgages, notes, bonds payable in 1 year or more		1,818,406		1,791,577
20 Other liabilities (attach schedule) . . . . See . St . 3 .		16,500		16,500
21 Partners' capital accounts		567,158		593,273
22 Total liabilities and capital		2,426,170		2,428,504

Schedule M-1 Reconciliation of Income (Loss) per Books With Income (Loss) per Return
(see page 23 of the instructions)

1 Net income (loss) per books.	67,180	6	Income recorded on books this year not included on Schedule K, lines 1 through 7 (itemize):		
2 Income included on Schedule K, lines 1 through 4, 6, and 7, not recorded on books this year (itemize):			a Tax-exempt interest $ _____		
3 Guaranteed payments (other than health insurance)		7	Deductions included on Schedule K, lines 1 through 12a, 17e, and 18b, not charged against book income this year (itemize):		
4 Expenses recorded on books this year not included on Schedule K, lines 1 through 12a, 17e, and 18b (itemize):			a Depreciation $ _____		
a Depreciation $ _____					
b Travel and entertainment $ _____		8	Add lines 6 and 7		
		9	Income (loss) (Schedule K, line 25a).		
5 Add lines 1 through 4	67,180		Subtract line 8 from line 5	67,180	

Schedule M-2 Analysis of Partners' Capital Accounts

1 Balance at beginning of year	567,158	6 Distributions: a Cash	54,700
2 Capital contributed during year		b Property	
3 Net income (loss) per books	67,180	7 Other decreases (itemize): _____	
4 Other increases (itemize): _____			
		8 Add lines 6 and 7	54,700
5 Add lines 1 through 4	634,338	9 Balance at end of year. Subtract line 8 from line 5	593,273

SCHEDULE K-1	**Partner's Share of Income, Credits, Deductions, etc.**	OMB No. 1545-0099
(Form 1065)	▶ See separate instructions.	
Department of the Treasury Internal Revenue Service	For calendar year 1996 or tax year beginning _____ ,1996, and ending _____ ,19___	**1996**

Partner's identifying number ▶ 95-123456789	Partnership's identifying number ▶ 95-4786646
Partner's name, address, and ZIP code JB MANAGEMENT, INC	Partnership's name, address, and ZIP code SUBURBAN OFFICE PARTNERS II, L.P. 4715 MAIN ST ORANGE, CA 92668

A This partner is a ☒ general partner ☐ limited partner
   ☐ limited liability company member
B What type of entity is this partner? ▶ **Corporation**
C Is this partner a ☒ domestic or a ☐ foreign partner?
D Enter partner's percentage of:

	(i) Before change or termination	(ii) End of year
Profit sharing	1%	1%
Loss sharing	1%	1%
Ownership of capital	1%	1%

E IRS Center where partnership filed return: _____

F Partner's share of liabilities (see instructions):
   Nonrecourse .... $ _____
   Qualified nonrecourse financing .... $ _____
   Other .... $ _____
G Tax shelter registration number .... ▶ _____
H Check here if this partnership is a publicly traded partnership
   as defined in section 469(k)(2) .... ☐
I Check applicable boxes: (1) ☐ Final K-1 (2) ☐ Amended K-1

J Analysis of partner's capital account:

(a) Capital account at beginning of year	(b) Capital contributed during year	(c) Partner's share of lines 3, 4, and 7, Form 1065, Schedule M-2	(d) Withdrawals and distributions	(e) Capital account at end of year (combine columns (a) through (d)
5,672		672	(547)	5,797

		(a) Distributive share item		(b) Amount	(c) 1040 filers enter the amount in column (b) on:
Income (Loss)	1	Ordinary income (loss) from trade or business activities...............	1	-40	
	2	Net income (loss) from rental real estate activities ....See Line 25	2	682	} See pages 5 and 6 of Partner's Instructions for Schedule K-1 (Form 1065).
	3	Net income (loss) from other rental activities	3		
	4	Portfolio income (loss):			
	a	Interest...	4a	30	Sch. B, Part I, line 1
	b	Dividends...	4b		Sch. B, Part II, line 5
	c	Royalties..	4c		Sch. E, Part I, line 4
	d	Net short-term capital gain (loss)........................	4d		Sch. D, line 5, col. (f) or (g)
	e	Net long-term capital gain (loss)	4e		Sch. D, line 13, col. (f) or (g)
	f	Other portfolio income (loss) (attach schedule)	4f		Enter on applicable line of your return.
	5	Guaranteed payments to partner	5		} See page 6 of Partner's Instructions for Schedule K-1 (Form 1065).
	6	Net gain (loss) under section 1231 (other than due to casualty or theft).....	6		
	7	Other income (loss) (attach schedule)	7		Enter on applicable line of your return.
Deductions	8	Charitable contributions (see instructions)	8		Sch. A, line 15 or 16
	9	Section 179 expense deduction.............................	9		} See page 7 of Partner's Instructions for Schedule K-1 (Form 1065).
	10	Deductions related to portfolio income........................	10		
	11	Other deductions (attach schedule)	11		
Investment Interest	12 a	Interest expense on investment debts	12a		Form 4952, line 1
	b	(1) Investment income included on lines 4a, 4b, 4c, and 4f above	b(1)	30	} See page 7 of Partner's Instructions for Schedule K-1 (Form 1065).
		(2) Investment expenses included on line 10 above	b(2)		
Credits	13 a	Low-income housing credit:			
		(1) From section 42(j)(5) partnerships for property placed in service before 1990.......	a(1)		} Form 8586, line 5
		(2) Other than on line 13a(1) for property placed in service before 1990	a(2)		
		(3) From section 42(j)(5) partnerships for property placed in service after 1989........	a(3)		
		(4) Other than on line 13a(3) for property placed in service after 1989..............	a(4)		
	b	Qualified rehabilitation expenditures related to rental real estate activities..	13b		} See page 8 of Partner's Instructions for Schedule K-1 (Form 1065).
	c	Credits (other than credits shown on lines 13a and 13b) related to rental real estate activities....................................	13c		
	d	Credits related to other rental activities............................	13d		
	14	Other credits	14		

For Paperwork Reduction Act Notice, see Instructions for Form 1065.

KFA

Schedule K-1 (Form 1065) 1996

Partner 1

Schedule K-1 (Form 1065) 1996 SUBURBAN OFFICE PARTNERS II, L.P.   95-4786646   Page 2

(a) Distributive share item	(b) Amount	(c) 1040 filers enter the amount in column (b) on:
SELF-EMPLOYMENT 15a Net earnings (loss) from self-employment	15a	Sch. SE, Section A or B
b Gross farming or fishing income	15b	See page 8 of Partner's Instructions for Schedule K-1 (Form 1065).
c Gross nonfarm income	15c	
ADJUSTMENTS AND TAX PREFERENCE ITEMS 16a Depreciation adjustment on property placed in service after 1986	16a	98	See pages 8 and 9 of Partner's Instructions for Schedule K-1 (Form 1065) and Instructions for Form 6251.
b Adjusted gain or loss	16b	
c Depletion (other than oil and gas)	16c	
d (1) Gross income from oil, gas, and geothermal properties	d(1)	
(2) Deductions allocable to oil, gas, and geothermal properties	d(2)	
e Other adjustments and tax preference items	16e	
FOREIGN TAXES 17a Type of income ▶		Form 1116, check boxes
b Name of foreign country or U.S. possession ▶		
c Total gross income from sources outside the U.S.	17c	Form 1116, Part I
d Total applicable deductions and losses (attach sch.)	17d	
e Total foreign taxes (check one): ▶ ☐ Paid ☐ Accrued	17e	Form 1116, Part II
f Reduction in taxes available for credit (att. schedule)	17f	Form 1116, Part III
g Other foreign tax information (attach schedule)	17g	See Instructions for Form 1116.
OTHER 18 Section 59(e)(2) expenditures: a Type ▶		See page 9 of Partner's Instructions for Schedule K-1 (Form 1065).
b Amount	18b	
19 Tax-exempt interest income	19	Form 1040, line 8b
20 Other tax-exempt income	20	See page 9 of Partner's Instructions for Schedule K-1 (Form 1065).
21 Nondeductible expenses	21	
22 Distributions of money (cash and marketable securities)	22	547	
23 Distributions of property other than money	23	
24 Recapture of low-income housing credit:		Form 8611, line 8
a From section 42(j)(5) partnerships	24a	
b Other than on line 24a	24b	

25 Supplemental information required to be reported separately to each partner (attach additional schedules if more space is needed):

Line 2
Rental Real Estate Activities

Description of Property	Gross Income	Net Expenses	Net Income	Passive NonPass	Section 1231
COMMERCIAL BUILDING	4,776	4,095	681	Passive	
		Rounding	1		
		Total	682		

Partner 1: JB MANAGEMENT, INC   95-123456789

SCHEDULE K-1 (Form 1065) Department of the Treasury Internal Revenue Service	**Partner's Share of Income, Credits, Deductions, etc.** ▶ See separate instructions.	OMB No. 1545-0099 **1996**

For calendar year 1996 or tax year beginning ,1996, and ending ,19

Partner's identifying number ▶ 123-45-6789	Partnership's identifying number ▶ 95-4786646
Partner's name, address, and ZIP code JOHN BUILDER 15 PARADISE LANE LAGUNA HILLS, CA 92653	Partnership's name, address, and ZIP code SUBURBAN OFFICE PARTNERS II, L.P. 4715 MAIN ST ORANGE, CA 92668

A This partner is a ☐ general partner ☒ limited partner
  ☐ limited liability company member
B What type of entity is this partner? ▶ *Individual*
C Is this partner a ☒ domestic or a ☐ foreign partner?
D Enter partner's percentage of:

	(i) Before change or termination	(ii) End of year
Profit sharing	20%	20%
Loss sharing	20%	20%
Ownership of capital	20%	20%

E IRS Center where partnership filed return:

F Partner's share of liabilities (see instructions):
  Nonrecourse .... $ _____
  Qualified nonrecourse financing .... $ _____
  Other .... $ _____
G Tax shelter registration number .... ▶
H Check here if this partnership is a publicly traded partnership as defined in section 469(k)(2) .... ☐
I Check applicable boxes: (1) ☐ Final K-1 (2) ☐ Amended K-1

J Analysis of partner's capital account:

(a) Capital account at beginning of year	(b) Capital contributed during year	(c) Partner's share of lines 3, 4, and 7, Form 1065, Schedule M-2	(d) Withdrawals and distributions	(e) Capital account at end of year (combine columns (a) through (d)
113,432	13,436		(10,940)	115,928

		(a) Distributive share item		(b) Amount	(c) 1040 filers enter the amount in column (b) on:
Income (Loss)	1	Ordinary income (loss) from trade or business activities................	1	-825	
	2	Net income (loss) from rental real estate activities ....See..Line..25	2	13,630	} See pages 5 and 6 of Partner's Instructions for Schedule K-1 (Form 1065).
	3	Net income (loss) from other rental activities	3		
	4	Portfolio income (loss):			
	a	Interest...	4a	631	Sch. B, Part I, line 1
	b	Dividends...	4b		Sch. B, Part II, line 5
	c	Royalties..	4c		Sch. E, Part I, line 4
	d	Net short-term capital gain (loss)........................	4d		Sch. D, line 5, col. (f) or (g)
	e	Net long-term capital gain (loss)	4e		Sch. D, line 13, col. (f) or (g)
	f	Other portfolio income (loss) (attach schedule)	4f		Enter on applicable line of your return.
	5	Guaranteed payments to partner	5		} See page 6 of Partner's Instructions for Schedule K-1 (Form 1065).
	6	Net gain (loss) under section 1231 (other than due to casualty or theft).....	6		
	7	Other income (loss) (attach schedule)	7		Enter on applicable line of your return.
Deductions	8	Charitable contributions (see instructions)	8		Sch. A, line 15 or 16
	9	Section 179 expense deduction	9		} See page 7 of Partner's Instructions for Schedule K-1 (Form 1065).
	10	Deductions related to portfolio income.....................	10		
	11	Other deductions (attach schedule)	11		
Investment Interest	12 a	Interest expense on investment debts	12a		Form 4952, line 1
	b	(1) Investment income included on lines 4a, 4b, 4c, and 4f above	b(1)	631	} See page 7 of Partner's Instructions for Schedule K-1 (Form 1065).
		(2) Investment expenses included on line 10 above	b(2)		
Credits	13 a	Low-income housing credit:			
		(1) From section 42(j)(5) partnerships for property placed in service before 1990.......	a(1)		} Form 8586, line 5
		(2) Other than on line 13a(1) for property placed in service before 1990	a(2)		
		(3) From section 42(j)(5) partnerships for property placed in service after 1989........	a(3)		
		(4) Other than on line 13a(3) for property placed in service after 1989..............	a(4)		
	b	Qualified rehabilitation expenditures related to rental real estate activities...	13b		} See page 8 of Partner's Instructions for Schedule K-1 (Form 1065).
	c	Credits (other than credits shown on lines 13a and 13b) related to rental real estate activities................................	13c		
	d	Credits related to other rental activities.....................	13d		
	14	Other credits	14		

For Paperwork Reduction Act Notice, see Instructions for Form 1065.

KFA

Schedule K-1 (Form 1065) 1996

Partner 2

Schedule K–1 (Form 1065) 1996 SUBURBAN OFFICE PARTNERS II, L.P.   95-4786646   Page **2**

	(a) Distributive share item		(b) Amount	(c) 1040 filers enter the amount in column (b) on:
S E L F – E M P L O Y	**15a** Net earnings (loss) from self–employment	15a		Sch. SE, Section A or B
	b Gross farming or fishing income	15b		See page 8 of Partner's Instructions for Schedule K–1 (Form 1065).
	c Gross nonfarm income	15c		
A D J U S T M E N T S **P R E F.** **T A X I T E M S**	**16a** Depreciation adjustment on property placed in service after 1986	16a	1,975	See pages 8 and 9 of Partner's Instructions for Schedule K–1 (Form 1065) and Instructions for Form 6251.
	b Adjusted gain or loss	16b		
	c Depletion (other than oil and gas)	16c		
	d (1) Gross income from oil, gas, and geothermal properties	d(1)		
	(2) Deductions allocable to oil, gas, and geothermal properties	d(2)		
	e Other adjustments and tax preference items	16e		
F O R E I G N T A X E S	**17a** Type of income ▶			Form 1116, check boxes
	b Name of foreign country or U.S. possession ▶			
	c Total gross income from sources outside the U.S.	17c		Form 1116, Part I
	d Total applicable deductions and losses (attach sch.)	17d		
	e Total foreign taxes (check one): ▶ ☐ Paid ☐ Accrued	17e		Form 1116, Part II
	f Reduction in taxes available for credit (att. schedule)	17f		Form 1116, Part III
	g Other foreign tax information (attach schedule)	17g		See Instructions for Form 1116.
O T H E R	**18** Section 59(e)(2) expenditures: **a** Type ▶			See page 9 of Partner's Instructions for Schedule K–1 (Form 1065).
	b Amount	18b		
	19 Tax–exempt interest income	19		Form 1040, line 8b
	20 Other tax–exempt income	20		See page 9 of Partner's Instructions for Schedule K–1 (Form 1065).
	21 Nondeductible expenses	21		
	22 Distributions of money (cash and marketable securities)	22	10,940	
	23 Distributions of property other than money	23		
	24 Recapture of low–income housing credit:			
	a From section 42(j)(5) partnerships	24a		Form 8611, line 8
	b Other than on line 24a	24b		

25 Supplemental information required to be reported separately to each partner (attach additional schedules if more space is needed):

Line 2
Rental Real Estate Activities

Description of Property	Gross Income	Net Expenses	Net Income	Passive NonPass	Section 1231
COMMERCIAL BUILDING	95,524	81,894	13,630	Passive	
		Total	13,630		

Partner 2: JOHN BUILDER   123-45-6789

Form **8825**	**Rental Real Estate Income and Expenses of a Partnership or an S Corporation**	OMB No. 1545–1186
Department of the Treasury Internal Revenue Service	▶ See instructions on back. ▶ Attach to Form 1065 or Form 1120S.	**1996**

Name	Employer identification number
SUBURBAN OFFICE PARTNERS II, L.P.	95-4786646

1 Show the kind and location of each property. See page 2 for additional properties.

A COMMERCIAL BUILDING, 200 S. MAIN ST , TUSTIN CA 92680

B

C

D

			Properties			
			A	B	C	D
Rental Real Estate Income						
2 Gross rents		2	477,622			
Rental Real Estate Expenses						
3 Advertising		3				
4 Auto and travel		4				
5 Cleaning and maintenance		5				
6 Commissions		6				
7 Insurance		7	2,512			
8 Legal and other professional fees		8				
9 Interest		9	196,905			
10 Repairs		10	18,480			
11 Taxes		11	18,420			
12 Utilities		12	26,311			
13 Wages and salaries		13				
14 Depreciation (see instructions)		14	46,470			
15▶ Management Fees			33,413			
Building Services			31,078			
Administrative			35,882			
		15				
16 Total expenses for each property. Add lines 3 through 15		16	409,471			

17 Total gross rents. Add gross rents from line 2, columns A through H	17	477,622
18 Total expenses. Add total expenses from line 16, columns A through H	18	(409,471)
19 Net gain (loss) from Form 4797, Part II, line 20, from the disposition of property from rental real estate activities	19	
20a Net income (loss) from rental real estate activities from partnerships, estates, and trusts in which this partnership or S corporation is a partner or beneficiary (from Schedule K-1)	20a	

  b Identify below the partnerships, estates, or trusts from which net income (loss) is shown on line 20a. Attach a schedule if more space is needed:

    (1) Name   (2) Employer identification number

21 Net income (loss) from rental real estate activities. Combine lines 17 through 20a. Enter result here and on Schedule K, line 2	21	68,151

KFA **For Paperwork Reduction Act Notice, see back of form.**

Form **8825** (1996)

1996	Federal Statements	Page 1

SUBURBAN OFFICE PARTNERS II, L.P.   95-4786646

Statement 1
Form 1065, Line 20
Other Deductions

Administrative	$	273
Insurance		1,414
Legal and Professional		1,638
Total	$	3,325

Statement 2
Form 1065, Schedule L, Line 17
Other Current Liabilities

	Beginning	Ending
Current Portion LT Debt	$ 24,106	$ 26,829
Total	$ 24,106	$ 26,829

Statement 3
Form 1065, Schedule L, Line 20
Other Liabilities

	Beginning	Ending
Security Deposits	$ 16,500	$ 16,500
Total	$ 16,500	$ 16,500

1996	Supplemental Information	Page 1
	SUBURBAN OFFICE PARTNERS II, L.P.	95–4786646

BALANCE SHEET
TRADE NOTES AND ACCOUNTS RECEIVABLE

Skipper Strickland	$	6,000
Builder Construction		40,000
Total	$	46,000

Community Bank

Serving YOUR Community Since 1873

```
                                                    PAGE:  1
                        DATE:   02/07/1997          ACCOUNT   4416852
```

```
                    SUBURBAN OFFICE PARTNERS II
                    A CALIFORNIA LIMITED PARTNERSHIP          30
                    4715 MAIN STREET                                      0
                    ORANGE, CA  92668                                     9
```

```
===================================================================================
    ANAHEIM OFFICE                              TELEPHONE: 714-555-1222
    4301 N STATE COLLEGE DR
    ANAHEIM CA 92805
===================================================================================
                    FIRST INTEREST CHKNG ACCOUNT 4416852
===================================================================================
    MINIMUM BALANCE          53,457.41   LAST STATEMENT              74,250.00
    AVG AVAILABLE BALANCE    69,869.66              3 CREDITS
    AVERAGE BALANCE          69,869.66             10 DEBITS
                                         THIS STATEMENT              81,533.41
```

```
          - - - - - - - - - - - OTHER CREDITS - - - - - - - - - - -
    DESCRIPTION                                         DATE      AMOUNT
    DEPOSIT                                             01/22   15,700.50
    DEPOSIT                                             01/22   18,316.38
    INTEREST                                            02/07      320.00
```

```
          - - - - - - - - - - - - - CHECKS - - - - - - - - - - - -
    CHECK #  DATE......AMOUNT    CHECK #  DATE......AMOUNT   CHECK #  DATE......AMOUNT
       5067  01/14  18,417.59       5070  01/22   1,324.60      5073  01/22      985.26
       5068  01/15     450.00       5071  01/22     187.11      5074  01/28      772.10
       5069  01/20     600.40       5072  01/28   1,469.63
```

```
              - - - - - - - - - - - - BALANCE - - - - - - - - - - -
          DATE.....BALANCE          DATE.....BALANCE          DATE.....BALANCE
          01/08  74,250.00          01/22  69,157.91          01/28  84,060.19
          01/14  55,832.41          01/22  68,970.80          02/03  81,624.41
          01/15  55,382.41          01/28  67,501.17          02/05  81,213.41
          01/20  54,782.01          01/22  66,515.91          02/07  81,533.41
          01/22  53,457.41          01/22  84,832.29
```

```
          - - - - - - - - - - - - - INTEREST - - - - - - - - - - -
    AVERAGE LEDGER BALANCE:    69,869.66   INTEREST EARNED:                320.00
    INTEREST PAID THIS PERIOD:    320.00   DAYS IN PERIOD:                     31
    INTEREST PAID 1997:           320.00   ANNUAL PERCENTAGE YIELD EARNED:    5.5%
```

Distribution History for Suburban Office Partners, II	
1997	$32,194
1996	54,700
1995	47,100
1994	42,600
1993	0

Partnership Profiles Data

A publication of Partnership Profiles, Inc., *THE Source For Partnership Information*   May/June 1997

PARTNERSHIP RE-SALE DISCOUNTS DIMINISHING

IN THIS ISSUE

DEPARTMENTS

The real estate gold rush has officially spilled over into the secondary market for real estate partnerships where buyers of "used" partnership units are paying higher prices than ever before in terms of discounts to net asset values.

According to a new study by *The Partnership Spectrum*, investors tapping the partnership secondary market for their real estate fix are buying units of real estate partnerships at an average price-to-value discount of 30%. This compares to the results of similar studies published in this newsletter in 1996 and 1995, which reported average price-to-value discounts of 38% and 41%, respectively.

While values for many real estate partnerships have improved in recent years as the nationwide real estate recovery has continued, secondary market prices have outpaced these gains, causing price-to-value discounts to shrink. A study published in the January/February 1997 issue of this newsletter revealed that prices for a sample group of 200 real estate partnerships rose an average of 35% during the year ended January 31, 1997.

Higher secondary market prices reflect investor optimism about real estate in general - a perception supported by increasing cash flows and property values for most partnerships - and the potential for near-term liquidations in particular. While secondary market buyers certainly factor current distribution yields into their pricing models, the potential for reaping near-term capital gains from partnership liquidations is even more appealing than quarterly distributions which help pass the time until the big check arrives in the mail at liquidation time.

This year's price-to-value discount study features 130 real estate partnerships owning real estate assets ranging from insured mortgages to debt-laden apartment complexes. This represents a decrease from the 167 partnerships in last year's discount study, due primarily to partnership liquidations in the past year. Since price-to-value discounts tend to shrink considerably when a partnership announces definitive, near-term liquidation plans, efforts were made to exclude such partnerships from the discount study.

All of the partnerships included in this year's discount study are publicly-registered with the Securities and

Continued Next Page

RE-SALE DISCOUNTS.......... *Continued*

Exchange Commission, though none of the partnerships are publicly-traded on any formal securities exchange. Instead, units of the partnerships are bought and sold in the informal partnership secondary market. This market is comprised of 12 to 15 independent firms that serve primarily as intermediaries in matching up buyers and sellers of non-listed public partnerships of all types.

In this year's price-to-value discount study, the 1996 year-end unit values reported by the sample group of 130 partnerships were compared to the weighted average prices at which investors purchased units in these partnerships in the secondary market during the 60-day period ended May 30, 1997. The study incorporates a total of 928 actual purchase transactions reported to *The Partnership Spectrum* by the secondary market firms listed on the back page of this newsletter. These firms report transaction data bi-monthly to this newsletter which is compiled and reported in the "Secondary Spectrum" section.

The partnership unit values used in the study have been reported by the partnerships and represent either (i) valuations prepared internally by general partners, (ii) independent valuations prepared by third-party appraisers retained on behalf of the partnerships, or (iii) some combination of the two. Each unit value generally represents an estimate of the total amount of cash that would be distributed to limited partners on a per unit basis, based upon a hypothetical sale of the partnership's real estate assets at current market values and the liquidation of the partnership.

The results of this year's price-to-value discount study are consistent with previous studies published in this newsletter in that the two most important factors considered by secondary market buyers in pricing units of real estate partnerships is (i) whether the partnership is consistently paying periodic distributions and (ii) the degree of debt financing utilized by the partnership. This is evidenced by the paltry price-to-value discounts of debt-free insured mortgage and triple-net-lease programs which consistently deliver high distribution yields to buyers.

At the other end of the discount spectrum are debt-laden partnerships that are unable to pay cash distributions on a current basis and have no real prospects for doing so in the foreseeable future. Non-distributing partnerships have, however, registered the largest price increases over the past year among the various groups of real estate partnerships included in the study. This has resulted in a significantly lower average price-to-value discount for these partnerships compared to prior years, a primary factor in the precipitous decline in the average discount for all partnerships in the study from 38% last year to 30% this year. (Non-distributing partnerships comprised approximately 20% of the partnership sample group in both the 1996 and 1997 studies.)

DISCOUNTS AND YIELDS

To better understand the effect distribution yields have on price-to-value discounts, this year's study includes cash distribution data for each partnership. As would be expected, the study shows a clear link between discounts and cash distribution yields, with buyers giving up discounts in exchange for high current distribution yields, and vice versa.

For purposes of the study, the 130 partnerships were grouped into five categories. (Actual data for each partnership by category begins on page 8.) These categories and the average discount and distribution yield for each group of partnerships is provided in the table below, followed by a discussion of each group:

Partnership Category	# of Partnerships	Average Discount	Average Yield
Equity - Distributing (low or no debt)	48	28%	8.1%
Equity - Distributing (moderate to high debt)	24	37%	7.2%
Equity - Non-Distributing	27	42%	0%
Triple-Net-Lease	19	16%	10.1%
Insured Mortgages	12	20%	10.3%

Equity - Distributing (Average Discount: 31%)
Equity-based partnerships that consistently pay cash distributions comprise most of the secondary market trading volume in real estate partnerships. Of the 928 purchase transactions incorporated into this study, approximately 500 (54%) involve partnerships in this group.

The 72 partnerships in this category own primarily equity interests in income-producing real estate properties ranging from apartments to shopping centers. Capital structures of these partnerships range from debt-free to highly leveraged.

Higher secondary market prices have caused the average price-to-value discount for these partnerships to decline to 31%, compared to 37% last year. But depending upon the amount of debt financing employed, the price-to-value discount among the partnerships in this group tend to vary significantly.

With respect to the 48 partnerships in this group that are either debt-free or utilize low levels of financing, the average price-to-value discount is just 28%, while the average cash distribution yield is 8.1%. The "prototype" partnership in this group that best reflects this pricing model is Krupp Cash Plus LP which traded at an average price-to-value discount of 25% and a cash distribution yield of 8.11%.

As for the 24 partnerships in this group that employ moderate to high levels of debt financing, the average price-to-value discount is 37%, a full nine percentage
Continued Next Page

RE-SALE DISCOUNTS..........*Continued*

points higher than for distribution-paying partnerships utilizing little or no debt financing. While the price-to-value discount is higher for these partnerships, the average distribution yield is nearly one percentage point lower at 7.2%. The "prototype" partnership in this group that best reflects this pricing model is Uniprop Manufactured Housing Communities Income Fund II.

The higher average discount applicable to partnerships with significant debt financing reflects investor concerns that distributions from these partnerships can quickly evaporate when refinancing time rolls around or when major capital improvement projects require funding from operating cash flow. Investors are clearly willing to pay closer to net asset value for units of partnerships having little or no debt since the likelihood of these partnerships sustaining at least some level of distributions is much greater if problems are encountered.

The lower average distribution yield attributable to partnerships with moderate to high levels of debt financing is clear evidence of the trade-off that exists between discounts and distribution yields. Buyers of these partnerships expect to more than make up for the lower distribution yield, however, when the higher price-to-value discount is realized upon liquidation.

Leveraged partnerships also have a sort of "hidden yield" that occurs as debt is gradually paid down within a partnership which increases its overall equity value. It is clear, however, that secondary market buyers are willing to pay more for yields that show up in the form of predictable distribution checks, than for "hidden yields" resulting from debt reduction within a partnership.

To be sure, secondary market buyers seem to place a "premium" on partnerships that pay a predictable level of monthly or quarterly cash distributions, rather than paying distributions sporadically at unpredictable intervals. It's worth noting that the partnership in this category that traded at the highest price-to-value discount, HCW Pension Real Estate Fund (49%), pays distributions so sporadically and unpredictably that buyers are unable to yield-price this partnership due to the unreliability of its distributions. The result is an unusually high price-to-value discount compared to other equity-based, distribution-paying partnerships.

Equity - Non-Distributing (Average Discount: 42%)
Consistent with the results of prior years' discount studies, the real estate partnerships that traded at the highest average price-to-value discount are those partnerships that do not pay cash distributions. However, the average discount for these partnerships has declined from an average of 56% in last year's study.

The 27 partnerships in this group own income-producing properties similar to that owned by "Equity-Distributing" partnerships. All but one of these partnerships employ significant debt financing which is the primary reason they are unable to pay regular cash distributions.

The substantial decline in the average discount for the partnerships in this group is due to increased speculation

in these partnerships by secondary market buyers. As mentioned previously, prices for non-distributing partnerships have outpaced every other category of real estate partnerships over the past year.

Discounts among the partnerships in this group tend to vary significantly, however, based upon a partnership's prospects for resuming cash distributions in the near future. The six partnerships that seem capable of reinstating regular cash distributions in the near future - namely, Angeles Income Properties II (44%), Angeles Partners XII (32%), Hotel Properties LP (32%), Hutton/ConAm Realty Investors 2 (29%), New England Life Pension Properties I (32%), and Mid-Atlantic Centers LP (31%) - traded at an average discount of 33% which is very similar to price-to-value discounts for partnerships that are currently making distributions. The fact that these partnerships are being priced as though they were already making cash distributions reflects a change in secondary market pricing from what is now to what might be tomorrow.

The partnerships in this group that traded at the deepest discounts are those partnerships that seem to have no real prospects for resuming cash distributions for the foreseeable future. The five partnerships with this dubious distinction include Angeles Income Properties III (58%), Davidson Diversified Real Estate III (57%), First Capital Income Properties XI (49%), Outlook Income Fund 9 (55%), and PaineWebber Income Properties Eight (57%). While the average discount for these partnerships of 55% seems steep, it still represents a significant improvement from previous years when discounts ran as much as 80%.

Triple-Net-Lease Programs (Average Discount: 16%)
All or substantially all of the real estate properties owned by the 19 partnerships in this group are net-leased to tenants pursuant to long-term lease agreements, whereby the lessees are obligated to pay all insurance, taxes and day-to-day maintenance costs related to the properties. Unlike other real estate partnerships which actively manage their properties, triple-net-lease partnerships generally act as landlord only. While restaurants are the most common property type owned by these partnerships, other types of real estate include industrial/warehouse facilities, office buildings and travel plazas.

Units of triple-net-lease partnerships trade in the secondary market at relatively low price-to-value discounts because they typically pay cash distributions on a very predictable basis. Although the discounts may seem paltry, the cash distribution yields on these programs are very attractive, with the average yield on the 19 partnerships in the study coming in at a healthy 10.1%.

Triple-net-lease partnerships seem to be priced by secondary market buyers based primarily on current distributions, with the value of the underlying real estate given much less consideration due to the long-term nature of the leases and because these partnerships are not expected to be liquidated for many years.

It does appear, however, that the amount of debt financing utilized by a triple-net-lease partnership does have some bearing on the secondary market pricing of its units. With

Continued Next Page

RE-SALE DISCOUNTS.........*Continued*

respect to the 14 partnerships in this group that have little or no debt, the average price-to-value discount is 13%. This compares to the average discount for the five leveraged partnerships of 25%. Although the five leveraged partnerships represent a small sample group, the higher discounts being applied to leveraged triple-net-lease partnerships versus their debt-free counterparts is consistent with the pricing of "Equity-Distributing" partnerships where price-to-value discounts increase as more debt is factored into the equation, as previously discussed.

Insured Mortgage Programs (Average Discount: 20%)
Substantially all of the assets owned by the 12 partnerships in this group consist of mortgage loans and/or mortgage-backed securities secured by multi-family apartment complexes, whereby payment of principal and interest by the borrowers is fully, or at least substantially, guaranteed by the federal government or an agency thereof. To a lesser extent, some of the partnerships in this group also hold uninsured equity interests or subordinated loans relating to the properties securing their mortgages.

Because these partnerships consistently pay cash distributions, and because the mortgage loans are insured, units of these partnerships trade at relatively low price-to-value discounts. As with every other partnership group covered in the study, discounts on units of insured mortgage partnerships have shrunk in the past year, from 25% in the 1996 study to just 20% in this year's study.

Similar to triple-net-lease partnerships, buyers of units in insured mortgage partnerships forego price-to-value discounts in exchange for high cash distribution yields which average 10.3% for the partnerships included in the study. These yields can be misleading, however, since insured mortgage programs typically supplement their distributions with regular principal repayments on their mortgage loans and/or mortgage-backed securities which represents a return *of* capital rather than a return *on* capital.

The downside for insured mortgage programs would be a jump in interest rates since the loans held by these partnerships are almost always at fixed rates. This risk is somewhat mitigated, however, by the participation features of many insured mortgages which permit the partnerships to receive a piece of the action if the underlying property performs above certain levels or is sold at more than a certain price. These participation features were considered to be of little or no value just a few years ago, but the current real estate boom has resurrected these participations which has already made for some very pleasant surprises.

***

The partnership re-sale discount studies published annually in the May/June issue of this newsletter have caught the attention of secondary market investors and valuation professionals seeking a better understanding of how partnership units are priced in this market. As this study has become used more frequently by valuation professionals for its empirical data concerning price-to-

value discounts on non-publicly-traded partnerships, this has generated a fair number of questions. In a "Question and Answer" format, the following is an attempt to provide answers to the most commonly asked questions about the secondary market, the partnerships featured in the study, the methodology used in preparing the study, and the reasons for the discounts.

Q. What types of partnerships are included in the re-sale discount study?
A. All of the partnerships in the study are publicly-registered - meaning they all file annual and quarterly reports (10-Ks and 10-Qs) with the Securities and Exchange Commission - but they are not publicly-traded on any type of formal exchange or securities market. The partnerships are all finite-life. Most of the partnerships in the study were originally expected to operate for periods ranging from six to twelve years before liquidating and paying out the resulting net proceeds to the partners. Due to the lengthy real estate recession that began in the late 1980's and other factors, many of these partnerships are now operating beyond their originally anticipated time-frames.

Q. What is the partnership secondary market?
A. By way of background, during the 1980's an estimated $100 billion was poured into publicly-registered limited partnerships by the investing public. These partnerships were sold through broker-dealers ranging from Wall Street wire-house firms to small financial planning firms. The vast majority of these partnerships invested in real estate - and at the very top of the market.

As these partnerships have "aged" and continued operating well beyond their originally anticipated time-frames, this has resulted in an increasing number of investors desiring to sell their partnership units for a variety of reasons, not the least of which is their disappointment with this investment. What has evolved over the years is an informal group of independent firms that buy and sell interests in partnerships that were never intended to be traded. This group of firms has become known as the partnership secondary market.

As it stands today, the partnership secondary market is comprised of 12 to 15 independent firms, most of which operate primarily as intermediaries in matching up buyers and sellers of publicly-registered, non-traded partnership interests. The three most active firms - namely, Chicago Partnership Board, American Partnership Board and DCC Securities - generate roughly 75% of the secondary market's total trading volume. Total trading volume for 1996 was approximately $200 million, based upon trade data published in this newsletter.

Trading in real estate partnerships represents approximately 75% of secondary market trading volume. Other types of partnerships that change hands in this market include equipment leasing programs (14%), cable television system partnerships (5%), energy programs (1%), and venture capital programs (5%) which generally covers any partnership that invests in private companies.

Very small trades dominate the partnership secondary market, which is no surprise since the average original

Continued Next Page

RE-SALE DISCOUNTS.........*Continued*

investment in a publicly-registered partnership is in the neighborhood of only $10,000. According to transaction data submitted by secondary market firms for this issue, 17% of the transactions in this market are for less than $1,000, one-half are for less than $3,500, and fully two-thirds are for less than $6,000.

While 600 to 700 partnership issues typically change hands during any given 60-day period, the secondary market is still very "thin" in that trading in a mere 40 to 50 partnerships usually comprise one-half of the total trading volume during the same period. A partnership is considered "actively traded" if 3% of its total units change hands in the secondary market during a twelve-month period.

Q. How were the partnerships included in the re-sale discount study selected?
A. First, to be eligible for the study a partnership must report an annual unit value, and that value must be *meaningful*. Unfortunately, many partnerships do not report annual unit values to their investors which automatically excludes them from the study. In some instances, partnerships reporting unit values were excluded from the study because the methodology used to determine their annual unit values seems to have little, if anything, to do with the net asset value of the partnerships. These partnerships typically report book value, capital account value, or some sort of adjusted par value which makes for a very arbitrary estimate of value.

The second requirement for inclusion in the study is that the partnership's units must trade in the secondary market during the 60-day period covered by the study. Despite increased volume in the secondary market, a number of partnerships could not be included in the study since no trades were reported by secondary market firms during the study period.

Even if a partnership reports a *meaningful* unit value and its units trade in the secondary market during the period covered by the study, the partnership could still be excluded if it paid a "special" cash distribution during the study period. ("Special" cash distributions consist of unscheduled distributions usually stemming from a property sale or loan pay-off received by a partnership.) The reason for excluding these partnerships is that it is not possible to determine whether the price paid by the secondary market buyer included the special distribution. Without this information, the "net" price to the buyer cannot be determined which is critical to the study.

Finally, any partnership that has announced definitive plans to liquidate within the next 12 months was excluded from the study. Liquidating partnerships tend to trade at significantly smaller discounts as secondary market buyers are willing to pay more for the increased likelihood of realizing capital gains in the near future. Much of the price-to-value discount sought by secondary market buyers is due to the uncertainty over when the partnership will be liquidated and the "built-in" capital gains realized. This uncertainty and the resulting discount comprises the lack of control component of the price-to-value discount which

stems from the fact that limited partners are in a position of non-control.

The initial sample group for this year's re-sale discount study included approximately 180 partnerships. After excluding partnerships primarily for the reasons noted above, this year's study was whittled down to 130 partnerships.

Q. How can I obtain additional financial information and other data on the partnerships included in the study?
A. As noted above, all of the partnerships are publicly-registered and therefore file periodic reports with the Securities and Exchange Commission. In addition, detailed reports on approximately 90% of the partnerships in the study may be obtained from Partnership Profiles, Inc. for $180. (Subscribers to this newsletter may obtain the "Detailed Partnership Data" package for only $150.) Information for each partnership includes (i) property holdings, (ii) historical cash distribution data, (iii) debt levels and (iv) key operating statistics. The "Detailed Partnership Data" package is helpful for anyone needing comparables for valuation purposes.

In recognition of the need appraisers have for information on all types of partnerships, Partnership Profiles, Inc. has recently developed a CD-ROM product known as *PartnerDisc™* that provides on a single disc the most recent S.E.C. annual reports for virtually every publicly-registered (but non-publicly-traded) partnership operating today. The

Continued Next Page

5

RE-SALE DISCOUNTS..........*Continued*

partnerships included on *PartnerDisc™* own everything from aircraft to motion pictures to timberland, and interests in many of these partnerships trade in the informal partnership secondary market as reported in this newsletter. The files on *PartnerDisc™* can be opened, retrieved and printed through the use of virtually any word-processing software operating with a CD-ROM drive. The Table of Contents provided with *PartnerDisc™* doubles as a directory of "EDGAR" code-numbers for quickly locating partnership S.E.C. filings via the Internet.

Since *PartnerDisc™* is designed for use with the user's own word-processing software, this provides the user with the ability to run searches to locate partnerships having particular characteristics such as the type of assets owned. This can be easily accomplished with most personal software programs which have the ability to quickly search through an entire directory of files for a particular word or phrase. Such a search typically provides a list of those files having the word or phrase identified. For instance, a search for the phrase "shopping center" will provide a list of files for partnerships that have purchased shopping centers. This search capability is standard with most word-processing software programs.

Beginning with this year's Re-Sale Discount Study, *PartnerDisc™* has become a standard component of the "Detailed Partnership Data" package at no additional cost.

Q. What is the source of the price data used in the study?
A. This newsletter has compiled and reported partnership transaction data submitted by secondary market firms on a running 60-day basis since the first issue was published in April 1990. This price data appears on a regular basis in the "Secondary Spectrum" section of this newsletter. The back page of this newsletter contains a detailed explanation of this data and the terms on which it is collected.

Q. Why is the trading period April 1 - May 30, 1997 used for the study, when the partnership unit values are generally as of December 31, 1996?
A. Although the partnership unit values are typically as of year-end 1996, they are not actually reported by the partnerships until usually sometime between March 1 and April 15. (These unit values were reported in the March/April 1997 issue of this newsletter.) By using transaction data for the 60-day period ending May 30, 1996, it can be reasonably assumed that buyers and sellers had access to the 1996 year-end unit values for these partnerships and considered these values in making their price determinations. This presumably makes for more informed buyers and sellers.

Q. What do the unit values represent?
A. These values are generally based upon a hypothetical sale of the partnership's properties at appraised values, and the distribution of the resulting net proceeds (less estimated selling costs), together with the partnership's net other assets, to the partners based upon the allocation provisions set forth in the Partnership Agreement. In some instances, appraised values have been estimated by the general partners, and in other cases independent appraisal firms were retained by the partnerships.

Q. How do publicly-registered partnerships compare to private partnerships?
A. First, publicly-registered partnerships must file periodic financial reports with the S.E.C., while private partnerships do not. In addition, private partnerships typically place much more onerous restrictions on the ability of limited partners to transfer their units through re-sales. These two distinctions will ensure there will never be an active re-sale market for private partnerships such as has evolved for publicly-registered partnerships. Another distinction between public and private partnerships is that a publicly-registered partnership typically has thousands of small investors, while a private partnership may have only a handful of high net worth individuals who have each made a sizeable investment in the partnership.

Public and private partnerships are alike in that the liability of their limited partners is limited to the amount of their investment. In addition, limited partners have no role in their partnership's day-to-day management decisions and are at the mercy of their general partner when it comes to major decisions such as paying distributions or when to liquidate their partnership. (Limited partners are often given the opportunity to vote on a proposed liquidation, but only *after* their general partner has made the decision to liquidate.) Whether the partnership is publicly-registered or private, limited partners are purely passive investors who through the Partnership Agreement have granted the general partner with almost unlimited discretion to make decisions regarding most every aspect of the partnership's operations. This lack of control position accounts for most of the price-to-value discount sought by buyers of partnership units.

Q. Are the partnerships in the study required to pay out any minimum level of cash distributions?
A. While real estate investment trusts must distribute certain minimum amounts to their investors to retain their preferred tax status, no such requirement exists for limited partnerships. The decision whether and when to make distributions and in what amounts is entirely at the discretion of the general partner. Instead of using excess cash flow to pay distributions, a general partner may decide that the partnership should use this cash flow to reduce debt or to fund property improvements. (The only exception to this is that some partnerships are required to make minimum cash distributions in the event a property sale results in a taxable gain to the limited partners, *if* the general partner determines there is adequate cash on hand.)

Q. What unit transfer restrictions apply to publicly-registered limited partnerships?
A. The Partnership Agreements for most public partnerships grant general partners substantial discretion when it comes to recognizing unit transfers, especially when the transfer is the result of a re-sale. Assuming all the necessary transfer documents are in good order, however, general partners of publicly-registered partnerships rarely block unit transfers unless recognizing a transfer would jeopardize the tax status of the partnership. Even then, the transfer is typically only delayed until the beginning of the partnership's next tax year. Another exception is that some general partners will temporarily "freeze" all unit transfers upon the announcement of a major event involving a partnership such as a roll-up, the sale of significant assets or plans to liquidate the

Continued Next Page

RE-SALE DISCOUNTS..........*Continued*

partnership. The transfer restrictions for most publicly-registered partnerships are fairly similar, but interpretations can vary significantly from one general partner to the next. These restrictions are discussed in the Partnership Agreements contained in the original prospectuses for the partnerships, all of which are on file with the Securities and Exchange Commission and can be obtained through a service bureau such as Disclosure, Inc. (800-638-8241).

As previously noted, private partnerships generally have much more onerous transfer restrictions than publicly-registered partnerships. In some instances, investors selling their units in a private partnership are required to obtain a legal opinion that the transfer will not jeopardize the tax status of the partnership. Many private partnerships also have "right of first refusal" provisions requiring that the other limited partners and/or the general partner be given the opportunity to purchase the units before they can be sold to an outsider.

Q. What is a "triple-net-lease" partnership?
A. This is a partnership where all or substantially all of its real estate properties are leased under long-term leases whereby the tenants are responsible for paying all insurance, maintenance and taxes related to the properties. The partnership serves as landlord only and does not participate in the operations of the properties.

The most common property types owed by these partnerships are restaurants, retail stores, corporate headquarters and manufacturing facilities. The lessees use triple-net-leases as a financing technique. Lease terms often go beyond ten years, with a series of renewal options. The primary consideration of the partnerships owning these properties is the credit-worthiness of the lessee.

Q. What are the economic interests of the general partners of the partnerships included in the study?
A. With respect to most of the partnerships in the study, the general partners have only a nominal interest in the partnerships, say 1% or 2%. The partnerships were structured such that the general partners would receive a stepped-up economic interest after the limited partners received certain returns. Very few, if any, of these partnerships have been able to meet these preferred returns, however, meaning the general partners continue to have only a nominal interest in the partnerships. Since any unpaid preferred returns to limited partners typically accumulate throughout the life of a partnership, a general partner's prospects for receiving any significant proceeds from the liquidation of a partnership are remote. This has created a situation where many general partners are reluctant to liquidate their partnerships since the value of their partnership management fees and expense reimbursements far exceeds any proceeds they might receive upon liquidation of the partnerships.

Q. How much of the overall price-to-value discount is due to lack of marketability versus lack of control/minority interest considerations?
A. It is difficult and perhaps even impossible to precisely quantify the amount of discount corresponding to these two factors. It does seem, however, that the discount for lack of marketability has become the lesser portion of the

overall discount over the years since the growth of the partnership secondary market means that a buyer can now be found relatively quickly for virtually any publicly-registered partnership. The results of similar studies by this newsletter over the years seem to support this since overall discounts have declined as secondary market trading volume has increased. The first re-sale discount study published by this newsletter (May/June 1992) found that the average price-to-value discount for the 85 partnerships in that study was 44%; this compares to an average discount of 30% for the 130 partnerships in this year's study. Secondary market trading volume has more than doubled from 1992 to today.

While some portion of the overall discount is due to lack of marketability since the partnership secondary market is very informal and does not offer the liquidity of an established securities market, lack of control/minority interest considerations play a larger role in the composition of the total discount. This is evidenced by the fact that buyers are willing to pay more for the units of partnerships that have announced definite plans to liquidate in the near future. As previously mentioned, any partnership that has announced definitive plans to liquidate within the next 12 months was excluded from the study.

Q. Do the price-to-value discounts reported in the study apply to buyers or sellers?
A. The discounts reported in the study reflect the discounts at which investors have *purchased* partnership units in the secondary market. On a net basis, the price-to-value discounts to sellers are slightly higher since sellers must pay commissions and other transaction costs typically ranging from 5% to 10% of the transaction amount. ▪

EQUITY PARTNERSHIPS - DISTRIBUTING (LOW OR NO DEBT)

PARTNERSHIP	VALUE PER UNIT	AVERAGE TRADE PRICE	AVERAGE DISCOUNT	REGULAR DISTRIBUTIONS	TYPE OF REAL ESTATE	DEBT LOW, HIGH	DISTRIBUTION RATE $	DISTRIBUTION RATE %	COMMENTS
Aetna Real Estate Associates	$15.70-I	$11.88[16]	24%	Yes	C, MF, R	L	$0.72	6.1%	Huge asset management fees help keep distributions low.
Carlyle Income Plus II	$425-GP	$304[4]	28%	Yes	C, R	L	$32.00	10.5%	None
Century HillCreste Apartment Inv.	$6.90-GP	$5.34[4]	23%	Yes	MF	L	$0.32	6.0%	Third-party proxy could accelerate liquidation of this single-asset partnership.
Century Pension Income XXIV	$401-I	$232[10]	42%	Yes	C, R	L	$15.00	6.5%	Pricing shows trade-off between discount and current yield.
Commercial Properties 2	$273-I	$194[1]	29%	Yes	C	L	$17.00	8.8%	None
Commercial Properties 3	$302-I	$215[1]	29%	Yes	C	L	$12.00	5.6%	None
Copley Pension Properties VI	$732-I	$594[5]	19%	Yes	C, MF	L	$42.28	7.1%	None
Copley Pension Properties VII	$838-I	$670[6]	20%	Yes	C, MF, R	L	$61.88	9.2%	None
Copley Realty Income Partners 2	$588-I	$481[1]	18%	Yes	C	L	$50.00	10.4%	None
Copley Realty Income Partners 3	$789-I	$623[3]	21%	Yes	C	L	$65.00	10.4%	None
Damson/Birtcher Realty Income I	$367-I	$247[2]	33%	Yes	C, R	L	$10.40	4.2%	Discount reflects secondary market buyers' perception of open-ended liquidation plans.
Damson/Birtcher Realty Income II	$593-I	$397[2]	33%	Yes	C, R	L	$46.00	11.6%	Discount reflects secondary market buyers' perception of open-ended liquidation plans.
Dean Witter Realty Yield Plus I	$11.15-I	$6.65[5]	40%	Yes	C, R	L	$0.52	7.8%	Also holds a mortgage loan secured by property in bankruptcy.
Dean Witter Realty Yield Plus II	$245-I	$169[4]	31%	Yes	C	L	$12.50	7.4%	Also holds a mortgage loan secured by property in bankruptcy.
First Capital Growth Fund XIV	$51-I	$38.43[2]	25%	Yes	C	L	$3.20	8.3%	None
First Capital Instit. Real Estate 1	$477-I	$362[10]	24%	Yes	C	L	$28	7.7%	None

PARTNERSHIP	VALUE PER UNIT	AVERAGE TRADE PRICE	AVERAGE DISCOUNT	REGULAR DISTRIBUTIONS	TYPE OF REAL ESTATE	DEBT LOW, HIGH	DISTRIBUTION RATE $	DISTRIBUTION RATE %	COMMENTS
First Capital Instit. Real Estate 2	$487-I	$405[31]	17%	Yes	C, R	L	$36	8.9%	Secondary market pricing similar to that of a net-lease partnership.
HCW Pension Real Estate Fund	$731-GP	$367[4]	49%	Yes	C, MF	L	NSR	NSR	Pays distributions sporadically which makes pay-outs unreliable.
High Equity Partners Series 85	$92.03-GP	$64.77[39]	30%	Yes	C, R	L	$3.00	4.6%	Price will rise once management raises distributions to actual cash flow.
High Equity Partners Series 86	$98.87-GP	$64.26[46]	35%	Yes	C, R	L	$3.08	4.8%	Price will rise once management raises distributions to actual cash flow.
High Equity Partners Series 88	$145-GP	$90.28[22]	38%	Yes	C, R	L	$8.16	9.0%	None
Hutton/ConAm Realty Inv. 3	$203-I	$157[7]	23%	Yes	MF	L	$6.00	3.8%	Distributions recently temporarily reduced from $10 to $6 per unit (annualized) to fund capital improvements.
Hutton/ConAm Realty Inv. 4	$228-I	$173[3]	24%	Yes	MF	L	$15.00	8.7%	None
Hutton/ConAm Realty Inv. 5	$359*-I	$285[1]	21%	Yes	MF	L	$24.00	8.4%	None
Hutton/ConAm Realty Pension Inv.	$271-I	$210[8]	23%	Yes	MF	L	$10.00	4.8%	Distributions have been temporarily reduced from previous rate of $20/unit annualized.
John Hancock Realty Income LP	$265-GP	$208[7]	19%	Yes	C, R	L	$22.52	10.8%	Secondary market pricing is similar to that of a net-lease partnership.
John Hancock Realty Income II	$10.95*-GP	$8.43[3]	23%	Yes	C, R	L	$0.96	11.4%	None
Krupp Cash Plus LP	$9.02-GP	$6.80[6]	25%	Yes	R	L	$0.55	8.1%	Represents "prototype" pricing for partnerships in this category.
Krupp Cash Plus II	$10.41-GP	$8.05[4]	23%	Yes	MF, R	L	$1.00	12.4%	Distribution recently increased from $0.80 to $1.00/unit annualized.
Krupp Cash Plus V	$9.66-GP	$7.62[5]	21%	Yes	R	L	$1.00	13.1%	Single-asset partnership.

9

PARTNERSHIP	VALUE PER UNIT	AVERAGE TRADE PRICE	AVERAGE DISCOUNT	REGULAR DISTRIBUTIONS	TYPE OF REAL ESTATE	DEBT LOW, HIGH	DISTRIBUTION RATE $	DISTRIBUTION RATE %	COMMENTS
Murray Income Properties I	$764-I	$516¹	32%	Yes	R	L	$52.52	10.2%	Pricing reflects investor concerns over strip shopping centers.
Murray Income Properties II	$74-I	$56¹	24%	Yes	R	L	$5.75	10.2%	Pricing reflects investor concerns over strip shopping centers.
New England Life Pens. Props. II	$863-I	$649⁹	25%	Yes	C, R	L	$56.40	8.7%	None
New England Life Pens. Props. III	$401-I	$327¹¹	18%	Yes	C, MF	L	$26.80	8.2%	None
New England Life Pens. Props. IV	$603-I	$502¹⁸	17%	Yes	C, MF	L	$38.30	7.6%	None
New England Life Pens. Props. V	$804-I	$632¹⁵	21%	Yes	C, R	L	$57.75	9.1%	None
PaineWebber Equity Props. Two	$0.32-I	$0.26¹⁸	19%	Yes	C, MF, R	L	$0.022	8.5%	None
PaineWebber Independent Living I	$9.51-I	$7.42³	22%	Yes	MF	L	$0.75	10.1%	Non-traded REIT owning retirement/senior living centers.
PaineWebber Independent Living II	$9.69-I	$7.61¹⁰	21%	Yes	MF	L	$0.65	8.5%	Non-traded REIT owning retirement/senior living centers.
PaineWebber Mortgage Partners 5	$17.04-I	$12.62⁴	26%	Yes	R	L	$0.68	5.4%	None
Participating Development Fund 86	$16.02-I	$10.14⁷	37%	Yes	C	L	$1.20	11.8%	None
PS Partners V	$394-GP	$308⁵	22%	Yes	MW	L	$24.00	7.8%	None
Qualified Properties 80	$373-I	$241²	35%	Yes	C	L	$16.00	6.6%	Distributions have been temporarily reduced from previous rate of $26/unit annualized.
Rancon Income Fund I	$402-GP	$220²	45%	Yes	C, R	L	$3.84	1.7%	Minimal distribution has buyers pricing this partnership as though it were non-distributing.
Real Estate Income Properties III	$319*-I	$214⁴	33%	Yes	C, R	L	$12.00	5.6%	Discount reflects secondary market buyers' perception of open-ended liquidation plans.
Windsor Park Properties 3	$33-GP	$18.00⁶	45%	Yes	MH	L	$1.40	7.8%	None
Windsor Park Properties 4	$42-GP	$30.00¹	29%	Yes	MH	L	$2.24	7.5%	None
Windsor Park Properties 5	$17-GP	$8.82²	48%	Yes	MH	L	$0.82	9.3%	None
AVERAGE DISCOUNT =		28%					AVERAGE DISTRIBUTION YIELD =	8.1%	

10

EQUITY PARTNERSHIPS - DISTRIBUTING (MODERATE TO HIGH DEBT)

PARTNERSHIP	VALUE PER UNIT	AVERAGE TRADE PRICE	AVERAGE DISCOUNT	REGULAR DISTRIBUTIONS	TYPE OF REAL ESTATE	DEBT LOW, HIGH	DISTRIBUTION RATE $	DISTRIBUTION RATE %	COMMENTS
Davidson Diversified Real Estate I	$6,538-GP	$4,690¹	28%	Yes	MF	H	$504	10.7%	None
Davidson Growth Plus	$495-GP	$263³	47%	Yes	MF	H	$25	9.5%	Pricing hasn't yet caught up with 22% increase in unit value from 1995.
Davidson Income Real Estate	$503-GP	$304⁶	40%	Yes	MF	H	NSR	NSR	Quarterly distributions often fluctuate significantly.
First Dearborn Income Props. II	$240-GP	$110²	54%	Yes	MF, R	H	$8.28	7.5%	Reasoning behind high discount is unclear.
First Dearborn Income Props. LP	$186-GP	$127¹	32%	Yes	C, R	H	$7.50	5.9%	None
Hutton/ConAm Realty Inv. 81	$145-I	$105	28%	Yes	MF	H	$7.40	7.0%	None
Krupp Realty Fund III	$661-GP	$393²	40%	Yes	MF	H	$15.86	4.0%	Low yield reflects buyer optimism that this partnership will increase payout in near future.
Krupp Realty Fund IV	$573-GP	$449¹	22%	Yes	MF	H	$37.32	8.3%	None
Krupp Realty Fund V	$787-GP	$460¹	42%	Yes	MF	H	$40.00	8.7%	One apartment property also contains retail space.
Krupp Realty LP VII	$484-GP	$332⁴	31%	Yes	MF,R	H	$20.00	6.0%	None
PaineWebber Equity Props. One	$17.32-I	$11.15⁴	36%	Yes	C, MF	H	$0.50	4.5%	Distribution rate has since doubled due to improving operations.
PaineWebber Equity Props. Three	$402-I	$293⁹	27%	Yes	C, MF, R	H	$25.00	8.5%	Secondary market pricing is similar to a debt-free partnership.
PaineWebber Growth Props. LP	$581-I	$370⁴	36%	Yes	MF	H	$16.16	4.4%	None
PaineWebber Growth Props. Two	$720-I	$420¹	42%	Yes	C, MF	H	$15.40	3.7%	Good example of trade-off between discount and distribution yield.
PaineWebber Income Props. Seven	$545*-I	$286³	47%	Yes	MF, R	H	$24.00	8.4%	Resumed distributions this year after lengthy suspension.

11

PARTNERSHIP	VALUE PER UNIT	AVERAGE TRADE PRICE	AVERAGE DISCOUNT	REGULAR DISTRIBUTIONS	TYPE OF REAL ESTATE	DEBT LOW, HIGH	DISTRIBUTION RATE $	DISTRIBUTION RATE %	COMMENTS
PaineWebber Income Props. Six	$403*-I	$327[10]	19%	Yes	MF, R	H	$34.78	10.6%	Secondary market pricing is similar to a debt-free partnership.
PaineWebber Income Props. Three	$540-I	$294[3]	45%	Yes	R	H	$19.52	6.6%	None
Real-Equity Partners	$545-I	$247[4]	55%	Yes	MF	H	$20	8.1%	A good example of almost pure yield-pricing.
Shelter Properties IV	$589-I	$357[7]	39%	Yes	MF	H	$20	5.6%	Good example of trade-off between discount and distribution yield.
Shelter Properties V	$621*-I	$420[6]	32%	Yes	MF	H	NSR	NSR	Distributions fluctuate from one payment to the next.
Sierra Pacific Development II	$156-GP	$110[11]	30%	Yes	C	H	NSR	NSR	Distributions fluctuate from one payment to the next.
Uniprop Manufacturing Housing Communities II	$12.81-I	$8.23[1]	36%	Yes	MH	H	$0.60	7.3%	Discount and yield represent "prototype" pricing model for partnerships in this group.
USAA Income Properties III	$296-GP	$193[3]	35%	Yes	C, R	H	$8.00	4.1%	None
Windsor Park Properties 7	$102-GP	$64.29[6]	37%	Yes	MH	H	$7.50	11.6%	Unusually high yield for a leveraged partnership trading at such a discount.
		AVERAGE DISCOUNT =	37%				AVERAGE DISTRIBUTION YIELD =	7.2%	

EQUITY PARTNERSHIPS - NON-DISTRIBUTING

PARTNERSHIP	VALUE PER UNIT	AVERAGE TRADE PRICE	AVERAGE DISCOUNT	REGULAR DISTRIBUTIONS	TYPE OF REAL ESTATE	DEBT LOW, HIGH	DISTRIBUTION RATE $	DISTRIBUTION RATE %	COMMENTS
Angeles Income Properties 6	$313-GP	$182[1]	42%	No	MF, R	H	$0	0%	None
Angeles Income Properties II	$220-GP	$124[16]	44%	No	MF, R	H	$0	0%	Has potential to resume regular cash distributions near-term.
Angeles Income Properties III	$120-GP	$50.65[5]	58%	No	MF, R	H	$0	0%	No apparent prospects for resuming regular cash distributions in foreseeable future.

12

PARTNERSHIP	VALUE PER UNIT	AVERAGE TRADE PRICE	AVERAGE DISCOUNT	REGULAR DISTRIBUTIONS	TYPE OF REAL ESTATE	DEBT LOW, HIGH	DISTRIBUTION RATE $	DISTRIBUTION RATE %	COMMENTS
Angeles Income Properties IV	$106-GP	$79.77⁸	25%	No	R	H	$0	0%	Seems overpriced for a non-distributing partnership.
Angeles Partners IX	$494-GP	$313¹	37%	No	MF	H	$0	0%	None
Angeles Partners XI	$64-GP	$40²	38%	No	MF	H	$0	0%	None
Angeles Partners XII	$582-GP	$393⁸	32%	No	MF	H	$0	0%	Has potential to resume regular cash distributions near-term.
Davidson Diversified Real Estate III	$4,405-GP	$1,900¹	57%	No	MF	H	$0	0%	No apparent prospects for resuming regular cash distributions in foreseeable future.
First Capital Income Growth XII	$25-I	$13.91⁸	44%	No	C, R	H	$0	0%	None
First Capital Income Props. XI	$155-I	$78.44¹	49%	No	C, R	H	$0	0%	No apparent prospects for resuming cash distributions in foreseeable future
Hotel Properties LP	$8.13-GP	$5.50⁴	32%	No	HTL	H	$0	0%	Has potential to resume regular cash distributions near-term.
Hutton/ConAm Realty Inv. 2	$203-I	$145¹	29%	No	MF	H	$0	0%	Has potential to resume regular cash distributions near-term.
Mid-Atlantic Centers LP	$10.19-I	$7.02²	31%	No	R	H	$0	0%	Plans to resume distributions in 1997.
New England Life Pension Props. I	$415-I	$283¹	32%	No	C, R	L	$0	0%	Has potential to resume regular cash distributions near-term.
Outlook Income Fund 9	$0.11-GP	$0.05²	55%	No	C, HTL, MF	H	$0	0%	No apparent prospects for resuming regular cash distributions in foreseeable future.
PaineWebber Income Props. Eight	$0.093-I	$0.04²	57%	No	MF, R	H	$0	0%	No prospects whatsoever for resuming regular cash distributions.
PaineWebber Income Props. Five	$318-I	$213⁷	33%	No	MF, R	H	$0	0%	Seems overpriced for a non-distributing partnership.
PaineWebber Income Props. Four	$335-I	$199²	41%	No	MF	H	$0	0%	None

13

PARTNERSHIP	VALUE PER UNIT	AVERAGE TRADE PRICE	AVERAGE DISCOUNT	REGULAR DISTRIBUTIONS	TYPE OF REAL ESTATE	DEBT LOW, HIGH	DISTRIBUTION RATE $	%	COMMENTS
Rancon Realty Fund IV	$317-GP	$191[2]	40%	No	C, MF, R	H	$0	0%	Also holds significant undeveloped land for development or sale.
Rancon Realty Fund V	$340-GP	$190[8]	44%	No	C	H	$0	0%	Also holds significant undeveloped land for development or sale.
Shelter Properties I	$751*-GP	$402[3]	46%	No	MF	H	$0	0%	None
Shelter Properties II	$583-I	$313[3]	46%	No	MF	H	$0	0%	None
Shelter Properties III	$302-I	$165[4]	45%	No	MF	H	$0	0%	None
Shelter Properties VI	$539-I	$309[5]	43%	No	MF	H	$0	0%	Represents "prototype" pricing for partnerships in this category.
Shelter Properties VII	$634-I	$239[3]	62%	No	MF	H	$0	0%	Secondary market prices yet to catch up with increase in value from 1995 to 1996.
Shopco Regional Malls	$276-I	$177[11]	36%	No	R	H	$0	0%	Secondary market price reflects the partnership's huge cash reserves.
Sierra Pacific Instit. Props. V	$79.91-GP	$44.86[2]	44%	No	C	H	$0	0%	None
	AVERAGE DISCOUNT =		42%				AVERAGE DISTRIBUTION YIELD =	0%	

TRIPLE-NET-LEASE PARTNERSHIPS
(ALL DISTRIBUTING)

PARTNERSHIP	VALUE PER UNIT	AVERAGE TRADE PRICE	AVERAGE DISCOUNT	REGULAR DISTRIBUTIONS	TYPE OF REAL ESTATE	DEBT LOW, HIGH	DISTRIBUTION RATE $	%	COMMENTS
Carey Institutional Properties	$11.90-I	$9.71[17]	18%	Yes	C	H	$0.822	8.5%	Non-traded REIT.
CNL Income Fund II	$512-I	$430[1]	16%	Yes	RST	L	$47.50	11.0%	All-cash restaurants.
CNL Income Fund III	$488-I	$461[3]	6%	Yes	RST	L	$47.50	10.3%	All-cash restaurants.
CNL Income Fund IX	$10.73-I	$8.37[2]	22%	Yes	RST	L	$0.90	10.8%	All-cash restaurants.
CNL Income Fund V	$482-I	$449[2]	7%	Yes	RST	L	$46.00	10.2%	All-cash restaurants.
CNL Income Fund VI	$534-I	$482[2]	10%	Yes	RST	L	$45.00	9.3%	All-cash restaurants.
CNL Income Fund VII	$1.05-I	$0.96[2]	9%	Yes	RST	L	$0.09	9.4%	All-cash restaurants.
CNL Income Fund X	$10.77-I	$8.70[3]	19%	Yes	RST	L	$0.90	10.3%	All-cash restaurants.

14

PARTNERSHIP	VALUE PER UNIT	AVERAGE TRADE PRICE	AVERAGE DISCOUNT	REGULAR DISTRIBUTIONS	TYPE OF REAL ESTATE	DEBT LOW, HIGH	DISTRIBUTION RATE $	%	COMMENTS
CNL Income Fund XI	$10.53-I	$8.93[1]	15%	Yes	RST	L	$0.875	9.8%	All-cash restaurants.
CNL Income Fund XIII	$10.33-I	$8.77[2]	15%	Yes	RST	L	$0.85	9.7%	All-cash restaurants.
Corporate Property Associates 10	$10.00-I	$8.17[11]	18%	Yes	C	H	$0.702	8.6%	Non-traded REIT.
Corporate Realty Income Fund I	$14.96-I	$9.90[4]	34%	Yes	C	H	$1.20	12.1%	None
DiVall Insured Income Fund LP	$550-GP	$505[4]	8%	Yes	RST	L	$60.00	11.9%	Distributions often fluctuate from one payment to the next.
John Hancock Realty Income III	$16.61-GP	$13.29[5]	20%	Yes	C, R	L	$1.40	10.5%	Six of seven properties are net-leased.
Net 1 LP	$751-I	$537[4]	28%	Yes	R	H	$50.04	9.3%	None
Net 2 LP	$78.09-I	$56.98[4]	27%	Yes	C, R	H	$5.00	8.8%	None
Participating Income Props. 1986	$1,026-I	$891[11]	13%	Yes	R	L	$102	11.4%	Distributions fluctuate slightly from one payment to the next.
Participating Income Props. II	$983-I	$918[14]	7%	Yes	R	L	$101	11.0%	Distributions fluctuate slightly from one payment to the next.
Participating Income Props. III	$1,015-I	$899[1]	11%	Yes	R	L	$86.76	9.7%	Also holds a note receivable.
		AVERAGE DISCOUNT = 16%					AVERAGE DISTRIBUTION YIELD = 10.1%		

INSURED MORTGAGE PROGRAMS (ALL DISTRIBUTING)

PARTNERSHIP	VALUE PER UNIT	AVERAGE TRADE PRICE	AVERAGE DISCOUNT	REGULAR DISTRIBUTIONS	TYPE OF REAL ESTATE	DEBT LOW, HIGH	DISTRIBUTION RATE $	%	COMMENTS
Capital Mortgage Plus	$16.86-GP	$11.41[6]	32%	Yes	N/A	L	$1.40	12.3%	Distributions exceed actual cash flow.
Capital Source LP	$16.71-GP	$11.52[7]	31%	Yes	N/A	L	$1.01	8.8%	None
Capital Source LP II	$9.55-GP	$7.21[6]	25%	Yes	N/A	L	$0.81	11.2%	None
KP Wingate Insured Partners	$3.85-I	$3.10[2]	19%	Yes	N/A	L	NSR	NSR	Distributions fluctuate from one payment to the next.
Krupp Government Income Trust	$14.95-GP	$12.09[36]	19%	Yes	N/A	L	$1.30	10.8%	Distributions include principal payments.
Krupp Government Income Trust II	$14.88-GP	$11.90[40]	20%	Yes	N/A	L	$1.25	10.5%	Distributions include principal payments.

PARTNERSHIP	VALUE PER UNIT	AVERAGE TRADE PRICE	AVERAGE DISCOUNT	REGULAR DISTRIBUTIONS	TYPE OF REAL ESTATE	DEBT LOW, HIGH	DISTRIBUTION RATE $	DISTRIBUTION RATE %	COMMENTS
Krupp Insured Mortgage LP	$12.75-GP	$10.20^{72}	20%	Yes	N/A	L	$1.20	11.8%	Distributions include principal payments.
Krupp Insured Plus LP	$9.60-GP	$8.55^{13}	11%	Yes	N/A	L	$0.76	8.9%	Distributions include principal payments.
Krupp Insured Plus II	$14.02-GP	$11.71^{25}	16%	Yes	N/A	L	$1.12	9.6%	Distributions include principal payments.
Krupp Insured Plus III	$14.11-GP	$11.77^{14}	17%	Yes	N/A	L	$1.20	10.2%	Distributions include principal payments.
PaineWebber Insured Mortgage 1-B	$43.79*-I	$41.45^{6}	5%	Yes	N/A	L	$3.55	8.6%	Distributions include principal payments.
Wingate Government Mortgage II	$6.31-I	$4.90^{3}	22%	Yes	N/A	L	NSR	NSR	Distributions fluctuate from one payment to the next.
		AVERAGE DISCOUNT =	**20%**				**AVERAGE DISTRIBUTION YIELD =**	**10.3%**	

EXPLANATORY NOTES

The above unit values have been reported by the partnerships and have not been determined by Partnership Profiles, Inc. Under no circumstances does the publisher make any representation or warranty as to the accuracy or reasonableness of any of the above unit values. Unit values followed by an "I" represent estimates of value made or reviewed by independent, third-party appraisers. Unit values followed by the designation "GP" represent estimates of value made by the partnership's general partner. Unit values are generally as of the end of the partnership's 1996 fiscal year-end, which for most partnerships is December 31, 1996. Unit values are subject to change thereafter. A unit value followed by an asterisk (*) has been adjusted for a special distribution made by the partnership subsequent to the "as of" date of the unit valuation.

"Average Discount" represents the percentage difference between the partnership's value per unit and the weighted average trading price of the partnership's units based on transactions reported by various secondary market firms to Partnership Profiles, Inc. for the 60-day period ending May 30, 1997. The number of trades reported for each partnership during this period is provided in superscript with the average trade price of the partnership.

Cash distribution information reflects the annualized regular cash distribution rate of the partnership as of March 31, 1997. Percentage (%) information reflects the partnership's annualized cash distribution rate in dollar terms (as shown), divided by the weighted average trade price of the partnership's units. A designation of "NSR" (i.e., no set rate) has been provided for partnerships that make periodic distributions, but where such distributions often vary significantly from one payment to the next. Such partnerships were omitted in computing the "Average Distribution Yield" for each category of partnerships.

"Type of Real Estate" information describes the real estate holdings for each partnership in general terms as follows:

C = office buildings, industrial/warehouse facilities, research and development facilities, and business parks
MF = apartments and retirement centers
R = shopping centers, outlet malls and other retail-use space
MH = manufactured housing communities and mobile home parks
HTL = hotels and other lodging facilities
RST = restaurants
MW = mini-warehouses/self-storage facilities

"Debt" information is based upon the capital structure of the partnership in terms of the amount of debt financing utilized. The designation "L" has been provided for partnerships that are either debt-free or are operating subject to a relatively low amount of debt financing. The designation "H" has been provided for partnerships that operate subject to a moderate-to-high degree of debt financing.

16

SECONDARY SPECTRUM

APRIL 1, 1997 THROUGH MAY 30, 1997

REAL ESTATE PARTNERSHIPS

PARTNERSHIP NAME	ORIGINAL UNIT SIZE	WEIGHTED AVERAGE	TRADING PRICES HIGH	LOW	TOTAL UNITS TRADED	# OF TRADES	VOLUME	CURRENT YIELD $	%	UNIT VALUES
DSI Realty Income Fund VII	$500	$445.00	$445.00	/$445.00	8	1	$3,560.00	$40	8.99%	N/A
DSI Realty Income Fund VIII	$500	$395.00	$395.00	/$395.00	4	1	$1,580.00	$45	11.39%	N/A
DSI Realty Income Fund IX	$500	$445.00	$445.00	/$445.00	4	1	$1,780.00	$40	8.99%	N/A
DSI Realty Income Fund X	$500	$475.00	$475.00	/$475.00	10	1	$4,750.00	$40	8.42%	N/A
Damson/Birtcher Realty Income I	$1000	$246.64	$247.62	/$246.00	16.5	2	$4,069.53	$10.40	4.22%	$367-I
Damson/Birtcher Realty Income II	$1000	$397.43	$400.00	/$395.01	4	2	$1,640.26	$46	11.57%	$593-I
Davidson Diversified Real Estate I	$20,000	$4,690.41	$4,800.00	/$4,383.56	2.85	3	$13,367.67	$504	10.75%	$6,538-GP
Davidson Diversified Real Estate III	$20,000	$1,900.00	$1,900.00	/$1,900.00	2.5	1	$4,750.00	$0	0.00%	$4,405-GP
Davidson Growth Plus	$1000	$263.45	$328.00	/$226.00	73.5	5	$19,363.50	$25	9.49%	$495-GP
Davidson Income Real Estate LP	$1000	$304.00	$315.00	/$290.00	35	6	$10,640.00	N/A	N/A	$503-GP
DiVall Insured Income Properties 2	$1000	$467.93	$525.00	/$405.00	138	7	$64,574.00	N/A	N/A	$440*-GP
DiVall Insured Income Properties 3	$1000	$247.66	$302.38	/$200.00	85	5	$21,050.75	N/A	N/A	$216*-GP
Diversified Historic Investors VI	$1000	$39.94	$41.50	/$38.00	22.5	2	$898.75	$0	0.00%	N/A
Drexel Burnham Lambert Real Estate I	$500	$48.00	$50.00	/$46.00	40	3	$1,920.00	$0	0.00%	N/A
Drexel Burnham Lambert Real Estate II	$500	$91.80	$120.00	/$53.00	240	10	$22,031.20	$0	0.00%	N/A
Eagle Insured L.P.	$20	$9.90	$10.15	/$9.10	20,321	9	$201,172.48	$0.95	9.60%	N/A
Fairfield Inn By Marriott	$1000	$686.28	$707.50	/$645.00	231	13	$158,529.90	N/A	N/A	N/A
Fairway Funds LP	$500	$184.53	$184.53	/$184.53	20	1	$3,690.60	N/A	N/A	N/A
First Capital Growth Fund Series XIV	$100	$38.43	$39.07	/$38.00	250	2	$9,607.00	$3.20	8.33%	$51-I
First Capital Income Properties - Series VIII	$1000	$374.19	$391.20	/$350.00	292	23	$109,263.00	$26	6.95%	N/A
First Capital Income Properties - Series IX	$1000	$487.78	$500.00	/$460.00	362	23	$176,576.35	$42	8.61%	N/A
First Capital Income Properties - Series X	$1000	$132.00	$132.00	/$132.00	15	1	$1,980.00	$0	0.00%	N/A
First Capital Income Properties - Series XI	$1000	$78.44	$82.00	/$75.68	414	5	$32,472.26	$0	0.00%	$155-I
First Capital Income and Growth - Series XII	$100	$13.91	$15.30	/$12.80	2,165	8	$30,116.05	$0	0.00%	$25-I
First Capital Inst. Real Estate Ltd. - 1	$1000	$361.74	$370.00	/$335.00	95	10	$34,365.67	$28	7.74%	$477-I
First Capital Inst. Real Estate Ltd. - 2	$1000	$404.97	$418.09	/$361.00	220	21	$89,093.88	$36	8.89%	$487-'
First Capital Inst. Real Estate Ltd. - 3	$1000	$398.56	$415.00	/$380.00	107	11	$42,645.65	$28	7.03%	$459*-
First Capital Inst. Real Estate Ltd. - 4	$100	$42.32	$44.00	/$40.00	305	3	$12,909.00	$2	4.73%	$37.68*-I
First Capital Insured Real Estate	$100	$23.18	$26.00	/$22.00	750	5	$17,382.00	$1.80	7.77%	$20.14*-/
First Dearborn Income Properties LP	$500	$127.20	$127.20	/$127.20	20	1	$2,544.00	$7.50	5.90%	$186-G'
Growth Hotel Investors II	$1000	$1166.94	$1,250.00	/$1,030.00	101	9	$117,861.40	N/A	N/A	N/A
HCW Pension Real Estate Fund LP	$1000	$366.98	$405.48	/$320.00	71	4	$26,055.36	N/A	N/A	$731-GP
Healthcare Properties	$10	$8.51	$10.00	/$5.10	3,606	3	$30,668.92	N/A	N/A	N/A
High Cash Partners	$250	$62.97	$65.00	/$62.01	290	4	$18,262.40	$0	0.00%	N/A
High Equity Partners - Series 85	$250	$64.77	$80.00	/$57.00	1,032	39	$66,847.36	$3	4.63%	$92-GP
High Equity Partners - Series 86	$250	$64.26	$70.20	/$57.00	2,071	46	$133,072.32	$3.08	4.79%	$98.87-GP
High Equity Partners - Series 88	$250	$90.28	$96.58	/$83.40	2,330	22	$210,358.20	$8.16	9.04%	$145-GP
Hotel Properties LP	$10	$5.50	$5.50	/$5.50	2,500	4	$13,750.00	$0	0.00%	$8.13-GP
Hutton/ConAm Realty Investors 2	$500	$145.44	$148.00	/$144.00	86	4	$12,508.00	$0	0.00%	$203-I
Hutton/ConAm Realty Investors 3	$500	$157.19	$163.05	/$152.00	288	7	$45,272.05	$6	3.82%	$203-I
National Property Investors 5	$500	$76.33	$83.00	/$75.00	48	2	$3,664.00	$0	0.00%	N/A
National Property Investors 6	$500	$182.63	$233.00	/$155.00	140	7	$25,568.34	$0	0.00%	N/A
National Property Investors 7	$500	$191.49	$230.00	/$140.00	97	5	$18,574.10	$0	0.00%	N/A
National Property Investors 8	$500	$173.81	$200.00	/$150.00	21	2	$3,650.00	$0	0.00%	N/A
National Real Estate Income Props. II	$250	$93.00	$93.00	/$93.00	20	1	$1,860.00	N/A	N/A	N/A
National Tax Credit Partners	$2500	$705.36	$710.00	/$701.79	13	3	$9,169.68	$0	0.00%	N/A
National Tax Credit Investors II	$1000	$491.50	$500.00	/$470.00	105	5	$51,607.70	$0	0.00%	N/A
Net 1 LP	$1000	$537.40	$575.34	/$505.00	163	8	$87,596.60	$50.04	9.31%	$751-I
Net 2 LP	$100	$56.98	$61.00	/$54.80	1,749	8	$99,657.96	$5	8.78%	$78.09-I
PaineWebber Equity Partners Two	$1	$0.26	$0.27	/$0.17	386,004	18	$98,647.29	$0.022	8.61%	$0.32-I
PaineWebber Growth Properties L.P.	$1000	$369.55	$375.00	/$355.00	55	4	$20,325.00	$16.16	4.37%	$466*-I
PaineWebber Growth Properties II L.P.	$1000	$420.43	$430.00	/$401.18	55	4	$23,123.60	$15.40	3.66%	$720-I
PaineWebber Growth Properties III L.P.	$1000	$40.63	$62.00	/$25.00	95	6	$3,860.00	$0	0.00%	$131*-I
PaineWebber Income Properties Eight	$1	$0.04	$0.05	/$0.02	20,000	2	$850.00	$0	0.00%	$0.093-'
PaineWebber Income Properties Five	$1000	$212.74	$222.00	/$199.90	80	7	$17,019.00	$0	0.00%	$311
PaineWebber Income Properties Four	$1000	$199.04	$202.91	/$190.00	50	2	$9,951.85	$0	0.00%	$335-I
PaineWebber Income Properties Seven	$1000	$285.82	$290.00	/$258.00	146	5	$41,730.00	$24	8.40%	$545*-I
PaineWebber Income Properties Six	$1000	$326.71	$342.30	/$305.00	179	10	$58,481.48	$34.78	10.65%	$403*-I
PaineWebber Income Properties Three	$1000	$294.23	$295.93	/$293.00	20	3	$5,884.65	$19.52	6.63%	$540-I

A composite of pages 33-39

SPECIAL ADDENDUM COVERING REAL ESTATE PARTNERSHIPS INCLUDED IN THE 1997 PARTNERSHIP RE-SALE DISCOUNT STUDY PUBLISHED BY PARTNERSHIP PROFILES, INC.

Editor's Note: This Special Addendum includes detailed reports from the *Partnership Profiles* data base on all but nineteen partnerships included in the sample group for the **1997 Partnership Re-Sale Discount Study** as published in the May/June 1997 issue of *The Partnership Spectrum*. These detailed partnership reports and the Table of Contents that provides the page numbers for locating these reports is provided in the front section of this book.

The back section of this book (see colored divider) includes information and a directory for *PartnerDisc*, an information resource developed specifically for appraisers by Partnership Profiles, Inc. that provides on a single CD-ROM disc the most recent S.E.C. annual reports for virtually every publicly-registered (but non-publicly-traded) partnership and real estate investment trust operating today.

Partnership Profiles, Inc.
P.O. Box 7938
Dallas, Texas 75209
(800) 634-4614
Editor: Spencer Jefferies

WP: addendum.97

NOTICE TO USERS

TABLE OF CONTENTS

Editor's Note: Consistent with the 1997 Partnership Re-Sale Discount Study published in the May/June 1997 issue of *The Partnership Spectrum*, the partnerships featured herein have been placed into the following categories for purposes of this Table of Contents:

    Equity - Distributing (Low or No Debt)
    Equity - Distributing (Moderate to High Debt)
    Equity - Non-Distributing
    Triple-Net-Lease
    Insured Mortgages.

There are a total of 19 partnerships included in the 1997 Partnership Re-Sale Discount Study that are not included in this addendum because they are not covered in the *Partnership Profiles* data base. Detailed information on these partnerships - as well as virtually every publicly-registered partnership in existence - can be obtained from *PartnerDisc™* (see back section of this book at the divider).

EQUITY PARTNERSHIPS - DISTRIBUTING

```
PROGRAM:  Damson/Birtcher Realty Income Fund - I
SPONSOR:  Birtcher/Liquidity Properties
OFFERING COMMENCED:  1984
OFFERING CLOSED:  September 1985
OFFERING PROCEEDS:  $97,198,000
90% INVESTED:  1985
UNIT SIZE:  N/A
ADJUSTED UNIT SIZE:  N/A
VALUE PER $1,000 INVESTMENT: $367.40
     (AS OF 12/31/96-Independent)  (1,124,000 UNITS)
UNITS OUTSTANDING:  Capital not designated in units.
FYE:  December 31
DISTRIBUTION RATE:  1.05% (AS OF 06/15/97)
DISTRIBUTION FREQUENCY:  Quarterly
SPONSOR PHONE:  (212) 505-4460
```

°PARTNERSHIP PROFILES

PPI RATINGS:(1=HIGHEST,5=LOWEST)
FINANCIAL CONDITION.......2
CASH DISTRIBUTION.........5

DISTRIBUTION HISTORY (Per $1,000 Investment)

	1997-2Q	1997-1Q	1996	1995	1994	1993
Regular	$ 2.60	$ 2.60	$ 5.20	$ 7.80	$ 15.11	$ 19.22
Special	0	0	15.43	0	0	0
TOTAL	$ 2.60	$ 2.60	$ 20.64	$ 7.80	$ 15.11	$ 19.22

Cumulative: $330

> Note: Distribution information reflects the fiscal period during which distributions were actually paid to investors. Actual distributions may vary between investors in the Partnership based upon their actual date of admittance to the Partnership. Certain amounts may have been rounded. Distribution amounts have not been reduced to reflect any taxes withheld.

PROPERTIES

NAME/TYPE	LOCATION	SIZE	OCCUPANCY
Washington Technical Business Center - Phase I	Renton, WA	50,973 sf	94%/96%
Certified Distribution Center	Salt Lake City, UT	312,260 sf	100%/100%
Ladera Shopping Center-Phase I	Albuquerque, NM	89,742 sf	89%/95%
The Cornerstone Retail Center	Tempe, AZ	114,900 sf	56%/70%
Terracentre Office Building	Denver, CO	95,797 sf	78%/68%
Oakpointe Office Building	Arlington Heights, IL	96,213 sf	100%/76%
Arlington Executive Plaza Office Complex	Arlington Heights, IL	72,997 sf	SLD-'96

> Note: Property occupancy information is as of December 31, 1996 and December 31, 1995.

OPERATING DATA (through 12/31/96)
    (Dollars in 000's Except Per Unit Amounts)

	1996	1995	1994	1993	1992
PROPERTIES AT COST(1).......	$ 34,582	$ 88,455	$ 87,267	$ 86,557	$ 85,868
CAPITAL EXPENDITURES.........	$ 2,287	$ 1,188	$ 710	$ 689	$ 1,021
EQUITY IN NOTES RECEIVABLE..	----	----	----	----	----
PERCENTAGE LEVERAGE.........	8%	4%	4%	4%	5%
GROSS REVENUES..............	$ 6,185	$ 5,973	$ 6,307	$ 6,525	$ 7,403
NET INCOME (LOSS):					
Regular Operations.....	$ 236	$(4,972)	$(5,591)	$(195)	$(13,792)
With Extraord. Items...	$ 400	$(4,972)	$(5,591)	$(195)	$(13,792)
OPERATING SURPLUS (DEFICIT).	$ 2,225	$ 1,671	$ 1,845	$ 1,892	$ 3,405
CASH FLOW PER $1,000 UNIT:					
Before Capital Exp.....	$ 24.54	$ 18.74	$ 20.37	$ 19.88	$ 34.68
After Capital Exp......	-@-	$ 4.47	$ 11.19	$ 11.08	$ 22.26
DISTRIBUTION SOURCES:					
Operations............	0.5%	0.8%	1.5%	1.9%	1.2%
Prior Earnings........	----	----	----	----	----
Refinancing Proceeds...	----	----	----	----	----
Sale Proceeds.........	1.5%	----	----	----	----
Reserves..............	----	----	----	----	----
TOTAL DISTRIBUTIONS	2.1%	0.8%	1.5%	1.9%	1.2%

	1996	1995	1994	1993	1992
CUMULATIVE LP DISTRIBUTIONS:					
All Sources............	32.4%	30.3%	29.5%	28.0%	26.1%
Sales/Refinancings.....	1.5%	0%	0%	0%	0%
CASH AND EQUIVALENTS........	$ 711	$ 301	$ 648	$ 1,068	$ 2,415
WORKING CAPITAL.............	$(348)	$(994)	$(481)	$ 75	$ 1,587
ADVANCES BY AFFILIATES......	----	----	----	----	----
BOOK VALUE PER $1,000 UNIT:					
Properties At Cost.....	$ 336	$ 352	$ 666	$ 717	$ 716
Carrying Value/GAAP....	$ 336	$ 352	$ 411	$ 484	$ 505

Note: (1) Beginning with 1996, Properties At Cost information represents the net carrying value of the Partnership's properties for financial reporting purposes.

PROPERTY DISPOSITIONS

1996: On November 21, 1996, the Partnership sold Arlington Executive Plaza, an office complex composed of seven identical 10,428 square foot buildings located on 7.2 acres of land in Arlington Heights, Illinois to an unaffiliated third party. The gross sales price was $3,050,000 ($2,929,000 net of commissions and escrow fees) and the net proceeds of the sale, after all prorations and credits to the buyer, amounted to approximately $2,699,000. The General Partner was not paid a commission or disposition fee as part of this transaction.

SUPPLEMENTARY INFORMATION

1996: The increase in rental income for the year ended December 31, 1996, when compared to 1995, was primarily attributable to an increase in rental income at Oakpointe. A new lease was signed in February 1996 with Symbol Technologies, Inc. encompassing 22,801 square feet bringing Oakpointe to 100% leased.

The increase in interest and other income for the year ended December 31, 1996, as compared to 1995 was attributable to an increase in The Cornerstone's other miscellaneous income. This increase was partially offset by a decrease in interest income due to a decrease in the average level of working capital available for investment in 1996. Capital reserves were used to fund a portion of the renovation and tenant improvements at The Cornerstone and tenant improvements at Oakpointe.

On November 21, 1996, the Partnership sold Arlington Executive Plaza, an office complex composed of seven identical 10,428 square foot buildings located on 7.2 acres of land in Arlington Heights, Illinois to an unaffiliated third party. The sales price was $3,050,000 ($2,929,000 net of commissions and escrow fees) and the net proceeds of the sale amounted to approximately $2,699,000 after factoring in all prorations and credits to the buyer. In December 1995, the General Partner had adjusted the carrying value of the property in accordance with the guidelines of FAS 121, which resulted in a write-down of $1,250,000 and an adjusted carrying value of $2,740,000. The resulting gain on sale, after taking into consideration all costs of disposition, amounted to $164,000 as reflected in the Statement of Operations. The General Partner was not paid a commission or disposition fee as part of this transaction.

The decrease in operating expenses for the year ended December 31, 1996, as compared to 1995 was primarily attributable to the sale of Arlington Executive Plaza in November 1996 and reduced legal and professional fees at The Cornerstone and Terracentre.

Since the completion of its acquisition program in September 1985, the Partnership has been primarily engaged in the operation of its properties. The Partnership's original objective had been to hold its properties as long-term investments. However, an Information Statement, dated May 5, 1993, mandated that the General Partner seek a vote of the Limited Partners no later than December 31, 1996, regarding prompt liquidation of the Partnership in the event that properties with appraised values as of January 1993 which constituted at least one half of the aggregate appraised values of all Partnership properties as of that date are not sold or under contract for sale by the end of 1996. Given the mandate of the May 5, 1993 Information Statement, as of December 31, 1995, the General Partner decided to account for the Partnership's properties as assets held for sale, instead of for investment. In a Consent Solicitation dated February 18, 1997, the Partnership solicited and recieved the consent of the Limited Partners to dissolve the Partnership and sell and liquidate all of its remaining properties as soon as practicable, consistent with selling the Partnership's properties to the best advantage under the circumstances. The Partnership's properties were held for sale throughout 1996 and continue to be held for sale.

Regular distributions for the year ended December 31, 1996, represent net cash flow generated from operations of the Partnership's properties and interest earned on the temporary investment of working capital, net of capital reserve requirements. In December 1996, the Partnership made a special distribution of $1,500,000 representing a portion of net proceeds from the sale of Arlington Executive Plaza. Future cash distributions will be made to the extent available from net cash flow generated from operations and sales of the Partnership's properties and interest earned on the investment of capital reserves, after providing for capital reserves and payment for capital improvements and repairs to the Partnership's properties. The Partnership believes that the cash generated from its operations will provide the Partnership the funds necessary to meet all of its ordinary obligations.

The Partnership began renovation of The Cornerstone, located in Tempe, Arizona in August 1995 and those renovations were completed during third quarter of 1996. The cost of these capital improvements, which included the exterior facade modifications, hardscape and softscape changes and signage upgrades, was approximately $1,527,000. To pay for a portion of these improvements, the Partnership suspended distributions to its limited partners for the fourth quarter of 1995 and the first two quarters of 1996. Regular distributions resumed in the third quarter of 1996.

In September 1987, the Partnership borrowed $4,000,000 pursuant to a loan agreement secured by a First Deed of Trust on the Certified Distribution Center in Salt Lake City, Utah. The net proceeds were used primarily for capital improvements and leasing commissions on certain of the Partnership's properties, the Partnership's working capital reserves and certain general and administrative expenses. That loan matured on December 1, 1990, however, the General Partner obtained a loan extension that was to mature December 1, 1993. On July 20, 1993, the Partnership obtained a new loan secured by a First Deed of Trust on the Certified Distribution Center in Salt Lake City, Utah. The new loan, in the amount of $3,500,000, carries a fixed interest rate of 9% per annum over a 13-year fully amortizing term. The Partnership's first payment of $38,000 was paid on September 1, 1993, with monthly installments due thereafter.

In March 1996, the Partnership entered into a loan agreement pursuant to which it could borrow up to $1,500,000, evidenced by a note secured by a first deed of trust and financing statement on the Ladera I Shopping Center in Albuquerque, New Mexico. Pursuant to the note and loan agreement, the Partnership borrowed $700,000 in March 1996. The Partnership made interest only payments at the rate of 1% over prime (the

17

Executive Plaza. The net proceeds of the foregoing loan were used to fund a portion of the renovation and tenant improvements at The Cornerstone and tenant improvements at Oakpointe.

In accordance with the terms of the Partnership Agreement, each year the Partnership secures an independent appraisal of each of the Partnership's properties as of January 1. Prior to the January 1, 1995 appraisals, the independent appraiser had estimated each property's "Investment Value," utilizing a seven to ten-year cash flow model to estimate value based upon an income approach.

The amendment to the Partnership Agreement consented to by the Limited Partners in June 1993 mandates, among other things, that the General Partner seek a vote of (and provide an analysis and recommendation to) the Limited Partners no later than December 31, 1996 regarding the prompt liquidation of the Partnership in the event that properties with (then) current appraised values (constituting at least one-half of the total (then) current appraised values) of all of the Partnership's properties are not sold or under contract for sale by the end of 1996.

Given this mandate, the General Partner requested that the appraiser provide an assessment of value that reflects a shorter investment holding term. Although the General Partner does not know how long it will take to sell the Partnership's remaining properties, it requested that the appraiser assume that the entire portfolio would be sold over four years, in connection with the January 1995 appraisals, over three years in connection with the January 1996 appraisals and over approximately two years in connection with the January 1997 appraisals.

Using the shorter-term investment methodology that is consistent with the mandate of the 1993 amendment to the Partnership agreement, the appraiser estimated the value of the Partnership's remaining properties at January 1, 1997 to be $37,680,000.

The foregoing appraised value of the Partnership's remaining properties indicates an estimated net asset value of the Partnership of $35,711,000 or $3,674 per $10,000 of original investor subscription. (Net asset value represents the appraised value of the Partnership's properties, cash and all other assets less secured loans payable and all other liabilities.)

18

```
PROGRAM:    First Capital Growth Fund Series XIV
SPONSOR:    First Capital Financial Corporation
OFFERING COMMENCED:    December 1988
OFFERING CLOSED:    September 1990
OFFERING PROCEEDS:    $14,518,200
90% INVESTED: 1991
UNIT SIZE:   $100
ADJUSTED UNIT SIZE:  $100
VALUE PER UNIT: $51 (AS OF 12/31/96-Independent)
UNITS OUTSTANDING:   145,182
FYE:    December 31
DISTRIBUTION RATE:   3.2% (AS OF 06/15/97)
DISTRIBUTION FREQUENCY:   Quarterly
SPONSOR PHONE:   (800) 447-7364/(312) 207-0020
```

°PARTNERSHIP PROFILES

PPI RATINGS: (1=HIGHEST.5=LOWEST)
FINANCIAL CONDITION.......1
CASH DISTRIBUTION.........4

DISTRIBUTION HISTORY (Per $100 Unit)

	1997-1Q	1996	1995	1994	1993	1992
Regular	$ 0.80	$ 3.20	$ 3.00	$ 2.08	$ 0	$ 1.45
Special	0	0	0	0	0	0
TOTAL	$ 0.80	$ 3.20	$ 3.00	$ 2.08	$ 0	$ 1.45

Cumulative: $26.80

Note: Distribution information reflects the calendar quarter or year for which distributions were declared by the Partnership. The Partnership actually pays distributions to investors approximately 60 days after the end of the quarter for which the distributions have been declared. For instance, the Partnership pays its distribution for the first quarter on or about May 30. Actual distributions may vary between investors in the Partnership based upon their actual date of admittance to the Partnership. Certain amounts may have been rounded. Distribution amounts have not been reduced to reflect any taxes withheld.

PROPERTIES

NAME/TYPE	CONSTRUCTED	LOCATION	SIZE	OCCUPANCY
1800 Sherman Office Bldg. (50% Interest)	1986	Evanston, IL	134,541 sf	95%/97%
One Charles Center Office Bldg. (25% Interest)	----	Baltimore, MD	319,074 sf	F/C-'93

Note: Property occupancy information represents average occupancy levels during 1996 and 1995.

OPERATING DATA (through 12/31/96)
(Dollars In 000's Except Per Unit Amounts)

	1996	1995	1994	1993	1992
PROPERTIES AT COST..........	$ 8,361	$ 8,326	$ 8,153	$ 7,962	$ 16,803
CAPITAL EXPENDITURES........	$ 35	$ 174	$ 191	$ 764	$ 212
EQUITY IN NOTES RECEIVABLE..	----	----	----	----	----
PERCENTAGE LEVERAGE.........	0%	0%	0%	0%	37%
GROSS REVENUES..............	$ 1,654	$ 1,663	$ 1,598	$ 2,244	$ 3,133
NET INCOME (LOSS):					
Regular Operations.....	$ 429	$(857)	$ 410	$ 261	$(1,642)
With Extraord. Items...	$ 429	$(857)	$ 410	$(1,613)	$(1,642)
OPERATING SURPLUS (DEFICIT).	$ 679	$ 600	$ 646	$ 537	$ 708
CASH FLOW PER UNIT:					
Before Capital Exp.....	$ 4.21	$ 3.72	$ 4.00	$ 3.44	$ 4.62
After Capital Exp......	$ 4.00	$ 2.65	$ 2.82	-d-	$ 3.31
DISTRIBUTION SOURCES:(1)					
Operations.............	3.2%	3.0%	2.1%	----	1.4%
Prior Earnings.........	----	----	----	----	----
Refinancing Proceeds...	----	----	----	----	----
Sale Proceeds..........	----	----	----	----	----
Reserves..............	----	----	----	----	----
TOTAL DISTRIBUTIONS.	3.2%	3.0%	2.1%	0%	1.4%
CUMULATIVE LP DISTRIBUTIONS:					
All Sources............	26.0%	22.8%	19.8%	17.7%	17.7%
Sales/Refinancings.....	0%	0%	0%	0%	0%
CASH AND EQUIVALENTS........	$ 2,483	$ 2,365	$ 2,302	$ 2,270	$ 2,062
WORKING CAPITAL.............	$ 1,678	$ 1,566	$ 1,623	$ 1,444	$ 1,437
ADVANCES BY AFFILIATES......	----	----	----	----	----
BOOK VALUE PER UNIT:					
Properties At Cost.....	$ 61	$ 60	$ 67	$ 65	$ 80
Carrying Value/GAAP....	$ 52	$ 53	$ 62	$ 62	$ 73

Note: (1) Cash distribution information includes distributions accrued and payable as of the end of the period. Distribution information reflects only distributions allocated to Limited Partners.

PROPERTY DISPOSITIONS

1993: In regards to the mortgage loan collateralized by the One Charles Center located in Baltimore, Maryland, in lieu of making the June 1, 1993 payment, the General Partner proposed a debt restructuring. This plan was rejected by the mortgage holder. As a result, on August 17, 1993, the Partnership conveyed title to the property to the mortgage holder, and the Partnership was relieved of its obligation under the mortgage loan. The General Partner deemed this course of action necessary because of 1) an unwillingness to have the Partnership fund any additional operating deficits incurred by the property; 2) the lack of leasing activity in this property's market; 3) the projected investment for capital and tenant improvements was greater than the Partnership could recover through appreciation in the property's value and 4) the inability to sell this property in today's market or in the foreseeable future for an amount greater than the outstanding loan balance.

SUPPLEMENTARY INFORMATION

1996: Net income improved by $1,285,700 for the year ended December 31, 1996 when compared to the year ended December 31, 1995. The difference is the result of the recognition of a provision for value impairment of $1,200,000 during 1995 on 1800 Sherman. Exclusive of the provision of value impairment, net income increased by $85,700 for the comparable periods. The increase in net income was primarily the result of a decrease in real estate taxes and general and administrative expenses.

The decrease in general and administrative expenses was the result of a reduction in the costs associated with printing and mailing. Partially offsetting the increase in net income for the years under comparison was an increase in repair and maintenance expenses and property operating expenses.

Rental revenues remained stable for the year ended December 31, 1996 when compared to the year ended December 31, 1995.

Real estate tax expense decreased by $89,600 for the years under comparison. This decrease was primarily due to the successful appeal for a reduction of the assessed value of 1800 Sherman for the 1995 tax year.

Property operating expenses increased by $12,600 for the year ended December 31, 1996 when compared to the year ended December 31, 1995. The increase was primarily the result of an increase in management fees due to the fact that leasing related costs paid in 1995, which are ordinarily paid to and provided by an Affiliate of the General Partner as part of its property management fee, were paid to outside brokers and the expenditures were capitalized as lease commissions and amortized over the respective lease terms of new tenants.

Repairs and maintenance expenses increased by $10,000 for the year ended December 31, 1996 when compared to the year ended December 31, 1995. The increase was primarily due to increased costs resulting from hiring a more thorough and dependable contractor for the cleaning of the building. In addition, snow fall in 1996 was significantly higher than in 1995 resulting in an increase in snow removal costs.

1800 Sherman Office Building's ("1800 Sherman") operations are expected to be adversely affected by a potential leveling or reduction in rental rates resulting from an increased supply of vacant office space in its local area. The General Partner has learned that a competitive office property will shortly be vacated by its sole tenant. This event may cause an imbalance in the supply of office space available versus the demand for such space.

The increase in Cash Flow (as defined in the Partnership Agreement) of $79,200 for the year ended December 31, 1996 when compared to the year ended December 31, 1995 was primarily due to the increase in net income, as previously discussed, exclusive of depreciation and amortization expense and provision for value impairment.

The decrease in the Partnership's cash position of $378,500 was primarily the result of investments in debt securities, distributions paid to Partners and expenditures for capital and tenant improvements exceeding net cash provided by operating activities.

The General Partner continues to take a conservative approach to projections of future rental income and to maintain higher levels of cash reserves. The General Partner believes that Cash Flow (as defined in the Partnership Agreement) is one of the best and least expensive sources of cash. As a result of this, cash continues to be retained to supplement working capital reserves. For the year ended December 31, 1996, Cash Flow (as defined in the Partnership Agreement) retained to supplement working capital reserves was $163,200.

Distributions to Limited Partners for the quarter ended December 31, 1996, were declared in the amount of $116,200 or $0.80 per Unit. Cash distributions are made 60 days after the last day of each fiscal quarter. The amount of future distributions to Partners will ultimately be dependent upon the performance of 1800 Sherman as well as the General Partner's determination of the amount of cash necessary to supplement working capital reserves to meet future liquidity requirements of the Partnership. Accordingly, there can be no assurance as to the amount of cash for distributions to Partners.

Based upon the current estimated value of its assets, net of its outstanding liabilities, together with its expected operating results and capital expenditure requirements, the General Partner believes that the Partnership's cumulative distributions to its Limited Partners from inception through the termination of the Partnership will be less than such Limited Partners' original Capital Contributions.

28

PROGRAM: High Equity Partners L.P.-Series 86
SPONSOR: Integrated Resources, Inc.
           (now managed by Presidio Capital Corp.)
OFFERING COMMENCED: April 1986
OFFERING CLOSED: October 1987
OFFERING PROCEEDS: $147,003,500
90% INVESTED: 1988
UNIT SIZE: $250
ADJUSTED UNIT SIZE: $245
VALUE PER UNIT: $98.87 (AS OF 12/31/96-GP)
UNITS OUTSTANDING: 588,010
FYE: December 31
DISTRIBUTION RATE: 1.2% (AS OF 06/15/97)
DISTRIBUTION FREQUENCY: Quarterly
SPONSOR PHONE: (800) 678-7899

◎PARTNERSHIP PROFILES

PPI RATINGS:(1=HIGHEST.5=LOWEST)
FINANCIAL CONDITION.......1
CASH DISTRIBUTION.........5

DISTRIBUTION HISTORY (Per $250 Unit)

	1997-1Q	1996	1995	1994	1993	1992
Regular	$ 0.77	$ 2.48	$ 2.48	$ 2.45	$ 2.96	$ 5.64
Special	0	0	0	0	0	0
TOTAL	$ 0.77	$ 2.48	$ 2.48	$ 2.45	$ 2.96	$ 5.64

Cumulative: $90

Note: Distribution information reflects the calendar quarter or year for which distributions were declared by the Partnership. The Partnership actually pays distributions to investors subsequent to the end of the quarter for which the distributions have been declared. Actual distributions may vary between investors in the Partnership based upon their actual date of admittance to the Partnership. Certain amounts may have been rounded. Distribution amounts have not been reduced to reflect any taxes withheld.

PROPERTIES

NAME/TYPE	CONSTRUCTED	LOCATION	SIZE	OCCUPANCY
230 East Ohio Street OB	----	Chicago, IL	83,333 sf	74%/75%
Commonwealth Ind. Park	1972/1986	Fullerton, CA	273,500 sf	87%/66%
Commerce Plaza I Office Building	----	Richmond, VA	85,000 sf	95%/92%
Century Park I Off. Cmplx. (50% Interest)	1986	Kearny Mesa, CA	203,188 sf	74%/74%
Broadway Office Building (38.9% Interest)	1898	New York, NY	315,000 sf	100%/95%
Seattle Tower Office Bldg. (50% Interest)	1928	Seattle, WA	141,000 sf	96%/92%
Matthews Township Festival Shopping Center	1987	Matthews, NC	126,926 sf	86%/89%
Melrose Crossing Shop. Ctr.	1987	Melrose Park, IL	138,400 sf	18%/50%
Sutton Square Shop. Ctr.	----	Raleigh, NC	102,000 sf	100%/100%
TMR Industrial/ Warehouse Facilities (21% Interest)	----	Columbus, OH	1,010,500 sf	100%/94%
Melrose Land Parcel	----	Melrose Park, IL	18,000 sf	N/A
Commerce Plaza II OB	----	Richmond, VA	90,000 sf	SLD-'90

Note: Property occupancy information is as of January 1, 1997 and January 1, 1996. Occupancy information for Matthews Township Festival Shopping Center reflects economic occupancy. The former anchor tenant of the shopping center vacated in 1990 but continues to pay rent on its space.

OPERATING DATA (through 12/31/96)
    (Dollars In 000's Except Per Unit Amounts)

	1996	1995	1994	1993	1992
PROPERTIES AT COST.........	$ 133,750	$ 133,062	$ 130,862	$ 129,662	$ 128,347
CAPITAL EXPENDITURES........	$ 687	$ 2,200	$ 1,201	$ 1,328	$ 1,687
EQUITY IN NOTES RECEIVABLE..	----	----	----	----	----
PERCENTAGE LEVERAGE.........	0%	0%	0%	0%	0%
GROSS REVENUES..............	$ 12,075	$ 10,814	$ 10,426	$ 11,626	$ 11,963
NET INCOME (LOSS):					
Regular Operations.....	$ 2,245	$(22,085)	$ 936	$(16,512)	$(19,060)
With Extraord. Items...	$ 2,245	$(22,085)	$ 936	$(16,512)	$(19,060)
OPERATING SURPLUS (DEFICIT).	$ 4,022	$ 3,167	$ 3,195	$ 3,416	$ 4,546
CASH FLOW PER UNIT:					
Before Capital Exp.....	$ 6.50	$ 5.12	$ 5.16	$ 5.52	$ 7.34
After Capital Exp......	$ 4.66	$ 0.64	$ 2.84	$ 2.94	$ 4.21

40

Operating Data cont'd

DISTRIBUTION SOURCES:(1)	1996	1995	1994	1993	1992
Operations.............	1.0%	1.0%	1.0%	1.2%	2.3%
Prior Earnings.........	----	----	----	----	----
Refinancing Proceeds...	----	----	----	----	----
Sale Proceeds..........	----	----	----	----	----
Reserves...............	----	----	----	----	----
TOTAL DISTRIBUTIONS	1.0%	1.0%	1.0%	1.2%	2.3%
CUMULATIVE LP DISTRIBUTIONS:					
All Sources............	35.5%	34.5%	33.5%	32.5%	31.3%
Sales/Refinancings.....	2.0%	2.0%	2.0%	2.0%	2.0%
CASH AND EQUIVALENTS........	$ 7,410	$ 4,752	$ 5,750	$ 5,579	$ 5,066
WORKING CAPITAL.............	$ 3,870	$ 2,513	$ 3,701	$ 3,417	$ 3,379
ADVANCES BY AFFILIATES......	----	----	----	----	----
BOOK VALUE PER UNIT:					
Properties At Cost.....	$ 120	$ 117	$ 154	$ 152	$ 179
Carrying Value/GAAP....	$ 94	$ 93	$ 131	$ 132	$ 161

Note: (1) Cash distribution information includes distributions accrued and payable as of the end of the period.

ROPERTY DISPOSITIONS

90: On November 14, 1990, the Partnership sold Commerce Plaza II and 0.56 acres of vacant land located on Commerce Plaza I to the .ristian Children's Fund for $7,025,000. The Christian Children's Fund plans to occupy substantially all the space in Commerce Plaza II. From : proceeds of the sale, $3,094,790 was distributed to Unit holders as of date of record of October 1, 1990 as a return of capital, $1,791,025 of :viously deferred fees was paid to the Administrative General Partner and an affiliate in accordance with the deferred fee agreement, $236,827 s paid in connection with the closing and the remainder of $1,902,358 was set aside as a working capital reserve for future tenant improvement d leasing costs at Commerce Plaza I. The loss for financial statement purposes as a result of the Commerce Plaza II sale amounted to ,446,509. The Partnership's cost basis in the property sold was approximately $9,005,000.

IPPLEMENTARY INFORMATION

96: The Partnership experienced net income for the year ended December 31, 1996 compared to a net loss for the prior year due primarily the significant write-downs for impairment recorded during 1995 as previously discussed.

ntal revenue increased during the year ended December 31, 1996 as compared to 1995. The most significant increases in revenues occurred 568 Broadway, Century Park, Seattle Tower, Sutton Square and Commonwealth due to higher occupancy rates during 1996 as compared to : prior year. These increases, however, were partially offset by decreases in revenues during 1996 at Melrose Crossing and Matthews as certain ants vacated and/or filed for bankruptcy. Revenues at the other properties generally remained consistent in 1996 as compared to 1995.

sts and expenses decreased during the year ended December 31, 1996 as compared to 1995 due primarily to the significant write-downs for pairment recorded in 1995. Operating expenses decreased during 1996 due to decreases in real estate taxes at certain properties partially offset increases in repairs and maintenance and utility costs. Real estate taxes decreased significantly at 568 Broadway due to the receipt of refunds ated to the 1992-1995 tax years of which the Partnership's share was $353,500. Real estate taxes also decreased at Melrose I as the result of luction of the assessed value pursuant to on-going tax appeals. Repair and maintenance expenses increased at Century Park and Sutton Square e to the higher occupancy in 1996 compared to 1995. The cost of utilities increased at 568 Broadway due to increased occupancy in 1996 as mpared to the prior year. Depreciation expense for 1996 increased due to the significant capitalized improvements and tenant procurement costs urred and capitalized during the year ended December 31, 1995. The partnership asset management fee remained constant in 1996 as compared 1995. Administrative expenses increased due to the Partnership's reimbursement of the General Partners' litigation and settlement costs as :viously discussed and the property management fee increase was the direct result of higher revenues at the aforementioned properties.

r the year ended December 31, 1996, all capital expenditures and distributions were funded from cash flows. As of December 31, 1996, total naining working capital reserves amounted to approximately $5,763,000. The Partnership intends to distribute less than all of its future cash w from operations to maintain adequate reserves for capital improvements and capitalized lease procurement costs. In March 1997, the lministrative General Partner notified the limited partners of its intention to increase the annual distribution from $2.48 to $3.06 per it as a result of improved operating results. If the real estate market conditions deteriorate in any of the areas where the Partnership's properties : located, there is substantial risk that this would have an adverse effect on cash flow distributions. Working capital reserves are temporarily rested in short-term money market instruments and are expected, together with cash flow from operations, to be sufficient to fund future capital provements to the Partnership's properties.

iring the year ended December 31, 1996, cash and cash equivalents increased $2,657,554 as a result of cash provided by operations in excess capital expenditures and distributions to partners. The Partnership's primary source of funds is cash flow from the operations of its properties, ncipally rents received from tenants, which amounted to $4,879,769 for the year ended December 31, 1996. The Partnership used $687,199 : capital expenditures related to capital and tenant improvements to the properties and $1,535,016 for distributions to partners during 1996.

ie Partnership has budgeted approximately $3 million in expenditures for capital improvements and capitalized tenant procurement costs in 1997 iich is expected to be funded from cash flow from operations. However, such expenditures will depend upon the level of leasing activity and ier factors which cannot be predicted with certainty.

2GAL PROCEEDING

a or about May 11, 1993, the Partnership was advised of the existence of an action (the "B&S Litigation") in which a complaint (the "HEP mplaint") was filed in the Superior Court for the State of California for the County of Los Angeles (the "Court") on behalf of a purported class nsisting of all of the purchasers of limited partnership interests in the Partnership. On April 7, 1994 the plaintiffs were granted leave to file an iended complaint (the "Amended Complaint").

41

On November 30, 1995, after the Court preliminarily approved a settlement of the B&S Litigation but ultimately declined to grant final approval and after the Court granted motions to intervene by the original plaintiffs, the original and intervening plaintiffs filed a Consolidated Class and Derivative Action Complaint (the "Consolidated Complaint") against the Administrative and Investment General Partners, the managing general partner of HEP-85, the managing general partner of HEP-88 and the indirect corporate parent of the General Partners. The Consolidated Complaint alleges various state law class and derivative claims, including claims for breach of fiduciary duties; breach of contract; unfair and fraudulent business practices under California Bus. & Prof. Code Sec. 17200; negligence; dissolution, accounting and receivership; fraud; and negligent misrepresentation. The Consolidated Complaint alleges, among other things, that the general partners caused a waste of HEP Partnership assets by collecting management fees in lieu of pursuing a strategy to maximize the value of the investments owned by the limited partners; that the general partners breached their duty of loyalty and due care to the limited partners by expropriating management fees from the partnerships without trying to run the HEP Partnerships for the purposes for which they are intended; that the general partners are acting improperly to enrich themselves in their position of control over the HEP Partnerships and that their actions prevent non-affiliated entities from making and completing tender offers to purchase HEP Partnership Units; that by refusing to seek the sale of the HEP Partnerships' properties, the general partners have diminished the value of the limited partners' equity in the HEP Partnerships; that the general partners have taken a heavily overvalued partnership asset management fee; and that limited partnership units were sold and marketed through the use of false and misleading statements.

In January, 1996, the parties to the B&S Litigation agreed upon a revised settlement (the "Revised Settlement"). The core feature of the Revised Settlement was the surrender by the general partners of certain fees that they are entitled to receive, the reorganization of the Partnership, HEP-85 and HEP-88 (collectively, the "HEP Partnerships") into a publicly traded real estate investment trust ("REIT"), and the issuance of stock in the REIT to the limited partners (in exchange for their limited partnership interests) and General Partners (in exchange for their existing interest in the HEP Partnerships and the fees being given up). The General Partners believe that the principal benefits of the Revised Settlement were (1) substantially increased distributions to limited partners, (2) market liquidity through a NASDAQ listed security, and (3) the opportunity for growth and diversification that was not permitted under the Partnership structure. There were also believed to be other significant tax benefits, corporate governance advantages and other benefits of the Revised Settlement.

On July 18, 1996, the Court preliminarily approved the Revised Settlement and made a preliminary finding that the Revised Settlement was fair, adequate and reasonable to the class. In August 1996, the Court approved the form and method of notice regarding the Revised Settlement which was sent to limited partners.

Only approximately 2.5% of the limited partners of the HEP Partnerships elected to "opt out" of the Revised Settlement. Despite this, following the submission of additional materials, the Court entered an order on January 14, 1997 rejecting the Revised Settlement and concluding that there had not been an adequate showing that the settlement was fair and reasonable. Thereafter, the plaintiffs filed a motion seeking to have the Court reconsider its order. Subsequently, the defendants withdrew the revised settlement and at a hearing on February 24, 1997, the Court denied the plaintiffs' motion. Also at the February 24, 1997 hearing, the Court recused itself from considering a motion to intervene and to file a new complaint in intervention by one of the objectors to the Revised Settlement, granted the request of one plaintiffs' law firm to withdraw as class counsel and scheduled future hearings on various matters.

The Limited Partnership Agreement provides for indemnification of the General Partners and their affiliates in certain circumstances. The Partnership has agreed to reimburse the General Partners for their actual costs incurred in defending this litigation and the costs of preparing settlement materials. Through December 31, 1996, the General Partners had billed the Partnership a total of $824,511 for these costs which was paid in February 1997.

The Partnerships and the General Partners believe that each of the claims asserted in the Consolidated Complaint are meritless and intend to continue to vigorously defend the B&S Litigation. It is impossible at this time to predict what the defense of the B&S Litigation will cost, the Partnership's financial exposure as a result of the indemnification agreement discussed above, and whether the costs of defending could adversely affect the Managing General Partner's ability to perform its obligations to the Partnership.

```
PROGRAM:      Net 2 L.P.
SPONSOR:      Lepercq Capital Partners/The LCP Group
OFFERING COMMENCED:   January 1989
OFFERING CLOSED:   July 1990
OFFERING PROCEEDS:   $47,716,700
90% INVESTED: 1990
UNIT SIZE: $100
ADJUSTED UNIT SIZE: $100
VALUE PER UNIT: $78.09 (AS OF 12/31/96 - Independent)
UNITS OUTSTANDING:   477,167
FYE: December 31
DISTRIBUTION RATE:   5.00%   (AS OF 06/15/97)
DISTRIBUTION FREQUENCY:   Quarterly
SPONSOR PHONE: (800) 525-8904/(212) 692-7203
```

© **PARTNERSHIP PROFILES**

PPI RATINGS:(1=HIGHEST,5=LOWEST)
FINANCIAL CONDITION.......1
CASH DISTRIBUTION.........3

DISTRIBUTION HISTORY (Per $100 Unit)

	1997-2Q	1997-1Q	1996	1995	1994	1993
Regular	$ 1.25	$ 1.25	$ 5.00	$ 5.00	$ 5.00	$ 5.30
Special	0	0	0	0	0	0
TOTAL	$ 1.25	$ 1.25	$ 5.00	$ 5.00	$ 5.00	$ 5.30

Cumulative: $42

> Note: Distribution information reflects the fiscal period during which distributions were actually paid to investors. Actual distributions may vary between investors in the Partnership based upon their actual date of admittance to the Partnership. Certain amounts may have been rounded. Distribution amounts have not been reduced to reflect any taxes withheld.

PROPERTIES

NAME/TYPE(A)	CONSTRUCTED	LOCATION	SIZE	OCCUPANCY
Duracraft Corp. Office/ R&D Facility	1984	Southborough, MA	----	100%
Kohl's Department Stores Retail Facility	1994	Eau Claire, WI	----	100%
Transonic Office/Warehouse Facilities	1968/ 1981	Highland Heights, OH; Tempe, AZ	----	100%
Total Petroleum Stores(13)	----	Michigan	----	100%
Everest & Jennings Inc. Warehouse/ Manuf. Facility	1985	Earth City, MO	----	100%
Art Institute of Seattle Office/School Facility	1985	Seattle, WA	----	100%
National Convenience Stores Convenience-Type Grocery Stores (14)	----	San Antonio; El Paso, and Irving, TX	----	100%
Ameritech Services Industrial Facility	1989	Columbus, OH	----	100%
RCS (Intermedia) Office Facility	1988	Tucson, AZ	----	100%
A-Copy, Inc. Office/ Distribution Facility	1994	Milford, CT	----	100%
Frito-Lay Industrial Warehouse/Office/ Processing Facility	----	Beaverton, OR	----	SLD-'94

> Note: Unless otherwise noted, all of the Partnership's properties are leased under triple-net leases generally requiring the lessees to pay all taxes, insurance, maintenance and all other similar charges and expenses relating to the properties and their use and occupancy. The Partnership has classified all of the leases as operating leases.

OPERATING DATA (through 12/31/96)
(Dollars In 000's Except Per Unit Amounts)

	1996	1995	1994	1993	1992
PROPERTIES AT COST..........	$ 53,250	$ 53,533	$ 49,499	$ 46,703	$ 46,603
CAPITAL EXPENDITURES........	----	----	----	$ 100	$ 183
EQUITY IN NOTES RECEIVABLE..	----	----	----	----	----
PERCENTAGE LEVERAGE.........	32%	28%	30%	23%	23%
GROSS REVENUES..............	$ 5,913	$ 5,630	$ 4,614	$ 4,398	$ 4,233
NET INCOME (LOSS):					
Regular Operations.....	$ 2,308	$ 2,265	$ 1,352	$ 619	$ 1,293
With Extraord. Items...	$ 2,308	$ 2,277	$ 3,809	$ 619	$ 1,293
OPERATING SURPLUS (DEFICIT).	$ 2,824	$ 2,751	$ 2,226	$ 1,782	$ 3,001

247

Operating Data cont'd

	1996	1995	1994	1993	1992
CASH FLOW PER UNIT:					
Before Capital Exp.....	$ 6.50	$ 6.21	$ 4.83	$ 3.66	$ 4.15
After Capital Exp......	$ 6.50	$ 6.21	$ 4.83	$ 3.45	$ 3.49
DISTRIBUTION SOURCES:					
Operations.............	5.0%	5.0%	4.6%	3.7%	5.4%
Prior Earnings.........	----	----	0.4%	1.6%	----
Refinancing Proceeds...	----	----	----	----	----
Sale Proceeds..........	----	----	----	----	----
Reserves...............	----	----	----	----	----
TOTAL DISTRIBUTIONS.	5.0%	5.0%	5.0%	5.3%	5.4%
CUMULATIVE LP DISTRIBUTIONS:					
All Sources............	39.5%	34.5%	29.5%	24.5%	19.2%
Sales/Refinancings.....	0%	0%	0%	0%	0%
CASH AND EQUIVALENTS........	$ 4,125	$ 733	$ 1,704	$ 1,960	$ 3,050
WORKING CAPITAL..............	$ 3,423	$ 440	$ 1,265	$ 1,711	$ 2,909
ADVANCES BY AFFILIATES......	----	----	----	----	----
BOOK VALUE PER UNIT:					
Properties At Cost.....	$ 79.25	$ 77.88	$ 75.78	$ 72.41	$ 74.26
Carrying Value/GAAP....	$ 67.47	$ 67.73	$ 68.05	$ 65.20	$ 69.27

PROPERTY DISPOSITIONS

1994: On April 11, 1994, the Partnership sold one of the two vacant NCS stores. The Partnership realized a loss of $15,881 on the sale of the property.

On July 27, 1994, the Partnership sold the Beaverton, Oregon property to Frito Lay for $4,190,000. The Partnership realized net proceeds of approximately $4,190,000 from the sale of the property.
1995: On April 16, 1995, the Partnership sold the remaining vacant NCS store. The Partnership received net cash proceeds of $144,984 and realized a gain of $12,869 from the sale. This property was one of the two NCS stores which had been vacated by the tenant. The other vacated store was sold in April 1994.

SUPPLEMENTARY INFORMATION

1996: The results of operations for the years ended December 31, 1996, 1995 and 1994 are primarily attributable to the acquisition and operations of the real property investments.

Revenues for the year ended December 31, 1996 did not materially change from 1995. Revenues for the year ended December 31, 1995 increased $1,016,255 from 1994, due to the increase in rental revenue from leases on property acquisitions that occurred during 1994 and 1995.

Total expenses for the years 1995 and 1994 did not materially change. Interest expense for the year ended December 31, 1996 did not materially change from 1995. Interest expense for the year ended December 31, 1995 increased $336,464 from 1994, due to financing secured by a $12 million mortgage note. General and administrative expenses for the year ended December 31, 1996 increased $199,590 from 1995, due to increases in property operating expenses, including appraisals. General and administrative expenses for the year ended December 31, 1995 decreased $234,538 from 1994 due to non-recurring fees incurred in 1994 in connection with the refinancing of the closing loan.

Net income for the year ended December 31, 1996, did not materially change from 1995. Net income for the year ended December 31, 1995 decreased $1,531,129 from 1994. The decrease was primarily due to the settlement of the closing loan at a discount and the gain from the sale of the Oregon Property that occurred in 1994.

On April 2, 1996, the Partnership received financing secured by a $2.8 million mortgage note on the Massachusetts Property. The note has a 232-month term with an interest rate of 7.5 % per annum. Monthly payments of principal and interest in the amount of $22,895 are due on the first day of each month commencing on June 1, 1996.

As of December 31, 1996, the Partnership has made cumulative cash distributions to the Limited Partners totaling $18,850,004. The unpaid cumulative preferred return at December 31, 1996 totaled $18,468,053.

LONG TERM DEBT MATURITIES:

1997: $398,211
1998: $435,258
1999: $11,137,232
2000: $190,395
2001: $205,724

PROGRAM: PaineWebber Growth Properties Two L.P.
SPONSOR: PaineWebber Properties
OFFERING COMMENCED: October 1983
OFFERING CLOSED: October 1984
OFFERING PROCEEDS: $33,410,000
90% INVESTED: 1984
UNIT SIZE: $1,000
ADJUSTED UNIT SIZE: $363
VALUE PER UNIT: $720 (AS OF 12/31/96-Independent)
UNITS OUTSTANDING: 33,410
FYE: March 31
DISTRIBUTION RATE: 1.5% (AS OF 06/15/97)
DISTRIBUTION FREQUENCY: Quarterly
SPONSOR PHONE: 800-225-1174

PARTNERSHIP PROFILES

PPI RATINGS:(1=HIGHEST.5=LOWEST)
FINANCIAL CONDITION.......2
CASH DISTRIBUTION........4

DISTRIBUTION HISTORY (Per $1,000 Unit)

	1998-1Q	1997	1996	1995	1994	1993
Regular	$ 3.85	$ 17.53	$ 21.26	$ 8.68	$ 0	$ 0
Special	0	169.48	23.00	0	0	0
TOTAL	$ 3.85	$187.01	$ 44.26	$ 8.68	$ 0	$ 0

Cumulative: $689

Note: Distribution information reflects the fiscal period during which distributions were actually paid to
investors. Actual distributions may vary between investors in the Partnership based upon their actual
date of admittance to the Partnership. Certain amounts may have been rounded. Distribution amounts
have not been reduced to reflect any taxes withheld.

PROPERTIES

NAME/TYPE	CONSTRUCTED	LOCATION	SIZE	OCCUPANCY(1)
Portland Center Apts./ Office Complex (Majority Preferred Interest)(2)	1984	Portland, OR	525 units/ 28,328 sf	94%
The Hamlet Apts.	----	Montgomery Village, MD	864 units	SLD-'86
Hudson Apts. (Joint Venture Interest)(3)	1984	Tyler, TX	144 units	SLD-'95
Walker House Apts. (Majority Preferred Interest)(2)	1984	Montgomery Village, MD	196 units	SLD-'96

Note: (1) Property occupancy information represents occupancy levels at March 31, 1996.

(2) The Partnership has acquired its interests in the Maryland and Oregon properties through joint
venture arrangements. The Partnership generally has a preferred interest in the joint ventures with
respect to cash distributions from operations and sale or refinancing proceeds. Upon property sales,
the Partnership is generally entitled to all of the net proceeds (after repayment of debt and certain
venture partner loans, if any) until the Partnership has recouped its investment in the joint venture,
plus a cumulative annual preferred return. The Partnership does not have 100% control over the affairs
of the joint ventures; therefore, the Partnership accounts for its ownership interests in the joint
ventures based upon the equity method for financial reporting purposes.

(2) The Partnership accounts for its ownership interest in the joint venture owning the Hudson
Apartments based upon the equity method for financial reporting purposes.

OPERATING DATA (through 03/31/96)
(Dollars In 000's Except Per Unit Amounts)

	1996	1995	1994	1993
PROPERTIES AT COST(1).......	$ 31,078	$ 46,819	$ 44,966	$ 44,170
CAPITAL EXPENDITURES(1).....	$ 809	$ 1,911	$ 814	$ 484
EQUITY IN NOTES RECEIVABLE..	----	----	----	----
PERCENTAGE LEVERAGE(1)......	73%	66%	68%	59%
GROSS REVENUES(1)...........	$ 5,749	$ 7,990	$ 7,535	$ 7,279
NET INCOME (LOSS):				
Regular Operations.....	$(185)	$(2,245)	$(324)	$(324)
With Extraord. Items...	$ 4,041	$(2,245)	$(324)	$(324)
OPERATING SURPLUS(DEFICIT)..	N/A	N/A	$ 146	$ 112
CASH FLOW PER UNIT:				
Before Capital Exp.....	N/A	N/A	$ 4.34	$ 3.30
After Capital Exp......	N/A	N/A	$ 0.87	-d-

<u>Operating Data cont'd</u>

	1996	1995	1994	1993
DISTRIBUTION SOURCES:				
Operations.............	2.1%	0.9%	----	----
Prior Earnings.........	----	----	----	----
Refinancing Proceeds...	----	----	----	----
Sale Proceeds..........	2.3%	----	----	----
Reserves...............	----	----	----	----
TOTAL DISTRIBUTIONS	4.4%	0.9%	0%	0%
CUMULATIVE LP DISTRIBUTIONS:				
All Sources............	49.8%	45.4%	44.5%	44.5%
Sales/Refinancings.....	46.8%	44.5%	44.5%	44.5%
CASH AND EQUIVALENTS........	$ 6,278	$ 1,053	$ 514	511
WORKING CAPITAL..............	$ 6,423	$ 998	$ 506	477
ADVANCES BY AFFILIATES......	----	----	----	----
BOOK VALUE PER UNIT:				
Properties At Cost....	$ 200	$ 123	$ 199	$ 209
Carrying Value/GAAP....	$ 200	$ 123	$ 199	$ 209

Notes: (1) Information provided is based upon the consolidated financial statements of the joint ventures in which the Partnership owns interests. As discussed above under "Properties", the Partnership accounts for its interests in the joint ventures based upon the equity method for financial reporting purposes. Beginning with fiscal 1996, information includes only the joint venture owning the Portland, OR property.

PROPERTY DISPOSITIONS

1986:   On September 30, 1986, The Hamlet Apartments was sold for $38,000,000, with $36,000,000 paid in cash and the remainder paid in the form of a second mortgage note of $2,000,000. For its interest in the joint venture owning this property the Partnership received a distribution of $12,973,283. The Partnership distributed $400 per $1,000 unit to Limited Partners. The Partnership distributed an additional $45 per $1,000 unit to Limited Partners in fiscal 1992 as a result of the pay-off in September 1991 of the note receivable taken back on the sale of The Hamlet.
1995:   On September 12, 1995, the Partnership sold its joint venture interest in the Hudson Apartments, located in Tyler, TX, for $350,000 to its co-venture partner. While such proceeds are substantially less than the amount of the Partnership's original investment of $2,600,000, management believes that the offer is reflective of the current fair market value of the Partnership's interest.
1996:   On March 13, 1996, the joint venture which owned the Walker House Apartments sold the operating investment property to an unrelated third party for $10,650,000. The Partnership received net proceeds of $5.3 million from the sale of the Walker House Apartments after deducting closing costs, the repayment of the outstanding first mortgage loan and the co-venture partner's share of the proceeds. Due to the Partnership's policy of accounting for significant lag-period transactions in the period in which they occur, the gain on this transaction was recognized in fiscal 1996. The Partnership's share of the net proceeds was distributed to the Limited Partners as a special distribution on the amount of approximately $5,312,000, or $159 per original $1,000 investment, paid concurrently with the regular quarterly distribution on May 15, 1996.

SUPPLEMENTARY INFORMATION

1997:   The sales of the Walker House Apartments and the Partnership's interest in the Hudson Apartments during fiscal 1996 leave the Partnership with one remaining real estate investment, a majority interest in the joint venture which owns the Portland Center Apartments. While management continues to be optimistic about the near-term prospects of Portland Center and the downtown Portland apartment market, management believes that it may be the appropriate time to sell the property. There appears to be growing interest from institutional and local buyers for well-located, quality apartment properties like Portland Center. As a result, management has decided to market the property for sale with formal marketing efforts expected to begin in the fourth quarter of fiscal 1997. While there are no assurances that a sale transaction will be completed, a successful sale of the property would be followed by a liquidation of the Partnership.

The investment in the Portland Center joint venture comprised 41% of the Partnership's original investment portfolio. Portland Center is a 525-unit high-rise apartment building located in Portland, Oregon, which also contains 28,000 square feet of leasable commercial space. Management continues to be in the process of using the excess cash reserves from the December 1993 Portland Center loan refinancing to complete a major renovation program at the property, which includes upgrades to the common areas and many individual units. The property's individual apartment units are being upgraded on a turnover basis. Upgrades to the apartment interiors have been accelerated in recent months and continue to produce rental rates that are generally 10% above the rents generated by these units prior to their renovation. The implementation of the planned capital improvements at Portland Center, which will continue throughout calendar 1997, is expected to support management's ability to increase rents and add value to the property.

The mortgage debt obtained by the Portland Center joint venture in December 1993 contained a five-year prohibition on prepayment. The loan becomes prepayable beginning in December 1998 with a prepayment penalty which begins at 5% of the outstanding principal balance and declines by 1% annually over the next five years. While the loan cannot be prepaid prior to December 1998, it could be assumed by a buyer of the property for a fee, subject to approval by the lender and the U.S. Department of Housing and Urban Development, which insured the mortgage loan. The requirement that a buyer would have to assume the outstanding mortgage obligation could limit management's ability to effectively market the property for sale prior to December 1998 because of the reserve and reporting requirements associated with a HUD loan. However, the loan does have a favorable interest rate of 7.125% per annum and does not mature until January 1, 2029. In addition, management's analysis of market conditions completed during the current quarter to assess whether it might be in the best interests of the Limited Partners to seek a sale of the Portland Center property in the near term revealed favorable results. Market conditions for residential apartment properties in the Pacific Northwest in general and in the downtown Portland market in particular are very strong at the present time as a result of, among other factors, healthy employment gains, local restrictions on new construction, a limited amount of buildable land sites and several projects that have converted rental units into condominiums. Such favorable conditions may result in the Partnership receiving a greater return on the current sale of this investment property even prior to the completion of the ongoing improvement program and prior to the expiration of the loan prepayment restrictions.

The sales of the Walker House Apartments and the Partnership's interest in the Hudson joint venture during fiscal 1996, together with the planned marketing efforts for the Portland Center property, have positioned the Partnership for a possible liquidation within the next 1 to 2 years. However, there are no assurances that the Partnership will be able to successfully sell its remaining investment under favorable conditions within this time frame. Management's hold versus sell decisions with respect to the investment in Portland Center will be based on an assessment of the impact on the overall returns to the Limited Partners.

Common Tenancy Case Study

Community Bank
Serving YOUR Community Since 1873

DATE: 02/07/1997

PAGE: 1
ACCOUNT 4416844

```
                 JOHN BUILDER
                 ED HELPER
                 C/O JB MANAGEMENT CO., INC.              28
                 4715 MAIN STREET                                0
                 ORANGE, CA 92668                                7
```

```
================================================================================
  ANAHEIM OFFICE                                 TELEPHONE: 714-555-1222
  4301 N STATE COLLEGE DR
  ANAHEIM CA 92805
================================================================================
                 FIRST INTEREST CHKNG ACCOUNT 4416844
================================================================================
  MINIMUM BALANCE          8,907.41   LAST STATEMENT               29,250.00
  AVG AVAILABLE BALANCE   25,179.03          2 CREDITS
  AVERAGE BALANCE         25,179.03         10 DEBITS
                                     THIS STATEMENT               36,663.41
```

```
        - - - - - - - - - - - OTHER CREDITS - - - - - - - - - - -
  DESCRIPTION                                      DATE      AMOUNT
  DEPOSIT                                          01/22   15,700.50
  DEPOSIT                                          01/22   18,316.38
  INTEREST                                         02/07        0.00
```

```
        - - - - - - - - - - -  CHECKS  - - - - - - - - - - -
  CHECK #  DATE......AMOUNT   CHECK #  DATE......AMOUNT   CHECK #  DATE......AMOUNT
     5067  01/14  18,417.59      5070  01/22   1,324.60      5073  01/22     985.26
     5068  01/15       0.00      5071  01/22     187.11      5074  01/28     772.10
     5069  01/20     600.40      5072  01/28   1,469.63
```

```
        - - - - - - - - - - -  BALANCE  - - - - - - - - - - -
      DATE.....BALANCE           DATE.....BALANCE           DATE.....BALANCE
      01/08  29,250.00           01/22  24,607.91           01/28  39,510.19
      01/14  10,832.41           01/22  24,420.80           02/03  37,074.41
      01/15  10,832.41           01/28  22,951.17           02/05  36,663.41
      01/20  10,232.01           01/22  21,965.91           02/07  36,663.41
      01/22   8,907.41           01/22  40,282.29
```

SCHEDULE E (Form 1040) Department of the Treasury Internal Revenue Service (99)	**Supplemental Income and Loss** (From rental real estate, royalties, partnerships, S corporations, estates, trusts, REMICs, etc.) ▶ Attach to Form 1040 or Form 1041. ▶ See Instructions for Schedule E (Form 1040).	OMB No. 1545-0074 **1996** Attachment Sequence No. **13**

Name(s) shown on return	Your social security number
JOHN BUILDER	123-45-6789

Part I   **Income or Loss From Rental Real Estate and Royalties**   Note: Report income and expenses from your business of renting personal property on **Schedule C** or **C–EZ** (see page E-1). Report farm rental income or loss from **Form 4835** on page 2, line 39.

1	Show the kind and location of each rental real estate property:	2	For each rental real estate property listed on line 1, did you or your family use it for personal purposes for more than the greater of 14 days or 10% of the total days rented at fair rental value during the tax year? (See page E-1.)	Yes	No
A	Commercial Building 200 S Main St., Tustin, CA.		A		X
B			B		
C			C		

Income:		Properties			Totals (Add columns A, B, & C.)	
		A	B	C		
3 Rents received	3	477,622			3	477,622
4 Royalties received	4				4	
Expenses:						
5 Advertising	5					
6 Auto and travel (see page E-2)	6					
7 Cleaning and maintenance	7					
8 Commissions	8					
9 Insurance	9	2,512				
10 Legal and other professional fees	10					
11 Management fees	11	33,413				
12 Mortgage interest paid to banks, etc. (see page E-2)	12	196,905			12	196,905
13 Other interest	13					
14 Repairs	14	18,480				
15 Supplies	15					
16 Taxes	16	18,420				
17 Utilities	17	26,311				
18 ▶ Building Services Administrative Office Expense	18	31,078 35,882 273				
19 Add lines 5 through 18	19	363,274			19	363,274
20 Depreciation expense or depletion (see page E-2)	20	55,016			20	55,016
21 Total expenses. Add lines 19 and 20	21	418,290				
22 Income/(loss) from rental real estate or royalty properties. Subtract line 21 from 3 (rents) or 4 (royalties). If result is (loss), see page E-2 to find out if you must file **Form 6198**	22	59,332 X 0.2000 11,866				
23 Deductible rental real estate loss. Caution: Your rental real estate loss on line 22 may be limited. See page E-3 to find out if you must file **Form 8582**. Real estate professionals must complete line 42 on page 2	23	(	)(	)(	)	
24 **Income.** Add positive amounts shown on line 22. Do not include any losses					24	11,866
25 **Losses.** Add royalty losses from line 22 and rental real estate losses from line 23. Enter the total losses here					25	( )
26 **Total rental real estate and royalty income or (loss).** Combine lines 24 and 25. Enter the result here. If Parts II, III, IV, and line 39 on page 2 do not apply to you, also enter this amount on Form 1040, line 17. Otherwise, include this amount in the total on line 40 on page 2					26	11,866

KFA   **For Paperwork Reduction Act Notice, see Form 1040 instructions.**   Schedule E (Form 1040) 1996

| 12/31/96 | 1996 Federal Depreciation Schedule | | | | | | | | | | | | | Page 1 |

| Client 96XXXX | | | | | JOHN BUILDER | | | | | | | | | 123–45–6789 |

Schedule E · Commercial Building

No.	Description	Date Acquired	Date Sold	Cost/ Basis	Bus. Pct.	Current 179/ Bonus	Prior 179/ Bonus	Prior Dec. Bal. Depr.	Basis Reductn	Salvage Value	Depr. Basis	Prior Depr.	Method	Life	Rate	Current Depr.
	Buildings															
1				1733000							1733000	136,730	S/L	MM 31.5	.03175	55,016
				1733000		0	0	0	0	0	1733000	136,730				55,016
	Land															
2				767,000							767,000					0
				767,000		0	0	0	0	0	767,000	0				0
	Total Depreciation			2500000		0	0	0	0	0	2500000	136,730				55,016

APPENDIX E

Extracting the Necessary Data from Financial Statements and Tax Forms

A real property appraisal is often requested when an entity requires a business valuation. The most common reasons for the valuation are estate tax planning, a transfer of wealth, gifting, and, to a lesser extent, ownership changes at the entity level. It is very important that all professionals involved in the valuation process understand their role and level of involvement in the process and the standard of value to be addressed.

Ideally, the real property appraiser and the business valuation analyst should communicate with each other before either begins work. The real property appraiser should clearly understand the purpose of the report and how the business valuation analyst intends to use it. Conversely, the business valuation analyst should understand how the real estate appraiser arrived at the stated opinion of value and should be aware of the limiting statements and assumptions contained in the real property appraisal report.

This appendix item is intended to help the real property appraiser extract the appropriate income and expense items from the business's financial documents such as tax returns or compiled, reviewed, or audited financial statements prepared by a CPA or other qualified professional hired by management. Data extraction is often necessary to develop discounted earnings or cash flows for the property and helps the analyst forecast property income and expenses or project future cost items based on historical patterns. The tips included in this appendix can be used in any real property appraisal assignment in which it is necessary to extract financial data from business statements to create property income statements.[1] However, the focus of this appendix item is income-producing properties owned by investment groups or holding companies.

About the Author

Lari B. Masten, MSA, CPA,* CVA, is the Director of Business Valuation and Litigation Support Group of Ian D. Gardenswartz & Associates, P.C., Denver, Colorado. She is responsible for the valuation and related consulting services of private businesses and closely held stock. Lari is a certified public accountant and earned the Certified Valuation Analyst designation from the National Association of Certified Valuation Analysts (NACVA). Masten is also a member of the American Institute of Certified Public Accountants (AICPA), Colorado Society of Certified Public Accountants (CSCPA), and National Association of Forensic Economists (NAFE).

* Licensed in the states of Texas and Colorado

---

1. One use of these statements is for making income capitalization calculations.

Formats for Displaying Financial Information

The form that the appraiser fills out to request documents commonly contains a line item for several years' of financial statements, tax returns, or historical revenue data. Ownership or management will provide the actual historical income and expenses, but the data are presented in many different formats. The appraiser may receive internal statements prepared by management, tax returns, or financial statements issued by a CPA.

Internal Statements

The owners of the investment group, holding company, or management may provide their own spreadsheets that show historical data in the form of a property income statement. Such a statement shows actual expenses that are easily identifiable and can be used to arrive at the property's *NOI*. In this case, projections and forecasts are calculated using the historical data supplied by management for use in the real property appraisal report.

Ideally, management supplies the data in this form. The appraiser must be aware that management's property income data often will not have been adjusted, and management may rely on third parties to supply the adjusting items such as updated depreciation figures for the current year or reclassification of capital expenditures that had been recorded as expense items.

Frequently, management will supply tax returns or financial statements prepared by a third party for the holding or investment company. In this case, extracting the data needed to present a historical representation, cash flow analysis, or *NOI* projections for the specific property income is more difficult for the appraiser because these documents contain additional information that can distort the property income.

Income Tax Returns

Most investment or holding companies that hold income-producing real property as an underlying asset are formed as partnerships or limited liability companies (LLCs) and less often, as S corporations. Tax returns for partnerships and LLCs are filed on Form 1065 and those for S corporations are filed on Form 1120S. Both forms are submitted to the IRS. These three entities operate as "pass-through" entities, i.e., they pay no federal income tax. All of the income generated flows back to the partners, members, or shareholders, who then record their portions of the entity-level activity on their personal tax returns.

Appraisers who have access to the entity's tax returns and financial statements will often find that the net income reported on the tax return differs from what is reported on the financial statements. This difference can be attributed to differences in the reporting basis for financial statements, which can be cash, accrual, GAAP, tax, or other, depending on the entity type and underlying business activity, and the tax compliance-reporting basis, i.e., cash or accrual. A comprehensive explanation of varying tax and financial reporting compliance issues is outside the scope of this discussion.

When preparing the income capitalization section of an appraisal report and arriving at a value conclusion for the real property, the appraiser must determine the cash flow levels or specific property income levels. To do this effectively and consistently, it is essential that the appraiser understand the nuances of the data.

Forms 1065 and 1120S are only four pages long. The remaining pages of the tax return are supplemental schedules that are linked to these four pages. The schedules may include, but are not limited to

- Depreciation schedules (linked to the balance sheet on page 4 of Form 1065)
- K-1s for the individual partners (which together link to Schedule K)
- Specific transaction-reporting forms (such as Form 8825 for the rental real estate income and expenses of a partnership or S corporation)

Sometimes, these additional schedules itemize several different amounts that are subtotaled and entered on one of the four pages of the 1065 (or 1120S). These statements can often contain valuable information for extracting income and expense items that pertain to a specific property's activity.

Income and expense items. Partnerships, LLCs, and S corporations often are involved in activities unrelated to the rental of real property. If so, tax returns for these entities will contain income and expenses for the non-rental business operations, commonly referred to as "trade or business income and expenses." These items pertain to the operating business (i.e., a manufacturer, retailer, wholesaler, or service industry) and do not include income and expenses involving the real estate rental activity.

The non-cash items required to determine cash flow for the non-rental real estate activity, which are shown on the first page of the tax return, include depreciation expenses and other deductions. Other deductions are normally detailed on a supporting schedule and often will not affect the real property being valued. One item included in other deductions would be amortization expenses for intangible assets, e.g., goodwill, non-compete agreements, loan costs.

Real property activity. The net income and expenses for all income-producing real property that a partnership or S corporation owns are reported in total as "net income (loss) from rental real estate activities" on line 2 of Schedule K of the tax return.[2] In the subject case study Suburban Office Partners, II, this figure is $68,151.

Form 8825, "Rental Real Estate Income and Expenses of a Partnership or an S Corporation," lists detailed income and expense data for each rental property that is listed on Form 1065 or 1120S. (See page 276.)

Because Suburban Office Partners, II, has only one property, the net income reflected on Form 8825, line 21 is identical to that on line 2 of Schedule K ($68,151). The non-cash items that appear on the following lines of Form 8825 should be reviewed when the valuer prepares the cash flow analysis and projections for the specific property:

Line 14: Depreciation

Line 15: Other expenses, which can include amortization expense, often detailed in a supporting statement to the tax return.

In addition to the income and expense detail, other balance sheet items can also affect individual properties. Book balance sheet details for both the current year and the previous year are reported on Schedule L on page 4 of Form 1065 (see page

---

2. Schedule K is on page 3 of Form 1065 and on page 2 of Form 1120S.

271). This balance sheet includes all of the assets, liabilities, and capital for the entity and are listed in two sets of columns:

- "Beginning of Tax Year," columns (a) and (b)
- "End of Tax Year," columns (c) and (d)

Information items important to the valuation of a business or the appraisal of assets are listed on the following lines on Schedule L of Form 1065[3]

- Line 9a: Building and other depreciable assets
- Line 9b: Accumulated depreciation
- Line 12a: Intangible assets
- Line 12b: Accumulated amortization
- Lines 15–20: Debt, with the nonrecourse loans reported on line 18
- Line 21: Partners' capital

Because of the different structure and tax regulations for a partnerships and S corporations, some items either do not apply to both entities or are reported differently on the tax forms. Key differences between the reporting requirements for partnerships and S corporations are described below.

Form 1065. A partnership's book income is often different from its income for tax purposes. For example, a partnership may use different methods of calculating depreciation and useful lives for its depreciable assets for book and tax purposes. These differences, and others relative to income and expenses reported for book and tax purposes, are reflected in Schedule M-1, Reconciliation of Income (Loss) per Books With Income (Loss) per Return, on page four of Form 1065. This information is needed to determine all of the income that a partnership receives and the expenses that it incurs, which may not be reflected in the taxable income shown on pages one to three of Form 1065.

Information about the changes in partners' capital accounts can be found in Schedule M-2, Analysis of Partners' Capital Accounts, on page 4. Specifically, partners' cash contributions to the partnership and cash distributions to partners can be found on lines 2 and 6, respectively. Cash distributions to partners also can be found on Schedule K, line 22 on page 3 of Form 1065.

Form 1120S. Discussion of the various types of retained earnings[4] for an S corporation for tax purposes is beyond the scope of this appendix. An analysis of retained earnings for an S corporation is provided in Schedule M-2 on page 4 of Form 1120S. Total S corporation distributions (cash and property) are reported on line 7 of Schedule M-2. This same amount can also be found on Schedule K, line 20. Total retained earnings of the corporation reported on Schedule L, line 24, may not agree with the S corporation retained earnings reported on Schedule M-2, line 8. The difference might be the result of book- or tax-timing differences or C corporation retained earnings. Again, this is a somewhat complicated tax area, but if an S corporation has not been an S corporation from its inception, it may have C corporation retained earnings and potential net unrealized built-in gains on the sale of any asset

---

3. The line numbers are slightly different on Form 1120S, but the same data are shown.
4. Retained earnings are accumulated, undistributed past and current years' earnings, net of taxes and dividends paid and declared.

it holds. This can have significant tax implications upon the sale or liquidation of a corporation with prior C corporation retained earnings. To properly address this potential tax liability, the appraiser should consult a tax accountant.

Table E.1 summarizes the location of pertinent items on Form 1065 and Form 1120S.

Table E.1	**Tax Return Page and Line Number Reference***			
	Form			
	1065		**1120S**	
	Page	**Line**	**Page**	**Line**
Non-Rental Business Operations – Trade or Business				
Income and Expenses:				
Gross receipts or sales	1	1a	1	1a
Cost of goods sold	1	2	1	2
Gross profit	1	3	1	3
Other income	1	4-7	1	4-5
Operating expenses (deductions)	1	9-20	1	7-19
Depreciation expense	1	16	1	14
Other deductions	1	20	1	19
Income-producing real estate/Schedule K				
Net income (loss) from rental real estate activities	3	2	2	2

* As tax compliance rules change, the IRS modifies its forms from time to time. These line numbers are based on 2003 tax forms. The most recent tax forms are available at the IRS website, *www.irs.gov.*

Outsourced Financial Statements

When management outsources the preparation of financial statements to CPAs, public accountants, or bookkeepers, these preparers will often use different methods of accounting, provide different levels of service, and use different formats for the presentation of the data. They frequently use different titles for the financial statement. When using financial statements that have been developed externally, appraisers should first establish the degree of reliance that can be placed upon them.

CPAs offer three types of financial statements. Each is based on different procedures and provides a different level of assurance. They include:

- Compilation
- Review
- Audit

A compilation represents the minimal level of service provided, and the professional issuing it may not be a CPA. A compilation that is issued by a CPA will contain a cover letter that states that the CPA did not audit or review the underlying data supplied by management. An accountant reads the compiled financial statement and considers whether it is appropriate in form and free from obvious material errors. The term *errors* refers to mistakes in the compilation, including mathematical or clerical mistakes, and mistakes in the application of accounting principles, including inadequate disclosure.

Reviewed statements must be issued by a CPA and have been analyzed to some degree by the CPA. A cover letter states that no review of internal controls has been performed. Reviewed statements provide limited assurance that no material modifications have been made to the financial statements to achieve conformity with generally accepted accounting principles (GAAP), or other comprehensive bases of accounting (OCBOA). Reviewed statements include cash- and tax-based financial statements.

Audited financial statements provide the highest level of reliability. They are prepared by a CPA who is the auditor and who certifies that the financial statements meet the requirements of U.S. GAAP. An auditor can render an unqualified opinion[5] to indicate agreement with the way the company prepared the statements, or a qualified opinion,[6] which identifies aspects of the statements that he or she does not agree with. In extreme cases in which the scope of the audit is insufficient, the auditor may express no opinion at all.

The reporting requirements for financial statements not prepared by a CPA are neither standardized nor uniformly accepted. Thus, it may be more difficult to ascertain the basis of accounting used or the level of assurance provided for such financial statements.

An appraiser is likely to encounter three common methods of accounting, which are used to produce the three types of financial statements:

- Accrual basis (GAAP)
  Generally accepted accounting principles (GAAP) is an accounting term that normally refers to financial statements prepared on the accrual basis of accounting. Under this system, income is recorded when earned (i.e., accounts receivables are reported) and expenses are recorded when incurred (i.e., accounts payables are recorded).

- Cash basis
  Cash basis financial statements normally include only income collected and expenses paid in cash; they do not reflect accrued items such as accounts payable, dividends (distributions) payable, or accounts receivable.

- Tax basis
  Tax basis financial statements can reflect accrual or cash basis methods of accounting and should agree with the income and expenses reported on the tax return. When presented with tax basis financial statements and returns, the appraiser should verify that the documents agree. If they do not, the appraiser may want to note the differences and state them in the report to avoid disseminating misleading financial information.

The titles used in financial statements can also vary, depending on the method of accounting that the company and the preparer of the financial statements used. CPAs must follow specific rules when titling financial statements. Those not prepared by CPAs are not governed by the same rules. Although these preparers may employ titles that are similar to those used by CPAs, the financial statements may have been prepared using different accounting methods.

---

5. An auditor's unqualified opinion of a financial statement is given without any reservation. Such an opinion states that the auditor believes that the company followed all accounting rules appropriately and that the financial reports are an accurate representation of the company's financial condition.

6. An auditor's qualified opinion of a financial statement includes limitations, which may be based on the auditor's inability to gather certain information or a significant impending event pertaining to the company that may or may not occur.

Table E.2 shows common financial statement titles used for CPA-prepared financial statements featuring the use of GAAP, cash, and tax basis methods of accounting:

Table E.2	**Common Titles of CPA-Prepared Financial Statements**	
GAAP Basis Financial Statements	**Cash Basis Financial Statements**	**Tax Basis Financial Statements**
Balance Sheet	Statement of Assets, Liabilities, and Equity (Capital)—Cash Basis	Statement of Assets, Liabilities, and Equity (Capital) —Income Tax Basis
Statement of Income	Statement of Revenues and Expenses—Cash Basis	Statement of Revenues and Expenses —Income Tax Basis
Statement of Income and Retained Earnings	Statement of Revenues, Expenses, and Retained Earnings (Partners' Capital, Proprietor's Capital)— Cash Basis	Statement of Revenues, Expenses, and Retained Earnings (Partners' Capital, Proprietor's Capital)—Income Tax Basis
Statement of Retained Earnings	Statement of Retained Earnings—Cash Basis	Statement of Retained Earnings—Income Tax Basis
Statement of Changes in Stockholder's Equity	Statement of Changes in Stockholder's Equity (Partners' Capital, Proprietor's Capital)—Cash Basis	Statement of Changes in Stockholder's Equity (Partners' Capital, Proprietor's Capital)—Income Tax Basis
Statement of Cash Flows	Statement of Cash Flows—Cash Basis	Statement of Cash Flows—Income Tax Basis

In general, all information pertaining to assets, liabilities, and equity will be found on the balance sheet of a company's financial statements.

Typically, all income and expenses are reflected in the statement of income. Certain key expenses needed for cash flow analysis, such as depreciation, amortization, interest expense, and discretionary expense items, will generally be included in this statement or in supporting schedules.

Cash distributions to partners and/or shareholders are generally reflected in the statement of income and retained earnings or in the statement of retained earnings if it is prepared as a separate statement. Occasionally, distributions may be reflected in the equity section of the balance sheet.

In addition to extracting data from the supplied documents, the appraiser will often need to consider accruing items from cash basis financial statements or tax returns. As an example, the valuation date in the case study is January 1, 1997, and distributions based on the 1996 tax year have not been made. These questions must be answered.

- Would the hypothetical sellers of the interest be due their distribution for the 1996 year after the sale,
- Will the distribution flow to the new interest holder,
- Will the transaction price be adjusted accordingly (to include the distribution amount due to the seller)?

- Should the adjustment for the 1996 distribution be recorded as a liability of the partnership?

The answers to these questions depend on what the partnership or shareholder agreement stipulates as to distributions and sales of interests.

Is the agreement silent to this issue? If so, the appraiser must use his or her judgment as to how to value the interest accurately and arrive at a fair and reasonable opinion of value. Most likely, the seller will demand the distribution, as it was an amount due based on historical performance. In that case, the appraiser will likely accrue the distribution as a liability on the balance sheet, with a corresponding adjustment to the partner/shareholder capital.

Working with Attorneys and Other Client Intermediaries

The Uniform Standards of Professional Appraisal Practice (USPAP) require the appraiser to state the identity of the client and any intended users of the appraisal by name and type. However, common sense also requires that the appraiser consider other professionals who will read the report. In the real world, the client (e.g., the executor of an estate) often does not read the report or interface with the appraiser at all. It is an attorney or accountant who serves as an intermediary and provides information, works on planning issues and the valuation premise with the appraiser, and reviews the draft report. There are a number of steps that the appraiser should follow to maximize the efficiency of the process and the satisfaction level of both the intermediary and the client. The steps include making a written plan, defining the subject of the appraisal, identifying and verifying all material assumptions, providing a draft report for the client, being willing to make referrals when necessary, and asking questions when in doubt.

Create a Written Plan

Develop a plan for the appraisal. Provide the intermediary with a written list of documents that you will need to examine and a preliminary list of questions that you will need to resolve. Such a list allows the intermediary to efficiently parse out the various items among the people who will be providing information and documents to the appraiser, including the client, the attorney, the accountant, and/or whoever is managing the particular asset or business that is being appraised.

Define the Subject of the Appraisal

Exercise care when defining the property or interest in the property that will be the subject of the appraisal. This may seem obvious, but all too often appraisers end up valuing the wrong interest or property rights. For example, if the intermediary tells you that the interest to be appraised is a common tenancy interest, it is still prudent to ask whether there are any documents that might suggest the existence of a partnership agreement and whether any partnership tax returns have been filed. Although determining whether an arrangement constitutes a legal partnership should generally be left to the attorney, the appraiser can be an important and helpful team player by raising such issues at the earliest possible time.

About the Author

Gerald E. Lunn, Jr., J.D. is a certified specialist in estate planning, probate, and trusts, and a sole practitioner in Los Angeles, California. He is a member of the Los Angeles County and American Bar Associations and the State Bar of California.

Identify and Verify All Material Assumptions

Even the simplest appraisal involves making important assumptions regarding legal matters. For example, an appraisal of a 100% fee interest in real estate–perhaps the most straightforward set of property rights–would be clearly inaccurate if it ignored some material element of state or local law, such as a zoning restriction. When addressing such issues, it is appropriate to err on the side of caution in working with other members of the team. For example, if you become aware of a zoning or encroachment issue that might impact the valuation of the property, it would be both prudent and polite to discuss this with counsel as soon as it is known. When dealing directly with the client or with the client's accountant, it would be appropriate to suggest that an attorney get involved to address any legal issues that are not absolutely clear.

You should also be careful about relying on others for guidance on how to deal with legal issues. If the client or accountant provides instructions with respect to a legal question, it may be appropriate to suggest that an attorney be consulted. If this is not agreeable, then you should clearly document the source of the instruction on which you are relying.

Provide a Draft Report for the Client

Many situations have fixed due dates, but it is not unusual for the client and/or intermediaries to wait too long to initiate the appraisal process and then expect the appraiser to work overtime to meet the deadline. There are several good ways to address this issue. First, advise your clients and their advisors to initiate the process early. Second, set realistic delivery dates. Assume that whatever can go wrong will, and protect yourself by tying your schedule to the receipt of all necessary information and documents listed in your retainer agreement.

Generally, it is both wise and helpful to provide a draft of the report to be reviewed by the client or the client's intermediaries. Such a draft provides an opportunity to check all facts and assumptions for accuracy and to consider unforeseen legal, accounting, or other issues. A valuation report is a complex, multidisciplinary document, and an early opportunity to check the results will be much appreciated.

Ideally, a draft report will be provided at least one month prior to the due date, but there are no hard and fast rules in this regard. Also, when a deadline is looming, it might be wiser to provide a draft report that is not up to your usual standards, rather than to provide a more polished report later, when there is no time left for input from the client and the client's other professionals. However, any rough draft report should be clearly identified as such and, ideally, the portions that need additional work should highlighted to prevent unnecessary concern or editing on the part of the reader.

Be Willing to Make Referrals When Necessary

A client's valuation needs may sometimes extend beyond your expertise or the geographic range of your practice. For example, if you practice in California and are asked to help with the appraisal of a tenancy-in-common interest in land located in Alaska, it would usually make sense to engage an appraiser located in Alaska to value the underlying fee interest. The intermediaries (attorney and accountant) will be grateful if you find a competent and reliable colleague in Alaska and clearly delineate, in writing, the scope of such colleague's role in the engagement as well as your own. Be honest with your client about the basis for any referrals. If you do not know much about the person you are referring, be candid about it, and encourage the client to evaluate the appraiser's expertise independently.

When in Doubt, Ask

Appraisers face important challenges when working with legal and accounting documents. They can ask many questions about issues that should, perhaps, be understood by the valuation expert and risk revealing a lack of knowledge. Or they can make assumptions and risk making mistakes or practicing law without a license. Therefore, you should be sufficiently familiar with leases, partnership agreements, shareholder agreements, deeds and other documents to be able to converse with the experts who prepared them. However, you should also err on the side of caution if there is any doubt as to the meaning or potential impact of any document. Clauses whose meanings are readily apparent, such as voting provisions, methods of dividing proceeds of sale, methods of holding title, and the rental amount and allocation of expenses, do not necessarily require legal interpretation. However, problems often arise in the following situations:

- The document has provisions that appear to contradict each other or appear to be inconsistent.
- The language is vague or uses terms that are not clearly defined.
- The legal status of the subject interest is unclear (e.g., assignee vs. limited partner).
- The assumptions of the appraisal, while consistent with the document (such as the right of a partner to cause termination of the partnership), could lead to litigation under one or more causes of action that might not be apparent to the appraiser. (The hypothetical prudent buyer of the interest might see the presence of such a condition as risky—i.e., "buying a lawsuit.")
- The document is an old one, written in a style or with terms that are difficult to understand.

"When in doubt, ask!" Appraisers, like most experts, are proud of their knowledge of their field and may be reluctant to seem ignorant in the eyes of the client or other professionals. When one of these issues arises, however, bring the issue to the attention of counsel. You might be surprised to realize that even experienced attorneys may need to research an issue to fully understand its legal implications. If you identify more than one or two issues that are ambiguous, detail them in a letter to counsel for further consideration. It is annoying to bring these matters up verbally and force a note-taking session on your client's attorney or accountant. Moreover, you place yourself in a better position by documenting your concerns and the questions and asking for clear instructions.

Some areas in which appraisers may wish to help frame legal research include the reference in IRC Section 2703 to applicable restrictions and state law. You should, ideally, be familiar with this and other relevant tax concepts and be able to frame questions for counsel in the context of specified sections of the Internal Revenue Code. While this may not be required, it will improve your effectiveness and reputation if you can help frame the relevant issues. Other situations that involve interpretation and application of the Internal Revenue Code include characterization of an association as a partnership, the taxation of current and future income generated by the interest, and the taxability of the interest in the hands of a hypothetical purchaser.

Sometimes there are conflicting legal authorities, or the assumptions underlying value rest on legal interpretations (e.g., whether there is an assignee interest or or not, or whether a clause giving up a cotenant's absolute right to partition is valid, or whether a buyout provision can be enforced). In these cases it might be best to obtain a written opinion from counsel. When asking for a written opinion, be aware that your request may be costly to the client, and try to make the request as precise and clear as possible.

Summary

It is prudent to always consider the other parties and practitioners involved in an appraisal assignment and develop a plan for focusing their expertise and energy on working together efficiently. The appraisal process involves people as well as facts and issues. Therefore, you should be flexible in accommodating the client or the client's intermediaries but should also be prepared to take a lead role when no one else seems to be running the show.

APPENDIX F

REVENUE RULING 59-60

Rev. Rul. 59-60, 1959-1 C.B. 237

26 CFR 20.2031-2: Valuation of stocks and bonds.
(Also Section 2512)

(Also Part II, Sections 811(k), 1005, Regulations 105, Section 81.10)

In valuing the stock of closely held corporations, or the stock of corporations where market quotations are not available, all other available financial data, as well as all relevant factors affecting the fair market value must be considered for estate tax and gift tax purposes. No general formula may be given that is applicable to the many different valuation situations arising in the valuation of such stock. However, the general approach, methods, and factors which must be considered in valuing such securities are outlined.

Revenue Ruling 54-77, C.B. 1954-1, 187, superseded.

SECTION 1. PURPOSE.

The purpose of this Revenue Ruling is to outline and review in general the approach, methods and factors to be considered in valuing shares of the capital stock of closely held corporations for estate tax and gift tax purposes. The methods discussed herein will apply likewise to the valuation of corporate stocks on which market quotations are either unavailable or are of such scarcity that they do not reflect the fair market value.

SEC. 2. BACKGROUND AND DEFINITIONS.

.01 All valuations must be made in accordance with the applicable provisions of the Internal Revenue Code of 1954 and the Federal Estate Tax and Gift Tax Regulations. Sections 2031(a), 2032 and 2512(a) of the 1954 Code (sections 811 and 1005 of the 1939 Code) require that the property to be included in the gross estate, or made the subject of a gift, shall be taxed on the basis of the value of the property at the time of death of the decedent, the alternate date if so elected, or the date of gift.

.02 Section 20.2031-1(b) of the Estate Tax Regulations (section 81.10 of the Estate Tax Regulations 105) and section 25.2512-1 of the Gift Tax Regulations (section 86.19 of Gift Tax Regulations 108) define fair market value, in effect, as the price at which the property would change hands between a willing buyer and a willing seller when the former is not under any compulsion to buy and the latter is not under any compulsion to sell, both parties having reasonable knowledge of relevant facts. Court decisions frequently state in addition that the hypothetical buyer and seller are assumed to be able, as well as willing, to trade and to be well informed about the property and concerning the market for such property.

.03 Closely held corporations are those corporations the shares of which are owned by a relatively limited number of stockholders. Often the entire stock issue is held by one family. The result of this situation is that little, if any, trading is the shares takes place. There is, therefore, no established market for the stock and such sales as occur at irregular intervals seldom reflect all of the elements of a representative transaction as defined by the term `fair market value.'

SEC. 3. APPROACH TO VALUATION.

.01 A determination of fair market value, being a question of fact, will depend upon the circumstances in each case. No formula can be devised that will be generally applicable to the multitude of different valuation issues arising in estate and gift tax cases. Often, an appraiser will find wide differences of opinion as to the fair market value of a particular stock. In resolving such differences, he should maintain a reasonable attitude in recognition of the fact that valuation is not an exact science. A sound valuation will be based upon all the relevant facts, but the elements of common sense, informed judgment and reasonableness must enter into the process of weighing those facts and determining their aggregate significance.

.02 The fair market value of specific shares of stock will vary as general economic conditions change from `normal' to `boom' or `depression,' that is, according to the degree of optimism or pessimism with which the investing public regards the future at the required date of appraisal. Uncertainty as to the stability or continuity of the future income from a property decreases its value by increasing the risk of loss of earnings and value in the future. The value of shares of stock of a company with very uncertain future prospects is highly speculative. The appraiser must exercise his judgment as to the degree of risk attaching to the business of the corporation which issued the stock, but that judgment must be related to all of the other factors affecting value.

.03 Valuation of securities is, in essence, a prophecy as to the future and must be based on facts available at the required date of appraisal. As a generalization, the prices of stocks which are traded in volume in a free and active market by informed persons best reflect the consensus of the investing public as to what the future holds for the corporations and industries represented. When a stock is closely held, is traded infrequently, or is traded in an erratic market, some other measure of value must be used. In many instances, the next best measure may be found in the prices at which the stocks of companies engaged in the same or a similar line of business are selling in a free and open market.

SEC. 4. FACTORS TO CONSIDER.

.01 It is advisable to emphasize that in the valuation of the stock of closely held corporations or the stock of corporations where market quotations are either lacking or too scarce to be recognized, all available financial data, as well as all relevant factors affecting the fair market value, should be considered. The following factors, although not all-inclusive are fundamental and require careful analysis in each case:

(a) The nature of the business and the history of the enterprise from its inception.

(b) The economic outlook in general and the condition and outlook of the specific industry in particular.

(c) The book value of the stock and the financial condition of the business.

(d) The earning capacity of the company.

(e) The dividend-paying capacity.

(f) Whether or not the enterprise has goodwill or other intangible value.

(g) Sales of the stock and the size of the block of stock to be valued.

(h) The market price of stocks of corporations engaged in the same or a similar line of business having their stocks actively traded in a free and open market, either on an exchange or over-the-counter.

.02 The following is a brief discussion of each of the foregoing factors:

(a) The history of a corporate enterprise will show its past stability or instability, its growth or lack of growth, the diversity or lack of diversity of its operations, and other facts needed to form an opinion of the degree of risk involved in the business. For an enterprise which changed its form of organization but carried on the same or closely similar operations of its predecessor, the history of the former enterprise should be considered. The detail to be considered should increase with approach to the required date of appraisal, since recent events are of greatest help in predicting the future; but a study of gross and net income, and of dividends covering a long prior period, is highly desirable. The history to be studied should include, but need not be limited to, the nature of the business, its products or services, its operating and investment assets, capital structure, plant facilities, sales records and management, all of which should be considered as of the date of the appraisal, with due regard for recent significant changes. Events of the past that are unlikely to recur in the future should be discounted, since value has a close relation to future expectancy.

(b) A sound appraisal of a closely held stock must consider current and prospective economic conditions as of the date of appraisal, both in the national economy and in the industry or industries with which the corporation is allied. It is important to know that the company is more or less successful than its competitors in the same industry, or that it is maintaining a stable position with respect to competitors. Equal or even greater significance may attach to the ability of the industry with which the company is allied to compete with other industries. Prospective competition which has not been a factor in prior years should be given careful attention. For example, high profits due to the novelty of its product and the lack of competition often lead to increasing competition. The public's appraisal of the future prospects of competitive industries or of competitors within an industry may be indicated by price trends in the markets for commodities and for securities. The loss of the manager of a so-called `one-man' business may have a depressing effect upon the value of the stock of such business, particularly if there is a lack of trained personnel capable of succeeding to the management of the enterprise. In valuing the stock of this type of business, therefore, the effect of the loss of the manager on the future expectancy of the business, and the absence of management-succession potentialities are pertinent factors to be taken into consideration. On the other hand, there may be factors which offset, in whole or in part, the loss of the manager's services. For instance, the nature of the business and of its assets may be such that they will not be impaired by the loss of the manager. Furthermore, the loss may be adequately covered by life insurance, or competent management might be employed on the basis of the consideration paid for the former manager's services. These, or other offsetting factors, if found to exist, should be carefully weighed against the loss of the manager's services in valuing the stock of the enterprise.

(c) Balance sheets should be obtained, preferably in the form of comparative annual statements for two or more years immediately preceding the date of appraisal, together with a balance sheet at the end of the month preceding that date, if corporate accounting will permit. Any balance sheet descriptions that are not self-explanatory, and balance sheet items comprehending diverse assets or liabilities, should be clarified in essential detail by supporting supplemental schedules. These statements usually will disclose to the appraiser (1) liquid position (ratio of current assets to current liabilities); (2) gross and net book value of principal classes of fixed assets; (3) working capital; (4) long-term indebtedness; (5) capital structure; and (6) net worth. Consideration also should be given to any assets not essential to the operation of the business, such as investments in securities, real estate, etc. In general, such nonoperating assets will command a lower rate of return than do the operating assets, although in exceptional cases the reverse may be true. In computing the book value per share of stock, assets of the investment type should be revalued on the basis of their market price and the book value adjusted accordingly. Comparison of the company's balance sheets over several years may reveal, among other facts, such developments as the acquisition of additional production facilities or subsidiary companies, improvement in financial position, and details as to recapitalizations and other changes in the capital structure of the corporation. If the corporation has more than one class of stock outstanding, the charter or certificate of incorporation should be examined to ascertain the explicit rights and privileges of the various stock issues including: (1) voting powers, (2) preference as to dividends, and (3) preference as to assets in the event of liquidation.

(d) Detailed profit-and-loss statements should be obtained and considered for a representative period immediately prior to the required date of appraisal, preferably five or more years. Such statements should show (1) gross income by principal items; (2) principal deductions from gross income including major prior items of operating expenses, interest and other expense on each item of long-term debt, depreciation and depletion if such deductions are made, officers' salaries, in total if they appear to be reasonable or in detail if they seem to be excessive, contributions (whether or not deductible for tax purposes) that the nature of its business and its community position require the corporation to make, and taxes by principal items, including income and excess profits taxes; (3) net income available for dividends; (4) rates and amounts of dividends paid on each class of stock; (5) remaining amount carried to surplus; and (6) adjustments to, and reconciliation with, surplus as stated on the balance sheet. With profit and loss statements of this character available, the appraiser should be able to separate recurrent from nonrecurrent items of income and expense, to distinguish between operating income and investment income, and to ascertain whether or not any line of business in which the company is engaged is operated consistently at a loss and might be abandoned with benefit to the company. The percentage of earnings retained for business expansion should be noted when dividend-paying capacity is considered. Potential future income is a major factor in many valuations of closely held stocks, and all information concerning past income which will be helpful in predicting the future should be secured. Prior earnings records usually are the most reliable guide as to the future expectancy, but resort to arbitrary five-or-ten-year averages without regard to current trends or future prospects will not produce a realistic valuation. If, for instance, a record of progressively increasing or decreasing net income is found, then greater weight may be accorded the most recent years' profits in estimating earning power. It will be helpful, in judging risk and the extent to which a business is a marginal operator, to consider deductions from income and net income in terms of percentage of sales. Major categories of cost and expense to be so analyzed include the consumption of raw materials and supplies in the case of manufacturers, processors and fabricators; the cost of purchased merchandise in the case of merchants; utility services; insurance; taxes; depletion or depreciation; and interest.

(e) Primary consideration should be given to the dividend-paying capacity of the company rather than to dividends actually paid in the past. Recognition must be given to the necessity of retaining a reasonable portion of profits in a company to meet competition. Dividend-paying capacity is a factor that must be considered in an appraisal, but dividends actually paid in the past may not have any relation to dividend-paying capacity. Specifically, the dividends paid by a closely held family company may be measured by the income needs of the stockholders or by their desire to avoid taxes on dividend receipts, instead of by the ability of the company to pay dividends. Where an actual or effective controlling interest in a corporation is to be valued, the dividend factor is not a material element, since the payment of such dividends is discretionary with the controlling stockholders. The individual or group in control can substitute salaries and bonuses for dividends, thus reducing net income and understating the dividend-paying capacity of the company. It follows, therefore, that dividends are less reliable criteria of fair market value than other applicable factors.

(f) In the final analysis, goodwill is based upon earning capacity. The presence of goodwill and its value, therefore, rests upon the excess of net earnings over and above a fair return on the net tangible assets. While the element of goodwill may be based primarily on earnings, such factors as the prestige and renown of the business, the ownership of a trade or brand name, and a record of successful operation over a prolonged period in a particular locality, also may furnish support for the inclusion of intangible value. In some instances it may not be possible to make a separate appraisal of the tangible and intangible assets of the business. The enterprise has a value as an entity. Whatever intangible value there is, which is supportable by the facts, may be measured by the amount by which the appraised value of the tangible assets exceeds the net book value of such assets.

(g) Sales of stock of a closely held corporation should be carefully investigated to determine whether they represent transactions at arm's length. Forced or distress sales do not ordinarily reflect fair market value nor do isolated sales in small amounts necessarily control as the measure of value. This is especially true in the valuation of a controlling interest in a corporation. Since, in the case of closely held stocks, no prevailing market prices are available, there is no basis for making an adjustment for blockage. It follows, therefore, that such stocks should be valued upon a consideration of all the evidence affecting the fair market value. The size of the block of stock itself is a relevant factor to be considered. Although it is true that a minority interest in an unlisted corporation's stock is more difficult to sell than a similar block of listed stock, it is equally true that control of a corporation, either actual or in effect, representing as it does an added element of value, may justify a higher value for a specific block of stock.

(h) Section 2031(b) of the Code states, in effect, that in valuing unlisted securities the value of stock or securities of corporations engaged in the same or a similar line of business which are listed on an exchange should be taken into consideration along with all other factors. An important consideration is that the corporations to be used for comparisons have capital stocks which are actively traded by the public. In accordance with section 2031(b) of the Code, stocks listed on an exchange are to be considered first. However, if sufficient comparable companies whose stocks are listed on an exchange cannot be found, other comparable companies which have stocks actively traded in the over-the-counter market also may be used. The essential factor is that whether the stocks are sold on an exchange or over the counter, there is evidence of an active, free public market for the stock as of the valuation date. In selecting corporations for comparative purposes, care should be taken to use only comparable companies. Although the only restrictive requirement as to comparable corporations specified in the statute is that their lines of business be the same or similar, it is obvious that consideration must be given to other relevant factors in order that the most valid comparison possible be obtained. For illustration, a corporation having one or more issues of preferred stock, bonds or debentures in addition to its common stock should not be considered to be directly comparable to one having only common stock outstanding. In like manner, a company with a declining business and decreasing markets is not comparable to one with a record of current progress and market expansion.

SEC. 5. WEIGHT TO BE ACCORDED VARIOUS FACTORS.

The valuation of closely held corporate stock entails the consideration, of all relevant factors as stated in section 4. Depending upon the circumstances in each case, certain factors may carry more weight than others because of the nature of the company's business. To illustrate:

(a) Earnings may be the most important criterion of value in some cases, whereas asset value will receive primary consideration in others. In general, the appraiser will accord primary consideration to earnings when valuing stocks of companies which sell products or services to the public; conversely, in the investment or holding type of company, the appraiser may accord the greatest weight to the assets underlying the security to be valued.

(b) The value of the stock of a closely held investment or real estate holding company, whether or not family owned, is closely related to the value of the assets underlying the stock. For companies of this type the appraiser should determine the fair market values of the assets of the company. Operating expenses of such a company and the cost of liquidating it, if any, merit consideration when appraising the relative values of the stock and the underlying assets. The market values of the underlying assets give due weight to potential earnings and dividends of the particular items of property underlying the stock, capitalized at rates deemed proper by the investing public at the date of appraisal. A current appraisal by the investing public should be superior to the retrospective opinion of an individual. For these reasons, adjusted net worth should be accorded greater weight in valuing the stock of a closely held investment or real estate holding company, whether or not family owned, than any of the other customary yardsticks of appraisal, such as earnings and dividend-paying capacity.

SEC. 6. CAPITALIZATION RATES.

In the application of certain fundamental valuation factors, such as earnings and dividends, it is necessary to capitalize the average or current results at some appropriate rate. A determination of the proper capitalization rate presents one of the most difficult problems in valuation. That there is no ready or simple solution will become apparent by a cursory check of the rates of return and dividend yields in terms of the selling prices of corporate shares listed on the major exchanges of the country. Wide variations will be found even for companies in the same industry. Moreover, the ratio will fluctuate from year to year depending upon economic conditions. Thus, no standard tables of capitalization rates applicable to closely held corporations can be formulated. Among the more important factors to be taken into consideration in deciding upon a capitalization rate in a particular case are: (1) the nature of the business; (2) the risk involved; and (3) the stability or irregularity of earnings.

SEC. 7. AVERAGE OF FACTORS.

Because valuations cannot be made on the basis of a prescribed formula, there is no means whereby the various applicable factors in a particular case can be assigned mathematical weights in deriving the fair market value. For this reason, no useful purpose is served by taking an average of several factors (for example, book value, capitalized earnings and capitalized dividends) and basing the valuation on the result. Such a process excludes active consideration of other pertinent factors, and the end result cannot be supported by a realistic application of the significant facts in the case except by mere chance.

SEC. 8. RESTRICTIVE AGREEMENTS.

Frequently, in the valuation of closely held stock for estate and gift tax purposes, it will be found that the stock is subject to an agreement restricting its sale or transfer. Where shares of stock were acquired by a decedent subject to an option reserved by the issuing corporation to repurchase at a certain price, the option price is usually accepted as the fair market value for estate tax purposes. See Rev. Rul. 54-76, C.B. 1954-1, 194. However, in such case the option price is not determinative of fair market value for gift tax purposes. Where the option, or buy and sell agreement, is the result of voluntary action by the stockholders and is binding during the life as well as at the death of the stockholders, such agreement may or may not, depending upon the circumstances of each case, fix the value for estate tax purposes. However, such agreement is a factor to be considered, with other relevant factors, in determining fair market value. Where the stockholder is free to dispose of his shares during life and the option is to become effective only upon his death, the fair market value is not limited to the option price. It is always necessary to consider the relationship of the parties, the relative number of shares held by the decedent, and other material facts, to determine whether the agreement represents a bona fide business arrangement or is a device to pass the decedent's shares to the natural objects of his bounty for less than an adequate and full consideration in money or money's worth. In this connection see Rev. Rul. 157 C.B. 1953-2, 255, and Rev. Rul. 189, C.B. 1953-2, 294.

SEC. 9. EFFECT ON OTHER DOCUMENTS.

Revenue Ruling 54-77, C.B. 1954-1, 187, is hereby superseded.

Bibliography

Articles

Aschwald, Kathryn F. "Restricted Stock Discounts Decline as Result of One-Year Holding Period," *Shannon Pratt's Business Valuation Update* (May 2000): 1-5.

Chaffe III, David B. H. "Option Pricing as a Proxy for Discount for Lack of Marketability in Private Company Valuations." *Business Valuation Review* (December 1993): 182-188.

Cooper John R., and Richard Gore, "Built-in Gains Discount Calculation." *Valuation Strategies* (Jan/Feb 2001): 5-13, 44.

Emory, John D. Sr., ASA, and John D. Emory, Jr., "The Value of Marketability as Illustrated in IPOs: May 1997 – December 2000." *Shannon Pratt's Business Valuation Update* (October 2001): 1, 3.

Griffith, Reynolds, Ph.D., "Valuation of Restricted Stocks: An Option Theory Approach." *ASA Valuation* (February 1988): 96-102.

Hall, Lance. "Should the IRS Surrender Cost-to-Partition Discounts for Undivided Interests?" *Valuation Strategies* (January/February 1998): 25-27, 46, 48.

Harris, Don L., MAI, et al. "The Valuation of Partial Interests in Real Estate." *ASA Valuation* (December 1983): 63-73.

Humphrey, Walter H. "Unsyndicated Partial Interest Appraisals." *Valuation Insights and Perspectives* (Third Quarter 1998): 9-12.

Humphrey, Walter H., and Bruce B. Humphrey, MAI. "Unsyndicated Partial Interest Discounting." *The Appraisal Journal* (July 1997): 267-274.

Israel, Ted, CPA/ABV, CVA, "Discounts on Undivided Interests in Real Estate." *Valuation Strategies* (May/June 2003): 14-19, 47.

Johnson, Bruce, ASA, "Restricted Stock Discounts 1991-1995." *Shannon Pratt's Business Valuation Update* (March 1999): 1-3.

Johnson, Bruce, ASA. "Quantitative Support for Discounts for Lack of Marketability." *Business Valuation Review* (December 1999): 152-155.

Longstaff, Francis A. "How Much Can Marketability Affect Security Values?" *The Journal of Finance* (December 1996): 1767-1774.

Mercer, Z. Christopher. "Developing Marketability Discounts." *Valuation Strategies* (March/April 2001): 12-21, 46.

McConaughy, Daniel L. et al. "Factors Affecting Discounts on Restricted Stock," *Valuation Strategies* (Nov/Dec 2000): 14-23, 46.

Partnership Profiles, "Secondary Market Buyers Playing Arbitrage." *The Partnership Spectrum* (March/April 2000): 1-6.

Patchin, Peter J., CRE. "Market Discounts for Undivided Minority Interests in Real Estate." *Real Estate Issues* (Fall/Winter 1988): 14-16.

Seaman, Ronald M., ASA, CBA. "Valuation of Undivided Interests in Real Property." *Business Valuation Review* (March 1997): 32-40.

Secondary Spectrum, *The Partnership Spectrum*, a bimonthly newsletter. Dallas: Partnership Profiles (May/June 1992, and later issues).

Willis, Jr., Robert T., CPA, CFA. "Preparing Valuation Reports to Withstand Judicial Challenge," *Estate Planning* (December 1998): 455-462.

Books

Abrams, Jay B., ASA, CPA, MBA. *Quantitative Business Valuation: A Mathematical Approach for Today's Professionals.* New York: McGraw-Hill, 2000.

Appraisal Institute. *The Appraisal of Real Estate.* 12th ed. Chicago: Appraisal Institute, 2001. (Footnotes also refer to the 10th and 11th editions.)

Bogdanski, John A. *Federal Tax Valuation.* 1 5.01[2][e][iii]. Boston: Warren, Gorham & Lamont, Updated 2003.

The Dictionary of Real Estate Appraisal, 4th ed. Chicago: Appraisal Institute, 2002.

Fishman, Jay E., MBA, ASA, CRA, et al. *Guide to Business Valuations,* 7th ed. Fort Worth: Practitioners Publishing Company, 1997.

Haug, Espen Gaarder, *The Complete Guide to Option Pricing Formulas.* New York: McGraw-Hill, 1998.

Clewlow, Les and Chris Strickland, *Implementing Derivatives Models,* (New York: Wiley, 1998)

"Institutional Investor Study Report of the Securities and Exchange Commission," H.R. Doc. No. 92-64 part 5, 92nd Congress, 1st Session, pp. 2412-2475 (1971).

Johnson, Bruce A. and Spencer J. Jefferies. *Comprehensive Guide for the Valuation of Family Limited Partnership.* Dallas: Partnership Profiles, Inc., 2001.

Mercer, Z. Christopher, ASA, CFA. *Quantifying Marketability Discounts.* Memphis: Peabody Publishing, 1997.

Pratt, Shannon P., DBA, CFA, FASA, et al. *Valuing a Business: The Analysis and Appraisal of Closely Held Companies,* 4th ed. Chicago: Irwin Professional Publishing, 2000.